BYZANTIUM

1. VIEW OF CONSTANTINOPLE

BYZANTIUM

AN INTRODUCTION TO
EAST ROMAN CIVILIZATION

Edited by
NORMAN H. BAYNES
and
H. St. L. B. MOSS

OXFORD
AT THE CLARENDON PRESS

Oxford University Press, Amen House, London E.C.4

GLASGOW NEW YORK TORONTO MELBOURNE WELLINGTON
BOMBAY CALCUTTA MADRAS KARACHI LAHORE DACCA
CAPE TOWN SALISBURY NAIROBI IBADAN ACCRA
KUALA LUMPUR HONG KONG

FIRST PUBLISHED BY THE CLARENDON PRESS 1948
REPRINTED WITH CORRECTIONS 1949
REPRINTED LITHOGRAPHICALLY IN GREAT BRITAIN
AT THE UNIVERSITY PRESS, OXFORD
FROM SHEETS OF THE SECOND IMPRESSION 1953
FIRST ISSUED IN OXFORD PAPERBACKS 1961
REPRINTED 1962

NOTE

THIS book was being prepared for publication before the outbreak of war and all the translations of chapters written by foreign scholars had been approved by their authors. We desire to thank Miss Louise Stone (King's College, University of London) for her help in rendering into English the French texts. Mr. Moss, besides contributing the section of Chapter I on Byzantine history down to the Fourth Crusade, has throughout helped me in the preparation of this book for the press and is solely responsible for the choice of the illustrations. I have added a few bibliographical notes which are placed within square brackets.

N. H. B.

CONTENTS

CONTENTS

LIST OF PLATES

Heaven. At the top, an old monk is received by Christ. On the left, devils are trying to drag the monks from the ladder. Some monks fall headlong, carried away by devils. Below, a dragon, representing the jaws of Hell, is swallowing a monk. 1546. See p. 196. From G. Millet, ibid.

24. Refectory. Lavra, Mt. Athos. 1512. See p. 196. By kind permission of Professor D. Talbot Rice.

25. Fresco. Parable of the Talents. Monastery of Theraponte, Russia. In the centre, men seated at a table. On the left, the Master returns. His servants approach, three of them bearing a jar filled with money, a cup, and a cornucopia. On the right, the Unprofitable Servant is hurled into a pit representing the 'outer darkness' of Matt. xxv. 30. *Circa* 1500. From Ch. Diehl, *La Peinture byzantine* (Van Oest).

26. Miniatures. Story of Joseph. Vienna Genesis. (*a*) On the left, Joseph's brethren are seen 'coming down' into Egypt from a stylized hill-town. On the right, Joseph addresses his brethren, who stand respectfully before him. In the background Joseph's servants prepare the feast. (*b*) Above, Potiphar, on the left, hastens along a passage to his wife's chamber. Below, Joseph's cloak is produced in evidence. 5th century. See p. 176. From Hartel and Wickhoff, *Die Wiener Genesis*, vol. 2.

27. Miniature. Parable of the Ten Virgins. Rossano Gospel. On the left, the Foolish Virgins, in brightly coloured garments, with spent lamps and empty oil-flasks. Their leader knocks vainly at a panelled door. On the other side is Paradise with its four rivers and its fruit-bearing trees. The Bridegroom heads the company of Wise Virgins, clad in white and with lamps burning. Below, four prophets; David (three times) and Hosea. (Cf. A. Muñoz, *Il Codice Purpureo di Rossano*, Rome, 1907.) Late 6th century. See p. 177. *Photograph by Giraudon.*

28. Miniature. Abraham's sacrifice. Cosmas Indicopleustes. Vatican Library. See p. 176.

29. Miniature. Isaiah's Prayer. Psalter. Bibliothèque Nationale, Paris. Above is the Hand of God, from which a ray of light descends on the prophet. On the right, a child, bearing a torch, represents Dawn. On the left, Night is personified as a woman holding a torch reversed. Over her head floats a blue veil sprinkled with stars. Cf. H. Buchthal, *The Miniatures of the Paris Psalter*. See p. 407 *infra*. 10th century. See p. 186. From J. Ebersolt, *La Miniature byzantine* (Vanoest, Paris).

39. Ivory. Story of Joseph. 'Throne of Maximian' (detail), Ravenna. Above: Joseph sold to Potiphar by the Ishmaelites. Below: Joseph tempted by Potiphar's wife; Joseph thrown into prison. 6th century. See p. 177. *Photograph by Alinari.*

40. Ivory. Romanus and Eudocia crowned by Christ. Cabinet des Médailles, Paris. The two figures, formerly taken as representing Romanus IV (1067–71) and his consort, have recently been identified with Romanus II (959–63) and Bertha of Provence, who assumed the name of Eudocia on her marriage. 10th century. See p. 187. *Photograph by Giraudon.*

41. Ivory. Scenes from the Life of Christ. Victoria and Albert Museum: Crown copyright reserved. Above: Annunciation and Nativity. Centre: Transfiguration and Raising of Lazarus. Below: Resurrection. 11th–12th century.

42. Silver Dish from Kerynia, Cyprus. David and Goliath. By courtesy of the Metropolitan Museum of Art, New York. 6th century. See p. 177.

43. Reliquary. Esztergon, Hungary. See p. 188. Silver-gilt, with figures in coloured enamel. Above: mourning angels. Centre: Constantine and Helena. Below: the Road to Calvary; and the Deposition. 12th century. From L. Bréhier, *La Sculpture et les Arts Mineurs byzantins* (Les Éditions d'art et d'histoire, Paris).

44. Wool Tapestries from Egypt. (*a*) Hunting Scene. Victoria and Albert Museum: Crown copyright reserved. (*b*) Nereids riding on sea-monsters. Louvre. 4th–6th century. See p. 177. From L. Bréhier, *op. cit.*

45. Silk Textile. Riders on Winged Horses. Schlossmuseum, Berlin. On a cream background, two helmeted kings in Persian dress, embroidered in green and dark blue, confront one another across a *hom* or sacred tree. Though following earlier models of Sassanian type, this textile is probably to be assigned to the 10th century. *Photograph by Giraudon.*

46. 'Dalmatic of Charlemagne.' Vatican Treasury. Blue silk, embroidered in gold and silk. Christ summoning the Elect. Centre: Christ seated on a rainbow. Above: angels guard the throne of the Second Coming (Etimasia). Below: a choir of saints. On the shoulders: Communion of the Apostles. For the iconography see G. Millet, *La Dalmatique du Vatican*, Bibliothèque de l'École des Hautes Études, Sciences religieuses, vol. lx, Paris, 1945. 14th century. See p. 197.

MAPS (*at end*)

INTRODUCTION

'THERE are in history no beginnings and no endings. History books begin and end, but the events they describe do not.'[1] It is a salutary warning: yet from the first Christians have divided human history into the centuries of the preparation for the coming of Christ and the years after the advent of their Lord in the flesh, and in his turn the student of history is forced, however perilous the effort, to split up the stream of events into periods in order the better to master his material, to reach a fuller understanding of man's development. What then of the Byzantine Empire? When did it begin to be? When did it come to an end? Concerning its demise there can hardly be any hesitation—1453, the date of the Osmanli conquest of Constantinople, is fixed beyond dispute. But on the question at what time did a distinctively Byzantine Empire come into being there is no such agreement. J. B. Bury, indeed, denied that there ever was such a birthday: 'No Byzantine Empire ever began to exist; the Roman Empire did not come to an end until 1453'—of 'Byzantine art', 'Byzantine civilization' we may appropriately speak, but when we speak of the State which had its centre in Constantine's city the 'Roman Empire' is the only fitting term.[2]

But Bury's dictum obviously implies a continuity of development which some historians would not admit. Thus Professor Toynbee has argued that the Roman Empire died during the closing years of the sixth century: it was a 'ghost' of that Empire which later occupied the imperial throne. During the seventh century a new Empire came into being and stood revealed when Leo III marched from Asia to inaugurate a dynasty. That new Empire was the reply of the Christian East to the menace of the successors of Mahomet: the State as now organized was the 'carapace' which should

---

[1] R. G. Collingwood, *An Autobiography* (London, Oxford University Press, 1939), p. 98; and cf. his study of Christian historiography in *The Idea of History* (Oxford, Clarendon Press, 1946), pp. 49–52.

[2] J. B. Bury, *A History of the Later Roman Empire* (London, Macmillan, 1889), vol. i, p. v; *The Cambridge Medieval History* (Cambridge University Press, 1923), vol. iv, pp. vii–ix.

form the hard shell of resistance against the Muslim attack. Here there is no continuity with the old Roman Empire: there is but a reassertion of imperial absolutism and of administrative centralization to meet changed conditions.

Others, without employing Professor Toynbee's forms of presentation, have expressed similar views. The loss of Syria, Palestine, and Egypt to the Arabs in the seventh century led, as a counter-measure on the part of the Empire, to the building up in Asia Minor of a new military system: land grants were made to farmers subject to a hereditary obligation of service in the imperial armies. It was on this system and its successful maintenance that the defence of the Empire was henceforth to depend, and since the Empire was continuously assailed by foes through the centuries, it was this new system, Ostrogorsky has urged, which serves to date the beginning of a distinctively Byzantine Empire: all the preceding history was but a Preface and a Prelude which can be briefly summarized.[1]

Perhaps an editor may be allowed in this Introduction to express in a few words a personal opinion, if it be clearly understood that he has not sought in any way to enforce that opinion upon contributors. . . . If we ask the question can we still, despite Bury's objection, use the term 'Byzantine Empire'? that question may be answered in the affirmative, since thereby we are reminded of the historical significance of the fact that it was precisely at the Greek city of Byzantium and not elsewhere that Constantine chose to create his new imperial capital. Attempts have been made of recent years to minimize the importance of that fact; the capital, it is said, might equally well have been set in Asia Minor, just as the capital of the Turkish Empire has, in our own day, been transferred to Ankara. But Asia Minor of the Byzantines was overrun by hostile armies time and again and its cities captured by the foe. Constantinople, posted on the waterway between the continents and guarded by the girdle of its landward and seaward walls, through all assaults remained impregnable. At moments the Empire might be confined within the circle of the city's fortifications, but the assailants

[1] 'En 717 commence . . . l'Empire byzantin': Henri Berr in the preface to Louis Bréhier's *Vie et Mort de Byzance* (Paris, Michel, 1947), p. xiii.

retired discomfited and still the capital preserved the heritage
of civilization from the menace of the barbarian. The city
was Constantine's majestic war memorial: the Greek East
should not forget the crowning mercy of his victory over
Licinius. By its foundation Constantine created the imperial
power-house within which could be concentrated the forces
of a realm which was sustained by the will of the Christians'
God and which, in the fifth century, was further secured by
the acquisition of Our Lady's Robe, the palladium of New
Rome. It is well that we should be reminded of that act of
the first Christian Emperor.

And did the Roman Empire die at some date during the
closing years of the sixth century or in the first decade of the
seventh? Is it true that a 'ghost' usurped the imperial
throne? It is not every student who will be able to follow
Professor Toynbee in his essay in historical necromancy.
To some it will rather seem that, *if* the Roman Empire died,
its death should be set during the breakdown of imperial
power and the financial and administrative chaos of the third
century of our era. With Diocletian and with the *turbator
rerum*, the revolutionary Constantine, there is such a rebuilding that one might with some justification argue that a new
Empire was created. For here, as Wilamowitz-Moellendorf
wrote, is the great turning-point in the history of the
Mediterranean lands. But may it not be truer to say that the
Roman Empire did not die, but was transformed from
within, and that the factor which in essentials determined
the character of that transformation was the dream of the
Empire's future as Constantine conceived it? He had been
called to rule a pagan Empire; he brought from his rule in
the West the knowledge of the tradition of Roman government. At the battle of the Milvian Bridge he had put to the
test the Christian God, and the God of the Christians had
given him the victory over Maxentius: that favour made of
Constantine an Emperor with a mission, he was 'God's man',
as he called himself. When he went to the East he came into
lands where language, literature, and thought were all alike
Greek. There could be no idea of transforming the East into
a Latin world. That was the problem: a pagan Empire
based on a Roman tradition of law and government ruled by

a Christian Emperor who had been appointed to build up his realm upon the foundation of a unified Christian faith—an Empire centred in a Christian capital and that capital surrounded by a deeply rooted tradition of Hellenistic culture. Those are the factors which had to be brought 'to keep house together'. And this Christian Emperor, incorporating in his own person the immense majesty of pagan Rome, could not, of course, make Christianity the religion of the Roman State—that was unthinkable—but the man to whom the Christian God had amazingly shown unmerited favour had a vision of what in the future might be realized and he could build for that future. Within the pagan Empire itself one could begin to raise another—a Christian—Empire: and one day the walls of the pagan Empire would fall and in their place the Christian building would stand revealed. In a Christian capital the Roman tradition of law and government would draw its authority and sanction from the supreme *imperium* which had been the permanent element in the constitutional development of the Roman State; that State itself, become Christian and Orthodox, would be sustained through a Catholic and Orthodox Church, while Greek thought and Greek art and architecture would preserve the Hellenistic tradition. And in that vision Constantine anticipated, foresaw, the Byzantine Empire. And thus for any comprehending study of that Empire one must go as far back at least as the reign of Constantine the Great.

The factors which went to form Constantine's problem—the pagan Hellenistic culture, the Roman tradition, the Christian Church—were only gradually fused after long stress and strife. The chronicle of that struggle is no mere Preface or Prelude to the history of the Byzantine Empire; it is an integral part of that history, for in this period of struggle the precedents were created and the moulds were shaped which determined the character of the civilization which was the outcome of an age of transition. Without a careful study of the Empire's growing-pains the later development will never be fully comprehended.

And from the first the rulers of the Empire recognized the duty which was laid upon them, their obligation to preserve that civilization which they had inherited, to counter the

assaults of the barbarians from without or the threat from
within—the menace of those barbarian soldiers who were in
the Empire's service. It was indeed a task which demanded
the highest courage and an unfaltering resolution. 'If ever
there were supermen in history, they are to be found in the
Roman emperors of the fourth century.' And this duty and
the realization that Constantinople was the ark which
sheltered the legacy of human achievement remained constant throughout the centuries. The forms of the defence
might change, but the essential task did not alter. When in
the seventh century Egypt, Palestine, and Syria were lost,
the system of imperial defence had perforce to be reorganized,
but that reorganization was designed to effect the same
traditional purpose. It is this unchanging function of the
later Empire which, for some students at least, shapes the
impressive continuity of the history of the East Roman
State. Leo III is undertaking the same task in the eighth
century as Heraclius had faced in the seventh, as Justinian
had sought to perform in the sixth. It is this continuity of
function which links together by a single chain the emperors
of Rome in a succession which leads back to Constantine the
Great and Diocletian.

Professor Toynbee regards the reassertion of absolutism
and the centralization of government under Leo III as a
fatal error. But it is not easy to see what alternative course
was possible. In the West the Arabs overthrew imperial rule
in Africa and invaded Europe. What could have stayed the
far more formidable attack upon the Byzantine capital if
Leo III had not thrown into the scale the concentrated force
of the Empire and thus repelled the assault? Could the
Empire have survived? The ruler was but shouldering his
historic burden.

And even if the continuity of the history of the East
Roman State be questioned, the continuity of Byzantine
culture it is impossible to challenge. Within the Empire
the culture of the Hellenistic world which had arisen in
the kingdoms of the successors of Alexander the Great
lives on and moulds the achievement of East Rome. For
the Byzantines are Christian Alexandrians. In art they
still follow Hellenistic models; they inherit the rhetorical

tradition, the scholarship, the admiration for the Great Age of classical Greece which characterized the students of the kingdom of the Ptolemies. That admiration might inspire imitation, but it undoubtedly tended to stifle originality. Those who would seek to establish that at some time in the history of East Rome there is a breach in continuity, that something distinctively new came into being, must at least admit that the culture of the Empire knew no such severance: it persisted until the end of the Empire itself.

There are, however, scholars who would interpret otherwise the essential character of this civilization. For them East Rome was an 'oriental empire'; they contend that it did but grow more and more oriental until in the eighth century it became *étroitement orientalisé*. These assertions have been repeated many times, as though it were sought by repetition to evade the necessity for proof: certain it is that proof has never been forthcoming. It is true that Hellenistic civilization had absorbed some oriental elements, but the crucial question is: Did the Byzantine Empire adopt any *further* really significant elements from the East beyond those which had already interpenetrated the Hellenistic world? One may point to the ceremony of prostration before the ruler (*proskynesis*), to mutilation as a punishment, possibly to some forms of ascetic contemplation, to the excesses of Syrian asceticism, to Greek music and hymnody derived from Syrian rhythms and rhythmic prose, and to cavalry regiments armed with the bow—what more? The Christian religion itself came, it is true, originally from Palestine, but it early fell under Hellenistic influence, and after the work of the Christian thinkers of Alexandria—of Clement and Origen—Christianity had won its citizenship in the Greek world. Until further evidence be adduced, it may be suggested that the Empire which resolutely refused to accept the Eastern theories of the Iconoclasts was in so doing but defending its own essential character, that the elements which in their combination formed the complex civilization of the Empire were indeed the Roman tradition in law and government, the Hellenistic tradition in language, literature, and philosophy, and a Christian tradition which had already been refashioned on a Greek model.

What were the elements of strength which sustained the Empire in its saecular effort? They may be briefly summarized. Perhaps the factor which deserves pride of place is the conviction that the Empire was willed by God and protected by Him and by His Anointed. It is this conviction which in large measure explains the traditionalism, the extreme conservatism of East Rome: why innovate if your State is founded on Heaven's favour? The ruler may be dethroned, but not the polity; that would have been akin to apostasy. Autocracy remained unchallenged. And, with God's approval secure, the Byzantine Sovereign and the Byzantine State were both Defenders of the Faith. To the Byzantine the Crusades came far earlier than they did to the West, for whether the war was waged with Persia or later with the Arabs, the foes were alike unbelievers, while the standard which was borne at the head of the East Roman forces was a Christian icon—at times one of those sacred pictures which had not been painted by any human hand. The Byzantine was fighting the battles of the Lord of Hosts and could rely upon supernatural aid. The psychological potency of such a conviction as this the modern student must seek imaginatively to comprehend—and that is not easy.

And the concentration of all authority in the hands of the Vicegerent of God was in itself a great source of strength. On the ruins of the Roman Empire in western Europe many States had been created: in the East the single State had been preserved and with it the inheritance from an earlier Rome, the single law. In the West men's lives were lived under many legal systems—tribal law, local law, manorial law—and the law of the central State fought a continuing battle for recognition: in the East one law and one law alone prevailed, and that Roman law emanated from a single source, the Emperor; even the decisions of the Councils of the Church needed for their validity the approval of the Sovereign. The precedents established by Constantine were upheld by his successors, and under the Iconoclasts the challenge to imperial authority raised by the monks demanding a greater freedom for the Church was unavailing. The Patriarch of Constantinople lived in the shadow of the imperial palace: within the Byzantine Empire there was no room for an Eastern Papacy. The fact that the Book of Ceremonies of Constantine Porphyrogenitus has been preserved has tended to produce the impression that the life of an East Roman Emperor was spent in an unbroken succession of civil and religious formalities, that its most absorbing care was the wearing of precisely those vestments which were hallowed by traditional usage. That impression is misleading, for the Emperor successfully maintained his right to lead the Byzantine armies in the field, while the folk of East Rome demanded of their ruler efficiency and personal devotion. In the constitutional theory of the Empire no hereditary right to the throne was recognized, though at times hereditary sentiment might have great influence. When, under the Macedonian dynasty, that sentiment placed a student emperor upon the throne, a colleague performed those military duties which remained part of the imperial burden. That immense burdon of obligation imposed upon the ruler—the responsibility both for the temporal and spiritual welfare of his subjects—fashioned the Byzantine imperial ideal, and that ideal puts its constraint upon the Sovereign: it may make of him another man:

> The courses of his youth promised it not.
> The breath no sooner left his father's body,
> But that his wildness mortified in him
> Seemed to die too.

So it was with Basil II: 'with all sail set he abandoned the course of pleasure and resolutely turned to seriousness.'[1] It is to wrong the Byzantine Emperors to picture them as cloistered puppets: the Emperor was not merely the source of all authority both military and civil, the one and only legislator, the supreme judge, but it was his hand, as George of Pisidia wrote, which in war enforced the will of Christ.

The East Roman State demanded money—much money: no Byzantine Sovereign could 'live of his own'. During the chaos of the breakdown of the imperial administration in the third century of our era a prodigious inflation sent all prices rocketing sky-high and the economy of the Empire threatened to relapse into a system of barter. But the fourth-

---

[1] Psellus, *Chronographia*, vol. i, ch. 4.

century reform restored a money economy and taxation which could be adapted to the current needs of the Government. While the west of Europe under its barbarian rulers was unable to maintain the complex financial system of Rome, the needs of the East Roman State were safeguarded by a return to a system which enabled it to pay its soldiers in money, while, if military force should fail, the diplomacy of Constantinople could fall back upon the persuasive influence of Byzantine gold. It was the tribute derived from the taxation of its subjects which enabled the Empire to maintain a regular army schooled in an art of war—an art perpetually renewed as the appearance of fresh foes called for a revision of the military manuals. This small highly trained army must at all costs be preserved: no similar force could be hurriedly improvised on an emergency. War for the Empire was no joust, but a desperately serious affair. Therefore risks must not be run: ambushes, feints, any expedient by which irreplaceable lives could be saved were an essential element of Byzantine strategy. To us the numerical strength of East Roman armies seems preposterously small. As Diehl has pointed out, Belisarius reconquered Africa from the Vandals with at most 15,000 men; in the tenth century the great expeditions against Crete were carried out by a disembarkation force of 9,000 to 15,000. The grand total of the Byzantine military forces in the tenth century was at most 140,000 men.

The Empire was always inclined to neglect the fleet when no immediate danger threatened from the sea. During the first three centuries of our era the Mediterranean had been a Roman lake. The only barbarian kingdom formed on Roman soil which took to the sea was that of the Vandals in North Africa and before their fleets the Empire was powerless: the seaward connexions between the East and the West were snapped. The Emperor Leo even feared that the Vandals would attack Alexandria: Daniel, the Stylite saint whom he consulted, assured him that his fears were groundless, and in the event the holy man's confidence was justified. Justinian made an extraordinary effort in his sea-borne attack upon North Africa, but after the overthrow of the Vandal kingdom we hear of no further naval operations until the Arabs developed their sea-power in the seventh century. When Constans II reorganized the fleet and left Constantinople for Sicily (A.D. 662), his aim, as Bury suggested, must have been from a western base to safeguard North Africa and Sicily from the Arabs in order to prevent the encirclement of the Empire: 'If the Saracens won a footing in these lands Greece was exposed, the gates of the Hadriatic were open, Dalmatia and the Exarchate were at their mercy' (Bury). But Constans died, his successors kept the imperial navy in the eastern Mediterranean, and the Saracen fleet drove the Romans out of Carthage. North Africa was lost.

When the Caliphate was removed from Syria to Mesopotamia Constantinople was released from any serious menace from the sea; the navies of Egypt and Syria were in decline, and in consequence the Byzantine navy was neglected. Under the Macedonian house the East Roman fleet played an essential part in the imperial victories, but later the Empire made the fatal mistake of relying upon the navy of Venice and thus lost its own control of the sea. The naval policy of the Byzantine State did but react to external stimulus much as the Republic of Rome had done in former centuries.

Army and fleet defended the Empire from external peril, but the force which maintained its internal administration was the imperial civil service. Extremely costly, highly traditional in its methods, often corrupt, it was yet, it would seem, in general efficient: the administrative machine worked on by its own accumulated momentum. Under weak and incapable rulers it could still function, while the edicts of reforming emperors would doubtless be competently filed and then disregarded. We possess no adequate documentary evidence for the history of this imperial service: the historians took it for granted, and they tend to mention it only when some crying scandal aroused popular discontent. Yet its activity is one of the presuppositions which rendered possible the longevity of the Empire.

And the service of the Orthodox Church to East Rome must never be forgotten in any estimate of the factors which sustained the Byzantine State.

'The Latin Church', as Sir William Ramsay said in a memorable lecture in 1908, 'never identified itself with the Empire. So far as it

lowered itself to stand on the same level as the Empire it was a rival
and an enemy rather than an ally. But in the East the Orthodox
Church cast in its lot with the Empire: it was coterminous with and
never permanently wider than the Empire. It did not long attempt
to stand on a higher level than the State and the people; but on that
lower level it stood closer to the mass of the people. It lived among
them. It moved the common average man with more penetrating
power than a loftier religion could have done. Accordingly the Orthodox Church was fitted to be the soul and life of the Empire, to maintain
the Imperial unity, to give form and direction to every manifestation
of national vigour.'[1]

That close alliance between the Byzantine Empire and the
Orthodox Church, however, brought with it unhappy consequences, as Professor Toynbee has forcibly reminded us.
Church and State were so intimately connected that membership of the Orthodox Church tended inevitably to bring with
it subjection to imperial politics, and conversely alliance with
the Empire would bring with it subjection to the Patriarch of
Constantinople. The fatal effect of this association is seen in
the relations of the Empire with Bulgaria and with Armenia.
To us it would appear so obvious that, for instance, in
Armenia toleration of national religious traditions must have
been the true policy, but the Church of the Seven Councils
was assured that it alone held the Christian faith in its purity
and that in consequence it was its bounden duty to ride
roughshod over less enlightened Churches and to enforce
the truth committed to its keeping. And a Byzantine
Emperor had no other conviction: the order of Heraclius in
the seventh century that all Jews throughout his Empire
should be forcibly baptized does but illustrate an Emperor's
conception of a ruler's duty. The Orthodox Church must
have appeared to many, as it appeared to Sir William Ramsay, 'not a lovable power, not a beneficent power, but stern,
unchanging . . . sufficient for itself, self-contained and self-
centred'.[2]

But to its own people Orthodoxy was generous. The
Church might disapprove of the abnormal asceticism of a
Stylite saint; but that asceticism awoke popular enthusiasm

---

[1] *Luke the Physician* (London, Hodder and Stoughton, 1908), p. 145 (slightly
abbreviated in citation).
[2] Ibid., p. 149.

and consequently the Church yielded: it recognized St. Simeon Stylites and made of Daniel the Stylite a priest. That is a symbol of the catholicity of Orthodoxy. And through the services of the Church the folk of the Empire became familiar with the Old Testament in its Greek form (the Septuagint) and with the New Testament which from the first was written in the 'common' Greek speech of the Hellenistic world, and the East Roman did truly *believe* in the inspiration of the Bible and its inerrancy. When Cosmas, the retired India merchant, set forth his 'Christian Topography' to prove that for the Christian the only possible view was that the earth was flat, he demonstrated the truth of his assertion by texts from the Bible and showed that earth is the lower story, then comes the firmament, and above that the vaulted story which is Heaven—all bound together by side walls precisely like a large American trunk for ladies' dresses. If you wished to defend contemporary miracles it was naturally the Bible which came to your support: Christ had promised that His disciples should perform greater works than His own: would a Christian by his doubts make Christ a liar? 'The Fools for Christ's sake'—those who endured the ignominy of playing the fool publicly in order to take upon themselves part of that burden of humiliation which had led their Lord to the Cross—they, too, had their texts: 'The foolishness of God is wiser than men', 'the wisdom of this world is foolishness with God'. It was hearing a text read in Church which suggested to Antony his vocation to be the first monk: 'If you would be perfect, go sell all that thou hast and give to the poor, and come, follow me.' That summons he obeyed and it led him to the desert. In Byzantine literature you must always be ready to catch an echo from the Bible.

And thus because it was the Church of the Byzantine people, because its liturgy was interwoven with their daily lives, because its tradition of charity and unquestioning almsgiving supplied their need in adversity, the Orthodox Church became the common possession and the pride of the East Romans. The Christian faith became the bond which in large measure took the place of a common nationality. And was *their* Church to be subjected to the discipline of an alien Pope who had surrendered his freedom to barbarous Frankish rulers of the West? Variations in ritual usage might be formulated to justify the rejection of papal claims, but these formulations did but mask a profounder difference —an instinctive consciousness that a Mediterranean world which had once been knit together by a bilingual culture had split into two halves which could no longer understand each other. The history of the centuries did but make the chasm deeper: men might try to throw bridges across the cleft—communion between the Churches might be restored, even Cerularius in the eleventh century did not say the last word, but the underlying 'otherness' remained until at last all the king's horses and all the king's men were powerless to dragoon the Orthodox world into union with the Latin Church. That sense of 'otherness' still persists to-day, and it will be long before the Churches of the Orthodox rite accept the dogma of the infallibility of a Western Pope.

And, above all, it must be repeated, Constantinople itself, the imperial city (ἡ βασιλεύουσα πόλις), secure behind the shelter of its fortifications, sustained the Empire alike in fair and in foul weather. The city was the magnet which attracted folk from every quarter to itself: to it were drawn ambassadors and barbarian kings, traders and merchants, adventurers and mercenaries ready to serve the Emperor for pay, bishops and monks, scholars and theologians. In the early Middle Age Constantinople was for Europe *the* city, since the ancient capital of the West had declined, its pre-eminence now but a memory, or at best a primacy of honour. Constantinople had become what the Piraeus had been for an earlier Greek world; to this incomparable market the foreigner came to make his purchases and the Byzantine State levied its customs on the goods as they left for Russia or the West. Because the foreigner sought the market, New Rome, it would seem, failed to develop her own mercantile marine, and thus in later centuries the merchants of Venice or Genoa could extort perilous privileges from the Empire's weakness. Within the imperial palace a traditional diplomacy of prestige and remote majesty filled with awe the simple minds of barbarian rulers, even if it awoke the scorn of more sophisticated envoys. It may well be that the Byzantines were justified in developing and maintaining with scrupulous fidelity that calculated ceremonial. 'But your Emperor is a God' one barbarian is reported to have said—him, too, the magnet of Constantinople would attract and the Empire would gain a new ally.

Yet this magnetism had its dangers. All roads led to New Rome, and a popular general or a member of that Anatolian landed aristocracy which had been schooled in military service might follow those roads and seek to set himself upon the imperial throne. Prowess might give a title to the claimant, and the splendid prize, the possession of the capital, would crown the venture, for he who held Constantinople was thereby lord of the Empire. Yet though the inhabitants might open the gates to an East Roman pretender, the Byzantines could assert with pride that never through the centuries had they betrayed the capital to a foreign foe. That is their historic service to Europe.

It becomes clear that the welfare of the Byzantine State depended upon the maintenance of a delicate balance of forces—a balance between the *potentiores*—the rich and powerful—and the imperial administration, between the army and the civil service, and, further, a balance between the revenues of the State and those tasks which it was incumbent upon the Empire to perform. Thus the loss of Asia Minor to the Seljuks did not only deprive East Rome of its reservoir of man-power, it also crippled imperial finances. Above all, in a world where religion played so large a part it was necessary to preserve the balance—the co-operation—between Church and State. 'Caesaropapism' is a recent word-formation by which it has been sought to characterize the position of the Emperor in relation to the Church. It is doubtless true that in the last resort the Emperor could assert his will by deposing a Patriarch; it is also true that Justinian of his own motion defined orthodox dogma without consulting a Council of the Church. But that precedent was not followed in later centuries; an Emperor was bound to respect the authoritative formulation of the faith; and even Iconoclasm, it would seem, took its rise in the pronouncements of Anatolian bishops, and it was only after this episcopal initiative that the Emperor intervened. Indeed

the Byzantine view of the relation which should subsist
between Church and State can hardly be doubted: for the
common welfare there must be harmony and collaboration.
As Daniel the Stylite said addressing the Emperor Basiliscus
and the Patriarch of Constantinople, Acacius: 'When you
disagree you bring confusion on the holy churches and in the
whole world you stir up no ordinary disturbance.' Emperor
and Patriarch are both members of the organism formed by
the Christian community of East Rome. It is thus, by the
use of a Pauline figure, that the *Epanagoge* states the relation.
That law-book may never have been officially published, it
may be inspired by the Patriarch Photius, but none the less
it surely is a faithful mirror of Byzantine thought. But it is
also true that bishops assembled in a Council were apt to
yield too easily to imperial pressure, even though they might
reverse their decision when the pressure was removed. The
breeze passes over the ears of wheat and they bend before it;
the breeze dies down and the wheat-ears stand as they stood
before its coming. But such an influence as this over an
episcopal rank and file who were lacking in 'civil courage' is
not what the term 'Caesaropapism' would suggest; if it is
used at all, its meaning should at least be strictly defined.

One is bound to ask: How did these Byzantines live? It
was that question which Robert Byron in his youthful book
The Byzantine Achievement sought to answer; he headed his
chapter 'The Joyous Life'. That is a serious falsification.
The more one studies the life of the East Romans the more
one is conscious of the weight of care which overshadowed
it: the fear of the ruthless tax-collector, the dread of the
arbitrary tyranny of the imperial governor, the peasant's
helplessness before the devouring land-hunger of the powerful, the recurrent menace of barbarian invasion: life was a
dangerous affair; and against its perils only supernatural
aid—the help of saint, or magician, or astrologer could avail.
And it is to the credit of the Byzantine world that it realized
and sought to lighten that burden by founding hospitals
for the sick, for lepers, and the disabled, by building hostels
for pilgrims, strangers, and the aged, maternity homes for
women, refuges for abandoned children and the poor,

institutions liberally endowed by their founders who in their charters set out at length their directions for the administration of these charities. It is to the lives of the saints that one must turn, and not primarily to the Court historians if one would picture the conditions of life in East Rome. And because life was insecure and dangerous, suspicions were easily aroused and outbreaks of violence and cruelty were the natural consequence. The Europe of our own day ought to make it easier for us to comprehend the passions of the Byzantine world. We shall never realize to the full the magnitude of the imperial achievement until we have learned in some measure the price at which that achievement was bought.

At the close of this brief Introduction an attempt may be made to summarize in a few words the character of that achievement: (i) as a custodian trustee East Rome preserved much of that classical literature which it continuously and devotedly studied; (ii) Justinian's Digest of earlier Roman law salved the classical jurisprudence without which the study of Roman legal theory would have been impossible, while his Code was the foundation of the Empire's law throughout its history. The debt which Europe owes for that work of salvage is incalculable; (iii) the Empire continued to write history, and even the work of the humble Byzantine annalist has its own significance: the annalists begin with man's creation and include an outline of the history of past empires because 'any history written on Christian principles will be of necessity universal': it will describe the rise and fall of civilizations and powers: it will no longer have a particularistic centre of gravity, whether that centre of gravity be Greece or Rome:[1] a world salvation needed a world history for its illustration: nothing less would suffice. And to the Christian world history was not a mere cyclic process eternally repeating itself, as it was to the Stoic. History was the working out of God's plan: it had a goal and the Empire was the agent of a divine purpose. And Byzantine writers were not content with mere annalistic: in writing

[1] R. G. Collingwood, *The Idea of History* (Oxford, Clarendon Press, 1946), pp. 46–50.

history the East Roman not only handed down to posterity the chronicle of the Empire's achievement, he also recorded the actions of neighbouring peoples before they had any thought of writing their own history. Thus it is that the Slavs owe to East Rome so great a debt; (iv) the Orthodox Church was a Missionary Church, and from its work of evangelization the Slav peoples settled on its frontiers derived their Christianity and a vernacular Liturgy; (v) it was in an eastern province of the Empire—in Egypt—that monasticism took its rise. Here was initiated both the life of the solitary and the life of an ascetic community. It was by a Latin translation of St. Athanasius' Life of St. Antony, the first monk, that monasticism was carried to the West, and what monasticism—Egypt's greatest gift to the world—has meant in the history of Europe cannot easily be calculated. It was the ascetics of East Rome who fashioned a mystic theology which transcending reason sought the direct experience of the vision of God and of union with the Godhead (*theosis*). Already amongst the students of western Europe an interest has been newly created in this Byzantine mysticism, and as more documents are translated that interest may be expected to arouse a deeper and more intelligent comprehension; (vi) further, the Empire gave to the world a religious art which to-day western Europe is learning to appreciate with a fuller sympathy and a larger understanding. Finally, let it be repeated, there remains the historic function of Constantinople as Europe's outpost against the invading hordes of Asia. Under the shelter of that defence of the Eastern gateway western Europe could refashion its own life: it is hardly an exaggeration to say that the civilization of western Europe is a by-product of the Byzantine Empire's will to survive.

N. H. B.

I

THE HISTORY OF THE BYZANTINE EMPIRE:
AN OUTLINE

A. FROM A.D. 330 TO THE FOURTH CRUSADE

I

THE history of Byzantium is, formally, the story of the Late
Roman Empire. The long line of her rulers is a direct continuation of the series of Emperors which began with
Augustus; and it was by the same principle—consent of the
Roman Senate and People—which Augustus had proclaimed
when he ended the Republic that the Byzantine rulers
wielded their authority. Theoretically speaking, the ancient
and indivisible Roman Empire, mistress, and, after the
downfall of the Great King of Persia in 629, sole mistress of
the *orbis terrarum*, continued to exist until the year 1453.
Rome herself, it was true, had been taken by the Visigoths
in 410; Romulus Augustulus, the last puppet Emperor in
the West, had been deposed by the barbarians in 476, and
the firmest constitutionalist of Byzantium must have acknowledged, in the course of the centuries which followed, that
Roman dominion over the former provinces of Britain, Gaul,
Spain, and even Italy appeared to be no longer effective.
Visible confirmation of this view was added when a German
upstart of the name of Charles was actually, on Christmas
Day, A.D. 800, saluted as Roman Emperor in the West. But
there are higher things than facts; the Byzantine theory,
fanciful as it sounds, was accepted for many centuries by
friends and foes alike, and its influence in preserving the
very existence of the Empire is incalculable. Contact with
the West might become precarious; the old Latin speech,
once the official language of imperial government, might
disappear, and the Rhomaeans of the late Byzantine Empire
might seem to have little except the name in common with
their Roman predecessors. Liutprand of Cremona, in the
tenth century, could jeer at the pompous ceremonial and
ridiculous pretensions of the Byzantine Court; but the

B

Westerner failed, as did the later Crusading leaders, to comprehend the outlook of the classical world, strangely surviving in its medieval environment. For the ruler of Byzantium, the unshakable assurance that his State represented Civilization itself, islanded in the midst of barbarism, justified any means that might be found necessary for its preservation; while the proud consciousness of his double title to world-dominion—heir of the universal Roman Empire and Vicegerent of God Himself—enabled him to meet his enemies in the gate, when capital and Empire seemed irretrievably doomed, and turn back the tide of imminent destruction. Ruinous schemes of reconquest and reckless extravagance in Court expenditure were the obvious consequences of the imperial ideal; but what the latter-day realist condemns as the incorrigible irredentism of the Byzantine Emperors was not merely the useless memory of vanished Roman glories. It was the outcome of a confidence that the Empire was fulfilling a divine commission; that its claim to rule was based on the will of the Christian God.

II

When Constantine founded his capital city on the Bosphorus, his intention was to create a second Rome. A Senate was established, public buildings were erected, and the whole machinery of imperial bureaucracy was duplicated at its new headquarters. Aristocratic families from Italy were encouraged to build residences there, while bread and circuses were provided for the populace. The circus factions, transported from the other Rome, formed a militia for the defence of the city. The avowed policy was to produce a replica of the old capital on the Tiber.

One difference, indeed, there was. The new centre of administration was to be a Christian capital, free from the pagan associations of Old Rome, which had resisted, all too successfully, the religious innovations of Constantine. The Council of Nicaea, representing the Roman world united under a single Emperor, had given a clear indication of the main lines which subsequent sovereigns were to follow in dealing with the Church. The maintenance of religious unity was henceforth to form an even more essential principle of imperial policy. Rifts, however caused, in the structure of the Empire were a danger which, in view of the barbarian menace, the ruler could not afford to overlook. Constantinople was to be the strategic centre for the defence of the Danubian and Eastern frontiers; she was also to be the stronghold of Orthodoxy, the guardian of the newly-sealed alliance between Church and State.

At the same time, emphasis was laid on the continuity of Greek culture, rooted though it was in pagan memories. The rich cities of Syria and Asia Minor, the venerated island shrines of the Aegean were stripped of their masterpieces of sculpture, their tutelary images, to adorn the new mistress of the Roman Empire. Education was sedulously fostered by the authorities, and before long the University of Constantinople, with its classical curriculum, was attracting students from all parts. The process of centralization continued, and this was furthered by the closing in 551 of the school of law at Beirut, after the destruction of the city by earthquake.

From the first, then, the three main principles of the Byzantine Empire may be said to have manifested themselves —Imperial Tradition, Christian Orthodoxy, Greek Culture. These were the permanent directing forces of Byzantine government, religion, and literature.

III

The administrative reforms of Diocletian and Constantine had given to the Roman Empire a renewed lease of life, a restoration, dearly bought though it was, of stability after the chaos of the third century. Important, however, as these reforms were, it is possible to regard them as the logical conclusion of existing tendencies. The two acts of policy, on the other hand, by which Constantine became known to posterity—the foundation of Constantinople and the imperial favour increasingly shown to Christianity—may justly be considered a revolution, which set the Empire on new paths. That revolution took three centuries for its full development, but its final consequence was the creation of the East Roman or Byzantine State. Thus from Constantine (d. 337) to Heraclius (d. 641) stretches a formative period, during which Byzantium gradually becomes loosened from her Western interests, until, with the transformation of the Near East in the seventh century and the accompanying changes in her own internal structure, she assumes her distinctive historical form.

In this period the reign of Theodosius the Great (379–95) marks a turning-point. He was the last sole ruler of the Roman Empire in its original extent. Within a generation of his death, Britain, France, Spain, and Africa were passing into barbarian hands. Under his two sons, Arcadius and Honorius, the Eastern and Western halves of the Empire were sundered, never again to be fully reunited in fact, though remaining one in theory. In the relations of Church and State the reign was no less decisive. Constantine's initiative had, in 313, led to an announcement by the joint Emperors, himself and Licinius, of toleration for the Christian faith, and at the Council of Nicaea (325) he had, in the interests of imperial unity, secured the condemnation of Arius. Constantine's sons were educated as Christians, and Constantius II (337–61) zealously championed his own interpretation of the Christian faith; but the pagan reaction under Julian the Apostate (361–3), though finally ineffective, demonstrated the strength of the opposition. Julian's immediate successors displayed caution and forbearance in matters of religion, and it was not until the reign of Theodosius I that the Roman Empire officially became the Orthodox Christian State. Henceforth legal toleration of paganism was at an end and Arianism, outlawed from Roman territory, spread only among the barbarian invaders.

New heresies emerged during the fifth century; Trinitarian controversy was succeeded by Christological disputes. The rift between East and West, steadily widening as their interests diverged, enhanced the political significance of the Church's quarrels, and emperors could less than ever afford to remain indifferent. In the East the metropolitan sees had been placed in the chief centres of imperial administration; with the rise of Constantinople to the status of a capital, her ecclesiastical rank was exalted till she stood next in importance to Rome herself. A triangular contest ensued between Rome, Constantinople, and Alexandria, forming the background against which the Nestorian and Monophysite controversies were debated. The Council of Chalcedon (451), in which Rome and Constantinople combined to defeat the claims of Alexandria, ended the danger of Egyptian supremacy in ecclesiastical affairs, but it left behind it a legacy of troubles. Egypt continued to support the Monophysite heresy, and was joined by Syria—two provinces where religious differences furnished a welcome pretext for popular opposition to the central Government. Meanwhile the Roman see, uncompromisingly Chalcedonian, commanded the loyalty of the West. The problem which taxed all the resources of imperial statecraft was the reconciliation of these opposing worlds. The Henoticon of the Emperor Zeno (482), the Formula of Union which should reconcile Monophysite and Orthodox, did, it is true, placate the Monophysites, but it antagonized Rome. Justinian, in the sixth century, wavered between the two, and Heraclius, in the seventh, made a final but fruitless effort at mediation. The Arab conquest of Syria and Egypt ended the hopeless struggle by cutting off from the Empire the dissident provinces. The ecclesiastical primacy of Constantinople was now secure in the East, and with the disappearance of the political need for compromise the main source of friction with the West had been removed. By this time, however, the position of the two bishops at Old and New Rome had become very different. Church and State at Byzantium now formed an indissoluble unity, while the Papacy had laid firm foundations for its ultimate independence.

The German invasions of the fourth and fifth centuries were the principal cause of the differing fortunes of East and West, and the decisive factor was the geographical and strategic position of Constantinople, lying at the northern apex of the triangle which included the rich coast-line of the eastern Mediterranean. The motive force which impelled the Germanic invaders across the frontiers of Rhine and Danube was the irresistible onrush of the Huns, moving westwards from central Asia along the great steppe-belt which ends in the Hungarian plains. This westward advance struck full at central Europe; but only a portion of the Byzantine territories was affected. Visigoths, Huns, and

Ostrogoths successively ravaged the Balkans, dangerous but not fatal enemies, and passed on to dismember Rome's provinces in the West. The weakness of Persia, likewise harassed by the Huns, and the timely concessions made to her by Theodosius I in the partition of Armenia (*c.* 384–7), preserved the Euphrates frontier intact, while the ascendancy of the barbarian *magistri militum*, commanders of the Germanized Roman armies, was twice broken at Constantinople, by the massacre of the Goths in 400, and again by the employment of Isaurian troops as a counter-force in 471. Very different was the fate of Rome. In 410 the city itself was held to ransom by the Visigoths, and during the course of the fifth century Britain, Gaul, Spain, and Africa slipped from the Empire's weakening grasp. In 476 came the end of the series of puppet emperors, and the barbarian generals, who throughout this century had been the effective power, assumed the actual government of Italy.

In the economic sphere the contrast between East and West is yet more striking. Even under the earlier Empire, the preponderance of wealth and population had lain with the Eastern provinces. Banking and commerce were more highly developed in these regions, and through them passed the great trade-routes carrying the produce of Asia to the Western markets. The prosperous cities of Asia Minor, Syria, and Egypt were still, in the fifth century, almost undisturbed by the invader, and their contributions, in taxes or in kind, flowed in full volume to the harbours and Treasury of Byzantium. In western Europe the machinery of provincial government had broken down under the stress of anarchy and invasion. Revenues were falling off; long-distance trade was becoming impossible; the unity of the Mediterranean had been broken by the Vandal fleet, and even the traditional source of the corn-supply of the city of Rome was closed when the Vandals took possession of north-west Africa. With the establishment of the barbarian kingdoms, the organization of a civilized State disappears from the west of Europe. The centralized government of Byzantium could levy and pay its forces, educate its officials, delegate authority to its provincial governors, and raise revenue from the agricultural and trading population of its

Empire. The German kings had only the plunder of conquered lands with which to reward their followers; standing
armies were out of the question, and the complications of
bureaucracy were beyond their ken, save where, as in the
Italy of Theodoric, a compromise with Roman methods had
been reached.

IV

In 518 a Macedonian peasant, who had risen to the command of the palace guard, mounted the imperial throne as
Justin I. His nephew and successor, Justinian the Great
(527–65), dominates the history of sixth-century Byzantium.
For the last time a purely Roman-minded Emperor, Latin
in speech and thought, ruled on the Bosphorus. In him the
theory of Roman sovereignty finds both its fullest expression
and its most rigorous application. It involved, in his view,
the reconquest of the territory of the old Roman Empire,
and in particular of those Western provinces now occupied
by German usurpers. It involved also the imperial duty of
assuring the propagation and victory of the Orthodox faith
and, as a corollary, the absolute control of the Emperor over
Church affairs.

In pursuance of this policy Africa was retaken from the
Vandals (534), Italy from the Ostrogoths (537). The south
of Spain was restored to the Empire, and the whole Mediterranean was now open to Byzantine shipping. A vast
system of fortifications was constructed on every frontier;
the defensive garrisons were reorganized, and the provincial
administration was tightened up. Public works and buildings of every description, impressive remains of which are
still visible in three continents, owed their origin, and often
their name, to the ambitious energy of Justinian.

The same principles inspired his two greatest creations,
the codification of Roman law and the building of St. Sophia.
Conscientious government required that the law, its instrument, should be so arranged and simplified as to function
efficiently; and the immense expenditure incurred by the
Western expeditions could be met only by the smoothest and
most economical working of the fiscal machinery. Imperial
prestige was no less involved in the magnificence of the

Court and its surroundings; and the position of the Emperor, as representative of God upon earth, gave special emphasis to his responsibility for the erection of the foremost church in Christendom. The centralization of all the activities of the Empire—political, artistic, literary, social, and economic—in its capital city was now practically complete, and the first great period of Byzantine art is nobly exemplified in the Church of the Holy Wisdom.

The reverse of the medal, unhappily, stands out in higher relief when subsequent events are considered. The Western conquests, though striking, were incomplete, and ended by draining the resources of the Empire. Heavily increased taxation defeated the honest attempts of Justinian to remedy abuses in its collection, and alienated the populations of the newly regained provinces. The interests of East and West were now widely divergent, and to the Italian taxpayer the Byzantine official became a hateful incubus. Further, the main artery of communication between the Bosphorus and the Adriatic was threatened by the Slav incursions into the Balkan peninsula, which increased in frequency towards the end of the reign.

Even before his accession Justinian had departed from the conciliatory policy of Zeno and Anastasius with regard to the Monophysites, and with an eye to Western goodwill had taken measures to close the schism between Rome and Constantinople caused by Zeno's attempts to secure a working compromise in the dogmatic dispute. This, however, did not end all troubles with the Papacy, for Justinian's 'Caesaropapism' demanded absolute submission of the pontiff to all pronouncements of the imperial will; and to enforce this, violent measures, moral and even physical, were required, as Pope Vigilius found to his cost. A more serious consequence was the persecution of Monophysites in Egypt and Syria. The influence of Theodora, the Empress, who possessed Monophysite sympathies and an understanding of the Eastern problem, prevented the policy from being consistently carried out; but enough was done to rouse the fury of the populace against the 'Melchites', or supporters of the Emperor, and the results of such disaffection were seen before long when Persian and Arab invaders entered these regions.

At the death of Justinian it became evident that the vital interests of Byzantium lay in the preservation of her northern and eastern frontiers, which guarded the capital and the essential provinces of Anatolia and Syria. The rest of the century was occupied by valiant and largely successful efforts to mitigate the consequences of Justinian's one-sided policy. Aggression in the West had entailed passive defence elsewhere, supplemented by careful diplomacy and a network of small alliances. This had proved expensive in subsidies, and damaging to prestige. Justin II in 572 boldly refused tribute to Persia, and hostilities were resumed. The war was stubbornly pursued till in 591 the main objectives of Byzantium were reached. Persia, weakened by dynastic struggles, ceded her portion of Armenia and the strongholds of Dara and Martyropolis. The approaches to Asia Minor and Syria thus secured, Maurice (582–602) could turn his attention to the north. The Danube frontier—barely 200 miles from Constantinople—was crumbling under a new pressure. The Avars, following the traditional route of Asiatic nomad invaders, had crossed the south Russian steppes and established themselves, shortly after Justinian's death, in the Hungarian plains. Dominating the neighbouring peoples, Slav and Germanic, they had exacted heavy tribute from Byzantium as the price of peace. Even this did not avert the fall of Sirmium (582), key-fortress of the Middle Danube, and the Adriatic coasts now lay open to barbarian attacks. After ten years of chequered warfare Maurice succeeded in stemming the flood, and in the autumn of 602 Byzantine forces were once more astride the Danube. Meanwhile the Lombards, ousted by Avar hordes from their settlements on the Theiss, had invaded Italy (568), and by 580 were in possession of more than half the peninsula. Byzantium, preoccupied with the East, could send no regular assistance, but efforts were made to create a Frankish alliance against the invaders, and with Maurice's careful reorganization of the Italian garrisons a firm hold was maintained on the principal cities of the seaboard.

All such precarious gains won by the successors of Justinian were swept away by the revolution of 602, which heralded the approach of the darkest years that the Roman

Empire had yet known. Angry at the prospect of wintering on the Danube, the troops revolted. Phocas, a brutal centurion, was elected Emperor, and Maurice and his family were put to the sword. A reign of terror ensued, which revealed the real weakness of the Empire. Internal anarchy and bankruptcy threatened the very existence of the central power, while Persian armies, in a series of raiding campaigns, captured Rome's outlying provinces and ravaged even her vital Anatolian possessions. The ruinous heritage of Justinian was now made manifest, and the days of Byzantium were, it seemed, already numbered.

V

The forces of revival found their leader in Africa, perhaps at this time the most Roman province of the Empire. In 610 Heraclius, son of the governor of Carthage, sailed for Constantinople. Phocas was overthrown, and the new Emperor entered upon his almost hopeless task. The demoralized armies were refashioned, strict economy repaired the shattered finances, and the turbulent city factions were sternly repressed. The Sassanid forces, however, could not be faced in open combat, and a Persian wave of conquest, more overwhelming than any since Achaemenid days, rolled over the Near East. In 611 Antioch fell, in 613 Damascus; in the following year Jerusalem was sacked, and its Patriarch carried off to Persia, together with the wood of the True Cross, the holiest relic of Christianity. In 619 came the invasion of Egypt, and with the fall of Alexandria, the great centre of African and Asiatic commerce, Byzantium lost the principal source of her corn-supply. Palestine, Syria, and Egypt were gone, Anatolia was threatened, and meanwhile the Avars ravaged the European provinces, and in 617 were hardly repulsed from the walls of the capital.

By 622 Heraclius had completed his preparations, and the age-old history of the struggle between Rome and Persia closed in a series of astonishing campaigns. Boldly leaving Constantinople to its fate, the Emperor based his operations on the distant Caucasus region, where he recruited the local tribes, descending at intervals to raid the provinces of northern Persia. In 626, while he was still gathering his forces for decisive action, a concerted attack was made on Constantinople by the Avar Khagan, supported by Slav and Bulgarian contingents, and by the Persian army which had occupied Chalcedon. Fortunately there was no disaffection within the city; Heraclius had united Church and State in eager support for his crusade, and the inhabitants put up a desperate defence. Byzantine sea-power in the straits was perhaps the decisive factor in averting disaster. The Slav boats which had entered the Golden Horn were disabled, and effective contact between the European and Asiatic assailants was rendered impossible. After suffering heavy losses, the Khagan was forced to withdraw. The defeat was significant, for Avar supremacy in the Balkans declined from this point. The Slav tribes successively gained independence, and until the rise of the Bulgarian Empire no centralized aggression endangered the Danubian provinces.

The following year saw the advance of Heraclius into the heart of Persia. A glorious victory was gained near Mosul, and although Ctesiphon, the Sassanid capital, could not be reached, the next spring brought news of Persian revolution and the murder of the Great King. His successor was obliged to conclude peace, and all the territory annexed by Persia was restored to the Empire. Egypt, Syria, and Asia Minor were freed from the invader, and the True Cross returned to its resting-place at Jerusalem. In 629 Heraclius entered his capital in a blaze of glory, and the triumph of the Christian Empire was universally recognized. Rome's only rival in the ancient world had been overthrown, and six years of fighting had raised Byzantium from the depths of humiliation to a position unequalled since the great days of Justinian.

The defeat of Persia was followed closely by events even more spectacular, which changed the whole course of history, and ushered in the Middle Ages of Byzantium. At the death of Muhammad in 632 his authority scarcely extended beyond the Hedjaz. Within a few years, however, the impetus of his movement, reinforced by economic conditions in the Arabian peninsula, had produced a centrifugal explosion, driving in every direction small bodies of mounted raiders in quest of food, plunder, and conquest. The old empires were in no state to resist them. Rome and Persia had exhausted each other in the final struggle. The Sassanid realm, torn by palace revolutions, fell an easy victim, while the absence at Constantinople of Heraclius, disabled by fatal illness, disorganized the defence of the Asiatic provinces. By 640 both Palestine and Syria were in Muslim hands; Alexandria fell to the Arabs in 642, and with Egypt as a base the conquerors crept slowly along the North African coast. Here they encountered more effective resistance, and it was not till the close of the seventh century that the capture of Carthage laid open the way to Spain. Meanwhile from the naval resources of Egypt and Syria a formidable sea-power developed. Cyprus and Rhodes were taken, and became centres of piracy from which the Muslims plundered the Aegean islands, ruining Mediterranean commerce. Constantinople itself was not immune, and a series of attacks from the sea (673–7) was repulsed only after desperate efforts and with the aid of the famous 'Greek Fire'. Asia Minor, the last non-European possession of Byzantium, was fiercely contended for throughout the century; Armenia and the Caucasus regions finally succumbed, but in the south the Taurus passes, the principal gateway to the peninsula, were successfully held.

Under the pressure of invasion the Byzantine Empire took on its medieval, and final, form. The days of Rome as a great land-power were now over. Apart from Asia Minor and the immediate hinterland of the capital, Byzantine territory was reduced practically to the fringes of the northern Mediterranean coast. During the course of the seventh century her Spanish outposts had been ceded to the Visigoths, and north-west Africa fell at length to the Saracens. Sicily and south Italy, the Magna Graecia of classical times, still owned allegiance to their Greek-speaking rulers; Naples, Venice, and Istria were still in Byzantine hands, and by her hold on the districts of Rome and Ravenna, joined by a narrow corridor, New Rome had succeeded in preventing the complete Lombard conquest of Italy. These, however, were all that remained of the Western conquests of Justinian. Between them and Constantinople the Slav tribes had established themselves in the Balkan peninsula, driving the

Roman population to the Dalmatian islets or the coastal cities, and severing the great highway which connected East and West. Nearer home, a new menace had arisen. About 680 the Bulgars, an Asiatic people, had crossed the lower Danube, and for the next three centuries their aggression was to prove a constant danger to the capital.

To meet these altered conditions the imperial administration was adapted for defence. The territories occupied by the Byzantine armies became provinces known as 'Themes', and their commanders exercised as governors both military and civil functions—an experiment first tried in the 'exarchates' of Italy and Africa. The heart of the Empire now lay in Asia Minor, and here the armies were recruited from farmers to whom were given grants of land on a hereditary tenure with the obligation of military service. This new system of imperial defence was organized during the course of the seventh century, but the poverty of our sources for this period makes it impossible to trace the development in detail. By the early years of the eighth century the new army was already in being.

Byzantium henceforth faced eastwards. The Latin element in her culture declined, though, in spite of its disappearance (apart from a number of technical terms) even from official language, the legal conceptions of Rome continued to form the basis of her constitution. Shorn of the greater part of her Asiatic and Western territories, she had become predominantly Greek in speech and civilization, and a yet closer bond of unity within the Empire was found in common devotion to Orthodox Christianity. With the loss of the dissident provinces, a main obstacle to agreement with the Papacy had been removed, and in 681, after many storms, union was temporarily re-established by the Sixth Oecumenical Council.

Constantine IV (668–85), under whom this result was achieved, had not only done much for the safety of the Western provinces, but had also administered an important check to the advance of Islam towards Constantinople. His reign was the high-water mark of Byzantine success during this period. The Heraclian dynasty ended with his successor, Justinian II, and with its disappearance palace revolutions, culminating in anarchy, filled the years from 695 to 717. As ever, the foes of Byzantium seized their opportunity. Revolts in Italy became more frequent and more serious. Carthage fell at last to the Islamic invader. The Bulgarians, profiting by political discord within the Empire, established themselves south of the Danube. In Asia Minor the loyalty of the Byzantine troops and of their leaders had been sapped by constant rebellions, while from Damascus the Umayyads, whose Empire was now approaching its zenith, mercilessly ravaged the unguarded provinces. In 717 the spearhead of the Islamic advance threatened the capital. A determined investment of Constantinople by land and sea followed, and for twelve months victory hung in the balance. In the same year Leo III (717–41) came to the throne, and the saving of Constantinople from the concentrated thrust of the first great Muslim Empire was the earliest achievement of the new dynasty.

VI

The birthplace of the so-called 'Isaurian' rulers is not certainly known, though northern Syria appears most probable. Their Asiatic origin is generally admitted, and many aspects of their policy, which, owing to the meagre and hostile character of the sources, has been much debated, seem to display an alien challenge to the Graeco-Roman traditions of the Empire. Of the military services of the Isaurian Emperors there can be no doubt; even their bitterest opponents gratefully remembered them as saviours of the commonwealth in its direst need.

The contraction of the frontiers of East Rome had brought with it a straitening of her financial resources, a slowing-down of her commercial activities, and a narrowing of her intellectual and spiritual life. Under the stress of constant warfare, art and letters had declined, and the seventh century is perhaps the most barren period in the history of Byzantine civilization. The resulting paucity of records has left many gaps in our knowledge. Fuller information would reveal the transformation of the Empire, and the heroic efforts which must have been necessary to adapt it to the new and perilous conditions brought about by the invasions. It was these efforts which formed the foundation of the Isaurian successes.

From the standpoint of European history Leo III's most important work was accomplished in the first year of his reign, when he repulsed the Arab forces from the walls of . the capital. Even Charles Martel's great victory of Poitiers in 732 was less decisive, for Byzantium had met the full force of the Umayyad Empire at the gateway of Europe. With the succession of the Abbasid dynasty in 750, after a period of internal strife, the centre of Muslim power moved eastward to Bagdad, and Asia's threat to the Bosphorus was not renewed for many centuries. Constantine V was able to recover Cyprus in 746 and to push back the Anatolian frontier to the eastern boundary of Asia Minor. For the fortunes of the Roman Empire Leo's initial success is comparable with that of Heraclius, who overcame the Avars and Persians in the hour of their greatest strength. But the Bulgarians, who had replaced the Avars in the Danube region, found themselves on this occasion in the pay of Byzantium, and such was the military prowess of the Isaurian rulers that it was not until the close of the eighth century that Bulgaria began to present a real problem.

The administrative policy of Leo and Constantine appears to have followed approved methods of safeguarding the central power, and to have included an extension of the theme-system which their predecessors had instituted for the defence of the threatened provinces. The publication of the *Ecloga*, a new legal code modifying the law in the direction of greater 'humanity', was a more radical measure. *Philanthropia* was a traditional duty of Rome's sovereigns towards their subjects, but the new code signified a departure from the spirit of Roman law, especially in the sphere of private morals and family life, and an attempt to apply Christian standards in these relations. It is a proof of the latent strength of the legacy left by pagan Rome that, despite the renewed influence of the Church, a reversion to the old principles took place later under the Macedonian regime.

Most revolutionary of all, in Byzantine eyes, were the Iconoclastic decrees. The campaign opened in 726, when

Leo III issued the first edict against images, which in the Greek Church was directed specifically against the icons. Under Constantine V the struggle became more embittered, and in 765 a fierce persecution was set on foot. In 787 the Empress Irene, an Athenian by birth, succeeded in re-establishing the cult of images, but an Iconoclast reaction under three Emperors of Asiatic origin (813–42) renewed, though with more limited scope, the measures of Leo and Constantine. In 843 the images were finally restored.

The Iconoclast movement can be treated neither in isolation from the secular reforms, nor as subordinate to them. In its later stages the attack was directed primarily against the power and influence of the monasteries, as being the strongholds of the cult of images; and the monks retaliated by boldly challenging the Emperor's constitutional supremacy in Church affairs. But the Isaurians were neither rationalist anti-clericals nor dogmatic innovators. The use of images had not been favoured by the Early Church, and puritan tendencies had appeared sporadically in the fourth and sixth centuries. Asia Minor was their particular centre at this time, and Jewish or Muslim hostility in these parts to a religious use of an art of representation may not have been without effect, as the abusive epithet 'Saracen-minded', hurled at Leo III by his opponents, possibly indicates. Christological issues were deeply involved on either side, and it must always be emphasized that for the Byzantines the question was primarily a theological one. Popular feeling and the immense power of tradition were ultimately the deciding factors. The triumph of the icon-defenders was a victory for popular religion and popular ways of thought. The defeat, on the other hand, of the movement towards a separation between the spheres of State and Church reflected no less accurately the Byzantine conviction of the indissolubility of civil and religious government.

The reign of Irene, first as regent, and later as Empress after the deposition and blinding of her son, appears at first sight to be merely an interlude between two periods of Iconoclasm. Actually, however, the Second Council of Nicaea (787), which temporarily restored the images, formulated the theory of icon-worship with such success that the improved organization and tactics of the monastic party finally won the day.

A sensational development at this time in the West may have appeared less important to the Byzantines than it does to us. On Christmas Day, 800, Charlemagne was proclaimed Emperor in the basilica of St. Peter at Rome. The constitutional significance of the coronation has been variously interpreted in modern days, and the views of contemporaries were in many cases no less divergent. So far as Byzantium was concerned, the situation in the West was hardly affected by the new pronouncement. In theory Charles was no more than an unusually troublesome pretender. Practically, the decisive period had lain in the middle of the previous century. Italian antagonism to Byzantine rule had been sharpened by the Iconoclast controversy, but the Papacy had continued to support the Exarchate as a check to the Lombard overlordship of Italy. In 751 Pippin assumed the crown of France, and in the same year Ravenna, the centre of Byzantine defence, was captured by the Lombards. The dénouement was swift. In 754 Pippin, in answer to the Pope's appeal, invaded north Italy. Lombardy became a vassal state of the Franks, until in 774 it was finally conquered by Charlemagne. The Exarchate was delivered to the Pope, and Byzantine rule, save in a few coastal districts, in the southern extremity of the peninsula and in Sicily, came to an end.

The position was not improved with the advent of the Amorian dynasty (820–67), for Campania and Venice remained largely independent of Constantinople, while Sicily soon fell to the Arab invaders from North Africa. In the East, Byzantine arms met with greater success. Asia Minor was recovered after a dangerous insurrection under Thomas the Slav (820–3), and his Arab supporters were disappointed of their prize. A fixed frontier-line was established from Armenia to northern Syria, and the relations between the Christian and Muslim Empires came to resemble those which had formerly prevailed between Rome and Persia. Similar tactics and armament were employed on both sides; raids became periodical but produced no decision; mutual understanding and respect were engendered—

conditions which are reflected in the epic of Digenes Akritas (see p. 245). Meanwhile, however, Muslim sea-power menaced the whole Mediterranean basin, and the capture of Crete (825) by the invaders was even more disastrous than the loss of Sicily, for the Aegean now lay open to sudden and destructive raids from the swift corsairs which gathered there. On the northern frontier the Bulgarians under their first great leader, Krum, had become a formidable enemy. A Byzantine army was ambushed and cut to pieces in the Balkan defiles (811); the Emperor Nicephorus was slain, and his head used as a drinking-cup by the savage conqueror. Only the strong walls of Constantinople prevented Krum from assaulting the capital, and perhaps it was only his death in 814 which saved it from destruction. The Frankish invasions of Croatia occupied Bulgaria for the next few decades, and decreased the immediate threat to Constantinople, much as, in the East, Turkish inroads had paralysed Byzantium's other foe, the Caliphate.

The Isaurian house had ended with the death of Irene: from 802 to 867 no dynasty had established itself securely, and a number of ferocious palace murders punctuated the continual series of revolts. Of these latter, the rebellion of Thomas the Slav had been the longest and most dangerous, approaching at times the dimensions of a civil war. Asia Minor had been the worst sufferer, and the small peasant-farmers, a class which the Isaurian Emperors had carefully fostered, were reduced to dependence on the powerful land-owners. The feudal tendencies thus encouraged were destined subsequently to prove a serious problem for the State. The Amorian period, however, was not all loss. Against military reverses in the West must be set the successful maintenance of the Eastern frontier. Against the bitterness of the Iconoclast controversy must be reckoned the marked revival of art and learning and the renewed missionary activities of the Orthodox Church, which carried, at the hands of Constantine and Methodius, her most potent civilizing agencies to the Slavs of Moravia. Finally, the conversion of Bulgaria (864) brought Byzantine influence to bear, with decisive effect, on the most immediate enemy of the Empire.

VII

The greatest period in medieval Byzantine history is the double century spanned by the reigns of the Macedonian dynasty. It may justly be called the Macedonian period, for the unity thus implied was a real, though curious, phenomenon. During the whole period members of the Macedonian house occupied the imperial throne. Few of the direct heirs played a leading part in the military and administrative triumphs of the Empire; apart from the two Basils the heroic figures are for the most part usurping generals, such as Nicephorus Phocas or John Tzimisces, whose imperial titles were gained by murder or threats, or by politic marriages into the royal house. Yet the need for such marriage alliances proves clearly the strength of the dynastic sentiment which swayed the population at this time. Loyalty to the families of Constantine and Heraclius had been witnessed in the fourth and seventh centuries; but so deep-seated a feeling as that evoked by the Macedonians was a new development in Byzantium. Strangest of all was its final demonstration, when two elderly princesses, Zoe and Theodora, last scions of the Macedonian house, were carried to power on the crest of that astonishing tumult which Psellus has so vividly described. Palace intrigues, assassinations, and conspiracies were rife throughout this violent and romantic period; but they did not break that fundamental loyalty to the house of Macedon, which, reinforced by the majesty of ceremonial and the semi-divine character of the Emperor—treason had now become a veritable act of impiety—formed the background of the Byzantine achievement.

The beginnings of that achievement were slow. Byzantium, centre of stability amid the swirling currents of three continents, had preserved her heritage and guarded her difficult frontiers only by superior skill in the manipulation of her limited military resources.[1] For over a century she had been fully occupied in holding her own, and the forward movement was now made possible only by the weakness of the surrounding nations. In the West the Carolingian Empire was in process of dissolution. Byzantine relations

[1] The total strength of the Byzantine army in the ninth century has been estimated at 120,000.

with the Papacy, though chequered, were no longer embittered by the Iconoclast dispute, and common cause was
found in the defensive measures against Islam. The Saracen
conquest of Sicily continued, but the imperial possessions in
south Italy were firmly held, and spirited counter-attacks on
the Muslim pirates in Tyrrhenian and Adriatic waters gave
welcome signs of a revival of Byzantine sea-power. Nearer
home the Bulgarians at this time presented no real menace,
and Russia was beginning to admit Byzantine influences.
The security of the Empire, both military and financial,
rested, as ever, on the integrity of Asia Minor, and here, too,
the position was favourable for Byzantium. The Abbasid
dynasty, which had overthrown the Umayyads in 750, had
removed the capital of Islam from Damascus to Bagdad,
and with it the sword's point from the throat of Europe. The
Caliphate, which had hitherto been in the hands of able
generals and politicians, supported by Syrian Arabs, soon
fell under the dominance of Persian nobles or Turkish
mercenaries. The Western provinces of Islam—Spain,
North Africa, and Egypt—threw off in turn their political
allegiance to Bagdad, and powerful rulers in Syria and
Mesopotamia eventually rendered themselves independent
of the Caliph.

Asia Minor was vitally affected by these changes. Its
traditional defences were two. In the south the formidable
passes of the Taurus and Anti-Taurus had been successfully
held by the Byzantines against repeated Saracen inroads.
In the north control of the Armenian massif was necessary
for any permanent conquest of the Anatolian hinterland.
For nine centuries the mountain kingdom of Armenia had
been a bone of contention between Rome and the successive
rulers of Hither Asia. It had been partitioned at intervals
into spheres of influence; its princes had been supported in
turn, or its territories temporarily annexed, by the rival
Empires. From the accession of the Macedonian dynasty
dates the beginning of its Golden Age, when the ascendancy
of the great Bagratid family enabled it to assert a large
measure of independence for two glorious centuries.

Basil I was not slow to seize his opportunity. A treaty
was made with Armenia, and intrigues were set on foot

with a view to promoting Byzantine influence. In the south successive campaigns cleared the way from Cappadocian Caesarea—the starting-point for all Byzantine operations—to the Cilician plain, recovery of which was a necessary prelude to the advance on Syria. At the same time Byzantine garrisons were posted in the Taurus defiles, and a foothold was secured on the upper Euphrates. These advantages were held under Basil's successor, Leo VI (886–912), more through the weakness of his enemies than for any other cause, since the Empire was preoccupied elsewhere. Muslim corsairs from Crete were terrorizing the Aegean, and in 904 Salonica, the second city of the Empire, which had survived so many assaults by land and sea, was captured and barbarously sacked, while a large Byzantine naval expedition against Crete in 910 ended disastrously for the assailants. Even more dangerous was the rise of Bulgaria, under her greatest ruler, Simeon (893–927), whose ambition it was to wrest the sovereignty of the Balkans from East Rome. Until his death no security was possible for the Empire.

Meanwhile internal recovery from the troubled period of Iconoclasm continued. The reigns of Basil I and Leo VI are the last of the creative ages of Roman legislation. In the great collection known as the *Basilica* the legal heritage of the past was selected and arranged to suit the requirements of the new times, and it is significant that one of its main characteristics was a return to the laws of Justinian, and an abrogation of the revolutionary principles introduced by the Iconoclast rulers. The absolutism of the imperial supremacy over both Church and State is the underlying conception, and the governing ideals of the Macedonian house are further displayed in the laws protecting the peasant class against the depredations of the rich landowners. Tradition—the aesthetic legacy of Hellas, its delight in form and colour, its many-sided knowledge—is also apparent in the revival of art and letters at this time. Its effect is seen in the churches and palaces, with their exquisite proportions and balanced schemes of decoration, and in the classical studies of the University, where its scholars were dominated by the encyclopaedic Photius, the most remarkable figure in the long story of Byzantine learning.

Leo VI died in 912, leaving an infant son known to posterity as the Emperor Constantine VII Porphyrogenitus (912–59), to whose scholarly industry we owe much of our knowledge of medieval Byzantium. In 920 the admiral Romanus Lecapenus, succeeding where others had already failed, seized the supreme power, and was invested with the imperial title, legitimating himself in some degree by marrying his daughter to the youthful Constantine. Public opinion was exasperated by subsequent insults to the representative of the Macedonian house, and with its support Constantine was eventually able to drive out the usurping family (945).

The series of Byzantine triumphs in the East starts from this time, but it is doubtful whether it owed much to the personal efforts of Constantine VII. During the earlier part of the tenth century the Bulgarian problem had monopolized attention. Simeon, whose armies had more than once occupied the outskirts of the capital, died in 927. Under the rule of his son Peter (927–68) amicable relations were re-established, and Romanus Lecapenus, who had skilfully defended Byzantine interests in Europe, had been able to divert his forces in order to attack Rome's principal enemy in Asia. Here the continual frontier warfare of cavalry raids, ruses, and reprisals was breeding a race of brilliant leaders, whose sound strategy and tactical successes were steadily laying the foundations for the great advance. Chief among these was Nicephorus Phocas (Emperor 963–9), whose capture of Crete (961) restored at one stroke the Byzantine supremacy at sea which had been lost for 150 years. Four years later Cyprus was retaken, and the fall of Tarsus at length placed Cilicia in the power of Byzantium. All was now ready for the invasion of Syria, and the rich, strongly-walled centres of Muslim commerce fell before the conquering armies of Nicephorus. In 969 the great city of Antioch, one of the jewels of the old Roman Empire, and further ennobled by its Apostolic see, was stormed by the Byzantine troops. Aleppo was taken and became a vassal state, and north Syria once more, after a lapse of three centuries, returned to Roman rule.

The prestige of the Empire was now at its height, and the results were seen not only in Asia. To the demands of Otto I, restorer of the Western Empire, to be recognized as overlord of the Italian peninsula, Byzantium opposed her prior claim as the true heir of Rome, and open hostilities were at once begun. Nor would Nicephorus continue the annual tribute to Bulgaria which had been paid since the settlement of 927. Taking advantage of the disturbances which followed the death of Peter, he advanced into Thrace, and summoned the Russian hosts from Kiev to aid in completing the destruction of Bulgaria. This dangerous policy was soon reversed, when the Russians proved only too successful; their leader, not content with the occupation of Bulgaria, prepared to move on Constantinople itself.

A new crisis faced the capital, and a new Emperor was called upon to resolve it, for Nicephorus had been brutally murdered in the palace by John Tzimisces (969–76), his most brilliant general, with the connivance of the Empress, whose lover he is reputed to have been. Fortune still favoured the Romans, for Tzimisces proved equal to the opportunity. Peace was hurriedly patched up in the West, and sealed by the marriage of the Byzantine Princess Theophano to the future Emperor Otto II. Tzimisces next turned on the Russians, whom his generals had already thrown back into Bulgarian territory. Pursuing them northwards, he forced them to capitulate and to take their final departure from the Balkan peninsula. The eastern parts of Bulgaria were then annexed, and the Emperor concluded his short-lived and impetuous career with two memorable campaigns in the East. In 974 he ravaged Mesopotamia, capturing Edessa and Nisibis, two of the principal strongholds. In the following year it was Syria's turn, and his irresistible armies pushed southwards beyond Damascus and Beirut. It is clear that the objective was Jerusalem, and the language used by Tzimisces leaves no doubt of the crusading character of the expedition. But this final effort of East Rome to recover the Holy Places was destined to fail. In 969 the strong Fatimid dynasty, who had seized possession of Egypt, established themselves also in Palestine, and thus formed an insuperable barrier against permanent conquest.

The untimely death of Tzimisces in 976 cleared the stage for the greatest of the Macedonian Emperors, Basil II, 'the

Bulgar-slayer' (963–1025). The precarious tenure of a Byzantine ruler, menaced from without by hostile armies along every frontier, and from within by the fierce competition of powerful nobles, ambitious for the throne, is well illustrated by the events of his reign. Dangerous revolts in Asia Minor, lasting for several years, were crushed only after long and exhausting struggles. Meanwhile Samuel, ruler of western Bulgaria, had united his people once more, and in successive conquests had extended his boundaries from the Danube to the Adriatic. Thirty years of stubborn fighting in the last and fiercest of the Bulgarian wars ended in the great Byzantine victory of 1014, when 15,000 Bulgarian prisoners were blinded and sent back to their sovereign. With this terrible vengeance the ruin of the Bulgarian Empire was consummated, and its territories were placed under Byzantine rule.

The achievements of Basil II did not end here. In 999 he secured the Empire's hold upon northern Syria, and in 1001 a treaty was concluded with the Fatimid Caliph of Egypt, which lasted until the end of the reign. This in effect interpreted the limits of Byzantine reconquest. The duchy of Antioch was recognized as an imperial possession, and a rather shadowy suzerainty over Aleppo was admitted; south of this, the Fatimid sovereignty was acknowledged. The effects of this treaty were seen in the Crusading era.

Byzantine action in regard to Armenia was no less decisive. In 1021 one of the Armenian chieftains, menaced by Turkish invaders from the east, was persuaded to cede his dominions to the Roman Empire. By 1045 the whole plateau had been annexed, and the Empire now held in its grasp both northern and southern entrances to the vital provinces of Asia Minor. Meanwhile in the West all Byzantine territory was placed under the control of a 'catapan', an officer combining military and civil powers. The weakness of the Papacy and of the Germanic Empire at this time contrasted unfavourably with the new solidarity of East Rome, whose star, even in western Europe, appeared once more in the ascendant.

At the death of Basil in 1025 the Empire had reached its apogee. By the conquests of the preceding century, less

extensive but more practical than Justinian's, Roman territory had been more than doubled, and the prestige thus
acquired had surrounded it with a periphery of semi-
dependent states. Naples and Amalfi acknowledged the
imperial position in south Italy, while Venice, favoured by
privileged trading concessions, patrolled the Adriatic in the
Byzantine interest. Roman dominance was strongest in the
coastal districts of the Empire, and the fortress of Durazzo
in the West helped to secure the alliance of Serbs and
Croats against possible Bulgarian uprisings, while in the
north-east the Crimean city of Cherson was the centre of
Byzantine diplomacy, playing successfully on the mutual
rivalries of Patzinaks, Russians, and other peoples bordering
on the Black Sea. The Caucasian tribal rulers were heavily
subsidized, and Armenia, as we have seen, passed into
Byzantine hands shortly afterwards, thus forming the
northern bastion of the long eastern frontier.

No less remarkable was the economic prosperity of the
Empire. Basil II had filled the Treasury to overflowing, and
its resources were maintained by the revenue of the new
provinces, and by the dues levied on trade and industry,
both of which were elaborately controlled by the State—a
continuous development of those Roman principles which
had found their first systematic expression in the edicts of
Diocletian. Constantinople, the greatest commercial city of
the Middle Ages, was at this time not only the chief pur-
veyor of Asiatic luxuries to the West, but also the most
important single formative influence on the budding arts of
medieval Europe. In contrast with the semi-barbaric kingdoms of the West, the Byzantine Empire presents the appearance of a fully civilized State, equipped with the scientific
government and public services of the ancient world,
administered by a cultured and literary bureaucracy, and
guarded by troops whose tactical efficiency has perhaps
never been surpassed.

The end of the Macedonian house must be told briefly.
Once the strong hand of Basil was removed, all the centrifugal influences which he had checked resumed their sway.
For thirty years after his death (1025–56) the Empire rested
on the strength of its dynastic loyalties, while Zoe and

Theodora, childless daughters of Constantine VIII, gave the
supreme authority to a succession of mediocre rulers. The
extinction of the Macedonian family was followed by a
period of disastrous anarchy (1057–81) which lasted until
the advent of the Comneni. This period was significant for
the fortunes of Byzantium; it sets the stage for the concluding scenes of the drama. Norman adventurers and Seljuk
Turks make their appearance; the Western powers take the
offensive against Islam; the Italian seaports extend the range
of their commerce. The East Roman Empire suffered an
eclipse all the more striking by reason of its recent glories.
Seldom had the personal influence of its rulers been more
clearly demonstrated than in the contrast between the effective if high-handed methods of Basil II, and the unfortunate
compromises of his successors.

The outstanding service rendered by the house of Macedon had been the healing of the wounds left in the body
politic by the Iconoclast dispute. Basil I had perceived the
danger which lay in a final separation of the Roman and the
Orthodox Churches, and had deposed Photius, the Patriarch, at a time when a breach with Rome was threatened by
his aggressive personality. Successive emperors had maintained their supremacy in Church affairs, despite the steady
growth of ecclesiastical wealth and monastic influence. A
contrast is seen in the events which culminated in the
schism of 1054. Once more a conflict had arisen between
Pope and Patriarch; but no Basil sat upon the throne. The
Emperor Constantine IX, well-intentioned but feeble of
character, was powerless to control his formidable Patriarch,
Michael Cerularius, and the gradual estrangement of Greeks
and Latins, accentuated by differences of language, ritual,
and organization, resulted in a dramatic rupture. Political and personal ambition formed the real obstacle to reunion,
for no fundamental dogmatic principles separated the two
Churches, or prevented co-operation between the rank and
file. But Byzantium was destined to rue bitterly her decision,
when in the following century the help of the hated Westerners became necessary to her existence.

East Rome, a vulnerable Empire of heterogeneous territories and peoples, had preserved her integrity only by sub-

mission to absolute authority. The Macedonian dynasty had curbed not only the Church but also the aristocracy. Its decadence gave an opportunity for the disruptive forces represented by the lords of the big estates. The only centralizing principle which could counteract this anarchy was the Roman bureaucracy, that skilled machine of administration which had worked without intermission for over a millennium. So the 'civil party' came into existence, with a ministry of scholarly officials. Necessarily anti-militarist (for the great landowners of Asia Minor, with the levies of their tenants, formed the military caste), it aimed at decreasing the influence of the army. Expenses were cut down, regardless of defensive needs. The frontiers were denuded of troops, and their commanders could hope for no advancement at Court. The fatal consequences of this policy were soon apparent.

The era of Byzantine reconquest had ended in 1043, when Maniakes, the brilliant general who had triumphed on the Euphrates and even for a brief moment held Sicily, was goaded into rebellion and perished in Macedonia, a victim of the suspicion of unwarlike rulers. Further attempts by the military party were defeated, and when Isaac Comnenus, their representative, after holding the supreme power for two years (1057-9), felt obliged to abdicate, the civil servants resumed their sway. Everywhere the boundaries of the Empire receded. In Italy the Normans overwhelmed the Byzantine garrisons, and with the fall of Bari in 1071 the last remnant of Roman sovereignty in the West disappeared. Croatia regained her independence; Dalmatia and Serbia revolted; Bulgaria was seething with rebellion, and Hungarians and Patzinaks devastated the Danube territories.

Far more serious was the position in Asia Minor. The situation which had made possible the great Byzantine triumphs of the tenth century was now reversed. A new ruler at Bagdad—Tughril Beg, the Seljuk sultan (1055-63)—had inherited the Abbasid Empire, and imparted a fresh cohesion and driving force to the armies of Islam. Armenia, recently annexed by East Rome, was no longer a buffer-state, alert to preserve its independence. Weakly garrisoned by discontented forces, it succumbed to the invaders. The Byzantine counter-thrust, led by the Emperor Romanus IV Diogenes in person, ended in the disastrous battle of Manzikert (1071)—one of the blackest days in the long history of Byzantium. Despite the capture of the Emperor and the annihilation of his troops, all was not yet lost; but the disorganized government at Constantinople failed to initiate any effective resistance. Asia Minor was rapidly overrun, and by 1081 the Turks ruled from the Euphrates to the Sea of Marmora, where Nicaea became the first capital of the Seljuk sultanate of Anatolia.

Once more the Asiatic conqueror faced Constantinople across the narrow waters, and once more the Roman Empire found its saviour. Alexius Comnenus, member of one of the most powerful families in Asia Minor, was proclaimed Emperor by the military aristocracy, and inaugurated the brilliant dynasty which preserved the fortunes of East Rome for what must in truth be called the final century of her imperial existence.

VIII

The stage was now set for the last act, and the reign of Alexius Comnenus (1081–1118) revealed the main lines of its development. It marked the victory of the great land-owners over the civil servants of the capital—a victory of the forces held in check for so long by a succession of strong emperors. Its opening years witnessed the attack of Robert Guiscard the Norman on Durazzo, the fortress which guarded the western end of the *Via Egnatia*, the great Roman road leading from the Adriatic to Constantinople. This has been called a prelude to the Crusades, and it helps to explain the Byzantine attitude to the Crusaders, of whom the Normans formed a prominent part. The attack was defeated, with help from the Venetian fleet; Venice could not afford to see the mouth of the Adriatic occupied on both sides by the Normans. But the price paid by the Roman Empire was the opening of all ports to Venetian shipping, and freedom for Venetian commerce from the dues which contributed so greatly to Byzantine revenues. This concession made manifest the fatal error of Byzantine trading policy. In later centuries the Empire for overseas trade, both export and import, had come increasingly to rely on foreign shipping to convey its merchandise. Its wealthy classes had preferred to invest in land rather than risk the losses of maritime venture. The stranglehold of Venice tightened during the whole of this century, and to the mutual hatred of Greeks and Latins which resulted was due in no small measure the final catastrophe. Ominous, too, was the condition of Byzantine finances. The loss of her rich Asiatic provinces had deprived the Empire of the principal sources of taxation, and it is significant that the gold byzant, the imperial coin which had retained its full value in the markets of three continents since the days of Diocletian, was first debased under the Comnenian dynasty. It speaks well for the diplomatic and military genius of Alexius that, despite these difficulties, he was able to win back much of the European territory lost in the preceding period, to repulse a combined attack on the capital by Turks and Patzinaks, and by 1095 to be preparing for a sustained assault on his chief enemies, the Seljuks of Asia Minor. But in the following year the first Crusaders from the West made their appearance. Eastern and western Europe, more complete strangers to one another than perhaps at any other period in history, were suddenly thrown together by the impetus of this astonishing movement. Byzantium, drawn into the orbit of the Western States, and struggling to maintain her position amid changing coalitions of the Mediterranean powers, entered upon a tortuous policy of which only the barest outlines can be given here.

To the realist outlook of East Rome the Crusades were largely incomprehensible. In a sense all her wars had been Holy Wars, for she was, almost by definition, the champion of Christianity against the barbarians. Her own survival was thus bound up with the future of Christian civilization, and it therefore behoved all Christians to fight on her behalf. She, too, had tried to recover the Holy Places, and Antioch, the limit of her success, had remained Byzantine until only a few years before. It was reasonable to suppose that the Western armies would help her, in return for generous subsidies, to regain her essential Anatolian and north Syrian provinces. Western contingents had for some time formed a considerable part of the Byzantine forces, and the Crusaders might well, on this analogy, prove useful mercenaries; while if their idealism were genuine, they should surely be eager to assist the Empire which for so many centuries had held the gates of Europe against Asiatic heathenism. Alexius was soon undeceived. These undisciplined armies marching through his territories cared little for the security of Byzantium. Idealism led them to the conquest of Jerusalem; other motives urged them to carve out principalities for themselves. But Byzantine military science had not failed to study the psychology and tactics of the Westerners, and Alexius's astute diplomacy, utilizing the Western concept of the oath of fealty, established Byzantine rights over much of the reconquered territory.

The First Crusade, after initial setbacks, proved a brilliant success. The Seljuk rulers, mutually suspicious, failed to combine, and Bagdad gave no effective aid. Nicaea fell in 1097, and the Crusaders marched through Asia Minor. Antioch was taken in 1098, and in the following year the object of the expedition was attained with the capture of Jerusalem. Alexius had recovered most of western Anatolia, and Crusading States came into existence shortly afterwards at Jerusalem, Antioch, Tripoli, and Edessa. A new situation had arisen in the Near East. The Western conquerors entered into a complex system of balanced alliances which was necessary to maintain their existence, and Turco-Arab emirs soon became useful allies against the claims of Sultans, Caliphs, or Byzantine Emperors. Alexius had long been at home in this world, and his aims were consistently pursued. Asia Minor was essential to the Empire, and Antioch, which had been in imperial hands only ten years earlier, was recognized by most of the Crusaders as a Byzantine fief. Only the Normans, implacable enemies of Byzantium, proved recalcitrant, and Bohemond, son of Robert Guiscard, after his intrigues in Antioch and his attack on Durazzo, was finally crushed by Alexius.

John II Comnenus (1118–43) continued the foreign policy of his father; Cilicia and the Taurus, where Armenian refugees had begun to found independent States, were subdued, and Byzantine suzerainty over Antioch was successfully demonstrated. His efforts were wisely concentrated on the East; but the crowning of Roger II at Palermo in 1130, which united the realms of south Italy and Sicily, constituted a new threat, in face of which an alliance was concluded between Byzantium and the Germanic Emperor.

This alliance was destined to play an important part during the reign of Manuel I Comnenus (1143–80), which saw a complete change in Byzantine policy. It can be roughly summarized as a diversion of interests and activities to the western Mediterranean. Manuel hoped to check the Normans, who in 1147 had invaded Greece, by a united front of both Empires; and the policy seemed successful when a dangerous coalition, which was headed by Roger II, of France, the Papacy, Hungary, and Serbia failed to win over the Western Emperor. But in 1154 Byzantine troops once more landed in Italy; Venice, alarmed at the threat to her Adriatic trade, joined the Normans, and the Emperor Barbarossa followed suit. It was clear that Rome's last bid for Western dominion had failed, and in 1158 Byzantine troops left the Italian shores for ever. Manuel, reversing his policy, made overtures to the Papacy, and supported the Lombard cities in their successful struggle against Barbarossa. But the futility of this was shown in 1177, when the Congress of Venice reconciled the Pope, the German Emperor, and the cities of north Italy. Venice had been alienated by the harsh treatment of her merchants in Constantinople, and Manuel had thus made enemies of all his Western allies. Nor were events in the East more favourable. In the preceding year the disastrous defeat of Myriokephalon in the Phrygian mountains had destroyed all hopes of reconquering Asia Minor from the Seljuks, and the defence of the coastal districts was henceforth the limit of Byzantine endeavour.

A sunset glow pervaded the Court of the later Comneni. Art and letters flourished under this brilliant dynasty, and it is significant that even at the eleventh hour the poets, historians, and philosophers of ancient Greece continued to inspire their spiritual descendants. But within the capital there festered a fatal feud between the Greeks and the men of the West. Manuel's policy had raised many Latins to places of influence, and this brought to a head the accumulated hatred of the Greeks for the 'barbarian' soldiers and merchants whose insolence and rapacity had invaded all sections of Byzantine life. Its fruits were shown in the accession to power of Andronicus I Comnenus (1183–5) on a wave of nationalist feeling, which had already found vent in a bloody massacre of the Latins in Constantinople (1182). The revenge of the West was the sack of Salonica by the Normans (1185) and, when their forces approached the capital, Andronicus, who had lost influence by his oppression of the aristocracy, was deposed and murdered. The Comnenian house was replaced by the incapable Angeli, and the Western powers, further consolidated by the politic betrothal of the heirs of the Germanic Emperor and the Sicilian kingdom, waited only for an opportunity to humiliate Byzantium.

That opportunity was furnished by the Fourth Crusade. The complicated issues involved cannot be discussed here. The objective was Egypt, where Saladin had rallied the forces of Islam. But the controlling spirit of the Crusade was Venice, whose ships constituted the only means of transport. With the Crusading armies was a Byzantine prince, whose father, Isaac II Angelus, had recently been ousted from the throne. His presence, and the influence of Venice, turned the Crusade from its original purpose, and the fleet sailed for Constantinople to restore the fallen ruler. A popular anti-Latin tumult was the result. Isaac II and his son met their deaths, and the Crusaders assaulted the capital by land and sea.

On 13 April 1204 Constantinople fell. Three days of pillaging and outrage followed, and the palaces and churches of western Europe were presently filled with the stolen treasures of the East Roman Empire. Its territories were divided among the conquerors, Venice receiving the lion's share. Feudal principles determined the government both of the capital and of the petty principalities which came into being in Greece and the Aegean. Thus the decentralizing forces which, with the barbarian invasions, had destroyed the fabric of Roman organization in western Europe, extended their influence to the East, erasing the last vestige of Rome's unification of the ancient world.

H. ST. L. B. MOSS

THE HISTORY OF THE BYZANTINE EMPIRE
B. FROM A.D. 1204 TO A.D. 1453

I

In the history of the Byzantine Empire the taking of
Constantinople by the Latins is an important date. It was
the first time, since its foundation, that the Byzantine capital
had fallen into the hands of the foreigners attacking it, and
the result of this event was the dislocation of the monarchy.

The victorious Latins settled on the ruins of the Byzantine
Empire. A Latin Empire was established at Constantinople,
of which Baldwin, count of Flanders, one of the leaders of the
Crusade, was the first sovereign; a Latin Kingdom of
Thessalonica was formed for Boniface of Montferrat. Latin
States were founded in Greece, of which the principal were
the duchy of Athens, governed by the Burgundian family of
La Roche, and the principality of Morea or Achaia, which,
under the Villehardouins, was undoubtedly the most lasting
consequence in the East of the Crusade of 1204. Finally
Venice, which had for a moment thought of appropriating
the entire Byzantine heritage, established in the Mediterranean a wonderful colonial empire, both by directly occupying the most important strategic points, Crete, Euboea,
Gallipoli, and a whole quarter of Constantinople, and by
enfeoffing the islands of the Archipelago to her Patrician
families. The appearance of the Eastern world was completely transformed.

Some Greek States, however, remained, and at first, in the
collapse of the Empire, they were multiplied to infinity. But
among the ambitious, eager to carve out principalities for
themselves, three only were to succeed in forming permanent
States. At Trebizond there were two princes, descendants of
the Comneni, whose empire was to continue until the middle
of the fifteenth century. In Epirus there was Michael
Angelus Comnenus, a bastard of the family of the Angeli,
who founded a 'despotat' extending from Naupactus to
Durazzo. Lastly, at Nicaea, Theodore Lascaris, son-in-law
of Alexius III Angelus, collected together what remained of
the aristocracy and the higher ranks of the clergy of Byzantium, and in 1206 had himself crowned by the Patriarch as

'Emperor of the Romans'. And in these States, where the Latin victory had had the effect of reawakening patriotism and national feeling, it was but natural that all the Greek sovereigns should be filled with the same ambition; at Nicaea, as in Epirus, they were dreaming of the recapture of Constantinople, the holy city, from the usurpers who occupied it. Which of the two rival Greek Empires, that of Epirus or that of Nicaea, would realize this dream was, at the beginning of the thirteenth century, difficult to foresee. Faced by these two rival states, and menaced by Bulgaria, the feeble Latin Empire was in a singularly dangerous position. In fact during the sixty years of its miserable existence (1204–61), its fate was, as has been said, that 'of a city perpetually besieged and knowing full well that it is destined to fall'.[1]

Yet in the first moments of confusion which followed the fall of Constantinople it seemed as if the Latins would triumph everywhere. But the invasion of the Bulgarian Tsar Johannitsa and the defeat which he inflicted on the Emperor Baldwin at Adrianople (1205) saved Theodore Lascaris from what appeared certain ruin. For a time under Henry of Flanders, the successor of Baldwin (1205–16), without doubt the best prince amongst the rulers of the Latin Empire of Constantinople, it was possible to believe that the Latins would consolidate their position and that a sort of tetrarchy, formed by the four empires of Constantinople, Nicaea, Epirus, and Bulgaria, united by marriages and alliances, would definitely divide between them the Near East.[2] The premature death of Henry ruined these hopes. Henceforth Greeks and Bulgarians, allied for a joint enterprise, had their hands free to combat the feeble Latin State.

At first it might have been thought that to Epirus would fall the glory of re-establishing the orthodox Empire. The despot of Epirus, Theodore (1214–30), who had succeeded his brother Michael, had greatly extended his dominions at the expense of the Latins and the Bulgarians, conquering Durazzo and Corfu, Ochrida and Prilep, seizing Salonica, where he had himself crowned Emperor, advancing into the

---

[1] Iorga, *Histoire de la vie byzantine*, vol. iii, p. 110.
[2] Cf. Iorga, op. cit., vol. iii, pp. 108–9.

neighbourhood of Adrianople and Philippopolis and threatening Constantinople. But Bulgaria, which he imprudently
attacked, was ruled by an intelligent and energetic sovereign,
John Asên (1218–41). The Greek Empire in Europe
dashed itself unavailingly against him. Beaten and taken
prisoner at Klokotnitza (1230), Theodore was forced to
abdicate, and his brother Manuel, who succeeded him, lost
most of the conquests made by Theodore, retaining only
Salonica and Thessaly.

During this time, under Theodore Lascaris (1205–22),
and under his successor, John Vatatzes (1222–54), the most
remarkable of the sovereigns of Nicaea, the Greek Empire in
Asia was growing in strength and in extent. Master of almost
the whole of western Asia Minor, Vatatzes had retaken from
the Latins all the large islands of the Asiatic littoral, Samos,
Chios, Lesbos, Cos, and had extended his authority over
Rhodes. He then decided to enter Europe, and with the
Bulgarians as his allies attempted to take Constantinople
(1236). The capital of the feeble Latin Empire was saved
for the time by the intervention of the West, but despite this
intervention Vatatzes succeeded in re-establishing Byzantine
unity in face of the hated foreigner.

The Greek Emperor of Salonica had to renounce his
imperial title and acknowledge himself the vassal of Nicaea
(1242), and four years later Vatatzes took possession of
Salonica (1246). From the Bulgarians, who had been much
weakened since the death of John Asên, he took a large part
of Macedonia. Finally the despot of Epirus, Michael II,
accepted the suzerainty of Nicaea and promised to cede
Serbia, Albania, and Durazzo to Vatatzes (1254). As ally
of Frederick II of Hohenstaufen, whose daughter he had
married, and of the Seljuk sultan of Iconium, Vatatzes when
he died left the Empire of Nicaea rich, powerful, and
prosperous. The sojourn of the Byzantine monarchy in
Asia had, as it were, spiritually purified the State of Nicaea
and had given to it a national character which Constantinople
no longer possessed. 'A faithful nobility, active and pious
Emperors, had governed and led for half a century a people
of shepherds and peasants of simple manners and customs.'[1]

[1] Iorga, ibid., p. 120.

A new spirit was born there, and it was to this spirit that the restored Byzantine Empire was to owe for two more centuries 'a life which was not always humble and threatened'.

It only remained for the rulers of Nicaea to recapture Constantinople. The Mongol invasion, which forced Theodore II Lascaris (1254–8), the son of Vatatzes, to return to Asia, postponed for a time the Byzantine restoration. Further, Theodore was compelled to subdue the Bulgarians, who were seeking their revenge (1256), and later to repress the revolt of the intriguing despot of Epirus, Michael II. The latter, who was allied with the king of Sicily, Manfred, and the prince of Achaia, Guillaume de Villehardouin, was crushed, after an obstinate resistance, at the battle of Pelagonia (1259). This was the first victory of Michael Palaeologus, who on the death of Theodore II had usurped the throne of Nicaea. Shortly afterwards he crossed the Hellespont and took from the Latins all that they still possessed outside Constantinople, whilst, by the treaty of Nymphaeum (1261), his able diplomacy secured the alliance of the Genoese, who were jealous of the Venetians. Henceforth the Greeks only needed an opportunity and the capital was won. This opportunity was given to the Caesar Alexius Strategopoulus on 25 July 1261. The Latin Emperor Baldwin II, followed by the Latin Patriarch and the Venetian settlers, fled without any attempt at resistance, and on 15 August 1261 Michael Palaeologus made his formal entry into 'the city protected by God'. Kneeling before the Golden Gate, the Emperor and his soldiers listened to the thirteen prayers composed by Acropolites as a thanksgiving to God. Then, preceded by the image of the Virgin, the imperial procession went on foot to the monastery of Studius. Michael then mounted his horse, and rode amidst popular acclamation to St. Sophia, there to renew his thanksgiving to the Lord; this done, he took up his residence in the imperial palace. Some days later, in the 'Great Church', he solemnly reinstated the orthodox Patriarch, and in words of deep emotion expressed his faith in the destiny of the Empire. The Byzantine monarchy seemed to be reborn under the national dynasty of the Palaeologi, which was to govern it for nearly two centuries. Popular enthusiasm, intoxicated by this unhoped for success, hailed in the new reign the sure promise of a glorious age.

II

In actual fact this restored Byzantine State was but the pitiful remains of an empire. The Latins were driven from Constantinople; but they were still masters of the duchy of Athens and the principality of Achaia; the Venetians still held Euboea, Crete, and most of the islands of the Archipelago; the Genoese occupied Chios and had important colonies on the coast of Anatolia and on the Black Sea. Elsewhere, side by side with the reconstituted Empire of Constantinople, other Greek States existed which were to be feared as rivals: the empire of Trebizond in Asia, the despotat of Epirus in Europe. And above all, confronting the old Byzantine Empire, other States, young and vigorous, made their appearance on the stage of history and were quite ready to contend with Byzantium for the hegemony that it had once possessed. There were the Bulgarians who, in the course of the thirteenth century, under great sovereigns such as the three Johannitsas and John Asên, had risen to prominence in the Balkan peninsula. There were the Serbians who, under Stefan Nemanja (1151–95) and his immediate successors, had established themselves as an independent State with its own national dynasty and its own Church freed from the authority of the Patriarchate of Constantinople, and who were to become, in the fourteenth century, the great power in the Balkans. In Asia there were the Ottoman Turks, who were daily becoming a greater menace to the territories which the Greeks still retained in Anatolia. Thus with diminished territory, labouring under financial exhaustion and military weakness, and above all having no longer 'that moral energy which had so vigorously maintained itself in the isolation of Nicaea',[1] the Byzantine Empire, in spite of the efforts of several great sovereigns, sank slowly towards its ruin. Michael VIII (1261–82), John VI Cantacuzenus (1347–55), and Manuel II (1391–1425) were alike unable to arrest the decline. In fact, during the last two centuries of its existence, there was no longer anything to be found in

[1] Iorga, op. cit., vol. iii, p. 155.

Constantinople 'but a brilliant sovereign fallen in prestige and splendid in externals, ceaselessly squabbling monks, and foreigners exploiting the riches of the State'.[1] And the situation was all the more tragic and lamentable since to external dangers were added internal difficulties—political, religious, social, and economic—which were, in fact, insurmountable.

Michael VIII Palaeologus made a heroic effort to put things to rights, but by his surrender to the Papacy he did but awake the bitter opposition of his own subjects.

From the day of his accession Michael VIII had shown his intention of reconquering from the Greeks as well as from the Latins the provinces that had been taken from the Empire. He forced the prince of Achaia, who had fallen into his hands at the battle of Pelagonia, to cede to him, as the price of his freedom, the three strongholds of Monemvasia, Mistra, and Maîna, and thus he regained a footing in Frankish Morea (at the end of 1261). He seized Janina from the Epirots (1264); he recovered from the Bulgarians Mesembria, Anchialus, Philippopolis, and Stenimachus, while, to ensure the defence of the northern frontier, a march of Adrianople was created. The Emperor reoccupied several of the islands of the Archipelago belonging to the Venetians; he repressed the insolence of the Genoese whom he forced to leave Constantinople and settle in Heraclea. At the same time, very skilfully, by a whole series of family alliances, he brought into subordination to Byzantium the sovereigns of Bulgaria and Epirus, and even the powerful Tartar Khan Nogai, whose support he secured by giving to him in marriage his natural daughter Maria. A little later (1272) he once more placed the Bulgarian and Serbian Churches under the authority of a Greek prelate. These were great successes, and already at Constantinople the moment was foreseen when the despotat of Epirus—still regarded as part and parcel of the Roman Empire—should be recovered in its entirety.

But very soon Michael VIII came into collision with the hostility of the West. The Papacy and Venice had in fact by no means abandoned the hope of restoring the Latin Empire,

[1] Iorga, op. cit., vol. iii, p. 157.

and the Emperor Baldwin II had been favourably received at the court of Manfred, the king of Sicily. The situation became still more grave when Charles of Anjou became master of southern Italy (1266). In 1267, by the treaty of Viterbo, the new sovereign forced Baldwin II to surrender to him all his rights over the Latin Empire and married his daughter to the son of the fallen Emperor. By the marriage of his son to the heiress of Villehardouin he made sure of the suzerainty and eventual possession of the principality of Achaia. Soon his ambitious designs on the East and his policy towards Byzantium became even more clearly manifest. He seized Corfu (1267), sent troops into the Peloponnesus, occupied Durazzo and the coast of Epirus (1272), and even assumed the title of King of Albania. At the same time he allied himself with all the enemies of the Empire in the Balkans. Bulgarian and Serbian ambassadors appeared at Naples; the despot of Epirus and the prince of Great Wallachia promised their support to the Angevin sovereign.

In this terrible crisis Michael VIII showed his diplomatic skill by preventing a general coalition of the West against Byzantium. At first, to obviate this danger, he had thought of soliciting the help of St. Louis, and had sent ambassadors to ask for his intervention 'in support of the reunion of the Greek and Roman Churches'. After the death of the king he adopted the same policy in dealing with the Papacy. Adroitly taking advantage of the anxiety of the sovereign pontiff, who had no wish to see an unlimited increase in the power of Charles of Anjou, and playing upon the constant desire of the Papacy to re-establish the authority of Rome over the Greek Church, he concluded with Gregory X, at the Council of Lyons (1274), the agreement by which the Eastern Church was again subjected to the Papacy. But in exchange Michael VIII obtained the assurance that Constantinople should be his without dispute, that he should be left a free hand in the East, and that, to reconquer territory that had once been part of the Empire, he should be allowed to fight even the Latins themselves. Thus, in 1274, he took the offensive in Epirus against the Angevin troops; he intervened in Thessaly where he besieged Neopatras (1276); he fought the Venetians in Euboea and made further advances

in Achaia, where the death of Guillaume de Villehardouin
(1278) had greatly weakened the Frankish principality.
Charles of Anjou, kept very busy at this moment by his
difficulties with Genoa, and secretly thwarted by the policy of
the Papacy, looked on impotently at the triumphs of Byzantium.

Unfortunately the Greeks' inveterate hostility towards
Rome defeated the Emperor's ingenious schemes. It was in
vain that Michael VIII, in order to force the acceptance of
the Union upon the Byzantine clergy, replaced the uncompromising Patriarch Joseph by John Bekkos (1275), a
prudent man who was of the opinion that one could attain
truth without first insulting one's opponents, and who considered that many of the points under discussion between
Byzantium and Rome were only 'the sound of poor words'.
A violent opposition spread throughout the East. At
Constantinople and in the monasteries of Mount Athos
impassioned pamphlets were published against the union
with the Latins. Outside the Empire all the adversaries of
Michael VIII pronounced against his religious policy. A
council held in Thessaly condemned the Emperor and his
Patriarch; in Epirus, in Bulgaria, in Serbia, and even in
distant Jerusalem the censure was decisive and unanimous.
A veritable schism was produced within the Eastern Church,
and John Bekkos, defeated, was compelled finally, at the
death of Michael, to abandon the patriarchal see. The
demands of Pope Martin IV, who was strongly attached to
Charles of Anjou, still further aggravated the situation.
Michael VIII had hoped to mitigate the antagonism between
the two worlds; he had only made it more acute and more
formidable.

Moreover Charles of Anjou did not disarm. He reorganized the forces with which he dominated Epirus (1278),
won over the Papacy to his views, and formed, 'for the
recovery of the Empire of Romania which Palaeologus was
withholding from them', a league with Rome and Venice
which was joined by the Serbians, the Bulgarians, and even
by the Greeks of Thessaly and Epirus. The Byzantine
Emperor everywhere opposed this alliance with determination. He defeated the Angevin army at Berat; and above

all, to crush the ambition of Charles of Anjou, he helped to prepare the Sicilian Vespers (March 1282). In the end he did thereby, it is true, succeed in holding the West in check, but, when he died in 1282, he left the Empire in an anxious situation. Too exclusively preoccupied by his Latin policy, he had been neglectful of Asia; the danger from the Turks was becoming more and more menacing. By allowing, for financial reasons, the Empire's system of defence to become disorganized and by transporting to Europe the best Asiatic troops, Michael VIII at the end of his reign, in the words of a Byzantine chronicler, had lost almost the whole of Anatolia. Thus his undeniable successes were dearly bought. And although his reign seemed to mark for the Empire the beginning of a renaissance, decadence was to follow, swift and irremediable. It has been said, not without reason, that Michael Palaeologus 'was the first and also the last powerful Emperor of restored Byzantium'.

III

The sovereigns who succeeded Michael VIII were, in fact, nearly all mediocre: and this was a primary cause of the monarchy's weakness. Andronicus II (1282–1328) was a well-educated prince, eloquent, devoted to learning, and very pious, but weak, and susceptible to every influence, especially to that of his second wife, Yolande de Montferrat. He was devoid of any political qualities. It has been justly said of him that he 'had been destined by nature to become a professor of theology; chance placed him on the throne of Byzantium'. Andronicus III (1328–41) was intelligent, but frivolous, restless, and fond of his pleasures. After him the throne passed to his son John V, a child of scarcely eleven years, and this minority was the cause of prolonged disturbances, which had at least the happy result of bringing to the throne John VI Cantacuzenus (1347–55), the only really remarkable prince that Byzantium had in the fourteenth century. He made an energetic attempt to restore the Empire. Too intelligent not to understand that the glorious days of domination could return no more, he realized that 'what Byzantium had lost whether in material power, territory, finance, military strength, or economic prosperity, could be regained in two ways; through the Byzantine civilization which continued to preserve and develop the Hellenic inheritance, and through the oecumenical sovereignty of its Church over the whole of the East'.[1] Because of this his stormy reign is of real historic importance. But Cantacuzenus only governed for a few years. In 1355 John V Palaeologus, whom he had put into the background, overthrew the usurper; but his long reign (1341–91) only precipitated the decadence of the Empire. And although his son Manuel II (1391–1425) was a distinguished prince of whom it could be said 'that in more favourable times he would have saved the Empire', it was now only too clear that the Empire could no longer be saved. Manuel II and after him his son John VIII (1425–48) could only devote themselves to the utmost of their ability to postponing the inevitable catastrophe. The last emperor of the dynasty, Constantine XI (1448–53), could do no more than die a heroic death in defence of his capital when the walls were stormed by the Turks. The fact was that even men of ability were unable to arrest the decadence; circumstances were stronger than their good intentions. There was no longer any remedy for the conditions both external and internal which threatened the Empire with ruin.

In face of the dangers from without, domestic unity, tranquillity, and strength were essential. The period of the Palaeologi, on the contrary, was full of civil strife, of political, religious, and social struggles. First there were incessant wars for the possession of the throne. Against Andronicus II rose up his grandson, the future Andronicus III, whom the old Emperor sought to deprive of his rights to the throne, and for several years war laid waste the Empire (1321–8); the final result was the fall of Andronicus II. Then during the regency of Anne of Savoy there was the usurpation of John Cantacuzenus (1341) followed by the six years of conflict (1341–7) which divided the Byzantine world and ended in the triumph of Cantacuzenus. During the latter half of the fourteenth century the Empire suffered from a succession of revolutions, and the serious thing in all these civil wars was that the opposing parties

[1] Iorga, op. cit., vol. iii, p. 193.

without scruple called to their aid external enemies, Serbians, Bulgarians, Turks, Genoese, and Venetians, thus opening the door to those very nations which were contemplating the destruction of the monarchy. And this shows clearly to what extent all patriotism, all political sense even, had disappeared in these conflicts, the result of ambitions which had lost all scruple.

This was not all, for the Empire was further troubled by social and religious quarrels. About the middle of the fourteenth century a profound social agitation was disturbing the monarchy. The lower classes rose up against the aristocracy of birth and of wealth. At Constantinople, at Adrianople, and elsewhere as well, the populace attacked the rich and massacred them. At Salonica the party of the Zealots filled the city with terror and bloodshed, and the town, in fact, became an independent republic, which maintained itself for seven years (1342-9); its tempestuous history is one of the most curious episodes in the life of the Empire of the fourteenth century.

This was the victory of 'democracy in rags'. The dispute of the hesychasts was the victory of 'democracy in a cowl'. . . . For ten years (1341-51) this dispute disturbed and divided the Empire, bringing oriental mysticism, represented by the monks of Mount Athos and their defender Gregory Palamas, into conflict with Latin rationalism, the champions of which, Barlaam and Akindynus, were brought up on St. Thomas Aquinas and trained in the methods of Western scholasticism. And since Cantacuzenus sided with Athos, just as he sided with the aristocracy, the struggle, in appearance purely theological, soon became political and thus added to the confusion.

But the question of the union of the Churches caused the dying world of Byzantium still more trouble. From the time of Michael VIII the East Roman Government had realized the political advantage of friendship with the Papacy, which would thus secure for the Empire that support of the West which it so sorely needed. From this had resulted the agreement of Lyons. In order to conciliate public opinion Andronicus II had thought it wise to denounce the treaty concluded with Rome. But political necessity forced the Emperor's hand. To combat the Turkish menace the help of the West was for the Empire indispensable. To procure it John V went to Italy and was even solemnly converted to Roman Catholicism (1369); Manuel II negotiated with Rome for the same end (1417). And lastly, at the Council of Florence (1439), John VIII signed the agreement with Eugenius IV which put an end to the schism between the two Churches. But imperial policy still came into conflict with the stubborn resistance of the Byzantine clergy, who could not bring themselves to accept the supremacy of Rome, with the fierce opposition of the nationalist Orthodox party, who were convinced that the Latins, in spite of their promises, were seeking only the 'destruction of the Greek city, race and name', and with popular hatred, which was fanned by violent controversialists who represented all sympathy for Latin ideas as a betrayal of the Church. In vain did John VIII and his successor Constantine XI attempt to impose by force a union which was made even more difficult by the tactless demands of the Papacy. Clamours of discontent were heard even under the dome of St. Sophia itself (1452). On the eve of the catastrophe which was to overwhelm Constantinople, in spite of the tragic situation of the Empire, the question of the Union seemed to be the essential problem, and some prominent folk did not hesitate to declare that they 'would rather see the Turkish turban reigning in Byzantium than the Latin mitre'.

In addition to all this there was the financial distress. In an Empire ruined by war and possessing ever less and less territory, taxation no longer yielded adequate resources; the treasury was empty, and the Government was reduced to debasing the currency and, in order to procure a little money, to pawning the crown jewels with the Venetian bankers. The Empire no longer had an army with which to defend itself, and it was forced to have recourse to the services of mercenaries. On sea there was the same weakness. Michael VIII had attempted to reconstitute the fleet. His successors considered it a useless expense, and from this time the command of the Eastern seas passed to the squadrons of Venice and Genoa, who also dominated the whole economic life of the monarchy. The Empire stood at bay, and the most surprising thing is perhaps that it should have lasted so long, especially if the external perils by which it was threatened are taken into consideration.

After the death of the Tsar John Asên (1241) the Bulgarian Empire became much weaker, and thus less dangerous to Byzantium. But in its place a great State had arisen in the Balkans. Serbia, under ambitious princes such as Stephen Milutin (1282–1321) and Stephen Dushan (1331–55), boldly contended with Byzantium for supremacy in the peninsula. Milutin, relying on his alliance with the Epirots and the Angevins, seized Upper Macedonia from the Greeks, and by the occupation of the districts of Seres and Christopolis gained access to the Archipelago; Andronicus II was obliged to recognize all his conquests (1298) and to give him in marriage his daughter Simonis. The defeat which the Serbians inflicted on the Bulgarians at Velboudj (1330) further increased their power. Dushan could thus dream of greater things. An able general and a skilful diplomat on good terms with Venice and the Papacy, he began by completing the conquest of Macedonia, where the Byzantines now held no more than Salonica and Chalcidice, and where the Serbian frontier on the east reached the Maritza. He seized part of Albania from the Angevins, and part of Epirus from the Greek despot. In 1346, in the cathedral of Skoplie, he had himself crowned 'Emperor and Autocrat of the Serbians and Romans'. The Serbian Empire now extended from the Danube to the Aegean and the Adriatic, and its ruler was recognized as the most powerful prince in the Balkans. In 1355 he attempted to seize Constantinople. He had already taken Adrianople, and conquered Thrace, when he suddenly died—unfortunately for Christendom—in sight of the city which he had hoped to make his capital. After his death his Empire soon disintegrated. But from this struggle which had lasted for half a century Byzantium emerged in a singularly weakened condition. In 1355 the Venetian envoy at Constantinople wrote to his Senate: 'This Empire is in a bad state, even, to be truthful, in a desperate one, as much because of the Turks who molest it sorely on all sides, as because of the Prince and his government with which there is general discontent; the people would prefer the rule of the Latins, mentioning as their first choice our seigniory and commune, if they could obtain it. For in truth they cannot remain as they are for anything in the world.'

The Venetians and Genoese did, in fact, occupy in the dying Empire a place that was daily more important. The former, driven from Constantinople in 1261, had soon returned, and, having lost hardly any of their possessions in the Archipelago, were all-powerful in the eastern Mediterranean. The Genoese, established since 1267 at Galata on the Golden Horn, with settlements on the coast of Asia Minor, at Chios, Lesbos, and Phocaea, and on the Black Sea at Caffa and Tana, were no less to be feared. And although the rivalry of the two great maritime cities often brought about strife between them, they were united in exploiting the Empire and in profiting from its distress, 'closing to the Romans', as a Byzantine historian wrote, 'all the maritime trade routes'. Confident in their strength, the two republics treated the Empire as if they had conquered it, defying the Byzantine Emperors and imposing their will upon them. When they thought they had a grievance, they did not hesitate to attack Constantinople itself. Involved in all the internal affairs of the Empire, they spread trouble everywhere in the capital, provoking revolutions, and intervening on every hand. The Byzantines, although angered, bore with these indignities, while the dominating influence of the Latins was more and more completely pervading the Empire, yet instead of borrowing from the West 'the virtues of work, economy and enterprise', they permitted, almost without resistance, the completion of the economic ruin of their country.

But it was from Asia that the most terrible danger came. From the end of the thirteenth century the Osmanli Turks, who, after having been subjects of the Seljuk sultans, had gained their independence owing to the Mongol invasion, began to attack the Byzantine possessions in Anatolia. In vain had Michael VIII attempted to stop them; in vain in order to resist their advance had Andronicus II taken the Catalan Grand Company into his pay. Commanded by energetic leaders, Osman (1289–1326) and Orkhan (1326–59), in less than half a century the Turks had made themselves masters of nearly the whole of Asia Minor. Brusa fell into their hands in 1326, Nicaea surrendered in 1329, and Nicomedia in 1337. The fleet built up by the Ottomans ravaged the islands of the Archipelago, and the Crusade which in 1343 reconquered Smyrna produced no permanent results. Already the Turks were hoping to settle in Europe. Soon, summoned by the Byzantines themselves, they crossed the Hellespont. John Cantacuzenus, who had solicited the alliance of the Ottomans and given his daughter in marriage to the son of the Sultan Orkhan, allowed the Turks to establish themselves in Gallipoli in 1354. The Balkan peninsula was open to them. Soon they had occupied Didymotica and Tzouroulon (1357), and then a large part of Thrace, including Philippopolis and Adrianople, which the Sultan Murad I (1359–89) made his capital (1365). Constantinople, isolated, encircled, and cut off from the rest of the Empire, appeared only to await the final blow which seemed inevitable.

Two circumstances prolonged the existence of the Byzantine State for a century. Murad I next turned to attack the other Christian States in the Balkans, crushing the southern Serbians and the Bulgarians on the Maritza (1371), invading Albania (1385), and destroying the Serbian Empire at the battle of Kossovo (1389). In his relations with the Byzantines he insisted only that John V should acknowledge himself as his vassal and, after having for a moment threatened Salonica (1374), he was content to surround Constantinople with an ever closer investment.

Bajazet (1389–1402) from the moment of his accession appeared inclined to act more vigorously; so much so that, as early as 1390, the Venetians were wondering if he would not very soon be master of Constantinople. However, in spite of the prolonged attack (1391–5) which he made on the Greek capital, in spite even of the disastrous defeat which, at the battle of Nicopolis (1396), was inflicted on the Crusade undertaken by the West to save Byzantium, the Sultan failed; the valour of Marshal Boucicaut, sent by Charles VI to the Greek Emperor, protected Constantinople against the attacks of the Turks for two more years (1397–9). But the situation remained singularly critical. Manuel II decided to go to the West to ask for help (1402). He was courteously welcomed at Venice, Paris, and London; but he obtained only fair promises. Happily for the Greeks, at this precise moment a serious event took place in the East. The Mongol invasion and the resounding defeat which Timur inflicted on the Turks at Angora (1402) gave the Empire a few years of respite. Bajazet had fallen into the hands of his conqueror; his sons fought with each other for the succession, and Byzantine diplomacy, seconded by the personal influence of the Emperor Manuel, skilfully took advantage of their quarrels. The existence of the Empire was thus prolonged for another half century.

But, in 1421, Murad II (1421–51), having triumphed over the other pretenders, again took the offensive. He unsuccessfully attacked Constantinople, which resisted heroically (1422); he captured Salonica (1430), which in 1423 the Venetians had bought from the Greeks; one of his generals penetrated into the Morea (1423) where the Greek despotat of Mistra remained one of the parts of the Empire which had suffered least from invasion; he himself led his forces into Bosnia and Albania, and imposed the payment of tribute upon the prince of Wallachia. In spite of the heroic efforts of John Hunyadi and Scanderbeg, the Ottomans followed up their advantage. The situation was so serious that eventually even the West was alarmed. In consequence of the visit of John VIII to Italy, Pope Eugenius IV preached a new Crusade; but the expedition met with utter disaster at the battle of Varna (1444). It was the last attempt made by the West to save the Empire of Byzantium in its agony; henceforth Constantinople was left to its fate.

Murad II followed up his successes. The duchy of Athens submitted to the Turks; the principality of the Morea, invaded in 1446, was forced to acknowledge itself their tributary; John Hunyadi was defeated at the second battle of Kossovo. Constantinople alone, behind the formidable defence of its walls, appeared impregnable. Ever since his accession in 1451 it had been the chief ambition of Muhammad II to capture the city. On 5 April 1453, with an immense army supported by heavy artillery, he marched against the Byzantine capital. On 29 May 1453 the city was taken by storm; at the Gate of St. Romanus the Emperor Constantine XI died heroically, thus shedding a last ray of beauty on the closing scene of Byzantine history. The next day Muhammad II entered Constantinople and in St. Sophia gave thanks to the God of Islam.

IV

Thus ended the Byzantine Empire, after more than a thousand years of often glorious existence. But what should be remembered—for this is as unexpected as it is remarkable —is that, in spite of the almost desperate external situation, in spite of internal troubles, the period of the Palaeologi still occupies an important place in the history of Byzantine civilization. Although Constantinople had ceased to be one of the centres of European politics, it remained nevertheless one of the most beautiful and renowned cities in the world, the metropolis of Orthodoxy and Hellenism, and the centre of a magnificent literary and artistic renaissance, which clothed the dying city with a glorious light. In this period can be observed a new spirit, more comprehensive and more humane, which distinguishes these cultured Byzantines of the fourteenth and fifteenth centuries and makes them the forerunners of Humanism—the circle of John Cantacuzenus or the University world are proofs of this. Here, too, in this city which had so long claimed to inherit the Roman tradition, it is important to notice the surprising revival of memories of the past of Hellas, and to observe the birth of a Greek patriotism, which, on the eve of the final catastrophe, might seem only a vain illusion, but which is none the less an expression of one of the ideas that eventually led to the restoration of modern Greece in the nineteenth century. And lastly one must not forget that artistic renaissance, the originality of which is proved by the remarkable works of art which it produced, and through which Byzantium exerted, for the last time, a powerful influence over the whole of the Eastern world.

But Constantinople was by no means the sole centre of this civilization. At Mistra, the capital of the Greek despotat of Morea, there was to be found a brilliant, artistic, and cultured Court, not unlike the Italian Courts of the fifteenth century, a real home of Hellenism and Humanism, and rendered illustrious by the name of Gemistus Pletho. On the Black Sea Trebizond, the birthplace of Bessarion, was, under the dynasty of the Comneni, another centre of Hellenic civilization. The despotat of the Morea and the Empire of Trebizond survived the fall of Constantinople by only a few years. The first was conquered by the Turks in 1460, and the second succumbed in 1461. With the latter disappeared for nearly four centuries the last remembrance of Byzantine greatness. But it was no small glory for this dying Empire that it was able 'to summon all its spiritual energies at the moment of the final collapse and thus to fall in sunset radiance'.

CHARLES DIEHL

II

THE ECONOMIC LIFE OF THE BYZANTINE EMPIRE

POPULATION, AGRICULTURE, INDUSTRY, COMMERCE

I. POPULATION

Two English writers, E. A. Foord[1] and W. G. Holmes,[2] are, to my knowledge, the only historians who have attempted to estimate the entire population of the Empire. But their calculations refer to the end of the fourth and the beginning of the fifth century—before the distinctively Byzantine form of the Empire had come into being. Moreover, the figures that these writers give are entirely conjectural and therefore worthy of little confidence. The truth is that the elements which might serve as a basis for a scientific calculation are lacking. One can indicate only what was the demographic evolution of the Empire and furnish a few data concerning the population of its capital.[3]

The population of Western Europe diminished very greatly after the break-up of the Roman Empire. Did a similar phenomenon occur in the provinces which the Greek Emperors succeeded in saving from the Arabs and from the northern barbarians? If we consider the effects of the barbarian invasions and of piracy, of epidemics and famines and of the growth of monasticism, it is probable that we should answer that question in the affirmative.

The invasions of the Muslims and the Bulgars, accompanied, as they were, by massacre, mass enslavement, and the headlong flight of the population, were a terrible scourge. It is true that the fortified coast-cities and the islands were often spared these horrors, but they suffered from the not

[1] *The Byzantine Empire* (London, A. & C. Black, 1911), p. 10.
[2] *The Age of Justinian and Theodora* (2nd ed., 2 vols., London, Bell, 1912), vol. i, p. 137.
[3] Cf. A. Andréadès, 'De la population de Constantinople sous les empereurs byzantins' (in the statistical review *Metron*, vol. i, no. 2, 1920). In the present chapter no attempt will be made to go back farther than the seventh century. It would be futile to include in our calculations provinces later lost to the Empire or, on the other hand, to consider the period after the twelfth century when the Byzantine State retained but the shadow of its former greatness.

less formidable scourge of piracy.[1] When the Arabs established themselves in Crete, even cities as large as Salonica
were sacked.

The Greek Church has placed in the first rank of the
evils that it prays Heaven to avert from the faithful pestilence and famine (*loimos* and *limos*). This conjunction of
words is not due to a mere love of alliteration. Both evils
were equally formidable and constantly menaced the population of the Empire. One can appreciate the extent of their
ravages by a single instance: in the reign of Constantine V
the pestilence so greatly reduced the population of Constantinople that the Emperor did not hesitate to fill up the gap
by a forcible settlement in the capital of folk from several
provinces, chiefly from the Peloponnesus. The pestilence
of A.D. 746–7 was, in point of fact, the most terrible epidemic
known to medieval Hellenism, but there were many others.
Similarly, famines, general or local, were frequent.

'Celibacy', says St. Jerome, 'populates Heaven.' This is
beyond dispute. But it does not populate our earth, especially when practised on so vast a scale as it was in the Byzantine Empire. The attraction exercised by the monasteries
upon all classes of society, from the members of the imperial
family down to the lowliest peasant, was indescribable.
Undoubtedly the reaction against this evil contributed not a
little to the Iconoclast movement. But the persecutions of
the monks under the Isaurian and Amorian dynasties were
of small effect. Even before the restoration of icon-worship
the Lives of the Saints give examples of whole families
embracing the monastic life. And later on, the enormous
growth in wealth of the monasteries added material temptations to the hope of celestial rewards.

The population of the Empire would, indeed, have
suffered a very large reduction, if a series of circumstances
had not diminished the effects of the factors which we have
just enumerated, and if a series of favourable factors had not
in turn played their part in counteracting these effects. Thus
for many centuries the 'themes'—the frontier provinces—

---

[1] So widespread was this evil that a tariff of ransoms was established (cf. Th.
Reinach, *Un contrat de mariage du temps de Basile le Bulgaroctone*, Mélanges
Schlumberger, Paris, 1924, vol. i, pp. 118–32).

both in Asia Minor and in Europe were protected from invasion, while during the prosperous reigns it was the Byzantines who invaded foreign territories. Even piracy was repeatedly restricted, notably when Crete was delivered from the Arabs.

Further, famine, which was one of the most terrible scourges of western Europe during the Middle Ages, seems to have had much less serious effects in the Eastern Empire, thanks to the measures taken for the revictualling of the cities and to the aid distributed in emergencies to the peasantry.

Among positive factors tending to increase the population it will suffice to mention three:

(i) Statistics teach us that the population increases in countries where there is no birth-control and where the prosperity of commerce and industry favours the development of urban centres. Now, at about the time of the downfall of Paganism, the voluntary restriction of births, which had been so prevalent both in Greece and in Italy, ceases. In all classes of society large families appear to become the rule; Christianity established afresh the sanctity of marriage and thus served to compensate for the spread of celibacy caused by monasticism. On the other hand, industry and commerce were more highly developed in the Empire of the East than in any other medieval State. Also the number of cities was very large. Benjamin of Tudela found them on his route in almost every day's journey; the Golden Bull of the Comneni conceded to the Venetians the right of establishing privileged communities in twenty-eight provincial towns,[1] while other sources reveal the existence of a large number of towns not mentioned either by the Jewish traveller or in the Venetian charter.[2] This would indicate a very considerable urban population, doubtless exceeding several millions, especially if one bears in mind that the population of Constantinople in its palmy days cannot have been under 500,000 souls and occasionally, perhaps, was in excess of that figure.

[1] Nine in Asia, nineteen in Europe.
[2] This fact merits special attention, because often mention is made only of Salonica and of Trebizond, which were merely the most important provincial cities.

(ii) The loss of numerous provinces to Arabs and barbarians brought about, by way of compensation, a reinforcement in wealth and population within the remaining provinces. The commerce of Tyre and Alexandria, says Gibbon,[1] was transferred to Constantinople, and Christians from Africa, Syria, Armenia, and the Danubian districts flocked to reinforce the population of the Empire.[2]

(iii) Gibbon praises the imperial Government for having utilized these refugees for the creation of new towns and for the cultivation of deserted lands, and still more for having gradually subjected to the laws of Church and State the barbarian tribes which had forced their way *vi et armis* into the Empire. This raises the important question of the imperial policy in home-colonization. Prof. P. Boissonade has ably outlined the essential features of this policy.[3] He has shown that it employed a great variety of methods. Asylum was afforded to the Christian refugees; lands were distributed to soldiers, accompanied by the obligation of military service; to the provinces which it was desired to repopulate the Government transported either religious dissenters (e.g. Manichaeans, Jacobites, and Paulicians) or persons of foreign race (Avars, Bulgars, and Turks), while slaves were emancipated on condition that they would colonize deserted districts. Sometimes individuals, at other times large masses, were thus settled in depopulated districts.[4] This policy of colonization was extended to nearly all parts of the Empire, including Italy, but its results were felt chiefly in the Balkan peninsula.

From all these facts one may conclude that the diminution of population, which is recorded in the provinces of the Western Empire, did not extend to the Eastern Empire, or, at least, not in anything like the same degree. It is, however,

---

[1] *The Decline and Fall of the Roman Empire*, ch. 53 (ed. J. B. Bury, vol. vi, 1898, p. 69).

[2] This movement continued nearly to the end. Also, in the ninth century many Christians of Sicily and southern Italy found refuge in Greece.

[3] *Le travail dans l'Europe chrétienne au Moyen-Âge Ve–XVe siècles* (Paris, Alcan, 1921), pp. 40–1.

[4] Thus, Justinian II at one time settled 70,000 Slav prisoners in Asia Minor. On another occasion 14,000 Turkish prisoners were established as settlers in Macedonia.

impossible to estimate even approximately the number of the inhabitants of the Byzantine Empire.[1]

II. AGRICULTURE

The agricultural question presents itself under a double aspect. The one, which one might call the *legal* aspect, concerns the form of land tenure. The other is the *economic* aspect, in other words, the nature and the conditions of agricultural production. Of these two aspects the latter is one of the most obscure; but even as to the first there is much less information than is generally supposed.

On the strength of various imperial constitutions promulgated during a period of about ten centuries, it has frequently been contended that landed property underwent the following evolution. Concentrated at first in the hands of great landowners in the early days of the Empire, the land is seen, in the time of the Iconoclasts, to be divided between the agriculturists and the peasant communities; later there is a reversion to the earlier system of large estates. The struggle for the protection of small holdings, which was carried on vigorously from the days of Romanus I Lecapenus to those of Basil II, finally ended in failure. This summary is exact only in general outline; the dates of the beginning and close of each of the periods are very uncertain and neither form of ownership (great or small) ever prevailed absolutely over the other. Thus, apart from the fact that we do not know whether the Rural Law really dates from the time of the Isaurians, it seems certain that great landed estates continued to exist while this law, which concerns only the small holdings, was still in force. And, on the other hand, from the time of Justinian to the period of the Palaeologi, small holdings seem never to have completely disappeared. Further, though we know why small

[1] Formerly Professor Andréadès had conjectured that under the Comneni the population of the Empire may have numbered from 10 to 15 millions; later he felt that it was safer to refrain from attempting any estimate. See his paper on 'La Population de l'Empire byzantin', in *Bulletin de l'Institut archéologique bulgare*, vol. ix (1935), pp. 117-26, which was read at the Byzantine Congress in Sofia (September 1934).

holdings were protected by the central Government, the causes which led at first to the development of the system of small holdings and later to the disappearance of that system are much less clear. The struggle against the landed aristocracy undertaken by the Macedonian dynasty, and before them by certain other Emperors, is generally explained by reference to military, political, and fiscal considerations. If the 'military lands' were swallowed up in the large private estates, then the Empire would be compelled to maintain an army of mercenaries which would prove both costly and unreliable.

The great landed proprietors, who had become veritable 'feudal' barons, frequently rebelled and occasionally claimed the imperial throne. It was important to prevent the growth of their power, while the East Roman State found that it was much easier to collect from small holders than from large landowners the various taxes and the numberless contributions in kind.

To these reasons one must add another, which the materialistic interpretation of history too often overlooks, although it is clearly apparent in the text of the laws. Byzantine society was impregnated with the spirit of Christianity. The Government felt itself in duty bound to protect the weak and humble. It should be noted that Romanus I Lecapenus, who led the struggle against the 'powerful', was himself distinguished by his philanthropic activity.

One can only conjecture how it was that the system of moderate and small holdings came to be prevalent in the eighth century. This fact was formerly explained as due to the substitution of Slav settlers for the original cultivators. But this 'Slav' theory, which moreover could apply only to a part of the Empire, has been abandoned by the Slavs themselves. The tendency to-day is to believe that the great diminution in the number of large estates (they never disappeared entirely) was due to the terrible invasions in Europe of the barbarians of the north and in Asia of the Persians and the Saracens, and also perhaps to the oppressive administration of Phocas and of Justinian II. Concurrently, the composition of the agricultural class was completely altered by the migrations into the Empire of populations from beyond its frontiers and from province to province—migrations which were partly due to the policy of internal colonization, of which we have already spoken. Consequently in nearly all the provinces (even those which suffered comparatively little from the invasions) one saw peasant immigrants arriving who were dependent upon no lord of the soil. At about the same period the administration of the Empire assumed a military character,[1] and the organization of a provincial army composed of nearly 60,000 holders of 'military lands' must have entailed a parcelling-out of the vast domains which in one way or another had come into the hands of the State.

The later return to a system of large estates which began in the ninth and tenth centuries may be attributed to a variety of causes, economic, administrative, political, and religious. From the beginning of the ninth century, certainly from the reign of Theophilus (829–42), one notes an economic expansion; the precious metals become more plentiful and prices rise. The big landed proprietors, owing to the rise in the prices of agricultural products, a number of high public functionaries, owing to imperial favour or to the elasticity of their conscience, and many private individuals find themselves in command of considerable capital. In our day they would have invested this capital in portable securities, have laid it out at interest, or employed it in trade or industry. But in the East Roman world portable securities were unknown; money-lending at interest was forbidden by law or subject to very rigorous restrictions;[2] commerce and industry, while not attended with loss of social position, as in the West, yielded but limited profits owing to the guild system and the State control of production, as well as of prices.[3] Thus, only agriculture remained; and when the country had less fear of invasion and the urban and rural population developed rapidly, agriculture must

[1] On the constitution of the themes see p. 297 *infra*.
[2] [Cf. Grégoire Cassimatis, *Les Intérêts dans la Législation de Justinien et dans le Droit byzantin* (Paris, Recueil Sirey, 1931); G. Ostrogorsky, *Geschichte des byzantinischen Staates* (Munich, Beck, 1940), p. 131.]
[3] See p. 65 *infra*.

have become more and more profitable, especially for those who had the means of purchasing slaves.

While economic reasons thus led the 'powerful' to acquire landed property, the 'poor' were forced by fiscal, or rather by administrative, reasons to sell their lands. The *humiliores* were burdened by taxes payable in cash, rendered still more oppressive by the *epibolē*, the forced labour and contributions in kind, that were even heavier than the taxes.[1] Beyond these there were, in addition, various obligations which a policy of State intervention imposed upon the people.[2] In theory, no doubt, the fiscal and administrative laws did not discriminate between the rich and the poor, but in practice, the 'powerful', who possessed ready capital, could pay the taxes with infinitely greater ease;[3] moreover, by reason of their social position, being better able to withstand the tax-collector, they frequently evaded fiscal contributions or administrative regulations and, in any case, saw to it that these measures did not degenerate into oppressive exactions. This was so generally the case that the free peasant came to envy the serf of the great landowner or of the monastery, who lived protected against the State official and who, in case of a bad harvest, could look to his master to supply his needs; and no doubt, in many cases, this comparison induced the freeman voluntarily to embrace the state of serfdom.

In the sphere of politics Emperors might themselves belong to the landed aristocracy or might be too dependent upon the support of that class to combat it with any determination. This was the case with the weak successors of Basil II and even, to a certain degree, with the Comneni. Moreover, the example of the West, with which the Crusades brought the Comneni into contact, the powerful attraction exercised by Western chivalry,[4] the abandonment of the system of 'military lands' for the semi-feudal system of

---

[1] For details, see pp. 83–4 *infra*.

[2] Some of these obligations were very unexpected, as, for example, the obligation of widows to marry barbarians settled by the Emperor in the district.

[3] It is well known, even in our day, how heavy a burden the taxes payable in cash constitute for the farmer, who is always short of ready money.

[4] On the development of this idea, cf. N. Iorga, *Histoire de la vie byzantine* (Bucharest, 1934), vol. iii, chap. 1.

pronoiai, were in themselves sufficient to cause that dynasty to relinquish a struggle which neither the Emperors of the early centuries nor the great sovereigns of the Macedonian line had succeeded in bringing to a successful issue.

Lastly, one must not forget that foremost amongst the great landed proprietors were the monasteries. In a nation so piously inclined, not to say so bigoted, as the Byzantine, it was to be expected that the monastic establishments would be the recipients of many donations and bequests; and the monasteries themselves were not backward in soliciting such pious gifts; indeed one may say that in this method of enrichment they demonstrated the greatest ingenuity.[1] For the development of the large estates the monasteries were thus largely responsible.

When we turn to consider the condition of agriculture we find that our evidence is contradictory. The material collected by Boissonnade[2] shows that agriculture in the eighth and ninth centuries was in a state of 'astounding' prosperity and was able not only to feed the Empire but also to provide for an 'active exportation'. The Byzantines did not confine themselves to growing cereals and cultivating the vine, but devoted themselves with like success to the cultivation of fruits, medicinal herbs, cotton, and mulberry trees (whence the name 'Morea' given to the Peloponnesus). A flourishing bee-culture supplied the place of a sugar industry, while abundant horned cattle, sheep, and pigs were bred as well as horses for the racecourse and for the needs of the army. The forests gave the material necessary for house construction and shipbuilding.

Other sources, however, some of them official, tell us of an agricultural population harassed by Muslim and Bulgarian invasions, decimated by pestilence and famine, crushed by fiscal burdens, and exploited by the 'powerful' and by the monks. The latter two classes of landed proprietors are also accused of negligent farming and of leaving their domains partly uncultivated.

---

[1] Amongst other sources cf. *Episkepsis Biou Monachikou*, by Eustathius, the learned Bishop of Salonica (twelfth century); of this L. Fr. Tafel published in 1847 a German translation under the title *Betrachtungen über den Mönchsstand*.

[2] Op. cit. See note 3, p. 54 *supra*.

Probably neither of these two pictures, although contradictory, is wholly untrue. Doubtless there were periods and districts in which agriculture was prosperous, while in others it was in a miserable condition. The great landed estates were not *always* prejudicial to agriculture.[1] In the absence of documentary data, it is not easy to say what was the exact situation in normal times.

Yet it is difficult to believe that misery was the rule and not the exception. Agriculture benefited both by the absence of foreign competition and by the presence of a large urban population. After the loss of Egypt, the numerous cities of the Empire derived their means of subsistence from the national agriculture. Good communications by sea and surprisingly good roads in the interior[2] facilitated the exchange of commodities. In the twelfth century foreigners were struck by the abundance of provisions of every kind to be found in Constantinople. In the eighth century one landed proprietor, who did not belong to the aristocracy, owned 100 yoke of oxen, 500 grazing oxen, 80 horses and mules, 12,000 sheep, and a large number of serfs. Another indication of the agricultural resources of the Empire is the land-tax, which was one of the two main sources of public revenue.[3]

But one must avoid all exaggeration, and the complaints of the misery of the peasants offer sufficient ground for surmising that, apart from certain exceptional periods, agriculture enjoyed but a relative prosperity and that often the lot of the peasant was far from enviable.

---

[1] On principle the great estates are better fitted than the small holdings to organize the production and the distribution of agricultural products. There are indications that certain big landowners and monasteries realized this fact.

[2] At least in Asia Minor. The network of roads in Asia Minor was due in large measure to military considerations. [Cf. W. M. Ramsay, *The Historical Geography of Asia Minor*, Royal Geographical Society, Supplementary Papers, vol. iv (London, Murray, 1890); D. G. Hogarth and J. A. R. Munro, *Modern and Ancient Roads in Eastern Asia Minor*, Royal Geographical Society, Supplementary Papers, vol. iii, part 5 (London, Murray, 1893); and cf. W. Leaf, 'Trade routes and Constantinople', *Annual of the British School at Athens*, vol. xviii (1911-12), pp. 301-13; J. A. R. Munro, 'Roads in Pontus, Royal and Roman', *Journal of Hellenic Studies*, vol. xxi (1901), pp. 52-66 (with map).]

[3] The other being the customs.

III. INDUSTRY

In the Byzantine Empire industry occupied as important a place as did agriculture. But its forms underwent much fewer disturbances; and, in general, Byzantine industry presents much fewer historical problems than Byzantine agriculture.

THE CHARACTER OF BYZANTINE INDUSTRY

Given the density of the urban population, it is probable that the manufacture of articles of common use employed infinitely more hands than the manufacture of luxuries. Nevertheless, if Byzantine industry is usually associated with the idea of the manufacture of luxuries, this is not due solely to the fact that Byzantine *articles de luxe* (owing to their artistic character) have a special interest for modern students, but also to the fact that such articles undoubtedly had in the Byzantine world an importance relatively greater than they have in our own times. As a matter of fact, such articles, much sought after by the Churches of the West and by foreign grandees (both Christian and non-Christian), constituted the most important item of Byzantine exports. On the other hand, the home demand for such articles was also very great. The numerous ceremonies of the Byzantine Court have aptly been compared to a succession of theatrical representations (Kondakov); they required an enormous quantity of costumes, fabrics, vases, and ornaments of all kinds. The monuments and ceremonies of the Church demanded an even greater supply; for while there was only one Court, there were tens of thousands of churches, monasteries, and chapels; the treasures of the richest of them literally dazzled the Westerners, but even the smallest contained many objects of great value.[1]

The descriptions given by travellers and the lamentations of Church Fathers prove that luxury was very widespread in society. Benjamin of Tudela tells us of rich Byzantines clad in sumptuous fabrics; they also loved to live in grand houses and to adorn their tables with gold and silver ware.[2]

[1] Cf. O. M. Dalton, *Byzantion*, vol. i (1924), p. 595.

[2] This custom prevailed to the very last [cf. R. Guilland, 'Le Palais de Théodore Métochite', *Revue des études grecques*, vol. xxxv (1922), pp. 82–95]. For the

To meet this great demand at home and from abroad, the artisans of a number of towns, and principally those of Constantinople, Salonica, Thebes, Corinth, and Patras, were obliged to manufacture incessantly the articles, which are still the admiration of connoisseurs—the magnificent silk fabrics, the heavy gold brocades and fine cloths, the wonderful products of the goldsmith's art (jewellery, enamelled *cloisonné* plates, reliquaries, and other objects of religious devotion, bronzes, &c.), elegant glass-ware, ivories—in brief, to quote Diehl,[1] 'everything that was known to the Middle Ages in the way of precious and refined luxury'.

The Organization of Industry

Thanks to the publication by J. Nicole of the *Edict on the Guilds of Constantinople*, more generally known under the name of the 'Prefect's Book' (*eparchikon biblion*), one can form an approximate idea of the organization of Byzantine industry and petty trade.[2]

The guild system was in full force. Every branch of industry formed a corporation and some of the corporations (such as those concerned with the silk industry) were subdivided into several guilds. Each guild enjoyed a real monopoly but, on the other hand, was subject to a rigorous control by the State, which fixed the profits, the conditions of admission of new members, the restrictions upon the exportation of goods, and a number of other points, including (in certain cases) even the localities where booths and workshops could be established. The prefect of Constantinople also exercised a close surveillance over the members of corporations and had the right to inspect their workshops.

This order of things, combining economic monopoly and State intervention, shocked the learned scholar who discovered and published the Edict. Had Professor Nicole been an economist living in our day, he would have been much less surprised.[3] He called Byzantium 'the paradise of

luxury of the banquet-table see the exhaustive article by Prof. Phaedon Koukoulès, Ἐπετηρίς Βυζαντινῶν Σπουδῶν, vol. x (1933), pp. 97–160.

[1] *Byzance. Grandeur et Décadence* (Paris, Flammarion, 1919), p. 95.

[2] For studies on the *Book of the Prefect*, see p. 397 *infra*.

[3] For what follows see my article: 'Byzance, paradis du monopole et du privilège', *Byzantion*, vol. ix (1934), pp. 171–81.

monopoly and privilege', and this has become an everyday phrase. In reality, a legislation resembling in many respects that of Byzantium may be found wherever the *régime corporatif* has been tried, whether in the Eastern Roman Empire or in western Europe of the Middle Ages or in Japan under the Tokugawas. In most of these cases the system has had a less liberal form than at Byzantium. Certainly, in the long run, the guild system impedes progress and breeds abuses. But it possesses some important advantages; thus, it assures the quality of the goods produced, it does away with middlemen, it also forestalls both the exaggerated advance of prices and the crises of over-production. That is why this system seems to be a necessity in certain stages of economic development. In any case, it appears to have worked in the Greek Empire without arousing any complaints. Nor does it seem to have excited unfavourable criticism on the part of foreigners. Ganshof has discovered in the Western laws of the twelfth century a number of provisions which resemble those of the Prefect's Edict;[1] and the Turkish Sultans appear to have copied that Edict slavishly.[2]

IV. INTERNATIONAL TRADE

The Byzantine Empire was situated at the junction of the communications between Asia and Europe, and Europe and Africa; all routes, by land, sea, or river, connecting eastern Europe with the Mediterranean passed through Byzantine territory. This geographical position was a veritable calamity from a political point of view; for no Italian State nor any region in the Danube lands or in Hither Asia could develop without being tempted to invade Greek territory. On the other hand, from the commercial standpoint, that geographical position was of inestimable benefit, for automatically it made Byzantium the centre of international trade.

Nature had also favoured the Empire by endowing it with a great number of ports, on all its coasts, from Trebizond to

---

[1] *Byzantion*, vol. iv (1928), p. 659.

[2] Father Jannin pointed out that certain provisions of that Edict were still in force in the Istanbul of Mustafa Kemal Pasha.

Dyrrachium and from Crete to Anchialos. Some of these ports were the natural outlets of vast inland territories. Thus, Trebizond and Salonica were the ports not only of Persia and the centre of the Balkan peninsula respectively, but also of the hinterland of those regions.[1] Cherson, a sort of colonial possession, occupied for Russia a similar position.[2] But indisputably the greatest trade centre was Constantinople, with its unique situation and its incomparable harbour.

In the course of centuries man had completed the work of nature. We have already seen that for a long time Byzantium monopolized the trade in *articles de luxe*, so important in an age in which international trade relied for its customers to a great extent upon churches, royal palaces, and seigneurial castles; it may also be remarked that some agricultural products, such as certain wines and dried fruits, were much sought after, even by the barbarians.[3] We shall see, in the chapter on public finances, that at least down to the eleventh century the Emperors maintained the intrinsic value of their gold coinage, whence the *nomisma* or *besant* became a truly international coin and supplied the Empire with an indispensable instrument for drawing to itself the trade between the various nations. In the same chapter we shall speak of the great public edifices, where merchandise was stored; these bazaars or caravanseries were to be found in fortified cities, which afforded protection against invaders and pirates and thus furnished commerce with that security which is as necessary to it as a sound currency.

One must also remember that, beside the efficacious measures taken at various times against piracy, the Byzantines possessed a large mercantile fleet. Down to the Mussulman era this fleet was mistress of the seas; after centuries of reverses, it succeeded in developing a new prosperity, and its decadence did not really set in until the

[1] 'Trebizond became the great port of the East.' S. Runciman, *Byzantine Civilisation* (London, Arnold, 1933), p. 167.

[2] Direct relations between Constantinople and Russia do not date farther back than the ninth century.

[3] Thus the Russians brought their furs, honey, wax, and slaves, and received in exchange articles of the goldsmith's art, silk fabrics, wine, and fruits. Cf. A. Vasiliev, 'Economic Relations between Byzantium and Old Russia', *Journal of Economic History*, vol. iv (1932), pp. 314–34.

twelfth century. Even during the period of reverses, the Emperors strove to protect their merchant shipping by special laws,[1] and, it would seem, relaxed, in favour of ship-owners, the law against lending money at interest. Lastly, though we possess only fragmentary information on this point, it seems to be incontrovertible that international trade was encouraged by diplomacy and even by treaties. The treaties concluded with the Russians contributed, in no less a degree than the occupation of Cherson and the possession of the Straits, to make of the Black Sea a 'Greek sea', to use the expression of the Arab geographer Ibn Khordadbeh. In a more general way Byzantine policy towards foreigners contributed to making Constantinople and, in a lesser degree, certain other cities extremely busy centres of a re-exportation trade. That is why in the capital one saw 'strangers from every quarter of the world'. For nations that were of special importance special warehouses and even special quarters were reserved.[2]

Such are, in brief summary, the reasons why the Empire of the East remained for several centuries the centre of international trade. The imperial administration has been accused of hampering the development of that trade not only through the interference of its officials but also by a series of legislative measures. Some of these criticisms are well founded; others are more or less exaggerated. Too little account is taken of those economic ideas which, after having prevailed in the Middle Ages and down to the eighteenth century (Mercantilism), have now reappeared in another form in these times of 'State-controlled economy'.

Thus, it is probable that the customs authorities applied in a meddlesome and vexatious spirit the measures for regulating trade; and it is also probable that the customs duties (10 per cent. both on exports and on imports) were too high.

On the other hand, criticisms of the prohibitions placed upon imports and exports are much exaggerated. Prohibitions upon imports were practically unknown; those upon

---

[1] Cf. the Rhodian Law which has been attributed to the Isaurian Emperors. [It is not possible to say more than that the law was issued between A.D. 600 and 800: so Ostrogorsky.]

[2] This was notably the case with the Russians, the Venetians, and the Genoese.

exports were limited to a few cases and were justified by special reasons. Thus, only one article (soap) is cited the importation of which was forbidden—no doubt in order to protect manufacturers within the Empire. As for the goods whose exportation was forbidden (except by special permission), they can be classed under four categories: (a) ceremonial clothing, of which the State was in constant need for Court festivities, for distribution to high public functionaries, and for gifts to distinguished foreigners—together with unsewn fabrics (*arrapha*) and raw silk; (b) raw materials, which it was desired to reserve for home industries; (c) salt fish, which formed one of the staple foods of the capital; (d) gold, because of the State's anxiety not to deplete the monetary reserve—a principle thoroughly familiar to us to-day. To this same anxiety must be attributed the occasional recourse to barter or mutual exchange of products—the obligation imposed upon importers to pay for certain goods (e.g. Bulgarian honey and flax) not in cash but in goods. This system, which shocked us until recently, has to-day become once more the fashion.

Let us pass on to another class of criticisms. In the Byzantine Empire the guild system prevailed in commerce as much as in industry; lending at interest (at least from the time of the Iconoclasts) was forbidden or fixed at a low rate;[1] it was the public authorities, and not the law of supply and demand, that determined prices; admission to the capital was refused to certain aliens or subjected to very stringent regulations. It is but a few years ago that the conviction was prevalent that economic and commercial prosperity goes hand in hand with freedom in the matter of labour, prices, interest rates, and admission of aliens; one was asked to believe that one of the causes of the decadence of the Byzantine Empire was the absence of all forms of liberty. This is too sweeping a simplification of questions of economic history that are admittedly very complex. Doubtless the criticisms which we have mentioned are justified in theory. On the other hand, how can it be overlooked that the guild system and the principle of State intervention are, in certain stages of economic development, almost inevitable? Side by side

[1] See p. 57 *supra*.

with some manifest inconveniences, they possess many advantages. For instance, the regulation of prices forestalled speculation; while the guild system tended to encourage exports by assuring the good quality of industrial products and even to favour imports, since occasionally the guild was obliged to buy up whole stocks imported into the market of Constantinople[1]; and it must never be forgotten that the system of guilds and State intervention prevailed also in those great cities of the West which robbed Byzantium of its economic and commercial supremacy.

As for the aliens, whose sojourn in Constantinople was subjected to so strict a surveillance, they were mostly barbarians from the north, whom there was every reason to fear. Apart from these 'undesirables', foreigners appear to have obtained, without much difficulty, permission to sojourn and even to settle in Constantinople. Even before the formation of the strong Italian communities, foreigners (for instance, Syrians) resident in the capital were much more numerous than in any other city of the medieval world.

This is true to such an extent that one of the most generally accepted explanations of the economic decadence of Byzantium is that the Byzantines adopted the principle of not carrying their wares to foreign parts but of waiting for the foreign purchaser to come to them. The Italian communities were undoubtedly the cause of the Empire's political and financial ruin and also, perhaps, of its industrial decline. It was they who prompted the Fourth Crusade; by their privileges they deprived the imperial Treasury of the customs duties, which were its largest source of revenue; their industrial products little by little took the place of Greek manufactures; and it was their merchant shipping that supplanted the fleet of the Byzantine shipowners. Yet from the purely commercial standpoint these foreign communities had far less influence. As Charles Diehl says, 'Constantinople remained the great distributing centre of the world's trade up to the fall of the Byzantine Empire, even when it was no longer the Empire but the great Italian cities that profited by the situation'. In my opinion the truth is that

[1] For instance, all fabrics imported from Syria. Cf. *The Prefect's Book*, ch. v, § 4.

commercial decadence was not an independent phenomenon at Byzantium; it was the consequence of that economic decadence, the causes of which will be summarized in the concluding section of this chapter.

V. CONCLUSION

From the fifth to the end of the twelfth century the Byzantine Empire was indisputably the richest and most populous State in Christendom. Its prosperity was due in a large measure to its population, which was composed of citizens who were perhaps lacking in the political spirit, too much given to religious controversies and civil strife, but, on the other hand, were good heads of families, well endowed with the spirit of business enterprise, attracted by arts and commerce—in one word, marked by the virtues, as well as by the defects, of the Greek race. But this prosperity was equally due to the State, which took measures, often efficacious, against depopulation, or for the protection of small landowners or for the encouragement of industry and commerce. It was out of the combined efforts of Government and people that there grew again and again that wealth which, with the multitude of sacred relics, was what most impressed the foreign visitor. When Robert de Clari assures us that 'two-thirds of the world's wealth is to be found at Constantinople', when so many other travellers use the same, or nearly the same, expressions, and even cite details as to the wealth of various provinces,[1] doubtless they are exaggerating, but at least they attest that the richest Christian State of the West appeared poor in comparison with the Empire of the East. In the following chapter we shall see that the Byzantines themselves had the feeling that this national wealth, from which the public Treasury could draw sums that were enormous for those times, constituted one of the principal forces of their country.

---

[1] When, for instance, John Brompton and Arnold of Lübeck affirmed that the public revenues of Corfu and of Cyprus, toward the close of the twelfth century, amounted annually to 1,620,000 and 7,560,000 gold francs, respectively, they implied that the inhabitants of those islands had an annual income much larger than these sums, which to-day would have an infinitely greater (perhaps quintuple) purchasing value.

How did this Great Prosperity fall into Decline?

In many ways and for many reasons. In the first place, societies, like individuals, grow old. The Byzantine shipowners, merchants, and manufacturers, probably rooted firmly in antiquated methods of business, could not keep pace with their younger Italian competitors. On the other hand, as we have seen, the Byzantine economic organization was a State, and hence a bureaucratic organization, and bureaucracies are even more swiftly overtaken by decadence than communities. From the eleventh century the Byzantine administration was no longer capable of defending the small landowners; one may also conjecture that by the incessant interference of its officials (who themselves deteriorated, as time went on) the State caused more harm than good to commerce and industry. Oh the other hand, taxation, increasingly indulgent toward the monasteries and the powerful classes, became necessarily more and more oppressive for the mass of the people.

Nevertheless, all these causes of decadence weighed little in comparison with the political misfortunes which (with certain periods of respite[1]) continued to befall the Empire after the death of Basil II. The first of these successive disasters (each more terrible than the other) was the loss of the rich agricultural provinces of Asia Minor, in consequence of the rapid advance of the Seljuks. In the course of the twelfth century came the Norman invasions, one of which (that of the year 1147) was accompanied by the transfer to Sicily of the silk industries of Thebes and of Corinth. Almost simultaneously followed the first three Crusades, which, amongst other harmful consequences, brought about the displacement of the Syrian trade from Constantinople to Italy. In the reign of Isaac Angelus the restoration of the Bulgarian State brought about the loss of those Danubian provinces which for long had been a compensation for the loss of so many Asiatic provinces. The capture of Constantinople by the Crusaders and the partition of the Empire crowned this long series of disasters.

This last catastrophe was, from an economic point of view,

---

[1] Especially under the first three Comnene Emperors.

the death-blow of the Empire. Under the dynasty of the Angeli the Empire was in full political and military decline. Its wealth was less impaired, as shown by the testimony of the travellers quoted above, who belong to the times of that inglorious dynasty. So long as Constantinople remained intact, there was always the possibility of a revival like that which took place after the great Arab and Bulgarian invasions of the early Middle Ages. An example of this recuperation is to be found in Villehardouin's mention of Salonica as an extremely rich city, although only a few years before (1185) it had been sacked by the Normans. Constantinople can be considered the heart of the economic life of the Empire. It was there that for the most part the portable wealth and the principal branches of industry and commerce were concentrated; hundreds of thousands of working people lived within its walls. Of all this, after several days of pillage, massacre, and conflagration, hardly anything remained.

To sum up, and without overlooking the internal causes mentioned above, one may say that the economic decadence of the Empire was chiefly the work of its foreign enemies, who by fire and sword depopulated its cities and its lands, destroyed its industries, and took away its commerce, which had already been partly deflected to their own countries since the beginning of the Crusades. When the Palaeologi succeeded in reuniting under their sceptre a part of the old Empire, they found everything in ruins. The combined efforts of the enemy on the north, on the west, and (this time especially) on the east (the Turks) did not allow the Empire's economic life permanently to recover a portion of its ancient splendour.[1]

The Byzantine people paid a fearful price for the loss of their military virtues and for their passion for civil war.[2]

ANDRÉ M. ANDRÉADÈS

[1] The economic revival, which occasionally was noticeable, was both local and ephemeral (e.g. at Salonica).

[2] It was these civil wars which paved the way for the foreign invasions; as, for instance, the rivalries between Isaac II and his brother Alexius III, or between Andronicus Palaeologus and Cantacuzenus.

III

PUBLIC FINANCES

CURRENCY, PUBLIC EXPENDITURE, BUDGET, PUBLIC REVENUE

I. THE CURRENCY

OF the Byzantine coinage it will suffice to say that from Constantine to Alexius Comnenus the Emperors hardly ever had recourse to the practice, then so common, of debasing the coinage. In consequence, for many centuries the Byzantine gold piece, the *nomisma*, became a veritable international coin.

But from the time of the Comneni and especially under the Palaeologi, the practice of debasing the coinage became frequent and gradually the gold coin, now known as the *hyperpyron*, came to be worth but a third of its original value, which was about 15 gold francs.[1]

The precious metals at that time had, of course, a far greater purchasing value than they have in general to-day; it is estimated that that purchasing value was five times greater. Many modern historians, when quoting a figure from the sources, are in the habit of multiplying it by five. Thus Paparrigopoulos, who introduced this practice, reckons the revenues of Constantinople at 530 million gold francs because, according to the information of Benjamin of Tudela, the Emperor drew an annual revenue from the capital of 106 million gold francs. This method of calculation doubtless gives the reader a more concrete idea of what this or that item of revenue or expenditure would represent in present-day money, but it is perhaps safer simply to quote the figures as they are given by our sources. As a matter of fact, the purchasing value of gold and silver fluctuated very much during the ten centuries of the Empire; and what is more serious, there is no period during those centuries for

---

[1] Byzantine literary sources mention moneys of account, such as the gold pound (worth 1,080 gold francs) and the silver pound (worth 75 gold francs), while on the other hand, the gold *nomisma* was subdivided into *milliaresia* of silver, each of which was subdivided into *keratia*.

which one can determine with precision what that purchasing value was.[1]

II. PUBLIC EXPENDITURE

No Christian State in the Middle Ages and even few kingdoms of the Renaissance had to meet such great public expenditure as the Greek Empire of the East. This arose, on the one hand, from that Empire's geographical situation, which exposed it to countless dangers, involving enormous sums for national defence, while at the same time the political and social structure of the Empire demanded an expenditure at least as great as that required for national defence.

(a) NATIONAL DEFENCE

We have already pointed out the exceptional situation of the Empire at the junction of the great arteries of communication between Europe, Asia, and Africa. But this geographical position, while affording immense economic advantages, caused the Eastern Empire to be the object of attack from all sides. After the Persians came the Arabs, and then the Turks; after the Slavs, the Bulgars, and then the Russians; after the Goths and the Lombards, the Normans and then the Crusaders.

At first the Byzantines flattered themselves with the belief that they could stop these successive waves of invasion by a system of frontier and mountain-pass fortifications resembling the Great Wall of China, as well as by the fortification of every city of any importance. This system no doubt rendered great services; but besides being so costly as to call for special taxes, permanent or temporary, it was in itself inadequate. Therefore without abandoning it the imperial Government turned its attention more particularly to the creation of a strong army.

In fact, the Byzantines succeeded in forming an army and a navy superior in numbers and ships, as well as in organization, to those of most of the other States of the Middle Ages. But these land and sea forces, which repeatedly

[1] For the details see A. Andréadès, 'De la monnaie et de la puissance d'achat des métaux précieux dans l'Empire byzantin', *Byzantion*, vol. vii (1924), pp. 75–115; and cf. G. Ostrogorsky, 'Löhne und Preise in Byzanz', *Byzantinische Zeitschrift*, vol. xxxii (1932), pp. 293–333.

saved the Empire and enlarged its boundaries, were extremely costly.

It is true that the State reduced the annual charge on the budget by sacrificing large tracts of public land and distributing them to citizens in return for a hereditary obligation to serve in the army, but the charges on the budget continued to be very heavy. In the first place the Treasury had to provide for the building and upkeep of several hundreds of ships,[1] for arms and engines of war (including Greek Fire), and for the auxiliary services, which were so greatly developed that, as Manuel Comnenus wrote to Henry II of England, the Byzantine army, when on the march, extended for ten miles. Moreover, the 'military lands' did not furnish a sufficient number of soldiers. Hence, recourse was had to the enlistment of mercenaries, and the demands of these foreigners were exorbitant. We know, for instance, that the Scandinavian mercenaries used to return to their distant homes laden with riches.

If to all this expenditure we add the pay of the officers, who were numerous and well rewarded,[2] one can understand why the wars entailed heavy taxes in money and in kind, and why in consequence some of the most glorious Emperors (such as Nicephorus Phocas) were often so unpopular. One can also understand why the Byzantine Empire preferred to employ gold rather than the sword in its foreign policy. This employment of gold assumed two distinct forms. First, that of *tribute*. Tribute was in principle quite a wise arrangement; it was more economical to pay an annual sum than to expose the country to an invasion, even if that invasion were repulsed successfully. Thus the Bulgars paid to the Hungarians the greater part of the money they received from the Byzantines. Yet, as Procopius had already observed, if tribute kept away one set of barbarians from the frontiers, it attracted other races. It was, therefore, more profitable to utilize the great resources of the Empire in procuring allies amongst the neighbours of the Empire's enemies. The

[1] From the eighth to the twelfth century the historical sources repeatedly mention fleets of 500 to 1,000 ships, in addition to 1,000 to 2,000 transports.

[2] It may be estimated that their number amounted to 3,120 and their pay to 3,960 pounds (or, 4,276,800 gold francs) per annum.

Byzantine annals furnish many instances in which recourse was had to this latter method, which became a permanent element in East Roman foreign policy.[1]

The Emperors were also fond of creating a great impression of their wealth by the magnificence of their embassies. Thus, the chroniclers relate that Theophilus provided John the Grammarian with 400 pounds in gold, so that the latter was enabled to dazzle the Court of Bagdad by scattering 'money like sand'.

(b) Expenditure on the Civil Administration

The Byzantine Empire was a complex organism. It was at once a bureaucratic State, a semi-Oriental absolute monarchy, a Greco-Christian community, and, lastly, a nation in which the capital played a role almost as preponderant as in the States which, like Athens, Rome, or Venice, were the creation of one city. The budget being, as Napoleon said, the mirror of a country's political and social life, all the above traits were necessarily reflected in the finances and each of them formed a separate item of expenditure in the budget. We shall therefore examine in succession the expenditure for the administration, the Palace and Court, the churches and public charities, and the city of Constantinople. For lack of space we must pass over items of lesser importance such as, for example, universities, public works in the provinces, or the police force.

1. Diehl has justly praised the Byzantine administration as 'strongly centralized and wisely organized'. It was the administration no less than the army which placed the Empire of the East so far above the other States of the Middle Ages and which enabled it to survive the frequent changes of Emperors without lapsing into anarchy. On the other hand, this civil administration entailed heavy expenditure, inasmuch as the public officials were numerous and with few exceptions were paid by the State. Like the States of our own day the Empire of the East maintained a policy of 'State-directed economy' and insisted upon controlling and regulating all manifestations of the life of the community (production, labour, consumption, trade, movement

[1] See below what the ministers of Nicephorus Phocas said to Liutprand.

of the population, or public welfare). For this supervision a vast number of officials was needed. Further, the State possessed immense landed property and itself engaged in various industries. The kingdoms of the Renaissance, which also practised economic intervention, if not centralization, and also possessed State property, both agricultural and industrial, adopted the system of the sale of public posts. But in the Byzantine Empire only a few Court posts or empty titles were sold.[1] It was therefore necessary to give salaries to the public officials and each salary was composed of three parts: the *siteresion* (provisions), the *roga* (cash-payment), and the supply of clothing. The *roga* and the clothing were distributed once a year, to the higher functionaries by the Emperor himself, to the others by the *parakoimōmenos*. Liutprand (*Antapodosis*, vi. 10) tells us that the file past the Emperor lasted three days, while that past the *parakoimōmenos* lasted a week. From other sources we learn that the higher functionaries received a handsome *roga*[2] and costly clothing. Hence, while we lack evidence for the monetary value of the *siteresion* and the salaries of the lower officials, it is clear that the bureaucracy, like the army, constituted a heavy charge upon the public treasury.

2. In consequence of an evolution, which had its origin in Diocletian's time and was reinforced by the contact with the Caliphs of Bagdad, the Roman *principatus* had gradually changed into an Oriental monarchy. To this form of government corresponded the splendid palaces and the magnificent Court of Constantinople. From the financial standpoint alone it is difficult to estimate the cost of constructing the imperial residences (the chief Palace was in itself a small city) and the expense of the thousands of nobles, clerics, soldiers, eunuchs, and servants who swarmed therein. Yet it is certain that even under the most parsimonious Emperors what to-day we call the 'civil list' must have been enormous. It was swollen by all the largesses which the sovereign was expected to distribute to the army, the

---

[1] Cf. A. Andréadès, 'La Vénalité des charges est-elle d'origine byzantine ?', *Nouvelle Revue historique de droit français,* vol. xlv (1921), pp. 232–41.

[2] Thus the *roga* of the Dean of the Law School amounted to four gold pounds per annum (equivalent in purchasing power to £1,000 sterling at least).

Church, and the populace; these under prodigal Emperors, like Tiberius II,[1] reached extravagant sums. The banquets given on great feast-days or on the arrival of foreign monarchs or embassies entailed an expense much more considerable than in our day, seeing that the guests, whose number occasionally reached 240, received presents both in money and in kind.

3. But the Emperor was not only a prince, whose ideal of sovereignty had been influenced by the neighbouring Asiatic Courts; he was also the head of the Christian Church and as such he was expected to discharge many obligations and thereby to incur great expense. Even though the majority of the pious foundations were the work of private individuals, the churches and the monasteries must have cost the public treasury as much as the walls and fortifications. According to Codinus, St. Sophia alone cost 300,000 gold pounds—a sum much greater than the 60 million *scudi* spent on the erection of St. Peter's. The upkeep of churches and monasteries, which on principle was supposed to be at the expense of these institutions themselves, could not be overlooked by the *logothētēs* of the *genikon*, the imperial Minister of Finance. In the first place, the Emperor, in founding an ecclesiastical institution or church, endowed it with lands (thus, Justinian assigned to St. Sophia 365 domains, one for each day of the year, within the suburbs of Constantinople) or else with an income, as in the case of the monasteries founded by Nicephorus Phocas on Mt. Athos or that built by Manuel Comnenus at the entrance to the Bosphorus. Moreover, some of the more important churches were in receipt of an annual subvention. That to St. Sophia, fixed at first at 80 pounds, was raised by Romanus III to 160 pounds of gold. Likewise the Christian religion required the Emperor to be charitable, good, and merciful. Hence both he and his family competed with his wealthy subjects in the endowment of innumerable charitable institutions, such as hostels for pilgrims (*xenodocheia*), refuges for the poor (*ptochotropheia*), hospitals for the sick (*nosokomeia*), homes for the aged (*gērokomeia*), which were the ornament and pride of

---

[1] The successor of Justinian II, not content with reducing taxation by one-fourth, spent 7,200 gold pounds in largesses in one year.

the 'city guarded of God' and the administration of which represented one of the most important public services.

4. Alfred Rambaud has aptly remarked: 'Constantinople constituted the Empire, occasionally it reconstituted the Empire, sometimes it was the whole Empire.' This exceptional position of the capital is reflected in the enormous sums expended on its protection and embellishment, on the aqueducts, markets, and streets lined with arcades, which made Constantinople 'the sovereign of all cities', to use Villehardouin's phrase.

If Constantinople made and remade the Empire, its inhabitants made and unmade the Emperors. And that was a fact that the latter took good care not to forget; one of them, Isaac Angelus, compared the people of his capital to the wild boar of Calydon and all the Emperors were assiduous in cajoling the monster. The Roman tradition provided the populace with the games of the circus[1] and with free distributions of bread. These civic loaves (*artoi politikoi*) were indeed abolished by Heraclius, but reappeared in the infinitely more modest form of largesses in money or in kind, which were distributed on the occasion of happy events or at times of great scarcity.

III. THE BYZANTINE BUDGET

Paparrigopoulos, on the authority chiefly of foreign travellers and chroniclers, has estimated the budget of the Empire at 640 million gold francs, which, of course, had a far greater purchasing value. Ernst Stein puts it at only 100–115 millions. Elsewhere[2] I have discussed these figures at some length, and I still believe that both are equally erroneous, the former being too high, the latter too low. On the other hand, it seems to be impossible to suggest any definite figure, not only for the whole budget but even for any one of its principal heads. The data furnished by Byzantine sources

---

[1] Cf. Novel 81 of Justinian.

[2] Cf. A. Andréadès, *Le Montant du Budget de l'Empire byzantin* (Paris, Leroux, 1922). [This separate publication contains Appendixes which are not given in the article which appeared in the *Revue des études grecques*, vol. xxxiv (1921), no. 156. Cf. Ernst Stein, *Byzantinische Zeitschrift*, vol. xxiv (1923–4), pp. 377–87, and his *Studien zur Geschichte des byzantinischen Reiches* (Stuttgart, Metzler, 1919), pp. 141–60.]

are in some cases doubtful and in all cases fragmentary, and those given by foreigners are even more so. Moreover (and this is a point that has not been sufficiently emphasized) a considerable proportion of the expenditure was made in kind. This consisted of articles of every sort, including food-stuffs, derived from the land or the workshops owned by the State, or from requisitions made upon private individuals. It is manifestly impossible, after so many centuries, to say what value these supplies represented in cash; nor is it easier to estimate the cash value of the hours of forced labour (the *corvée*), which were a public burden laid upon the citizens.

An additional difficulty lies in the fact that though the principal heads of expenditure remained practically the same since the characteristic features of the Empire remained unchanged, the amounts raised under these different heads varied greatly according to the character of the reigning sovereign. Under an ambitious and magnificent Emperor like Justinian or Manuel Comnenus the expenditure entailed by campaigns and buildings predominated. Under a monarch more conscious of the real situation of the Empire, such as Constantine V, Nicephorus Phocas, or Alexius Comnenus, it was the expenditure for national defence. Under an Empress there would be heavy expenditure for the monasteries, for charities, and for popular largesses; lastly, under a stupid or debauched Emperor, favourites and buffoons absorbed a large part of the public treasury's resources.

But even after all this has been said, it is probable that, except in the days of the Palaeologi (1261–1453), when the Empire was but the shadow of its former greatness, and in certain peculiarly disastrous reigns, the State revenues must have exceeded, and sometimes greatly exceeded, the sum of 100 million gold francs. Those who assert the contrary forget, amongst other things,[1] that one must not take into account only the expenditure in money, since a part of the expenditure, as well as of the revenues, was in kind; that the

---

[1] As, for instance, the fact that from the ruins of the first Byzantine Empire sprang up a number of kingdoms and principalities, each of which had a luxurious Court and a costly army.

principal heads of expenditure in the budget (army, administration, Court, Church and charities, Constantinople) were not susceptible of great retrenchment, and that, taken in the aggregate, they necessarily amounted to a heavy total, and further, that vast wealth appeared, in the eyes of foreigners, to be the principal characteristic of the Empire. These outsiders considered Byzantium 'a kind of Eldorado' (Lujo Brentano). This wealth was also its principal weapon in the eyes of the Byzantines themselves; the ministers of Nicephorus Phocas said to Liutprand: 'We have gold and with this gold we shall rouse all peoples against you and break you like an earthen vessel' (*Legatio*, 58). It must also be remembered that all the information supplied by foreigners, as well as many data given by the Byzantine sources themselves, imply very great revenues and expenses. This is true also of the figures given by our sources of the wealth left by certain Emperors,[1] whose character and the circumstances of whose reigns (especially prolonged wars) did not permit them to adopt a policy of economy.

No comparison with the budgets of the medieval kings of the West can help us, since these princes reigned over feudal States and therefore knew nothing of most of the items of expenditure which we have enumerated above, especially expenditure for a paid army and a large body of bureaucratic officials. The only budget which could serve us for the purpose of comparison is that of the Caliphs of Bagdad; and the documents published by A. von Kremer tell us that under Harun-al-Rashid the budget amounted to a figure approximating to that given by Paparrigopoulos.[2]

Finally, it is to be noted that for the Byzantine Empire property belonging to the State had a much greater financial importance than it has to-day, while by taxation the Treasury absorbed a proportion of the national revenue which before 1914 would have seemed greatly exaggerated.

[1] Anastasius left 355,600,000 gold francs, Theophilus and Theodora 140 millions, Basil II 250 millions.

[2] Or 530 million dirhans, not counting taxation in kind. It is true that the territories of Harun-al-Rashid were more extensive than those of the Emperors, and his system of taxation more onerous; nevertheless, the official figures of the Caliph's revenue that we possess are an indication which we should not overlook.

IV. REVENUE

Public revenue was derived from the property of the State, the taxes properly so called, and the extraordinary contributions.

Property belonging to the State was of three kinds—industrial, agricultural, and urban.

Industrial property included both the manufacture of articles needed for the army and of articles of luxury, especially of fabrics. The products of the imperial factories were rarely sold; nevertheless they constituted an indirect revenue. Without them the State would have been obliged to purchase a multitude of articles indispensable to the army, the navy, the Court, and the administration. These factories furnished arms of all kinds (including 'Greek Fire') and the precious vestments which the Emperor required for his person and his Court, for gifts to foreign potentates and embassies, and also for the annual distributions, which, as we have seen, were one of the three forms of emolument received by public functionaries.

The Byzantine Emperors had inherited from their predecessors vast agricultural lands. These were reduced by the distribution of 'military lands', and by donations to churches, charitable institutions, relatives or favourites of the Emperor, and even to colonists of all kinds settled in the Empire. On the other hand, these agricultural domains were increased from time to time by conquest and especially by confiscation. Confiscations were plentiful in troubled times because the leaders of insurrections were often nobles, with great landed estates. This explains why, in spite of the many donations, the agricultural domains continued to be very extensive, while their products served to cover no inconsiderable part of the public expenditure. Thus, the public lands in the suburbs of Constantinople supplied with victuals the Court, comprising several thousands of officials and attendants.

The urban resources of the Byzantine State have often been overlooked by modern writers. To these resources a passage of Benjamin of Tudela should have called their attention. The Spanish traveller says that the daily revenue of 20,000 gold pieces, which Manuel Comnenus received from his capital, came from foreign traders (i.e. from customs duties), from the markets (i.e. from taxation of consumption), and from the caravanseries. To understand this passage, one must recollect that at Constantinople, as throughout the Empire,[1] merchandise was concentrated in vast buildings—bazaars or caravanseries. These belonged to the State and were not ceded gratis for the use of the merchants. If one considers also that all mines, quarries, and salt-pans, according to a tradition going back to Athens and to Rome, were the property of the State, one is convinced that the public property of the Empire of the East was much more varied and extensive and yielded much greater revenues than in modern States.

Since the time of Savigny much has been written on the Byzantine fiscal system. But these studies are confined almost exclusively to direct taxation; and indeed, it is chiefly of direct taxation that the Byzantine historical and legal sources treat.

Nevertheless, the only taxes mentioned by Benjamin of Tudela as levied at Constantinople are the customs duties and the tax on consumption. Nor do the Byzantine sources speak of a capitation tax or a house-tax in the capital or even, as far as the latter tax is concerned, in the provincial cities. On the other hand, the disastrous consequences which resulted for the public treasury from the customs privileges granted to Italian traders imply that the customs duties were of capital importance. Taken all in all, the direct taxes were not of the first importance except in places where there were neither ports nor markets—i.e., in the country districts. This need not surprise us. It is what one finds in the finances of Greek States from antiquity down to the present day. But why do the Byzantine sources speak chiefly of direct taxes? Probably because these taxes, always repugnant to the Greek temperament and rendered still more onerous to the rural population by reason of the scarcity of cash, were the most difficult to collect. Hence, the Emperors were forced from time to time to amend the legislation concerning

---

[1] This is proved by the Byzantine caravanseries of Salonica and Larissa, whose walls are preserved to this day.

these taxes[1] and also to exempt from their payment (temporarily or permanently) those to whom they wished to show
favour, especially the monasteries. On the other hand,
indirect taxation aroused much fewer protests and called for
much fewer fiscal reforms; whence it is seldom mentioned
by the chroniclers and legal sources.

The fiscal importance of indirect taxation in the Byzantine
Empire has, indeed, been insufficiently recognized.

Of the *direct taxes*, the most frequently mentioned are the
following:[2]

(*a*) The land-tax. This included, first, a tax on the land
itself, assessed according to the area, the value of the soil, and
the nature of its cultivation, and, secondly, a tax on the crops,
having its origin in the old Roman *annona* and varying
according to the number of ploughing animals employed.
Another peculiar feature of the land-tax was that each village formed a fiscal unit; if one landowner disappeared, the
Treasury was not the loser; it simply allotted the defaulter's
land to his nearest neighbour, who had to pay the tax
(*epibolē*).

(*b*) The tax on grazing-lands (*ennomion*) and animals other
than those used for ploughing (pigs, bees, &c.).

(*c*) The capitation tax. This assumed a family character;
it was laid upon each hearth, hence its name *kapnikon*. It
was levied only upon serfs.[3]

(*d*) All the foregoing taxes fell exclusively upon the rural
population. The direct taxes levied upon the urban population were the *chrysargyron*, the *aerikon*, and the tax on inheritances. But the first-named of these three, a sort of tax on
commercial profits, was abolished early in the fifth century
by the Emperor Anastasius and was replaced later by a
simple licence-tax. The *aerikon*, said to have been instituted
by Justinian, has called forth a whole literature,[4] but remains

---

[1] This may be observed also in modern Greece.

[2] Cf. Andréadès, *Byzantinische Zeitschrift*, vol. xxviii (1928), pp. 287-323.

[3] Another tax under the same name was levied occasionally upon freemen; but
it was a war contribution, an extraordinary tax. The sources mention a third tax,
which, as shown by its title (*kephalition*), was a real capitation tax. But, as Professor
Dölger has proved, this tax was levied only on non-Christians, chiefly Mussulmans
and Jews.

[4] Every self-respecting Byzantinologist thinks it his duty to give a new interpretation of this tax.

mysterious and the name seems to have been applied to several different taxes, while the tax itself would appear to have had a somewhat intermittent career. The same may be said of the tax on inheritances. As for the *chartiatikon*, it seems to have been a stamp-tax, i.e., an indirect tax. Hence, even if one admits that the *kensos*, the real estate tax properly so called, was levied on urban as well as agricultural land, the fact remains that the inhabitants of cities were at various times practically exempted from direct taxation. On the other hand, the *indirect taxes* fell heavily upon them in both forms—customs duties and excise.

Customs duties, as in ancient times, were levied both on exports and imports and the imported goods that had paid a customs duty were not thereby exempted from the payment either of the tax on retail sale or of port or transit dues (*skaliatikon*, *diabatikon*). Moreover, the customs duties were fixed at 10 per cent.,[1] whereas in ancient Athens they were only 2 per cent., and in Roman Italy $2\frac{1}{2}$ per cent. (*quadragesima*).

Since sea-trade was very highly developed, one can easily understand that under these conditions the customs revenues were of vital interest to the Empire. The *excise* (or tax on internal consumption of commodities) is set forth in detail in one document, Novel xxviii of Andronicus Palaeologus (1317), which has so far not been the subject of any special study. The fact that each tax bears the name of a commodity or group of commodities indicates that the amount of the tax was variable.[2] This Novel of Andronicus also mentions a tax on weights and measures, which was paid by the buyer, and lastly, the licence-tax paid by merchants for the exercise of their calling, which tax, too, varied according to each calling and was named after it.

Taken all in all, especially for the rural population, the Byzantine fiscal system would have been tolerable, if it had not been supplemented by a long series of extraordinary or supplementary obligations, on which a few words must here be said.

---

[1] At first, under Theodosius, the rate was $12\frac{1}{2}$ per cent.

[2] This method, in itself reasonable, is to be found in antiquity and in the Ionian Islands under the Venetian rule.

Anyone who peruses the charters of immunity from taxation granted to certain monasteries, notably that granted to the Nea Monê of Chios by Constantine Monomachus and to the Monastery of Patmos by Alexius Comnenus, sees how numerous and varied these supplementary burdens were. One may class them as contributions in kind for the benefit of the army, the officers, and the public functionaries, and as forced labour, *corvées*, properly so called, for public works, whether military (fortifications, &c.) or civil (roads, bridges, &c.).

Both classes are in conflict with Adam Smith's four rules of taxation. They were not equally distributed, because exemption was granted not only to a large number of privileged persons, but also to such cities and regions as for one reason or another were outside the circle of requisitions. They were not fixed, inasmuch as they varied according to circumstances. They were (by the force of circumstances) not collected at the time most convenient for the taxpayer. Lastly, their amount depended on the arbitrary decisions of the civil or military authorities; and this fostered numerous abuses to the detriment both of the taxpayers and of the Treasury.

The only excuse that one can plead for this pernicious legislation is that it was not an invention of the Byzantines. These contributions in kind and *corvées* were but a survival of the *munera extraordinaria et sordida*, of which the *Codex Theodosianus* gives us a list and enables us to appreciate the burden.

V. CONCLUSION

Byzantine finances could not be satisfactory. As in our day, expenditure was too great and in part unnecessary. The Government could not meet it except by a system of taxation which was more oppressive and certainly more arbitrary than anything we know of to-day.

One cannot, however, form an equitable judgement of the financial system of any State, except by comparing it with that of other States of the same period, or with that which the particular State had inherited. From these two points of view, the comparison is to the advantage of the Greek Empire of the East. In the first place one is struck by the fact that not only the monarchies which succeeded to the Empire of the West, but also the Bulgar and Russian Tsars, while failing to give their subjects a better administration, had the greatest difficulty in collecting revenues much inferior to those yielded without much effort by the smallest Byzantine 'province'. Their finances were in their infancy. The Caliphs of Bagdad did perhaps collect revenues which, at a given time, surpassed the revenues of the Byzantine Emperors, but they had a fiscal system even more crushing. Moreover, their financial prosperity was of brief duration.[1] Lastly, one must also bear in mind that, if the Greek Emperors retained in principle the fiscal system of the later Roman Empire, they improved upon it in many ways. They abolished certain taxes (notably the hated *chrysargyron*), reduced others, and took measures which ameliorated the collection of revenue and rendered the *epibolē* tolerable. They also strove, with more energy than their predecessors, to protect the small holders.

In a word, the Byzantine financial administration must be condemned; but there is good ground for a plea in extenuation of its faults.

ANDRÉ M. ANDRÉADÈS

[1] It reached its zenith under Harun-al-Rashid (768–809); during the ninth century revenue steadily fell off; in the tenth century it had fallen to insignificant sums. On the contrary, the yield of Byzantine revenue continued abundant for many centuries—a fact which demonstrates the efficiency of the imperial fiscal machine.

THE BYZANTINE CHURCH

THE Byzantine Empire being by definition the Roman
Empire in its Christian form, it goes without saying that in
Byzantium the Christian Church dominates at once both
political and social life, the life of letters and of art just as
much as the definitely religious life of the Empire. Its
special problems thus become affairs of State: its interests,
its grievances, its needs, its passions, its conflicts, whether
external or internal, fill the history of the Eastern Empire
both as that history was lived and still more as it was written.
Those disagreements which in their origin belong specifically
to the Byzantine Church have left deep marks upon the
civilization of the Christian peoples of the East and have
determined in many respects even down to our own day the
relations of these peoples amongst themselves and with the
West. To quote but two examples: the misunderstanding
which after the Yugoslav unification still divided Croats and
Serbs was in the last analysis the result of the breach between
the Byzantine Church and the Church of Rome which dates
from the year 1054; the antagonism between 'Orthodox'
Georgians and Monophysite Armenians which in the gravest
crisis of their history prevented them from co-ordinating
their efforts to secure their independence—that antagonism
was ultimately but a distant consequence of a Byzantine
theological dispute of the fifth century. To-day the Byzantine Church and the autocephalous communities which are
attached to it—or rather which have detached themselves
from it in the course of the centuries—appear to be the most
rigid, the most set of the Christian Churches; and it is true
that their rites and their dogmas have had for centuries past
a character of hieratic fixity. But the Byzantine Church has
been a living force, a moral force of the first order. And to do
it justice one cannot rest content to describe it merely in its
present attitude or in one only of the attitudes which it has
successively assumed. Nothing can be more superficial than
the reproach of 'Caesaropapism' with which it has at times

been branded; nothing more inexact so far as the Byzantine
Church is concerned than the charge of 'ceremonialism', of
formalism 'stifling the life of mysticism', for this mystic life
never ceased to inspire the ascetes and during the last century
of Byzantium even took possession of the masses.

It is essential to trace not only the internal evolution of
the Byzantine Church but also its external relations. For
most of its characteristic features result from the accidents of
these two aspects of its double history. These features we
shall do our best to emphasize, but first it is necessary to
bring before the reader the disorders and the tumults, the
conquests and the losses of which these characteristics
remain the witness, just as the motionless lines of a tor-
mented landscape are to be explained only by the convulsions
of which it has been the theatre in long past geological ages.
The plan of our chapter is determined by this consideration
which calls for a division into three parts: we shall first study
the Church as seen from within—the Church militant, the
Church finding itself, often divided against itself and often
opposing the State, seeking to assert or to define its dogma;
then we shall consider it from without, in its expansion
beyond the limits of the Empire, conquering and civilizing,
but also imperialist and even intransigent, provoking hatreds
and national reactions; finally we shall conclude by an attempt
—doubtless a rash attempt—at synthesis, an effort, perhaps
a vain effort, to attain to some understanding, through its
manifestations in history, of the essence of the Church of the
East, its spirit. . . .

THE TRIUMPH OF CHRISTIANITY IN THE EMPIRE.

THE ACCEPTANCE OF THE NEW FAITH BY THE STATE, AND
OF HELLENISM BY THE CHURCH.

THE TRIUMPH OF THE CATHOLIC CHURCH OVER THE
ARIAN HERESY: COMPROMISE BETWEEN PHILOSOPHY
AND THE FAITH.

The first great fact of the internal history of the Byzantine
Church is its 'march on Rome', its conquest of power, and
the foundation by Constantine of the New Rome on the
Bosphorus (inaugurated in 330) which is its striking symbol.
That triumph in which all the faithful saw and still see a

miraculous confirmation of the divine institution of the Church belongs, it is true, to all Christian Churches, but in especial it illumines the Church of which the city of Constantine was soon to be the capital and which identifies itself with the Empire reorganized by Constantine; and, through the centuries, that triumph ever gives anew to the Byzantine Church the highest idea of its own powers, the proudest confidence in its future. The Church is certain that it is at once eternal and unique, and this certitude welded it, as it were, to the Roman State which has the same conviction. Between Rome and Christ there had, indeed, never been any antagonism on grounds of principle: Jesus had from the first assigned to Caesar as of right his own sphere. Anatolia, which was the heart and the body of the Byzantine Empire, was predestined for Christian conquest, and the Apostle of the Gentiles knew well what he was doing when he carried the good news of redemption into a country which but a few years before had welcomed with enthusiasm the 'good news' of the appearance of Augustus, 'the Saviour God'. The whole history of Christian missions and of the spread of Christianity is, as it were, prefigured in the mission of Paul, the foe of the Greek idols, but the herald of the Unknown God—of whom thousands of the subjects of the first Caesars dreamed—and himself a loyal citizen of Rome. The peasants and the mountaineers of Asia Minor had only very superficially been won over to Hellenic polytheism and the higher culture of Greece. They knew ecstasy and religious fervour, personal devotion, the confession of sins, and the hope of the life beyond the tomb. The vulgar Greek spoken by Paul did indeed appear to them to be the language of the Holy Spirit. Amongst people such as these Christianity progressed almost without hindrance. The classical period of the orientalization of the Empire, that of the Severi at the beginning of the third century, saw upon the throne princes who were themselves half-Christian. The great persecutions, those of Decius and Valerian in the middle of the third century and that of Galerius and his colleagues at the beginning of the fourth, were but violent and desperate reactions against the peaceful conquest of the Empire by the new faith. These reactions sprang from the army of the Danube

recruited amongst Balkan barbarians who had remained
pagan—troops who were sacrificed in vast numbers for the
defence of the Empire. They were at once passionate and
interested defenders of the old religion, for the class-interest
of the officers appealed to all the anti-Christian prejudices.
The persecutions resemble the modern movements of anti-
semitism. The last persecution caused widespread disgust,
and the principal persecutor, Galerius, recognized his
failure by promulgating on his death-bed the great Edict of
Tolerance of the fourth century, the Edict of Sardica (Sofia,
A.D. 311). Five Emperors, at least, between the years 306
and 311 declared themselves more or less openly in favour of
Christianity. Their attitude proves that the Empire in order
to surmount a terrible economic and social crisis felt it
necessary to resort to a religious mysticism which might
buttress and sustain those political institutions which had
themselves been refashioned upon Eastern models.

That is not all: even such an enemy of Christianity as was
Maximin Daia (died 313)—who ended his reign like the
others with an edict of tolerance—as well as, half a century
later, the last imperial adversary of the new faith, Julian the
Apostate, sought in more than one point of their organization
of pagan worship to imitate that of the Christian Church. If
they had conquered the Galilaean, these Caesars would have
borrowed from His Church its hierarchy of metropolitans
and many another Christian institution.

Shaken to its foundations, within an ace time and again of
perishing in an unexampled cataclysm, the Empire realized
that in order to survive it needed not only a dynastic, military,
monetary, and administrative basis, it needed also a soul, a
core of religion. And, indeed, it had no longer any choice.
Christianity had on its side the mass of the people, at least in
the heart of the Empire. Here the Orient made its decisive
preponderance felt—a preponderance which was at once
demographic, economic, and cultural. And Christianity
brought to the Empire an organization already made, and
the Empire in identifying itself with Christianity had seen
in it a unifying factor. Christianity, however, had conquered
the world not in the form of a great river with a single stream,
but in the form of numerous torrents. These divisions had

not been suppressed by the victory of the Church. On the contrary, that victory only brought into full light the dogmatic differences between which the Emperors were forced to make their choice, while they found themselves faced by disciplinary disputes to which the persecution itself had given rise. Many ancient 'heresies' although they had struck deep roots—especially in Anatolia and Syria—such as Montanism in Phrygia or the dualist sects issuing from the Gnosis of Marcion and Manes—were henceforth no longer a serious danger for the 'Catholic' Church. But Constantine, so soon as he became master of Africa, found there a Christianity which was profoundly divided by Donatism; a movement which formed a rallying-point for the masses of the people who protested against the lukewarmness or the cowardice in the hour of persecution of those propertied classes who now, after the Christian victory, claimed their share of honours, though they had not shared the sufferings of the persecuted. And Constantine, such was the obstinacy of the schismatics, was forced to tolerate Donatism. Ten years later as conqueror of Licinius and master of the whole Empire he suffered his second disillusionment when he was faced with the Arian Controversy which was a far graver issue than Donatism, for Donatism divided only Africa, but Arianism divided the Roman world.

Arianism is the price paid for the early and fruitful alliance of Christianity with Greek philosophy. From the moment that Christ is identified with the Logos, His relations with the Father must be defined in terms of the Alexandrian conception of the Word. The 'savants', the philosopher-theologians—Antioch was then the great school of Christian philosophy—could not bring themselves to attribute to the Father and the Son the same essence, the same degree of divinity; to do so would have led, in their view, to a heresy which had already been condemned, to Sabellianism. A priest of Alexandria, Arius, had preached—not without indiscretions and extravagance of speech—had popularized and vulgarized the faith of Antioch. Bold and precise formulas such as 'There was a time when He was not' roused the passions of the crowd for and against this 'subordinationism'. His bishop Alexander excommunicated him, but the dispute began afresh. For the first time doubtless in the history of the world the inhabited universe—the *oikoumenē*—was divided into two camps on a point of religious metaphysics. An academic controversy was carried into the streets, a Church dissension became a political, a national, one might almost say a racial, issue, for it is generally true that while the hellenized East is Arian, the Latin West is solid in its opposition to Arianism. The bishops of Alexandria, at least Alexander and after him the great Athanasius, from the first took their stand against the position of the priest who had appealed to the mob, who spread his teaching through popular songs[1] chanted by sailors or artisans; in this great battle which lasted for more than half a century they were the allies of the West. Arian 'subordinationism', it should be observed, is the faith of those Eastern countries which had long since been Christian, solidly Christian; the formula of the 'Consubstantial'—the *Homoousion*—which the East will find such difficulty in accepting—will be imposed upon it—paradoxically enough—by the West which under Constantine and Constantius is still largely pagan, which can hardly boast of any theologians, since philosophy whether pagan or Christian was the concern of the Greeks. Faced by these subtleties, Constantine shows himself at once indifferent and ill-humoured. In a letter of undoubted authenticity he begins by describing the study of the relations between the Father and the divine Son as 'an idle inquiry'. But he soon saw that union between the hostile brothers in the faith would not come of itself, that he must throw his personal authority into the scale. He was compelled to turn theologian, and henceforth, until the fall of Byzantium, the Emperors of East Rome will never escape from this task which with many of them will become a passion, a mania: thus in the twelfth century Manuel Comnenus will raise a theological tempest over the text 'My Father is greater than I' (John xiv. 28). Constantius, son and successor of Constantine, will spend his life in the vain search, as his father would have called it, for a formula which might reconcile the differences of his Christian subjects. At Nicaea in 325 Constantine had wished, doubtless prematurely,

[1] *complaintes.*

to play the part of bishop; he had cut the Gordian knot by imposing the *Homoousion*—a formula suggested by the simple faith of a Spanish bishop which was repugnant to the philosophical conscience of the Orientals. A little later he came to realize the strength of that hostility. Emperor of Nicomedia and of Constantinople, in the end he took the part of the bishops of Asia against Athanasius. Constantius II, living in the East, passes through various shades of Arianism, while his brother Constans, Emperor of the West, defends the faith of Nicaea. This duality in the government of the Empire produces a kind of equilibrium: the bishops, both in East and West, maintain their positions; the Council of Sardica (343), assembled symbolically at the frontier where two Empires met, could not reconcile the differing points of view, though out of respect for each other the two brothers were not intolerant. In 350 Constans was assassinated; during the years 351 to 353 Constantius reconquered the West from the usurper Magnentius. More and more Constantius sets his heart upon forcing the Consubstantialists to accept the creed of the Eastern bishops, or formulas of compromise invented by ingenious Oriental theologians, or even Anhomoean formulas of the left wing of Arianism, until the day when at the two Councils of Ariminum and Seleucia a neutral confession which proscribed even the name of substance is imposed upon East and West alike.

The reign of Constantius is in many respects an anticipation of the whole course of the religious history of Byzantium. A theological difference ranges one half of the Empire against the other. The Emperor to settle the dispute summons council after council: the highways of the Empire are crossed and recrossed by 'galloping bishops': one sees now Court prelates or ecclesiastical assemblies won over or intimidated by the Government, now heroic athletes of the faith braving the Emperors themselves and gaining from these religious duels an immense popularity: one sees the Emperor seeking by any and every means to secure the support of the Bishop of Rome. And all this will recur— again and again. But in the fourth century the struggle between Christians is not without its danger: Constantius and Constans had thought that by their draconian edicts of the forties against superstition and sacrifices they could deal the death-blow to paganism, but paganism was not prepared to throw down its arms. Julian galvanizes it into new vigour: he turns to his own purposes the indignation aroused by the breakers of idols, by unlettered monks, by pamphleteers who in their hatred hurled their insults against the gods of Homer. But he did a disservice to the cause of humanism in claiming to exclude from the literary and artistic heritage of Hellas—and even from culture itself—those Christians of goodwill who had been trained at the great seats of learning of the Empire and who did not reject civilization along with paganism. From this time the moderates sought for a compromise which might preserve that which was of essential value, while amongst the Christians, weary of dogmatic disputes of which the reaction under Julian had proved the danger, there was an effort to reconcile the Christian faith of the West, attached by a primary anxiety for unity to the formula of the *Homoousion*, with the more subtle doctrine of the Orientals.

The peacemakers, the saviours of civilization, of the faith, and of the Empire, were the Cappadocians, Gregory of Nazianzus and Basil of Caesarea, men who had been brought up on the classics, themselves just as much rhetoricians and 'sophists' as they were theologians. Their work has a twofold aspect. On the one hand, they establish a new orthodoxy; while accepting the *Homoousion* they interpret that formula afresh, restoring the Logos theology. They admit in the Godhead, like the strict Nicenes, only one substance—a single *ousia*, but they distinguish three *hypostases*—three persons. They thus prepare the way for the return to Nicene orthodoxy of the moderate Arians, who had been startled by the excesses of Constantius and above all of Valens. On the other hand, by the literary charm of their writings which observed the canons of the schools and could be admired by a cultivated public they reconciled Christianity and Hellenism. By refounding, or rather by founding, religious unity on the basis of formulas which were not merely diplomatic, the great Cappadocians and their Latin disciples and allies, like St. Ambrose, once more assured, at the critical moment when the two Empires were finally taking their separate ways, through the unity of Christian thought the unity of the Christian world.

After the Council of 381 held under Theodosius the Great,[1] Arianism, repudiated by Greco-Roman society, was henceforth only a Christianity for German barbarians. Even after the fall of the Empire of the West in 476 the Latins reacted against this 'barbarous religion' with no less energy than did the Byzantines.

Finally Christianity, hellenized and philosophic, as it was presented by Gregory of Nazianzus and Basil of Caesarea, was well fitted to become 'a gentleman's religion', and the Empire could thus, without scandalizing men of intellect, persecute those who were still obstinately attached to pagan sacrifices and 'superstition', who refused to unite, as the State invited them to do, the cult of letters and the cult of the true God.

THE MONOPHYSITE AND MONOTHELITE CONTROVERSIES AND THEIR CONSEQUENCES

ALIENATION OF THE ARMENIAN, SYRIAN, AND COPTIC EAST

As fifty years of relative peace—the Pentekontaetia—separate the Persian Wars from the Peloponnesian War, so a dogmatic peace of like duration extends from the close of the Arian controversy to the beginnings of the dispute over the Two Natures. The dates, indeed, present striking analogies: 480 and 431 before Jesus Christ, 381 and 431 after Jesus Christ—the Councils of Constantinople and of Ephesus. Like the ancient quarrel, the Monophysite controversy will become an affair of State and will profoundly disturb the masses of the people. The Great Councils, the Parliaments of Christendom, will take an increasingly important place in the preoccupations of the world. The last refuge of free speech, they are, in a measure, the successors of the tumultuous assemblies of the Greek city-states. They proved, in general, to be less docile than were the synods presided over by the commissioners of Constantius. Moreover, the subject-matter of the dispute is perhaps of greater

[1] So called to distinguish him from his grandson Theodosius II.

import than the *Homoousion* or *Homoiousion*. And in any event the consequences of the century-long controversy will be very different from those of the Arian debate: the latter, as we have seen, finished by reinforcing the unity and the solidarity of the Romans, both Greek- and Latin-speaking, in face of the German invaders, while in the last analysis it is the Monophysite controversy which will detach from the Orthodox Church the majority of the Syrians, the whole body of the Copts and in their train the Ethiopians, and the Armenians, while this religious disaffection will facilitate the conquests of Islam and the dismemberment of the Empire. Further, the Monophysite dispute is more 'Byzantine' than the Arian controversy, inasmuch as it concerns especially the Eastern world. The West has other interests. A few dates set side by side will bring into relief this contrast between Latin Romania, victim of the great conflicts of peoples, and the Byzantine East distracted by the conflicts of bishops and of monks. The leading Latin doctor, St. Augustine, was summoned to the Council of Ephesus, but that summons reached him too late: he had died in Hippo while the Vandals were besieging the city.

The battle of the Catalaunian Fields, where all the West, Romans and Germans, stayed the advance of the Huns, was fought at about the same time as the great theological battle of Chalcedon. Still the West does not disavow all interest in the controversy; indeed, as in 325, it is the West which imposes a formula of too little subtlety—that of the two Natures without separation or confusion—which will remain the rock of orthodoxy but also a terrible rock of offence.

Nestorius himself spoke of his 'Tragedy': we may bear the word in mind and consider the whole history of the Monophysite controversy with its sequel the Monothelite dispute as a single drama in five acts of unequal length. The first act has for its central scene the Council of Ephesus (431). Nestorius, Patriarch of Constantinople, disciple of the school of Antioch, is a true representative of its theology, more speculative than mystical. He sets before himself the task of pursuing and overthrowing the followers of another heresy, Apollinarianism, which carried to excess its opposition to Arianism by minimizing the human nature in the Incarnate Word. Nestorius insisted on the Man-Christ, for on the humanity of Christ depended, it would seem, the reality of His redemptive death. He taught that the Virgin was not Mother of God, but of Christ—not *theotokos*, but *Christotokos*. Now their faith always led the most ardent of the faithful to 'go one better'. It was impossible, they thought, to give too much honour to the Mother of the Consubstantial Word, who had recently, it appears, become the object of a cult, full of tender emotion, which met a need of the Egyptians who, in spite of all, had not forgotten Isis and her worship. Just as Arius had seemed to humiliate the Word by saying 'There was a time when He was not', so Nestorius seemed to insult the divinity of the Redeemer, the more so as he permitted himself some irreverent and ill-timed sallies on 'The God at the breast'. When Nestorius affirmed that the divinity had come to dwell in the humanity of the Christ 'as in a temple', the devout indignantly protested that he was dividing, cutting into two, 'tearing asunder' the Christ. These protests came especially from Egypt: Egypt had every reason to keep a sharp lookout for errors of dogma or of language coming from a Patriarch of Constantinople. The bishops of Alexandria, absolute heads of the whole Egyptian episcopate, supported by a formidable army of monks and hospital attendants—the notorious *parabolani*[1]—were jealous of Constantinople, the proud upstart, once the humble suffragan-bishopric of Heraclea-Perinthus, but raised by the third canon of the Council of 381 above the glorious sees of Alexandria and Antioch. Every opportunity to humiliate his colleague was welcomed by the prelate whom men styled the 'Pharaoh' of Egypt. Although no theological question had been at stake, Theophilus of Alexandria had not failed to turn to account the feud between the Empress Eudocia and St. John Chrysostom: he had overthrown that generous Patriarch, the friend of the people and the bitter critic of the Court. Cyril, the nephew of Theophilus, in his turn was not slow to denounce the heresy of Nestorius. Behind him was the whole of Egypt, both Greeks and Copts.

[1] Really *parabalaneis*, or bath-attendants.

There had long been close connexion between Egypt and Rome: the Church of Alexandria had been founded, tradition said, by Mark, the disciple of Peter. It was at Rome that Athanasius had sought a refuge from persecution. It was thus natural that Pope Celestine should trust the orthodoxy and the energy of Cyril. The Council of Ephesus, summoned by Nestorius and by his protector the Emperor Theodosius II to judge Cyril, witnessed the triumph of the Egyptian and the decisive and final defeat of the 'Byzantine'. The assembly met 'in the church called Mary'—it was a symbol and a prophecy. And yet the result of the Council could not be easily foreseen. Cyril, in the eyes of many moderates, had gone too far in his attack upon Nestorius and his 'dyophysitism'. In his 'anathemas' he had made use of expressions which bordered on the left-wing heresy of the Single Nature in the Incarnate Christ—Monophysitism. But he manœuvred with supreme skill. Even at the Council of Ephesus itself he carried through—with the complicity of the Roman legates—a *coup d'église* by opening the proceedings before the arrival of the Eastern bishops who were favourable to his adversary whose condemnation he forced through without a moment's delay. Later every expedient was employed to influence the Court at Constantinople, particularly *baksheesh*. Cyril's 'benedictions' took the form of ivory tables, costly carpets, even ostriches, and thus gained for his theology the support of high officials and their wives. And at last when everyone including the Emperor had sacrificed the embarrassing and compromising Nestorius, Cyril made the necessary concessions to the theology of Antioch, spoke as did the Antiochene theologians of the Divinity which dwelt in the Christ as in a 'temple', and admitted that there had been 'a union of two natures'. The more fanatical of his partisans doubtless regretted the moderation of their great leader, but Mgr. Duchesne concludes that 'the Pharaoh had become a Saint'.

We have told the story of this first act at some length, because it both sets forth, as is fitting, the theme of the tragedy and is the prologue in which the characters are introduced. These, it is true, will at times change their names, will play different parts, but the rivalry between Alexandria and Constantinople, the arbitration of Rome, the vacillation of the Emperor, these remain throughout unaltered. We pass then to the second act.

Egypt under its new Patriarch Dioscorus wishes to drive home its victory: it regrets the moderation of Cyril. It now confesses the Single Nature without equivocation. At the Second Council of Ephesus (449) history repeats itself, at least in part, since Flavian, Patriarch of Constantinople, accused of having condemned the Monophysite monk Eutyches, is in his turn anathematized and deposed. At Rome the Pope, St. Leo, protests against a hazardous Christology, and in his famous dogmatic letter proclaims the 'orthodox' doctrine of the future: 'The true God is born with the complete and perfect nature of a true man, perfect in His own nature (divinity) and perfect in our nature (humanity).' Henceforward the Monophysites will be accused by the Great Church, as was Nestorius, of denying the humanity of the body of Christ, and, as a consequence, the Passion. Logically the Monophysites should have maintained that the death of Christ on the Cross had been only an appearance—a phantasia—unless they were prepared to confess that the God-Man had suffered 'by a miracle'. But in fact the Monophysite theologians and even Eutyches himself almost always declined to admit the extreme views which were imputed to them by their enemies. However that may be, passions had been unloosed in favour of a doctrine which exalted the divinity at the expense of the humanity of the Incarnate Christ. Almost throughout the East the masses of the people were in its favour, rising together with the monks against the Nestorianizing episcopate, while the feeble and vacillating Theodosius II, once the protector of Nestorius, impressed doubtless by the elemental force of the movement, gave to it his official support. His minister, the eunuch Chrysaphius, was the patron of Eutyches who, it was reported, had said that the body of Christ had descended from heaven.

But a change of sovereign reversed the course of religious policy: Theodosius II died, while hunting, in 450: his sister Pulcheria ordered the execution of Chrysaphius and then married Marcian who shared with her the government of the Empire. The new rulers set before themselves the task of imposing upon their subjects the creed of Pope Leo.

The third act of the tragedy begins: its scene is the Council of Chalcedon (451). The opening sessions of the Council were directed by a civil commission of nineteen high officials. But, despite this rigorous control, it was only with great difficulty that the assembly was brought to accept the new definition of the faith desired by Marcian and Pulcheria: 'We confess one Jesus, Lord, only Son, whom we acknowledge *in two Natures*.' There were those who had sought the golden mean by proposing the formula '*of two Natures*'. It was in vain that in later clauses of the creed emphasis was laid upon the indivisibility of the two natures: by admitting that they persisted without confusion after the union the doctrine of St. Cyril was implicitly rejected. It is for this reason that the definition of Chalcedon had on men's minds so provocative an effect. Throughout a large part of the East it was believed that the Government and the official Church had gone over to Nestorianism. Few ecclesiastical assemblies have been so hated and so anathematized by millions of the faithful as was the Council of Chalcedon: even to-day it is still a rock of offence. No sooner had 'the accursed Council' finished its work than a double revolution broke out against it—at Jerusalem and in Egypt. The influence of the monks, drawn for the most part from Asia Minor, and the prestige of a few great solitaries reconquered Palestine for Chalcedonian orthodoxy, but Egypt remains and will remain uncompromising. In the valley of the Nile there is constituted a solid Monophysite opposition which nothing can break, while in Syria after bloody conflicts and many disturbances the deep-seated Monophysitism of the masses of the people will shake the columns of 'the school of Antioch'.

Then there begins the interminable fourth act (476–565), the century during which the Emperors seek to disarm the hatred of the East against Chalcedon. Prodigies of ingenuity and of theological diplomacy were devised, but in the result it was almost completely labour lost. The Emperor Zeno in 484, in agreement with the Patriarchs of Constantinople and of Alexandria, published the *Henotikon* or Edict of Union,

the first in date of these subtle attempts to sacrifice Chalcedon
to the Anti-Chalcedonians without rejecting *expressis verbis*
the orthodox, but scandalous, Council. The *Henotikon*
repeated the official creeds, except that of Chalcedon, and
added: 'If anyone has taught otherwise, whether at Chalcedon
or elsewhere, let him be anathema!' But a silence which
failed to satisfy the Egyptians appeared to the Romans a
heretical pusillanimity; it caused a complete breach between
Constantinople and the Pope (484–518). This first schism,
known as the schism of Acacius from the name of the then
Patriarch of Constantinople, is a sign of the times: Byzantium, since the whole West is now taken captive by the
barbarians, prefers communion with Alexandria to union
with Rome.

Anastasius, the successor of Zeno, is a pure Monophysite,
although at times he may disguise his extreme views, since
the capital and the Balkans remain orthodox. One day the
general Vitalian presented himself before the gates of
Byzantium at the head of an army of Huns: he came as the
soldier of the Pope. Everywhere the two confessions
identified themselves with the political and social parties
which took as their emblems the colours of the 'factions' of
the circus: the Greens represented, as a rule, the lower classes
which were Monophysite, the Blues the orthodox *bourgeoisie*.
The latter triumphed with the Emperor Justin, a Latin of
Balkan origin as was Vitalian. Justin re-established union
with Rome and persecuted the Monophysites; his nephew
Justinian was, like his uncle, in principle a Blue and orthodox,
but vacillated now to one side, now to the other, under the
pressure of circumstances and still more under the influence
of his wife Theodora, a convinced Monophysite, who
united prudence with an unwavering purpose.

After the reconquest of Italy from the heretic Goths it was
essential for Justinian to pose as the champion of the orthodox
faith and the ally of the Pope; he thus, in concert with Pope
Agapetus, put an end to the Monophysite reaction of the
Patriarch Anthimus. But Theodora would not surrender
the hope of converting to her faith the Pope himself and the
whole of the regained West, and Justinian devoted ten
years of his life to this work—to 'the seduction of the

Papacy' and 'the reconciliation of the Orientals'. His idea was to expurgate Chalcedon: to eliminate from the Acta of the Fourth Council that which was most offensive to the nonconformists. In 451 three enemies of Cyril—Theodore of Mopsuestia, Theodoret of Cyrus, and Ibas of Edessa— had been absolved or justified. If one pursued the dead even in their tombs, the fierce hatreds of the Monophysites might be appeased: so thought the pious sovereigns and their advisers. And all the West, if the Pope of Rome consented thereto, would bow before this posthumous condemnation pronounced in the cause of peace.

Such was the affair of the 'Three Chapters' which is odious on more than one ground; it was a strange charity towards separated brethren which appealed to their hatred rather than their love: the Emperor's intervention in a purely theological dispute was direct, brutal, and repeated; the luckless Pope Vigilius was subjected to violence and mal-treatment: he was dragged from Rome to Constantinople: here he yielded, then resisted, retracted, again insisted, and at last at the Fifth Oecumenical Council (Constantinople 553) he ratified the condemnation of the 'Three Chapters', i.e. of the writings of the 'scandalous doctors'. Henceforth the Council of Chalcedon was emended, but nothing was gained thereby, for still the oriental dissenters refused their subscription. Moreover, in the course of the controversy over the Three Chapters the Monophysite Churches had reconstituted their hierarchy which had for a time been disorganized by 'the Catholic terror'. The enthusiastic missionary Jacobus Baradaeus has given his name to the Syrian 'Jacobites'. Coptic Egypt, in spite of the orthodox Patriarchs who had hardly any adherents save in Greek Alexandria, hesitated only between the different shades of Monophysitism. In 548 Theodora had died, doubtless full of hopes for the success of the great scheme of the Three Chapters and for the future of her co-religionists whom she sheltered and at need hid by hundreds in her palace. It was doubtless the memory of his wife which led the Emperor, exasperated by the failure of his efforts at conciliation, to join the extremists amongst the Monophysites and to profess Aphthartodocetism—to maintain the incorruptibility of the body of Christ. This imperial heresy was but the hallucination of a dying man; his successors returned to 'the catholic terror'. Yet in Egypt, as though to demonstrate the impossibility of repression in a country permanently disaffected, saints such as Eulogius and John the Almsgiver, who succeeded each other on the patriarchal throne of Alexandria, proved themselves veritable heroes of Christian charity. The fruits of their activity were disappointing: there were few whole-hearted conversions to orthodoxy.

Then there follows the fifth act of the great dispute: it, too, lasted for a century. Like Zeno and Justinian, Heraclius dreams of reconciling the dissidents. Never since Chalcedon had the prospects been more favourable for the re-establishment of religious peace. It must surely need a truly diabolical obstinacy in the Christians of the East to refuse to accept this peace from the hands of a holy Emperor, now crowned with victory, who after his overthrow of pagan Persia had restored in triumph the True Cross to Jerusalem (630). Heraclius was always henceforth in the eyes of Christians of the East and the West alike the Christian hero above all others, and his theological adviser, the Patriarch of Constantinople, Sergius, shared the Emperor's aureole, since it was he who with the favour of the Mother of God had defended the capital against Avars, Slavs, and Persians. Consequently more readily, more frankly than Vigilius, the Pope Honorius allowed himself to be won over to the pacific policy of the Emperor and the Patriarch of the East. It was a marvellous success! It was a triumph for Heraclius and he felt himself more truly victorious than on the day when he announced to the peoples of the Empire the destruction of Chosroes in 'the eternal fire'.

The peace for the souls of his subjects which Rome had sanctioned the Emperor owed to his faithful Armenian compatriots: for Heraclius was a son of this heroic nation. Two-thirds of Armenia had been reconquered from Persia by Maurice, it had been lost again in part under Phocas, it had been regained and delivered from the Iranian yoke by himself or rather by the prowess of its own warriors fighting in the service of Byzantium. Now Armenia, which for fifty years had been indifferent to the controversy on the Two

Natures, had, at the beginning of the sixth century, become Monophysite, or rather anti-Nestorian. This was not surprising, since Nestorianism was in Persia, as it were, a second national religion, the only recognized form of Christianity. Heraclius knew well his good 'Haikh'. After the hardships which they had shared with him, after the final victory, they asked for nothing better than to welcome as brothers both the Greek and the Latin Christians. But they desired to be reassured concerning Chalcedon which had divided the person of the Saviour. This Heraclius and Sergius undertook to do; without raising afresh the thorny problem of the Two Natures, they affirmed that in Christ there was at least only one energy. On this assurance the union with the Armenian Church was effected. Honorius went still further: he spoke of a single will and this latter formula was adopted in the imperial edict—the *Ekthesis*— of 638. But when that edict appeared, it was already too late. The fair dream had faded. The diplomacy of so many eminent and far-seeing men was rendered vain by the magnificent and disastrous obstinacy of one man, Sophronius (since 634 Patriarch of Jerusalem), who declared that belief in *two* energies and *two* wills was essential for orthodoxy. The Patriarch Cyrus, sent to Alexandria to win the Copts for the new *Henotikon*, soon found himself isolated between the Orthodox and the uncompromising Monophysites. The successors of Honorius, who died in 638, rejected with horror his 'Monothelitism'. And those for whom the subtle compromise had been framed, the Christians of Syria, Egypt, and Armenia, were either already conquered by the Arabs or would be subjected, one after the other, in the years which were to follow. Monothelitism which was designed to save the whole position in the East had ruined everything. But Armenia was not occupied until 652, and at first the Heraclian dynasty did not give up all hope. Still in 648 Constans II, the successor of Heraclius, endeavoured to render acceptable the essential point in the compromise by forbidding all discussion either of 'energies' or 'wills'. Pope Martin saw in this 'retreat' a heresy worse than all the others and, like Sophronius, demanded, with the inflexible logic of an intransigent Chalcedonian, the explicit recognition of two energies and two wills. All the efforts of a policy which aimed at peace and conciliation only served to make the 'dualism' more pronounced. The wish had been to translate, explain, expurgate, tone down the definition of Chalcedon of which the 'Two Natures' formed the stumbling-block. And in the result orthodoxy, more exigent than ever and more provocative, imposed on men's consciences three 'dyads' in place of one. At the same time the West revolted against the lawful Emperor. It is not difficult to understand the anger of Constans, the arrest, trial, and banishment of Martin and other martyrs of orthodoxy. But Monothelitism was defeated, because after the Arab conquest of Armenia it appeared to be at once useless and dangerous. Constantine IV surrendered: he accepted the Roman formulas, and at the Sixth Oecumenical Council (Constantinople 7 Nov. 680–16 Sept. 681) an 'aggravated Chalcedon'. This was a repetition, in the sphere of theology, of the adieu of Heraclius: 'Farewell Syria, farewell for ever!'; but that farewell was now extended to the Churches of all those territories which after centuries of religious disaffection were finally lost to the Empire.[1]

Conclusion

Chalcedon triumphed, but over ruins: it triumphed despite the power and the genius of Zeno, of Anastasius, of Justinian, of Theodora, and of Heraclius who for more than two centuries had sought with admirable devotion and perfect clear-sightedness to disarm hatreds, to conciliate the rival mysticisms. They had matched themselves against forces which were too strong for them. It has been urged that the losses sustained by the Empire in the seventh century did in one sense but strengthen the consciousness of Byzantine unity. It is certain that they made of it essentially a Greek State, its Latin possessions in the West being more and more eroded by invasion. And the faith of East Rome is crystallized. Men forgot the history of the 'sublime' controversies of the past: they remembered only the creeds of

[1] This fifth act of the Christological drama had a brief epilogue in 712 under an Armenian usurper, Philippicus Vardanes, the Julian the Apostate of Monothelitism.

the six canonical councils—regarding them as identical, or, like the Gospels, as complementary—recalled only the anathemas against the unhappy heroes of these theological disputes, Nestorius and Eutyches, Honorius and Sergius and, included in the medley, Theodoret of Cyrus and Ibas of Edessa. And since these condemned heresies exhaust almost all the possibilities of theological speculation, theology itself, living theology, henceforth ceases to play its preponderant part in the story of Byzantium.

THE ICONOCLAST CONTROVERSY

For it is in vain that some modern scholars have sought to extend into the eighth and ninth centuries the history of the beginnings of Christology. The controversies of the ancient schools count for nothing in Iconoclasm and in the defence of the icons, even though their champions employ *a posteriori* Christological arguments and hurl against each other charges of Nestorianism and Eutychianism. The disturbances which we must now recount are concerned with anything but philosophical speculation. Leo the Isaurian and his son Constantine V had saved Anatolia and Constantinople, threatened after the reign of Justinian II and his ephemeral successors by a great offensive from Islam. They needed for this defence, this laborious reconquest, the country-folk of Phrygia and of Pisidia fighting on their own soil which had now become a military frontier. It was necessary to reward these good soldiers, to make concessions in their favour. The puritan bishops of Phrygia were emboldened by the murmurings of their flocks who constantly affirmed that the defeats of the Christians were to be explained by the corruption of the Christian Church; they instinctively reverted to the language once used by St. Epiphanius condemning the abuse of images as idolatry. Iconoclasm arises from an examination of conscience made by Christians who doubtless for centuries past had kept alive their scruples on this point. Despite the agreement, sealed about 400, between Christianity and the arts—of which Epiphanius did not approve—protests were heard from time to time which recalled the prohibition of the Pentateuch. It needed only a convinced preacher to convert this latent protest into formal opposition. The bishops of Nakoleia and of other places who were the advisers of Leo III must at the bar of history bear the responsibility for a step which was at once natural and legitimate. The Emperor only followed with timidity a movement which he had not initiated: he satisfied these conscientious objectors, but that satisfaction was but partial, and belated. It needed another quarter of a century from the beginning of the movement before iconoclast theory was given dogmatic statement. This ratification legalized, one may say, an idea which since 729 had become very popular and very powerful, for it was recommended to the masses of the people by the striking military successes of the dynasty. The army stood almost solid behind Constantine V, who in his own lifetime became a legendary hero, and against the monks, the fanatical defenders of the images. On the other hand, by their overt resistance to the *Basileus*, certain ascetics for their part won a popularity which was perhaps somewhat questionable. They were in revolt, it must be remembered, not only against the decrees of the Emperor, but also against the canons of a council (753), and the cruelties of Constantine V were but a reply to a vast conspiracy hatched by these revolutionary monks.

Byzantium was never, at any period, totalitarian. Conquered parties, crushed under one reign or under one dynasty, revive and triumph under another reign, another dynasty. It is thus that, despite the martial glory of the great Isaurians, the religious revolution of 787 is to be explained. The military reigns, because of the burdens which they imposed upon the people and upon the monasteries, traditionally the foes of the imperial Treasury, always tended to provoke serious opposition. To secure power the ambitious Irene, widow of Leo IV, son of Constantine V, galvanized into action the anti-Constantinian, anti-militarist, iconophil party. In despite of the 'Old Guards' of Constantine V, in 787 she carried through the religious restoration (Second Council of Nicaea) and 'set up' once more the images which had for so long been proscribed. The Council took care not to blacken the memory of the great Isaurians; on the contrary it proclaimed the striking merits of these triumphant

Emperors. Irene feared their shades. The better to secure her position she sought to create in her favour a movement of greater strength than was at this time the reaction in favour of the images: she allowed the monks and the people to protest against the divorce of her son Constantine VI and his 'adulterous marriage' with the lady of the bedchamber Theodote. She was thus able to depose and blind an Emperor, who was her own son, without the loss of her prestige or her renown for saintliness. The 'Moechian Affair'—the 'Affair of the Adultery'—thus took precedence in the passions of the people over the 'Affair of the Images'. And Theodore of the monastery of Studius, an agitator beyond compare, will be able to arouse a greater enthusiasm than the champions of orthodoxy for having extorted from an Emperor respect for the moral law which bound all alike and from a Patriarch the strict application of canonical rules! Theodore henceforth will defend all good and holy causes: when Leo V began once more (815) to play the part of a Leo the Isaurian, Theodore had the honour of fighting for the sacred icons themselves. For Irene had fallen through the unpopularity of her eunuch camarilla; under her successors Nicephorus I, Stauracius, and Michael Rangabe, the Bulgarian victories of 811 and 813 had precisely the same effect as the great Arab invasion a hundred years before: cries were raised against the corruption of the faith. On the approach of the Bulgars, the people of Constantinople betook themselves to the tomb of Constantine V, the Iconoclast and victorious Emperor. The Council of 815 promulgated a kind of moderate Iconoclasm: it no longer ordered the destruction of the images: they were to be hung out of reach of the faithful. The Council made a distinction between 'images' and idols. To this doctrine Michael II and his son Theophilus, the princes of the Phrygian dynasty of Amorium, were content to adhere, until once more the opposition became a majority. And again a woman, a widow, an Empress, and a saint, Theodora, sees herself by the logic of events led to seek support in a party which she reorganizes. But the lessons of the past have told. In 843 orthodoxy was finally re-established, but the Festival of Orthodoxy is now in truth the festival of reconciliation: even the memory of the last heretical Emperor is saved as is that of those peace-loving Patriarchs who in spite of the Studites have given proofs of forbearance in the 'Moechian Affair'. Michael III, the son of Theodora, and the generals of his family together with the sovereigns of the Macedonian dynasty founded by Basil I (867) understood what part of the Iconoclast legacy should be preserved. Orthodox Byzantium keeps the enemy at bay; the Emperors lead the army in person and success-fully resist the monks. For the third time a long religious controversy is brought to a close and this time it ends in harmony. The Byzantine Church maintains intact the com-promise of the fourth century which reconciled art with the faith. Orthodox Emperors gird on the armour of the Icono-clasts. Culture wins a victory over the barbarous rudeness of the Isaurians, imperial order triumphs over the revolu-tionary spirit of undisciplined fanatics who had refused to communicate with Patriarchs and had declared that Emperors were not above the laws.

THE STRIFE OF PARTIES

The subjects on which turn the great disputes of the Church and of Byzantine society descend more and more from heaven to earth, from the heights of lofty speculation to practical morals and then to pure politics. From controver-sies on the divine consubstantiality of Christ and on the mystery of the Incarnation to those which debate the legiti-macy of images the distance and the difference are already sensible. When all these points of doctrine and of ritual are fixed, the militant passions of Byzantine society find new grounds of difference; but like our modern parties, formed from the same social strata, the folk of East Rome came into conflict over claims that were frequently changing, and in the name of principles which were very impermanent. One has the impression that the parties and their organization are the essential and enduring elements, much more at any rate than the issues for which they struggle. In the eighth century and at the beginning of the ninth we have seen Theodore the Studite and his monks in open feud with the hierarchy and with the authority of the Emperor: from Constantinople they appealed to Rome to defend the moral law and 'the

independence of the religious power'. The Patriarch
Methodius who suppressed this movement could rely upon
the support of the moderates and the politicians, of cultivated laymen, of the dynasty and the Court, and also of a
large number of monks who were weary of the pride and
dominating spirit of the men from the monastery of Studius.
Ignatius, his successor, was the tool of Studite bitterness.
Son of the dethroned Emperor Michael Rangabe, made a
eunuch in infancy, Ignatius had also on his side all those who
only unwillingly acknowledged the dynasty of Amorium.
No one can deny the heroic virtues of the ascete, but these
were accompanied by an inflexibility which dealt many
wounds. Ignatius seems to have taken as his model Theodore the Studite accusing Constantine VI of adultery; thus
he did not hesitate to impose a penance on the Caesar Bardas
(uncle of Michael III) who was suspected of 'incestuous'
relations with his niece. One can without difficulty conjure
up a picture of the party—heterogeneous enough—which
approved of the brutal reaction of the Government, a reaction
which culminated in the deposition of the eunuch Patriarch.
Bardas had as his allies the whole of the party which had
supported Methodius, from the loyal defenders of the
dynasty down to the anti-Studite monks, including the
intellectuals of the University of Constantinople. It was a
professor of this university, who was at the same time a high
official, a diplomat, a man of letters whose width of reading
was immense, the Byzantine who is most representative of
Byzantium, Photius, who was chosen to replace the ascetic
and impolitic Patriarch. We have reached the 25th of
December 858. Ignatius had been 'retired' five days before
and in the interval all the ecclesiastical orders had been conferred upon the layman Photius. The great dispute of the
ninth century had begun. Rome forthwith intervened. At
first Pope Nicholas I did not refuse to recognize this 'irre-
gular' election, since for this irregularity precedents were
not lacking; but he delayed his ratification. He hoped to
receive in exchange for his recognition some advantages—
he looked to recover jurisdiction over 'Illyricum', the
countries lying between Pope and Emperor that Leo III
after his quarrel with Pope Gregory II had withdrawn from

the latter in order to annex them to the Patriarchate of Constantinople. But Photius would not yield, and he was supported in his refusal by the Emperor Michael III and the Caesar Bardas. The Pope ostentatiously allied himself with the party of Ignatius which he thought to be the stronger. Ignatius, indeed, always denied that he had retired of his own free will.[1] In 863 Nicholas condemned and excommunicated Photius at the Lateran Council. Then Photius took the offensive with vigour. The conversion of the Bulgars, for long a matter of dispute between Rome and Byzantium, only embittered the quarrel. Photius transferred the controversy into the sphere of dogma and began to denounce not only to the Bulgars but to all the Churches of the East (866) the errors of Rome, such as the celibacy of the clergy and the corruption of its creed into which had crept the heretical addition of the *Filioque*.[2] He summoned to Constantinople a Council (867) where Nicholas in his turn was anathematized. At this Council the whole episcopate of the East was represented. Michael presided and doubtless also with him was the 'subordinate Emperor' Basil.[3] Photius was at the height of his success and glory. The Oriental patriarchates espoused his cause. Even in the West he had powerful allies in the Carolingian Emperor Louis II whom the Council acclaimed together with his wife Ingelberga; the latter was hailed as the 'new Pulcheria'. Photius had indeed everything on his side: learning, eloquence, imperial power, and incredible good fortune. Heaven seemed to bless his missions. The Moravians, the Bulgars, the Russians were converted. The aureole of Photius is associated with that of his imperial master Michael III who in 863 had exterminated the last great army of the Mussulmans of the Euphrates. By his side Photius, the *homo regius*, had become the national hero: his proud resistance to the pretentions of Rome had brought him that which he had previously lacked—popularity.

If none the less he fell, he fell together with the dynasty

---

[1] It would seem that on this point he was wrong, and that his resignation was a fact.

[2] The procession of the Holy Ghost from the Father *and the Son*.

[3] Michael and Basil had joined in the assassination of the Caesar Bardas in the preceding year.

itself. Basil the Macedonian, the murderer of Michael III, could not count upon any of the friends of this prince, his benefactor and his victim, and thus appealed to the adversaries of the fallen dynasty—to the Ignatians and their hero. Ignatius was re-established and at the Council of 869–70 (Eighth Oecumenical Council of the Latins), while avenging Rome, avenged his own wrongs: Photius was struck down. But there the triumph of the Pope was ended; after all Ignatius by an involuntary homage to his enemy continued the national policy of Photius which was an essential part of the renewal of the power of the Empire. Ignatius retained Bulgaria and—irony of history—avoided the excommunication of Rome only by his timely death, *felix opportunitate mortis*. Photius once more ascended the patriarchal throne and was recognized by Pope John VIII. Thus was peace concluded between Rome and Byzantium. At the Photian Council of 879–80 (Eighth Oecumenical Council for the Greeks) peace was solemnly proclaimed. Neither John VIII nor any of his successors will henceforth undo that which 'the good John' (as the Patriarch styles him in his last work) had done. If Photius fell yet again and without recovery (887), that was once more in consequence of a change of sovereign. The young Emperor Leo VI, whom his father Basil had sorely ill-treated, on his accession changed his ministers and in order to reconcile both parties and at the same time to secure his own control over the Church he made his brother Stephen Patriarch. Yet the Ignatians continued to fan the flame of the fierce hatreds of the past and pursued Photius in exile and in the tomb with a literature inspired by bitter animosity—a literature full of mangled citations and obvious forgeries. Until the year 898 they persisted in their refusal to communicate with the official Church, demanding from Rome and from the Patriarch a fresh condemnation of their enemy. It is they who have led men to believe in a 'second Photian schism'. At that time there was no schism save within the Greek Church itself—a consequence of an inexpiable party strife which is even continued under new names—the strife between Nicolaites and Euthymians.

That which gave rise to the feud between Nicolaites and

Euthymians was a repetition of the former 'Affair of Adultery'. The Emperor Leo VI wished in the Church's despite to marry as his fourth wife his mistress Zoe Carbonopsine, a beauty 'with eyes black as coal' who was already the mother of Constantine Porphyrogenitus. The Patriarch Nicholas, the Mystic, that is to say, the imperial secretary, twice dared to forbid the Emperor to enter St. Sophia. His place was taken by a monk Euthymius, a simple and saintly man who in the goodness of his heart and through love of peace settled the dispute. Thus on this occasion it is the 'Court prelate' Nicholas, a man of letters, a minister and a diplomat like Photius, whose pupil indeed he was, and who like Photius had passed directly from the 'world' to the Patriarchate, who contrary to all expectation takes up once more the heroic role of censor of an Emperor's morals, while the ascete Euthymius appears as the consecrator of a sacrilegious union. The Photian party which was that of Nicholas thus gains a new prestige while the former 'Ignatians' suffer from the complaisance of Euthymius. So when, on the death of Leo, Nicholas again becomes Patriarch, his pontificate was of a truly imposing magnificence. Regent during the minority of Constantine Porphyrogenitus, actually prime minister, a Byzantine Richelieu who conducted correspondence and negotiated with the Arabs and the Bulgars, he appears to Christendom at the same time as the moral superior of the Pope of Rome with whom he virtuously refuses to communicate, since Rome had sanctioned the scandal of the Emperor's fourth marriage. When in 920 the 'union of the Churches' was re-established it was as victor that Nicholas signed the famous 'Tome of Union', humiliating at the same time the Emperor Constantine who had been conceived in adultery. This moral superiority thus secured by the Byzantine patriarchate naturally caused the Government anxiety: after the pontificate of Nicholas, just as after that of Photius, the *Basileus* wishes to 'confiscate' the Patriarchate, by installing as Patriarch a prince of the blood royal: formerly it was Stephen, son of Basil I, now Theophylactus, son of Romanus Lecapenus. Had this precedent been followed, it would indeed have meant Caesaropapism. But these two attempts were not repeated in the sequel.

The second experiment was rendered particularly unfortunate by the character of Theophylactus who was an unworthy bishop, passionately interested in stables and horse-racing. Men grew accustomed to think that in all questions falling within his sphere, and above all whenever any moral issue was at stake, the Patriarch had undisputed rights even as against his master, the Emperor. Later Polyeuctus resumed this noble role of ecclesiastical censor when he forced John Tzimisces to repudiate the adulterous and criminal Theophano.

Under Sergius II, the great-nephew of Photius (beginning of the tenth century), the two great parties which we have seen at feud with each other since the end of the eighth century were finally reconciled. In the course of the years each had had its truth, and each its own greatness. They had had in turn, or even simultaneously, their *raison d'être*, their popularity. Each in its own way could justly claim to have incarnated the many-sided soul of Byzantium. And it was but logical that Byzantium should have adopted and canonized their leaders even while it opposed them. Whoever should speak ill of their combative Patriarchs—above all of Photius and Ignatius—was anathematized: Photius and Ignatius were at one in death and sanctity. When the final breach with Rome comes in 1054 it will find the Byzantine Church united: that breach is not caused by internal discords within Byzantium itself—the defeated party appealing to the arbitrament of Rome—as it had been previously in the Acacian and Nicolaite schisms. On the contrary, the energy of a Nicholas or a Polyeuctus doubtless inspired the action of the Patriarch Arsen Autorianus under Michael Paleologus when to the glorious founder of the last Byzantine dynasty, despite his reconquest of Constantinople from the Latins (1261), he refused pardon for having blinded the luckless Emperor John, the last of the Lascarids. Arsen was deposed, but the Arseniates, like the Ignatians of an earlier day, refused to recognize the new Patriarch and pronounced his ordinations invalid and sacrilegious. They became a fanatical and revolutionary sect, a kind of little Church avoiding all contact alike with the clergy and the laymen of the official Church. Like the Ignatians again they produced against their adversaries legends and forgeries. But in itself the movement—this protest of more than half a century against the crime of an Emperor—is not without its greatness. And the Patriarch Arsen, however narrow-minded he might be, certainly added to the glory of the oecumenical see: he has something of the stoic resolution of his great contemporaries, the popes who conquered Frederick II and Manfred.

PALAMISM

Before she perished Byzantium was to give to the world the spectacle of a last theological joust and the proof that she was to the end, even when hard pressed by the barbarians, capable of fighting against herself for high ideals. One might say that Byzantium had sworn to give the lie to her future reputation for dogmatic immobility, since fourteenth-century 'Palamism' is a doctrine of surprising boldness, of unexpected novelty. It is not that the mystical current which feeds Hesychasm—the movement of which Gregory Pala-mas was the theorist and the prophet—does not reach far back in the history of Byzantine religious thought; indeed, it derives in a straight line from Origen and there had ever been those in the Church of East Rome who had aspired to reach 'the delights of Contemplation'. But at an early date these speculations had been adjudged heretical. In the sixth century, at the very moment when the Great Council which was to condemn the Nestorian 'Three Chapters' was in session (553), anathemas had been launched against the errors of Origen and against the Origenist monks of Palestine. How comes it that eight centuries later practices and theories infinitely more hazardous not only appear openly in the light of day, but are straightway included amongst the treasured possessions of unchanging Ortho-doxy? The explanation of this paradox can be supplied by history alone. As we have seen, always, ever since the victory of Christianity, in the sphere of theology those opinions have triumphed, however daring they might be, which were held by the social strata of the population which circumstances had made the masters of the Empire. Egypt which for centuries was a necessity for the material existence of the

Empire, Armenia which fought its battles, Anatolia which repelled the Arab invasion forced Constantinople to come to terms with Monophysitism and with Iconoclasm. At Constantinople and Thessalonica, under Andronicus III Palaeologus, John V Palaeologus, and John Cantacuzenus, the people, exploited economically by the Latins, was roused to fury against the nobles and the intellectuals, who for political reasons were prepared to treat with the Westerners, and was torn by social convulsions, while Serbs and Turks were settling in the territories of the Balkan peninsula. Half betrayed and more than half invaded and subjugated, the Greek people defended only with greater passion its soul and its faith. The monks of Athos appeared to the folk of East Rome as the heroic champions of their cause. It is for this reason that when a stranger, a Calabrian monk, Barlaam, undertook to refute by means of the 'Western' syllogism and to ridicule with impious sarcasm the traditional methods of prayer employed on the Holy Mountain, popular sentiment immediately took the side of the Athonites. Gregory Palamas, an ascete of Athos, had built up a whole theology in justification of these methods of devotion: and this was unanimously adopted by the monks. John Cantacuzenus was at this time engaged in the struggle against his legitimate rival John Palaeologus: he desired to win over to his side the greatest moral force in the Empire now facing its death agony—the monks of Athos and the crowds which followed their lead: he therefore supported the innovator. The bishops, at first hostile or hesitant, saw in the new doctrine a rejuvenation of national orthodoxy, and the Council of St. Sophia gave to it its consecration (1351). At the outset the question was whether the Hesychasts were right in their claim that by holding the breath, by making the spirit re-enter into the soul, and by gazing fixedly upon the navel they could attain to the vision of the uncreated light which shone on Tabor. To justify their view Palamas, overturning the dogma which had been crystallized for centuries, proposed to distinguish between the divine essence and the operations of that essence. And the fathers of 1351 had the hardihood to see in his writings only a simple development of the ancient creeds. Palamism constitutes the most astonishing of paradoxes. Formally it has never been disavowed by the Byzantine Church. Gregory Palamas, who at his death was Archbishop of Thessalonica, is regarded as a holy doctor and as a worker of miracles. Thanks to him his Church, which prided itself on its fidelity to the tradition of the ancient Fathers and of the seven Councils—that tradition which it opposed to the sacrilegious *novelties* of the West—created in a fevered atmosphere as of a state of siege an entirely new transcendent theology, a disordered mysticism full of unfamiliar formulas which its author himself presented as a divine revelation. It is in truth a mystical Reformation, a new Christianity, which was perchance intended to supply spiritual armour to a nation on the threshold of a slavery which was to endure for half a millennium. Yet instead of scourging Palamism with the sarcasms of Barlaam, of Voltaire, and of Gibbon would it not be better rather to admire that depth of Christian sentiment which animated until the end the Byzantine people—a people which, whenever we see it stirred by a collective emotion, places those values which it considers eternal far above the chances and the changes of politics?

EXTERNAL HISTORY OF THE CHURCH

The Byzantine Church as a Christian Church and a State Church—rather as the Church of the universal State—had in double measure the duty of preaching the Gospel through the whole earth. Before the Church had conquered the Roman Empire it had already crossed the Empire's frontiers. The kingdom of Armenia submitted to Christ at a time when the Christians were still persecuted by Rome. It is certain that Constantine thought of using Christian Armenia to defeat Persia, the hereditary enemy of Rome in Asia. And henceforth Christian missionary activity, always in the service of the Empire, whether it springs from the sects or from the Great Church, will never cease. The Christological controversies which contributed to the political dismemberment of Byzantium had at first served to extend the empire of Christ. When Zeno expelled the Nestorians, particularly the scholars of Edessa, they fled into Persian territory and there the persecuted faith became what may be called the second national religion of the Sassanid State. This heroic body of Christians, this Church of the Martyrs, will remain attached, despite cruel memories, to its original home. It will spread in Sassanid Iran and later in Mussulman Persia the science of Greece and will carry its knowledge and its faith across the solitudes of central Asia as far as China, where the stele of Si-gnan-fu is a moving witness to its fidelity. This prodigious Nestorian missionary activity has been spoken of as a second Alexander's conquest of Asia. For Byzantium it is a sort of 'involuntary' mission. But on the other hand the conquests of the Monophysites have almost an official character. From Egypt, 'heretical' but passionately Christian, propaganda radiated towards Ethiopia (Axum) and Arabia, and Constantinople did not disavow the zeal of these heterodox missionaries. When the constancy of the Christians of Himyar is overborne by Jewish tribes, the Catholic Emperor Justin sends his Monophysite ally, the Ethiopian king, to deliver the heroic companions of the martyr Arethas. For the 'interior Mission'—the conversion of the pagans of Asia Minor—Justinian will make use of the Monophysite bishop, John of Ephesus, despite the brutality of his methods. Justinian and Theodora send concurrent missions to the tribes of Nubia, and the Monophysites, favoured by Theodora, will outdistance the Orthodox envoys dispatched by her husband. Henceforth the wars of Byzantium are holy wars, whether they are waged against pagans or against heretics. When the fleet of Belisarius sets forth for Carthage, on board the admiral's vessel there is placed a Vandal newly baptized according to the Orthodox rite. The great campaigns of Heraclius are the first Crusades. In the ninth century when the Amorian and Macedonian sovereigns begin anew the offensive against Islam, the enthusiasm of the reconquest gives birth to a fresh missionary ardour and these new missions will be amongst the most fruitful. In exceptional cases political considerations may prove unfavourable to Christian propaganda. The Chazars of southern Russia, allied with the Empire against the Mussulmans but fearing the imperial supremacy, reject the faith both of Irene and of Harun-al-Rashid and choose rather to adopt Judaism for their religion. It is under the victorious reign of

Michael III that Byzantium prepares its master-stroke, the conversion of the Slavs. The Court sends to Great Moravia, threatened by the German bishops, the two brothers from Thessalonica, Constantine and Methodius, who can speak the Slav language of Macedonia and who translate the scriptures into this tongue. And when in their turn the Bulgars to escape the weight of Byzantine arms accept Christianity, the disciples of Constantine and Methodius, the Apostles of the Slavs, ejected from Moravia, employ their zeal, their experience, and their books to make of Bulgarian Christianity the first-fruits of Great Slavia and in truth 'the eldest daughter of the Church of the East'.

Let us pause here for a moment. The adoption by the Greek Church of the Slav language for the use of its Slav converts is an important fact, yet it is not unnatural; it is indeed in conformity with its spirit and its liberal tradition. In the East the Church has always been polyglot, while in the West Latin was the sole liturgical language. The national liturgies, the diversity of ecclesiastical languages have at times been regarded as responsible for schisms and dismemberments of the Church; but Byzantium knew what was her true course. She had the merit of bearing no ill will towards Armenian, Copt, or Syrian for the secession of the Monophysite and Nestorian Churches: had not Georgia remained loyal? Byzantium granted freely to the Slavs that which Rome disputed or refused to them, and she had her reward. Along with the alphabet, the literature, even the thought of East Rome, the Slavs accepted Byzantine art in all its forms.

But this Slav mission was not complete until after the conversion of that people which both numerically and politically was destined in this great family to play the principal part—the Russian people, an amalgam of tribes which had been organized by the genius of Scandinavian adventurers. In 839 they came as friends to Constantinople in little groups, and then returned home, fearing the Magyars or the Petchenegs, by way of the territories of Louis the Pious. 'Home'? But where exactly was the residence of their chief or *hacan*? We cannot say. But twenty-one years later in 860 it is an immense fleet of *Rhōs* which all but captured Constantinople: it was only by a miracle, rendered famous by Photius, that the 'God-guarded city' was saved from this barbarian armada. Michael and Photius realized forthwith that they must convert these new neighbours now settled at Kiev, were it only to employ them against the terrible Petchenegs. The Rhōs accepted a bishop, but this first planting of Christianity was suppressed. In 957 the princess Olga visited the Byzantine Court: not only is this visit a fact of history, but we still possess in the *De Ceremoniis* the protocol which described the visit in full detail. Olga was converted to Christianity. In 989 Vladimir, Olga's successor, did not merely accept baptism for himself but baptized his people; by imperial favour he and his people became 'the first friends of the Basileus' and took the place of the Chazars as the allies of Rome in the far East. Vladimir had no cause to complain of his decision to reject both Islam which forbade wine to its converts—'To drink is a joy for the Russians and we cannot live without drinking'—and Judaism, circumcised Jews, like the Mussulmans, being dispersed throughout the world. The Russian Chronicle further tells of an embassy of six boyars whom the Emperors Basil and Constantine conducted to St. Sophia: 'We went to Greece,' so runs the story, 'and we were led to the place where they adore their gods and we knew not whether we were in heaven or on earth, for on earth nowhere are there such sights or such beauties.' On that day 'the third Rome' was born.

THE BYZANTINE CHURCH AND THE ROMAN CHURCH

The conquest of Russia may be regarded as compensation for the later breach with Rome. In the perspective of the centuries this schism is the most important fact in the *external* religious history of Byzantium. Since the period of the Crusades it has influenced and still influences profoundly the relations between the East and West: it has contributed and still contributes to form the very ideas of 'East' and 'West'—the concepts of the 'Oriental' Christian and the Christian of the Occident, of the 'Roman Catholic' on the one hand and the 'Orthodox' or 'schismatic' on the other. The dispute of the year 1054 determined the development of that conflict which has been waged through the centuries, of which the capture of Constantinople by the Latins in 1204 and by the Turks in 1453 are the most famous episodes and the most disastrous consequence. The mutual hatred caused by this quarrel produced during the sixteenth and seventeenth centuries the frescoes in the churches of Moldavia where the 'Latins' are represented amongst the damned, in the same way as to the average 'Catholic' the enslavement of the Greeks to the Ottoman yoke appeared as a divine punishment as fully deserved as was the dispersion of the Jews. The quarrel has been in the past and still remains stronger than the ties of blood. Even to-day in despite of their political interests it separates the Slavs who have followed the older Rome—Croats, Slovenes, Slovaks, Czechs, and Poles—from those whose religious centre is the New Rome of Constantine—whether they be Serbs, Bulgarians, Russians, or Latins of the Danube lands, the Roumanians, whose ecclesiastical language was for long the Old Slav. These profound divisions have produced the belief that long before 1054 the schism was predestined in the nature of things: it is considered to have been from the beginning inescapable, fatally conditioned by the opposition of nationality and of language. This view is false. The differences alleged between the rites of East and West are, for the most part, such as existed naturally in different Churches of which the ecclesiastical historian Socrates, in the fifth century, after the manner of Herodotus gives a curious catalogue. Divergent customs, contradictory practices were in no wise a hindrance to communion: they did not cause a breach of the peace. Too great importance has been attributed to the severances between Byzantium and Rome which occurred during the long controversy over the Two Natures—the Acacian schism, the Monothelite dispute. When the great debate was concluded, it left behind it no trace any more than did the ancient disagreements between Constantinople and Antioch or Alexandria. Of greater significance, at first sight, is the conflict between Leo III and Gregory II. It is thus summarized in the conventional story: Leo the Isaurian having endeavoured to enforce Iconoclasm upon the Church, the Pope stirred up revolt against him in Italy, while the

Emperor by way of reprisal confiscated the papal patrimony and attached to the diocese of his Patriarch Sicily, Byzantine Italy, and Illyricum. This seizure anticipates, it is contended, the policy of Photius and of Cerularius: the heresy of Leo III and of Constantine V led the Popes to betray the Empire and to throw themselves into the arms of the Franks. In short, Leo the Isaurian, when he tore down the icon of the Christ from the Brazen Gate, had conjured up Charlemagne seventy years before his time—that Western Emperor who as an imperial rival was to be the great scandal to Byzantine pride! But this conception of history is legendary. It is not Byzantine heresy which has emancipated the Papacy from the *Basileis*. The Popes of the eighth century never dreamed of freeing themselves from the sovereignty of the Emperor until it was proved that Byzantium had neither the strength nor the leisure to defend them against Lombards and Arabs. The religious question counted for nothing. The true touch-stone of the sentiments of the Papacy is the attitude of the Pope in 753-4 at the moment when Constantine V had assembled his great Iconoclast Council. Pope Stephen II so far from anathematizing the Emperor appealed to him for the dispatch of a fleet with reinforcements. The Pope, perfectly loyal to an Emperor at once 'heretic and perse-cutor', would not have asked for anything better than to remain such a loyal subject. If Stephen II did decide to betray Byzantium and call the Franks to his aid, that is solely because Constantine V was compelled to employ all his land and sea forces in his struggle against the Arabs and the Bulgars. Besides this, it is easy to show that the cause of the images, as Byzantium knew it, was not espoused by the West. If the heresy of the Isaurians had indeed produced the disaffection of the West, one should have seen in the West a movement of sympathy for Orthodoxy when it triumphed after the Council of 787. But almost the exact contrary actually occurred: the bishops of Charlemagne found that Byzantium of the Iconodules—the champions of the icons—was at least as much in the wrong as had been Byzantium of the Iconoclasts. The Pope himself was less unjust, and down to the time of Nicholas I, the enemy of Photius, it does not appear that either the confiscation of

Illyricum or the coronation of the usurper Charlemagne separated the two Churches from each other. Nicholas, as we have seen, taking advantage of the delicate position in which Photius was placed, thought that he could extort from the Patriarch the restitution of Illyricum. But that was to go against a *fait accompli* in the political sphere, and on this point St. Ignatius himself was just as obstinate or as powerless as was Photius. Nicholas, in his attack upon Photius and his Bulgarian mission and in general upon the distinctive practices of the Greek Church, showed a singular imprudence. Photius by his attack on the celibacy of priests and on the addition of the *Filioque* to the creed had no difficulty in proving to the Pope that alike in discipline and dogma it was the older Rome which was responsible for innovations: a great scandal would immediately be disclosed if only one should cease to keep the eyes shut in economic charity. We have seen how an intelligent Pope, John VIII, by recognizing Photius at the time of his second patriarchate allayed all these differences between Rome and Byzantium. It was agreed that the addition of the *Filioque* to the creed had been and should remain entirely unofficial, and the Papacy itself would see that the genuine text should be preserved. As is well known, to-day Rome on this point as on many others has returned to wisdom and truth, since it has authorized the Uniates to recite the creed without the *Filioque*. Charity on both sides could after all pass over minor differences: many of these had been charged against the Romans and denounced with great bitterness by the Byzantine Council in Trullo (691) and yet no breach between the Churches had ensued. But all the same the schism did come and persisted, like the Erinyes, as Aeschylus portrayed them, installing themselves in the house and refusing to be ejected. Why was there this schism?

We must reject completely the idea of those who seek to prove the existence of a schism already latent and to determine its 'terrain'; at the beginning of the eleventh century, it is urged, under Sergius II, great-nephew of Photius, it did but come once more to the surface: the Patriarch affirmed against Rome the sanctity of his great-uncle and re-edited the latter's encyclical addressed to the Eastern patriarchates on the errors of the Western Church. These theories which are still widely maintained form a sort of corollary to the legend of the second Photian schism. The schism of Cerularius, it is true, arose from no superficial causes. The main cause is the justifiable scorn of the Byzantines for the bad Popes of the ninth, tenth, and eleventh centuries. The folk of East Rome had never seen three oecumenical Patriarchs deposed by a single Emperor, as Henry III had deposed three Popes: they had never seen bishops fighting at the head of their troops, nor cases of simony as scandalous as those of the West. The comparison between Rome and Byzantium for the centuries which preceded the schism is all in favour of the latter. Contrary to that which is often ignorantly repeated, it is, in fact, the Popes who have fallen into slavery, it is the Patriarchs of Constantinople who are independent. Byzantium had a lively consciousness of its own strength, its dignity, and its privileges. Byzantium was in the right on most of those dogmatic and disciplinary questions which were in dispute, if in such matters it is *occupatio*, prescription, tradition which determine where right lies. But life also has its rights, and it is this fact which Byzantium failed to recognize. Here, indeed, is to be found the true cause of the schism. The Byzantines were fully justified in despising the bad Popes, but they did not realize with what kind of men they had to deal when they met Pope Leo IX and his advisers, Cardinal Humbert, Frederick of Lorraine, and their like. These men were not cowards, neither were they degenerate nor illiterate. Humbert, writing to the Patriarch of Antioch, approves the latter's creed, although it lacked the *Filioque*. These leaders of the West were full of life and enthusiasm, they were about to begin their great struggle for the purification of the Church, for its complete enfranchisement from civil authority, for the establishment of the celibacy of the clergy. They knew that the fight would be long and bitterly contested, and that it would be fought on more than one front.

The Norman conquests were already avenging Rome for the ecclesiastical annexations of Leo the Isaurian; as a consequence of these victories such towns as Otranto, Rossano, and Reggio had once more been attached to the Roman metropolitan see. As a counter-offensive, acting, it would seem, under orders from the Patriarch (Michael Cerularius), Leo, Bishop of Ochrida, indulged in an ill-timed attack upon the usages of the Latins. This was sent to the Bishop of Trani and by him transmitted to Rome. There it aroused sincere indignation. Leo had discovered a new ground of accusation which had been overlooked by Photius but which henceforth controversialists would never allow to be forgotten: besides fasting on the Sabbath, he censured the Latins for using unleavened bread in the eucharistic sacrifice, while another Greek disputant protested with violence against the celibacy of the clergy. The aggression of the Orientals was dangerous: it might compromise the whole work of the reformers, and arm against them the entire opposition of the West. It was for this reason that Rome's reaction was of an unlooked-for violence. The feeble government of Constantine Monomachus needed the Pope, for Italy was not yet lost beyond recall. An arrangement might have been possible: it was the wish of the Emperor himself. But Leo IX sent to Constantinople 'one of the violent men in Church history', Cardinal Humbert. On both sides old grievances were exploited: the encounter was brutal. Each party to the dispute excommunicated the other (1054). Michael Cerularius carried with him his whole people: Latin insolence had been such that this time Rome had no supporters in Byzantium: even the party of the philosophers, Psellus at its head, who were the foes of Cerularius applauded him. The Emperor who had disapproved his action narrowly escaped expulsion from the city when a riot broke out in the capital; he hastened to make his peace with the Patriarch.

This is not the place to recount the melancholy story of those fruitless efforts at union made almost without exception by the Emperors of Byzantium who were driven thereto by political necessity. All the Eastern patriarchates, all the Churches of the East had followed Constantinople into schism. The Latin conquest did but deepen the cleft between the two worlds. When the Latin Empire and the Latin Patriarchate fell in 1261, the repugnance of the Greeks for the Union, henceforth synonymous with alien domination, was stronger than ever. Yet Michael Palaeologus was a determined 'Unionist', especially during the years when under the menace of the Crusade of Charles of Anjou he sought on every side—whether at Rome or amongst the Arabs—to secure the help of allies against his redoubtable enemy. The Emperor gathered around him some prelates who wished him well; in particular the Patriarch Bekkos took his side. It is a curious fact: but at this time the prestige of the Latins and of their theological activity had a powerful effect upon some of the best minds in Byzantium. In all good faith these men were inspired by a Christian passion for unity and thus supported the policy of Michael which was crowned with success at the Council of Lyons (1274). But the union effected at Lyons had hardly more than a symbolic significance, and it further lost a great part of its value after the Sicilian Vespers of 10 March 1282. Charles of Anjou was thus deprived of his power to injure the Empire: Michael Palaeologus at the time of his death (December 1282) had won a complete triumph, and therefore his son and successor, Andronicus II (1282–1328), straightway renounced the Council of Lyons, made his peace with the Orthodox, and deposed Bekkos, the partisan of the Latins; the Patriarch, although a man of high character and of real independence of mind, was reviled as a traitor by the nation. Michael had negotiated and concluded the Union in order to disarm the West, to prevent a repetition of the Fourth Crusade. His successors revived the idea to stay the invasion of the Turks. But the danger must be instant and pressing before the rulers of Byzantium will decide to resort to so desperately unpopular an expedient. During the fourteenth and fifteenth centuries, indeed, both the intellectuals and the politicians may quite voluntarily be drawn towards the Latins, but as soon as the *pium votum* begins to take concrete shape, immediately it arouses against itself the fanatical opposition of the masses. During the disastrous quarrel of the two Johns (middle of the fourteenth century) in spite of the attitude of the people, solidly anti-Latin in its sympathies, the rival Emperors outdo each other in their zeal for the Union of the Churches. In 1348 an embassy of Cantacuzenus arrives at Avignon, in 1352 Cantacuzenus, although he welcomes the support of the monks and the crowds, yet writes to Clement VI. Stephen Dushan, the Serbian Emperor, precisely because he aspires to a rule which at least in the Balkans shall be universal, will for his part also affect an enthusiasm for the Union which, as he thinks, will win for him from the Pope the dignity of leadership in the Crusade as well as subsidies and reinforcements. The personal faith of John V Palaeologus, himself half-Latin through his mother Anne of Savoy, is beyond question, but all that he could do when in 1369 he visited Pope Urban V in Rome was to offer his individual 'conversion'. The terrible disasters of the years 1422 to 1430 brought John VIII and the representatives of the Greek Church to Florence, and it was in that city on 6 July 1439, after emotional debates in which the best Byzantine theologians together with the Patriarch Joseph participated, that there was signed that Act of Union which is to-day exhibited in the rotunda of the Laurentiana. The Union of Florence was to lead on 10 November 1444 to the catastrophe of Varna, while it also failed to preserve religious unity, for no sooner had the delegates of the Greek Church returned to their congregations than they were met by the reprobation of the monks and of the people. Many of the signatories withdrew their consent to the Union. But it remains a great religious transaction: it is on the basis of that Act of Union that to-day several millions of Oriental Christians are united with Rome. These 'Uniates' are particularly numerous in the Ukraine and in Transylvania, while in Greek territory the movement towards union with Rome has of recent years been slow and difficult, opposed, as it is, by a public sentiment which is inspired by the rancours and bitterness of the centuries. Still Rome never ceases to encourage Uniate propaganda: to each of the separate Eastern Churches it presents a Church which, while it acknowledges the supremacy of the Pope, yet retains the liturgy, the language, and, so far as possible, the customs and the costume of the national Church. Thus the Holy See is ever multiplying its concessions to the Byzantine tradition. In the matter of language it is almost as liberal as East Rome itself. The canonist Balsamon in the thirteenth century refused to exclude any language from liturgical use. To-day Catholics of the so-called Byzantine rite are granted, besides Greek, the use of the Old Slav, Georgian, Roumanian, and Arabic languages. Rome goes farther still: not only does she tolerate, she claims even to impose upon the Orientals united with her the preservation of their distinctive ritual. In 1931, on the occasion of the fifteenth centenary of the Council of Ephesus, there were celebrated at Rome and at Grottaferrata masses and solemn offices according to the different Oriental rituals. Such are the results of the Council of Florence.

THE ESSENTIAL CHARACTERISTICS OF THE BYZANTINE CHURCH

The Byzantine Church is the most important of Byzantine survivals. The Empire has disappeared, but the Church remains, and thanks to the Slavs it still has on its side the force of numbers. Despite the anti-religious persecutions in Red Russia and despite the multiplicity of the languages in which its liturgy is celebrated, it has kept an aspect, an appearance, just as characteristic as that of Islam, for example, and certainly much more traditional and more archaic than that of the Catholic Church which has been transformed almost beyond recognition by Jesuitic devotions and a kind of ritual Modernism. The preceding pages have shown the reader how the system of the Orthodox Church was constituted from century to century. Up to the time of the Iconoclast Controversy—up till the time of the Seventh Oecumenical Council (whose decisions alike for the Latin West and for the 'Orthodox' East are as canonical and binding as those of the other six)—Greek thought—the thought of Christianized Greek philosophy—provided the imposing 'structure' whence the entire Christian Church took its dogmatic definitions, the subtlest distinctions of its Christology. Despite the objections and the reservations of Rome, these Councils by their canons continuously consecrated and confirmed the hegemony of the Church of the capital, Constantinople, over all the other Churches comprised in the territories of the Eastern Empire, even over the Patriarchates of Alexandria, of Antioch, and of Jerusalem, although in the political sphere the first and the third of these were never regained by the Byzantine Emperors after their conquest by Islam. The ecclesiastical ascent of Constantinople was at first justified solely on political grounds. It was only later that it was based upon the apocryphal legend of St. Andrew, the first called amongst the Apostles, who became Bishop of Byzantium. The story is a fabrication of the sixth century. It is towards the end of the reign of Justinian that the Church of the capital adopts the title 'Apostolic'. If its head very early styles himself 'Patriarch', the epithet is at first only honorific and is used with great freedom by other metropolitans. The title 'oecumenical' or 'universal', by which Rome will on several occasions pretend to be scandalized, has in its origin but little significance. This qualification which is exactly equivalent to our 'general' or 'superior' only implies a relative and indeterminate authority: it may be granted to professors of the University or at times, like the term 'patriarch', to the ecclesiastical head of a province. The history of these titles does not differ from that of the word Pope to which the Bishop of Rome had no exclusive right, since it was borne and still is borne to-day by the Patriarch of Alexandria. But it is clear that the ambiguous term 'oecumenical' served to justify *a posteriori* a primacy of honour which is still respected by the different Orthodox Churches despite the decline of the see of Constantinople. The Arab conquest and the annexation of Illyricum in the eighth century make a reality of this 'oecumenicity', if the *oikoumenē* is to be identified with the State governed by the Basileus, and this ambitious predicate, precisely like the genitive 'Romaion'—'of the Romans'—which after the eighth century is regularly attached to the title of Basileus, permits the Church of Byzantium to grant to its daughter Churches of more recent formation Patriarchates which are more or less autonomous, just as the imperial chancery can recognize other Basileis. Thus after the political conquest of Bulgaria Basil II conferred his sanction upon the Bulgarian Patriarchate, and similarly to-day, in conformity with Byzantine tradition, the Phanar takes no offence at the title of Patriarch borne by the heads of several autocephalous Churches.

The organization of the Byzantine Church was from the outset modelled upon that of the Empire, and in particular upon the administrative divisions of the time of Diocletian or of Constantine. Even to-day the metropolitans can be said to be the bishops of the Constantinian provinces. In each city there was a resident suffragan bishop; in the Byzantine Empire the title of archbishop, if it is not merely an honorific synonym for bishop, denotes the head of an autocephalous bishopric, i.e. one which is directly dependent upon the Patriarch. It is only in Illyricum—which until the eighth century had for its ecclesiastical superior the Pope of Rome—that 'archbishop' has its Western sense of 'metropolitan'. In general the Byzantine Church had no bishops *in partibus*. One must come down almost until our own day to see residing in Constantinople prelates whose titles preserve the memory of those dioceses of Asia Minor where massacre or exchange of populations on a large scale has completely destroyed the former Christian congregations. While the dioceses, for example, attached to the Kingdom of Greece have already been or are in process of being emancipated according to the formula of the Oecumenical Patriarchate and thus incorporated in the national Church, in theory the episcopate is recruited by popular election, although more and more in the course of Byzantine history higher authorities and even the direct influence of the Emperor come to play a preponderant part in the choice of bishops. An ancient rule which for a long period does not admit of any exception and which is often adduced in the controversies between Rome and Byzantium declared that a bishop is elected for life, that he is wedded to his church and that a divorce from his see by way of translation to another bishopric is unlawful. After the fourth century at least, the bishop cannot be married: on the other hand, simple priests, deacons, and subdeacons can live with their wives on condition that they have been remarried on being created subdeacon. The celibacy of the clergy was often denounced as a heretical innovation which was due, according to Byzantine theologians, to the pernicious influence of Manichaeism. This essential difference in ecclesiastical discipline was one of those points of misunderstanding which were exploited by controversialists at the time of the schism. We have already said that nothing could be more false than the charge of

Caesaropapism which is generally brought against the Byzantine Church—the accusation that the Church rendered servile obedience to the orders of the Emperor even in the religious sphere. It is true that the Emperor always concerned himself with ecclesiastical affairs: he endeavoured to maintain or to impose unity in dogma but, as we have seen, his claims were by no means always submissively recognized. Indeed, the Byzantines became accustomed to the idea that organized opposition to the imperial will in religious matters was normal and legitimate. We have quoted some famous instances of opposition or victorious resistance to the Emperors of East Rome.

After the ninth century the Emperors no longer seek to attack orthodoxy: the orthodox faith is henceforward crystallized—it has, in a word, triumphed over the Emperors. Apart from a slight concession to the passions of the Monophysites at the time of the Fifth Oecumenical Council (553) nothing ultimately remained from the long-continued efforts —in themselves not without their own wisdom and nobility —by which the Emperors, from Zeno to Constantine III, sought to escape from the strict line of Chalcedonian orthodoxy. Neither did any trace of Iconoclasm survive, that movement which the Isaurian and Amorian sovereigns had sustained against a part of the nation which was later to become the majority of the Byzantine people. In the thirteenth, fourteenth, and fifteenth centuries the Basileis were unfortunately powerless to secure recognition from the clergy of the Union with Rome, and the last Palaeologi were so little Caesaro-Popes that they, together with a chosen few, belonged to the Uniate Greek rite, somewhat like some modern sovereigns who have been strangers to the religious faith of the majority of their subjects.

Such is the truth concerning the religious tyranny of the Byzantine Emperors. Without any suspicion of paradox the religious history of Byzantium could be represented as a conflict between the Church and the State, a conflict from which the Church emerged unquestionably the victor. Further, it is not true that intolerance and the persecution of dissenters are to be imputed primarily to the civil power which thus imposed upon the Church for political ends an attitude which was sadly lacking in Christian charity. From the time of the persecution of the last remaining pagans down to the vexatious measures directed against the Paulician dissenters and the Armenian Monophysites—measures which in the eleventh century weakened the resistance to the Seljuk Turks—there are numerous cases in which we see the Emperors subordinating the sectarian defence of orthodoxy to considerations of policy and of humanity. The Emperor Arcadius, the son of Theodosius the Great, has the reputation of having dealt the decisive blow against paganism. His legislation on this subject is indeed pitiless, but a contemporary document which chance has preserved for us shows the Emperor in October 400 refusing to the Bishop of Gaza his sanction for the destruction of the temple of Marnas for the same reasons which dissuaded Charles V from applying severe measures against the heretics in Antwerp, a commercial city and therefore of great moment to the State. 'I know well', said Arcadius, 'that this town is full of idols: but it pays its taxes loyally and contributes much to the Treasury. If, suddenly, we terrorize these people, they will take to flight and we shall lose considerable revenues.' We cannot catch in every case the echo of similar discussions in respect of those repressive measures which were constantly demanded by the Church against infidels and heretics. But, speaking generally, the policy of most of the Emperors of the fifth and sixth centuries is a policy of tolerance and of conciliation towards the heterodox. The Paulicians from 668 until about 875 sought to win over to their dualist faith the Armenians and Anatolians, especially in the regions of Pontus and the Euphrates; through their military virtues the Paulicians were the useful allies of the Empire. We know that at least one Emperor, Leo the Isaurian, refused to persecute the Paulicians, and that another, in spite of his Patriarch, listened to the counsels of moderation which were given him by the Studite monks. In the tenth century the Byzantine reconquest was accompanied and facilitated by the very liberal concessions granted to the Armenian and Syrian Monophysites. If these good relations are later disturbed and if in the end there was a return to the mistakes of the past, the fault assuredly lies not with the Emperors but with the local orthodox clergy. In a word, the civil power and the religious authorities have each of them kept to their proper roles. One may justly reproach the Byzantine Church for its dogmatic rigidity which has cost it many a disappointment, but it would be unjust to be surprised on that account. This rigidity is but one aspect of the orthodoxy of the Byzantine Church—an orthodoxy only crystallized after desperate and century-long conflicts. This rigid dogma was for the Byzantine Church a conquest of which she was proud. It was because she was the loyal trustee of this unadulterated faith that she could proclaim herself to be superior to the other Churches, that she could arrogate to herself the right to condemn the vicious practices of the Church of Rome. The reader who has observed in these pages the relations of politics and religion cannot fail to recognize that, however disastrous it may have been from the temporal point of view, Byzantine intolerance is in its essence an affair of the spirit: it is not inspired by any nationalism. Here lofty minds are at work who place above everything else the treasure of the faith. And if anything can lend beauty to the decline of the great Byzantine Empire after 1071—after the fatal day of Manzikert—it is precisely this impolitic and sublime refusal to compromise—it is the fact that the Byzantines were profoundly religious. The signature of their whole civilization is their faith. It is that which explains the character of their literature and of their art. It is true that Byzantium in its loyalty to the fourth-century compromise (see p. 93) preserved the essential works of profane literature, that it never ceased to transcribe them, to write commentaries upon them; Byzantium produced men of great learning, scholars of a curiosity which knew no bounds. History, for example, was passionately studied by an almost uninterrupted series of writers who at times were inspired by the great classical models. Yet almost all the Byzantine men of letters were first and foremost preoccupied with theology. Not only do the monastic chroniclers give pride of place to Church affairs, but the historians properly so called, like Nicephorus Gregoras, interrupt their narrative to recount through whole books high controversies over points of doctrine. Byzantine poets—or at least versifiers—are legion. But although some

of them have sought to sing of the great events of history—
and not merely of Byzantine history but of the history
of mankind—e.g. the glorious Crusades of the seventh
century—yet not one of them can claim a place in world-
literature—not even the Poet Laureate of Heraclius, George
of Pisidia, nor the Poet Laureate of Nicephorus Phocas,
John the Geometrician. There is no breath of the true spirit
either of epic or of lyric poetry in their elegant, frigid, and
pedantic works. If chance had not preserved for us some
fragments of popular songs from the ninth and tenth centuries of an inspiration similar to that of the klephtic ballads
of modern Greece, we might be tempted to believe that even
the heroism of the war against the Arabs never awoke in a
Byzantine bard that primitive enthusiasm which recurs in
the historical songs of almost all barbarian peoples. Even
the Armenians possess a large body of secular poetry. Such
poetry was denied to Byzantium, doubtless partly because
Byzantium neglected the language of the people which was
full of poetic possibilities in order to write almost exclusively
in a learned idiom. But the principal reason for this absence
of a poetic literature is to be sought in the almost complete
domination of the Byzantine by religious interests. The
true, the only Byzantine poets are those who in their
modesty styled themselves 'melodes', humble monks whose
sole aim was the enrichment of the liturgy. They indeed are
truly inspired, but the source of their inspiration is to be
found in the Scriptures and in the drama of the liturgy; and
it must also be said that their art does not follow classical
models or the rules which govern classical poetry. The
earliest of these poets are pupils of the Syrians whose
strophes, refrains, and acrostics they imitate. One great
name must be mentioned—that of Romanus 'the Melode'.
He was a deacon born in Syria who came to Constantinople
in the sixth century: to him the Greek Church is indebted
for hymns of deep feeling, though at times their effect is
spoiled by an excess of eloquence—by those peculiarly
Byzantine faults: superfluity of words and a prodigal misuse
of elaboration. And among prose-writers—apart from some
chroniclers using the vulgar tongue or some high functionary
relating without pretention his own memoirs—those who

escape from the conventional style which stifles true sentiment and simple expression are the mystics addressing themselves to a picked audience of ascetes, or the hagiographers,
happily fairly numerous, who are preserved by their ignorance from the well-worn expressions of a literary tradition
and who are almost the only Byzantines who can put us into
immediate contact with the life of their day. That religious
sentiment, however, which has saved from pedantry and
archaism a few pages of Byzantine literature could fashion
through art, above all through mosaic and painting, through
architecture also and at times, though very rarely, through
sculpture, a marvellously adequate expression of the Byzantine soul. But this art, like the poetry of the melodes, is only
a perpetual illustration of dogma or of the liturgy. The
theological and liturgical symbolism which was developed
after the seventh century is an original creation of Byzantium. Thanks to that creation the Byzantine Church has
something of beauty and of grandeur which can stand comparison with the cathedral of the West—that book of stone
with its wealth of spiritual teaching. In the West there are
the statues and the stained glass of the windows: in the
Byzantine East there are the frescoes and the mosaics which
present to the eye the scenes of the two Testaments and
the symbols which correspond to the different moments of
the Eucharistic Drama. Here in this Eucharistic Drama, the
Mystery of mysteries, the Sacrifice above all other sacrifices,
is the centre of Byzantine faith, the centre of Byzantine life
itself. Through the centuries Byzantine theologians sought
to determine precisely its sublime significance. It is because
in the Eucharist is contained man's supreme hope, because
here is the essence of Christianity, that the peoples of the
East have met in violent conflict seeking with passionate
intensity rigorously to define the dogma of their faith.
Christians were Christians only because Christianity brought
to them liberation from death. If one would penetrate to the
heart of Eastern Christianity one must be present on the
night when the Easter liturgy is celebrated: of this liturgy
all other rites are but reflections or figures. The three words
of the Easter troparion—the Easter hymn—repeated a
thousand times in tones ever more and more triumphant,

repeated to the point of ecstasy and of an overflowing mystic joy—θανάτῳ θάνατον πατήσας—'By His death He has trodden death beneath His feet'—here is the great message of the Byzantine Church: the joy of Easter, the banishing of that ancient terror which beset the life of man, this it is which has won and kept the allegiance of the masses: it is this creed of triumph which has been translated into all the languages of the Orient, and yet has never lost its virtue: this is the faith which found its material expression in the icon, so that even when the originality of the artist fell short, man's shortcoming could not veil the meaning of that joyous Mystery.

HENRI GRÉGOIRE

V

BYZANTINE MONASTICISM

IT would be difficult to over-estimate the part played by monasticism in the history of Byzantium. It was on the territory of the Eastern Empire that this institution took its rise and on that soil it flourished amazingly. We shall not attempt, as others have done, to look outside Christianity for the origin of an institution which was deeply rooted in the Gospel. 'If thou wilt be perfect', said the Lord, 'go and sell that thou hast, and give to the poor, and thou shalt have treasure in heaven.' This invitation, which any Christian could accept if he would, very early found an echo in the Church, and the state of perfection held up by Christ as an ideal met with a ready response in many hearts. Those who accepted the call did not at once separate themselves from the rest of the faithful. Ascetics of both sexes continued to live in the world, and like Origen, for instance, practised every form of self-discipline, without feeling bound to cut themselves off from all intercourse with their fellow men. It is in Egypt that we first hear of hermits. They began by building themselves huts in the outskirts of the towns and villages, and to these huts they withdrew in order to give themselves up to contemplation and the practice of ascetic exercises.

In this way St. Antony (about 270) began his life as a solitary, but after fifteen years he withdrew to Pispir in the desert and there shut himself up in an empty tomb, in which he lived for some twenty years. His reputation for holiness brought him many imitators, who came to settle in the neighbourhood of his retreat in order to profit by his example and advice; he was obliged to listen to their appeals and to busy himself in giving them some guidance and the rudiments of an organization. We need not consider whether any other hermit preceded him in the desert, as St. Paul of Thebes may perhaps have done. St. Antony was undoubtedly the first solitary of whose influence we may be certain, extending as it did beyond his place of retreat. But the company of his disciples had none of the characteristics of a religious community. Though they received instruction from him, they were not bound to obey him, nor were they committed to any uniformly regulated way of life. The development of monasticism known as semi-eremitical arose shortly afterwards in the deserts of Nitria and Scete in Lower Egypt. We have descriptions of these communities in the works of Palladius and Cassian. These monks lived in separate cells, and in Nitria sometimes three or four cells were grouped together. They met at church for the liturgy on Saturdays and Sundays only, and were subject to no rule, the authority of the elders being purely personal. When visiting each other they occupied themselves with the study of the Scriptures or discussed questions of spiritual doctrine. Cassian's *Collations* give us an idea of the nature of these conversations.

At about the same time that St. Antony, after twenty years of strict seclusion, began to concern himself with his disciples at Pispir, there appeared in Upper Egypt another famous ascetic, who was to give the monastic movement a new direction. St. Pachomius, a disciple of the hermit Palamon, having doubtless observed the disadvantages and even the dangers of complete isolation, proceeded to organize a community for the hermits of his neighbourhood, and founded at Tabennisi, near Dendera, the first monastery of the life in common (*koinobion*) to which disciples soon flocked. The monastery consisted of several separate buildings, each holding thirty to forty persons under the direction of a superintendent. The monks owed obedience to their Superior and were subject to a rule. Not only were their religious exercises, that is to say, prayer, instruction, and confession, strictly regulated, but manual labour, which consisted in the practice of different handicrafts, was also compulsory. This constitution of Pachomius met with very great success. Before his death in about 345 the Pachomian Congregation, as it may be called, comprised nine monasteries, containing a great number of monks, and two convents for women.

The work of Pachomius gave to monasticism its essential and final form. The hermit in his retreat practised continence and poverty, and to these virtues was added in the monasteries that of obedience. The religious was henceforth a man cut off from the world and obliged to exercise these three virtues: that obligation was soon to be enforced through the sanction of a vow. He was pledged to observe an austere discipline which regulated his relations with God, his superiors, and the monastic community. The independent life of a solitary did not lose its attraction all at once; still for a long time it remained the form of asceticism preferred by a minority, while it was found possible to combine it with coenobitism, i.e. with the life in a community. But the advantages of the latter were so great that it was bound before long to predominate. For in the common life there was found scope for the exercise of charity and for a rivalry in well-doing of every kind which was denied to the hermits, while it gave an opportunity to practise the virtues of religion without going into the wilderness.

In Egypt the monastic movement in all its forms met at first with incredible success. We need not discuss the fantastic figures given by certain authors. The *Historia Monachorum* would have us believe that there were more monasteries than private houses at Oxyrhynchus, and that, including those in the suburbs, monks numbered 10,000 and nuns 20,000. These exaggerated figures show that the number of the monks was large enough to strike men's imaginations and at the same time it is too large to allow us to believe that all who entered the monasteries were actuated by purely religious motives. It is therefore not surprising to find the Emperors Valentinian and Valens ordering the removal from the religious houses of those who had fled there in order to evade public duties.

Monastic life satisfied an aspiration so widespread that it could not long be confined to the land of its origin. It was natural that the adjoining countries of Palestine and Syria should have been the first to be influenced, especially as the Holy Places were becoming more and more a centre of attraction and the scene of an intense religious movement. Two names stand out among the pioneers of the religious life in Palestine in the first half of the fourth century, namely, St. Hilarion, who lived as a hermit in the Gaza desert, and

St. Chariton, to whom is attributed the foundation of the
Laura of Pharan, in the desert of Judaea, and of other lauras,
notably that of Souka, known as the Old Laura. The laura
was a form of ascetic life much favoured in Palestine. It
consisted of a group of hermits who lived in separate cells, but
were under the direction of an abbot. The centre of the
laura was often a monastery, where the hermits met on
Saturdays and Sundays, and to which young aspirants to
the solitary life were admitted in order first to undergo the
severe tests demanded of those who wished to embrace this
special vocation. During the fifth and sixth centuries
monastic life in Palestine developed remarkably. On this
movement we are exceptionally well informed through the
work of Cyril of Scythopolis (sixth century), the author of a
unique series of biographies of illustrious monks, among
them St. Euthymius, St. Sabas, and St. Theodosius. The
most famous of these monks, St. Sabas, founded no less than
seven lauras, among them the Great Laura, where he lived
until his death. At the beginning of the sixth century the
peace of the monasteries of Palestine was disturbed by the
Origenist disputes. The civil authority was forced to intervene, and the New Laura, which had become a centre of
heretical unrest, was cleared of its occupants and handed
over to the orthodox monks. Palestine admitted both the
established forms of monasticism, the coenobitic organization and the life of the hermit. The one did not exclude the
other, but the life of the solitary was generally more highly
esteemed. In the seventh century Palestine was cut off from
the Empire by the Arab invasion, and under the new government its monastic institutions suffered greatly, those which
survived losing all contact with the religious houses beyond
the frontier which had the same origin and observed the
same rite as themselves.

Syria and Mesopotamia were drawn into the movement
by an irresistible force. We are told that Eugenius, one of
the pioneers of Syrian monasticism, was apprenticed to the
religious life in Pachomius's monastery at Tabennisi, and
that from Egypt he brought a company of seventy monks to
Mesopotamia and founded a monastery near Nisibis.

A certain Julian, mentioned by St. Jerome, is said to have

introduced monasticism into Osrhoene. It is not recorded who first inhabited the desert of Chalcis, near Antioch, but it was there that St. Jerome is known to have lived as a hermit for several years. In Syria there were monasteries, properly so-called, of which mention is made by various historians. All the monks whose exploits were recounted by Theodoret in his *Philotheos Historia* were hermits. They gave themselves up to penitential exercises differing by their great austerity and other special characteristics from those practised by the monks of Egypt. These latter, it has been observed, performed penances which may be called natural, such as fastings, long vigils, and a strict isolation from the world. It is true that some of them, as for instance Macarius of Scete, were led through a competitive spirit to establish records in self-mortification and in consequence fell into obvious excesses. But in general Egyptian asceticism was governed by a spirit of moderation which took account of the limits of human endurance. In Syria it was otherwise; the hermits mentioned by Theodoret, living alone in the desert, their own masters, and subject to no control, tortured their bodies without check or restraint. Their asceticism took violent and at times extravagant forms. It was in Syria that St. Simeon the pillar-saint appeared, and his example was to prove infectious; it created a class of ascetes which persisted for centuries. If one disregards the bizarre form of his self-mortification, Simeon Stylites may be regarded as typical of Syrian monasticism, for unlimited austerities united with unceasing prayer, individualism, and complete isolation are its characteristic features.

The storms raised by heresy in the Patriarchates of Alexandria and Antioch, and the intervention of the Arabs, separated from Orthodoxy and later from the Empire nearly all the monasteries in the Nile valley and a great number of those in the Orontes, Euphrates, and Tigris regions. They formed themselves into isolated groups which had henceforth no share in the life of the great monastic family, the true heir of the traditions of Antony and Pachomius, which elsewhere was to exhibit so striking a development.

From Egypt and Syria monasticism spread, and the current must soon have reached Asia Minor. We know little more than that there were monks in Galatia before the end of the fourth century, and that there, as in the adjoining countries, the severity of the climate was unfavourable to the adoption of a hermit's life. We are better informed with regard to Armenia Minor, Paphlagonia, and Pontus, into which countries monastic life was introduced by Eustathius of Sebaste, whose indiscreet zeal nearly wrecked the whole future of the movement. Especially in Armenia monasticism assumed exaggerated forms. Several decrees of the Council of Gangra (in Paphlagonia) are inspired by the desire to remedy excesses which could not but be censured by the ecclesiastical authorities.

Cappadocia, which later sent into other countries such famous monks as SS. Theodosius and Sabas, gave to the Church one who may well be regarded as the lawgiver of the monastic life, namely, St. Basil of Caesarea. Under the influence of his sister Macrina, he resolved to leave the world, but before embracing the monastic life he determined to learn its secrets in the places where it had received its definite form. With this object he visited Egypt, Palestine, Syria, and Mesopotamia. On returning from his travels he withdrew to a retreat at Annesi on the River Iris in Pontus, and there proceeded to put into practice the ideal formed by his study of the lives of the anchorites on the one hand and of the coenobites on the other. The completely isolated life of the former could in his opinion be the goal only of the chosen few. Such a life was less in accordance with man's social nature, gave no scope for charity, and for most men was accompanied with serious disadvantages. Ordinary minds, uncontrolled by any supervision or rule of obedience, were apt to give way to pride and self-deception, and at times the cares of a man's mere material existence might become so absorbing as seriously to hinder communion with God. On these grounds St. Basil preferred coenobitism. But he fully realized the weakness of the Pachomian organization as it existed in Egypt, namely, that the number of monks in each group was too great. The Superior could consequently neither know them intimately nor direct them effectively; and it was not easy to free these necessarily self-supporting communities from preoccupation with material needs. Basil, therefore, in choosing the coenobitic system, amended it by reducing the number of monks in each monastery to more modest proportions. Still, while not encouraging the hermit's life, he did not altogether prohibit it.

Profiting by the experience gained in his travels, he regulated the lives of his monks in every detail. The hours given to prayer, study, work, meals, and sleep were all fixed, and even the details of dress laid down. Basil did not leave behind him any Rule, properly so called; and it is not easy to determine whether the ancient authorities who seem to attribute one to him are referring to the whole, or to a part of the *Ascetica* that have come down to us under his name. When writing to Gregory of Nazianzus[1] he traced in broad lines the life of the monk as he conceived it, and from the *Ascetica*, especially the 55 chapters known as *The Longer Rules*,[2] and from the monastic catechism in 313 questions and answers, known as *The Shorter Rules*, one could put together a series of fairly detailed regulations. In any case the tradition created by Basil and the writings which have circulated under his name have exercised a very great influence. The fame of the Bishop of Caesarea and the practical nature of his conception of the communal life assured the success of the moderate form of coenobitism and of the domestic discipline which he introduced into the groups under his control.

There was never in the Greek Church any 'Order of St. Basil', and the title 'Basilian' as applied to the monks of the Empire is an invention of Western scholars. But there is no doubt that his monastic system spread almost at once from Pontus into Cappadocia, Paphlagonia, Armenia, and the whole of Asia Minor; in these countries it enjoyed a remarkable success. We have unfortunately no satisfactory statistics of the number of monasteries which sprang up there during the following centuries. But judging from the allusions to them scattered through the Lives of the Saints, from the evidence of Procopius, and from the constant discovery in charters of fresh names of religious foundations whose history remains unknown to us the number of monasteries

---

[1] Ep. 8.   [2] *Regulae fusius tractatae.*

throughout Asia Minor must have been very considerable. It is particularly in this part of the Empire that one finds colonies of monks formed in mountainous districts corresponding to those 'Holy Mountains' which in Europe are still represented by Athos or the Meteora. The origin of these communities is nearly always the same. A holy man, having determined to shun the world, seeks out an accessible spot in the recesses of the neighbouring mountain, and there retires into a cave or builds himself a hut. His retreat is presently discovered, and disciples place themselves under his guidance. A community is thus formed and the building of a monastery begins. The reputation of the master and his disciples spreads, bringing fresh recruits, and it soon becomes necessary to enlarge the accommodation and also to add to the number of hermitages that generally spring up in the neighbourhood of a monastery. We may cite as an example Mt. St. Auxentius, above Chalcedon in Bithynia, which takes its name from the famous hermit who established himself there in the second half of the fifth century; here the religious life flourished for at least eight centuries. In Bithynia, too, was Mt. Olympus, one of the most important of monastic centres, the home through the centuries of many famous ascetes, among them the great St. Johannicius. Mt. Admirable, near Seleucia, owed its renown to St. Simeon Stylites the Younger and his disciples; and opposite to it, in the Black Mountains, was the Scopelos—the Rock—made famous by the Abbot Theodosius. Near Miletus, the mountain celebrated in antiquity under the name of Latmus was taken over by monks, the most noted of whom was St. Paul, who died in 955. Consecrated to the worship of God, the mountain henceforth takes the name of Latros.[1] Monasteries were founded on Mt. Galisius, near Ephesus, for the disciples of the monk Lazarus (*ob.* 1054), who lived several years upon a column. On Mount Kyminas, on the borders of Bithynia and Paphlagonia, we find in the tenth century several holy monks, notably St. Michael Maleinus and St. Athanasius. The latter went thence to found the monastery of Lavra on another holy mountain, destined to become yet more famous —Mt. Athos; and since we have now left the soil of Asia,

---

[1] *Latreuein,* to worship.

we may add a mention of Mt. Ganos in Thrace, of which little is known, and of the Meteora monasteries in Thessaly.

The capital of the Empire was not reached by the monastic tide as quickly as some have asserted. It has been maintained on documentary evidence of little value that the introduction of monasticism into Constantinople dates from the time of Constantine, and some fifteen monasteries are cited as having been founded there during his reign. From a study of more reliable sources, however, we are forced to the conclusion that the first monks established in the capital were heretics attached to the patriarch Macedonius, and that the few monasteries of those days had only an ephemeral existence. The true beginnings of Byzantine monasticism coincide with the reign of Theodosius. Jonas, a soldier from Armenia, founded the monastery of Halmyrissus in Thrace; and the oldest monastery in Constantinople itself, namely, that of Dalmatius, sprang from a hermitage founded by the monk Isaac. These two ascetes must be deemed to be the true fathers of monasticism in the capital. Isaac's foundation was followed by that of Dius, but of its early history little is known. One of the most important monasteries was that of Rufinianae, founded by Rufinus on the coast of Bithynia. Its monks were brought from Egypt, but on Rufinus's fall they returned to their own country. Later Hypatius, a Phrygian, came to Rufinianae and there with two companions he settled. Gradually a small community grew up; Rufinus's monastery was re-formed, and Hypatius was compelled to become its head. For forty years he governed the monastery with success.

A long history is attached to the monastery of the Akoimetoi. Its founder, Alexander, who came to Constantinople from the desert of Chalcis, bringing with him ideas of reform, introduced the practice of continuous prayer. The monks were divided into three choirs who relieved each other in singing the praise of God without ceasing by day or night. Hence the name Akoimetoi, those who never sleep. Under Alexander's successor the monastery was transplanted to Gomon, on the Black Sea, but it returned later to the neighbourhood of Constantinople and was re-established on the Bosphorus opposite the Bay of Sosthenes. Its founder,

Alexander, whose reputation in later years was not un-challenged, was outshone by one of his successors, St. Marcellus.

Once introduced into the capital, monasticism made rapid strides. In the Acts of the Council of 536 may be found the signatures of the representatives of sixty-eight monasteries in Constantinople and of forty in Chalcedon. Their number continued to increase and the list of the foundations that sprang up one after another in the city and its suburbs is interminable. Many of these have some history, some brief hour of fame, but we cannot give details here. It is interest-ing, however, to note that the strange form of asceticism originated by St. Simeon Stylites found its way to the capital. Daniel (*ob.* 518), the first successor of the famous Syrian penitent, lived for many years on a pillar near Anaplus. A number of disciples congregated at its foot and for them the Emperor Leo I built a monastery and provided accommodation for strangers. Daniel was not the only stylite in Constantinople, and even as late as the tenth century he had a successor in the person of St. Luke, whose column stood in the quarter of Eutropius.

With this great increase in the number of monks there immediately arose the necessity for a stricter discipline, and both the ecclesiastical authorities and the State were forced to take measures to correct or forestall abuses and to give a more solid foundation to the institution of monasticism. St. John Chrysostom, great champion as he was of the monastic state, was obliged to insist on the strict observance of the rule of seclusion and to admonish severely those monks who left their monastery and roamed through the streets of the city. More than one bishop doubtless had to recall to their duties the monks of his diocese who, for-getful of one of their principal obligations, were tempted to mingle with the world and busy themselves with secular matters.

Legislation on the part of the Councils was sometimes necessary. We need not discuss the decrees, of limited scope, passed by the Council of Gangra against the Eustathians. More general measures were taken by the Council of Chalcedon, which began by recognizing that for many men the monastic life was nothing more than a pretext for bringing confusion into the affairs of Church and State. Such persons were accused of going from one town to another with the sole object of building monasteries for themselves, and in future no one might found a monastery without the consent of the bishop of the diocese. Monks are to be entirely subject to the bishop, and may not leave their monastery save in case of necessity and with his authorization. Their duty consists in fasting and prayer within the precincts of the monastery. The monastic habit may not be given to a slave without the consent of his master. The religious of either sex, once vowed to God, can never marry. No regularly established monastery can be secularized, nor can its property be alienated.

At times circumstances gave to the Emperors the opportunity of passing laws governing the monks, but these, inspired as they were merely by the need of the moment, were soon disregarded. To Justinian is due the credit of having formulated in his later laws—the *Novels*—the code of monastic legislation. This code gives legal authority to the ecclesiastical canons, and, following in the tradition of St. Basil, regulates the statutes and the main details of the religious life. These dispositions were inspired by a genuine regard for the institution of monasticism. 'The monastic life', said the Emperor in his preface, 'with the contemplation which the monk practises is a holy thing; it leads men's souls to God, and not only does this life serve those who have adopted it, but its purity and its prayers make it useful to all.' Justinian deals mainly, and almost exclusively, with monasteries or coenobia, that is, with monks living, eating, and sleeping in common. He admits, however, a more perfect way, the life of hermits or solitaries, but refrains from detailed regulations for such. When the number of monks in a coenobium becomes very large, two or three buildings must be provided to house them. No religious house may be built without the permission and blessing of the bishop. The monastery must be surrounded by a wall, the door of which is guarded by some of the older and most trusted monks, and no one may pass in or out without the permission of the *Hegoumenos* (abbot). Communities of monks and nuns must have separate quarters, and every precaution is taken that the rule of separation should be strictly observed.

The monastery is placed under the authority of a Superior, elected by the monks. To four or five senior monks, who are in orders, is entrusted the regular performance of the religious services. If they have no church of their own, the monks must attend service in the neighbouring church and immediately afterwards return to the monastery. The noviciate is for three years, during which the postulant wears the dress of a layman. If at the end of that time he has given satisfaction and can prove that he is not a slave, he is granted the habit of a monk. Up to this time he has had the free disposition of his goods, but from the moment of his assuming the habit his property passes to the monastery. The proportion of his fortune that reverts to the wife or children whom the monk has left in the world is fixed by law.

A monk who leaves his monastery cannot be received into another, and property acquired by him reverts to his monastery and to that monastery he himself must be brought back. On a repetition of his offence he must be consigned to military service. No monk may accept the duties of a guardian or any other secular task that might turn him from the service of God. Property once in the possession of the monastery cannot be alienated. Rules are laid down to guide the Superiors in the administration of property, and to guard them against mistakes which might endanger the monastic endowments.

These laws were evidently not made without the cooperation of the ecclesiastical authority. State intervention in such matters is almost always accompanied by disadvantages which show themselves in the course of time. But in general Justinian's legislation was beneficial and well adapted to the regularization of the monastic life. It was definitive and Justinian's successors found little in it to alter. Nor did the Councils of the Church: the Council in Trullo laid down that no one might become a hermit who had not lived under coenobitic rule for three years. The Council of 787, in calling for the suppression of double monasteries, that is to say, of those in which the monks' dwelling was close to and under the same administration as the nuns', was merely restating an article of the original code.

Under these regulations monasteries continued to multiply throughout the Empire. Emperors, princes, wealthy merchants, and other persons of note built monasteries or hospices to the glory of God and as atonement for their sins. A desire for ostentation was sometimes a contributing factor. Nicephorus Phocas (963–9), though a great friend and benefactor of monks, held that the number of monasteries had already passed the bounds of moderation, and that the excessive increase in religious establishments was prejudicial to the institution of monasticism itself. He forbade the creation of new foundations and the enlargement and enrichment of those already in existence. He did not definitely prohibit the bequest of property to the Church, but ordained that the money must be used only to restore buildings fallen into ruin and not to erect new ones. These dispositions were annulled in the reign of Basil II.

Apart from legislation, in the strict sense of the term, the intervention of individuals had no small effect upon the development of the monastic life. The reformer who in the ninth and later centuries had most influence upon Byzantine monasticism was St. Theodore, of the monastery of Studius. Born in Constantinople, he left the world at the age of twenty-two and retired to an estate belonging to his family at Saccoudion on Mt. Olympus. Here, with several companions, he put himself under the guidance of his uncle, St. Plato, who had previously settled on the Sacred Mountain. As a monk Theodore made rapid progress and was soon fitted to assist his uncle in the control of the monastery. With the increasing number of postulants the burden became at last too heavy for the old man, and Theodore was called upon to take his place. When the monks of Saccoudion, headed by their Abbot, took up an uncompromising attitude towards the question of the Emperor Constantine VI's divorce, they brought on themselves a sentence of exile. For a brief interval they returned to Saccoudion, but were obliged once more to leave and take refuge in Constantinople. There they were invited to establish themselves in the Psamathia quarter, in a large monastery founded in

463 by the Consul Studius, and now almost abandoned as a result of the recent period of persecution which had only just come to an end. Under Theodore's control the monastery developed in an extraordinary degree, and we read that the number of 'Studite' monks soon reached a thousand.

But for the wise reforms instituted by Theodore, the weight of responsibility resting upon an abbot would have become well-nigh insupportable. He created a whole hierarchy of dignitaries, superintendents, and other monastic functionaries, each with well-defined duties, from choir-masters and stewards to cooks, infirmary attendants, and carpenters. Every head of a department had to render an account of his service to the abbot, who, by keeping the central control in his own hands, brought order and regularity into the working of the monastery. Theodore drew up a programme for each class of occupation. He even composed little pieces in verse, which summed up for each the duties of his charge, and thus recalled the particular virtues needed in his task. Many monastic regulations attributed to St. Theodore were in fact introduced at Saccoudion by St. Plato. Amongst these is the prohibition against admitting into the monastery not only women, but also female animals. In this Plato would seem not to have introduced any new rule, but only to have reinstated an ancient practice. It is well known how strict is the observance of this rule at Mt. Athos, and how greatly it adds to the austerity of the life in those monasteries. It is by no means certain that it was originally conceived as a safeguard of morality as it is usually interpreted. It would appear that St. Plato wished to remove the abuses that arose from too close an association of monks and laymen, and to remove any mercenary tendency that might easily result from trading in goods belonging to the monastery. In more than one monastery the breeding of cattle was carried on, obliging the monks to house lay servants within their walls. In banning all female domestic animals, Plato put an end to that particular form of trading which specially called for the employment of workers from the world without the monastery.

St. Theodore supplemented these regulations by

introducing a sort of penitential code, attaching punishments to breaches of the common rule or to failures in individual duty. Three times a week he called his monks together to be instructed by lecture or catechism in the virtues of the monastic life—piety, obedience and self-discipline, and the enthusiasm and the fervour which each should bring to the discharge of his own task. He established in the monastery of Studius (we must not call it the 'Studion', a term unknown to the ancients) a minute organization of the communal life, a rigorous discipline, and a severe though reasonable asceticism. These reforms, widely disseminated by his writings, especially by his will, the *Hypotyposis*, and his Catechisms, which last were frequently read in monasteries, gave a new vigour and a new lustre to the religious life of the Eastern Empire. Traces of Theodore's influence are found in the Rule that St. Athanasius of Mount Athos gave to the monastery of Lavra, and in the special monastic constitutions known as *typica*.

From a study of these charters of foundation, a certain number of which have been preserved to us, the oldest of them dating from the ninth century, we can form a vivid picture of life in the monasteries. The regulations of these *typica* are naturally adapted to the laws issued by Justinian which themselves were inspired by the Monastic Rules of St. Basil. As far as liturgical ordinances and the dates of fast-days are concerned they are content to follow the use of Jerusalem, or what is generally known as the *typicon* of St. Sabas. Taken as a whole, the details of these rules, as codified in the *typica*, though not expressly derived from the regulations of St. Theodore the Studite, are yet in such complete accord with his reforming spirit as to leave no doubt of his influence in their composition.

We may take as an instance the Rule of the Euergetis monastery in Constantinople, which was drawn up by Timothy, monk and priest, and later abbot. He was the brother of the founder, Paul, who died in 1054.[1] This *typicon* may usefully serve to illustrate the character of these monastic regulations since it was later used by other founders

---

[1] *Typica* of two kinds are here preserved together, the κτητορικόν and the λειτουργικόν. We have to deal here with the former only.

and had itself drawn material from analogous texts. This is what it tells us of the organization of the monastery.

Its essential part has reference to the life of prayer: the chanting of the services, private devotions, and the chief means of sanctification. The hours to be spent in prayer by day and night are laid down. Mass shall be celebrated daily; the more advanced monks may communicate three times and the others once a week, always by permission of the Superior. Communion must be preceded by confession. The sole confessor is the abbot, who must put himself at the disposal of the penitents twice a day, that is, in the morning and at evening after compline.

During meals, which are eaten in common, someone reads aloud; at no other time may any food or drink be taken. The dietary is specified for ordinary days, for Lent and the two lesser times of fasting, and also for certain days on which better fare is permitted. The food is the same for everyone, except in case of illness. The Brothers are lodged two in a cell; their clothing is supplied from the common stock. Monks in good health are allowed three baths a year, those who are unwell may have more. The number of monks in a monastery is in proportion to its income.

It was the founder's intention that his establishment should be self-governing, and that no one, not even the Patriarch or the Emperor, should be able to take possession of it. The authority of the abbot is paramount, he is the sole spiritual director of the monks, and all owe him respect and obedience. He chooses his steward (*oeconomos*), who, unless unworthy, will ultimately succeed him. Besides the steward, the chief officials to help him are the *skeuophylax* or sacristan, in charge of the church and the sacristy; the *dochiarios* (custodian, treasurer) of money, and the *dochiarios* of goods, such as linen, shoes, and food. To the *epistemonarchos* is confided the maintenance of order and regularity in the monastery. The *trapezarios* has the management of the refectory, and below him come those in charge of the cellar and the bakery.

Founder's Day must be observed, and the anniversaries of certain other benefactors. On these days alms are distributed, but apart from these distributions no poor man should ever

be sent away empty-handed. No women may be admitted
except ladies of very high rank. Travellers and the sick poor
are warmly welcomed and cared for in the hostel or hospital
maintained on their behalf.

The rules of the *typica* constituted a new consecration and
a stricter regulation of the monastic communities. We must
not expect to find in them any concrete details or special
conditions of the life in different monasteries, due to differences of time and place, which would give an individual
character to each establishment. The interior life of a
monastery as portrayed in the *typica* was everywhere the
same: an orderly contemplative existence, in which prayer
took the chief place and for which rules were laid down with
regard to fasting and abstinence, and also concerning manual
labour so far as this was compatible with the austerity of the
ascetic life. Everything was arranged with a view to the
personal sanctification of the monk, not with any idea of
pastoral ministry.

Some *typica* of nunneries have also come down to us.
These are the more important since we have little information on the subject of female monasticism, which is, however,
of very ancient origin and had a development as rapid as the
male branch. Vowed to a strict seclusion in a narrowly
limited field of action, nuns have naturally left less mark than
monks on the history of their times. In Greek hagiography
they play an unobtrusive part, and in order to measure the
attraction of the cloister for the women of East Rome we are
almost reduced to counting the number of convents. We
know that there were a great many, but we can give no
precise figures. Naturally a few special regulations occur, but
otherwise there is little essential difference between the
typica of the women's convents (of which unfortunately few
survive) and those of the monasteries. The most important
of these *typica* are the one long familiar to students which was
framed about 1118 by the Empress Irene for the convent of
the Virgin (τῆς κεχαριτωμένης) and that of Our Lady of
Good Hope, founded in the next century by Theodora and
her husband, the famous general John Comnenus. Like
most of the foundation charters, Theodora's was designed
to protect her new establishment from any hampering out-

side interference. She wished Our Lady of Good Hope to be a free and autonomous convent. To safeguard the religious spirit and the material interests of the house the nuns needed the protection of some influential personage, and, with this object in view, she appointed her sons its *ephoroi* (guardians). The number of nuns, limited at first to thirty, was afterwards raised to fifty. They were divided into two categories, corresponding to the choir nuns and the lay sisters of our days.

The nuns were to be on a footing of complete equality, and the rule permitted no mitigation of the rigour of the common life, except in illness, or in those special circumstances in which, according to the usage of the times, some relaxation of austerity was allowed. For the convent was often the refuge of the victims of great misfortune, while members of the nobility and of the imperial family sometimes sought to end their days in its shelter. Allowance was made for the former state of these ladies, used as they had been to lives of ease and luxury, and, if they so desired, they were permitted to employ a servant.

The convent should have a priest to celebrate the Holy Mysteries and to take the services. He must be of a certain age and of unquestioned honour and virtue. According to the *typicon* of Irene, priests attached to a convent must be eunuchs, but no such stipulation is made in that of Theodora. The obligations on which the foundress laid special stress were those of obedience and poverty. The nuns were not allowed to alienate any goods, and the fruit of their labour became the property of the convent. Rigorous seclusion was enforced and visits were strictly regulated. The day was divided between prayer and work, and it was impressed upon the nuns that they had not left the world in order to live in idleness. The Mother Superior, who is elected by the Sisters, has control of the convent with the help of several assistants, the chief of whom are the *ecclesiarchissa* and the steward. Less important duties are assigned to other nuns. The table fare on feast and ordinary days is regulated, as are also the details of dress.

It was a matter of course that charity should be shown to the poor, and we learn from the *typica* that religious houses often had benevolent institutions, such as hospices, hostelries, or hospitals, attached to them as annexes which were not served by the monks or nuns, but were maintained by the funds of the community. Pacurianus, a 'Great Domestic' of the West under Alexius Comnenus, founded a hospice for old men near the monastery of Petritzos (in Bulgaria). In other places he erected three hostels dependent on this same monastery, where the poor were lodged and cared for free of charge. He also established a monastic school in which six young men were trained in holy learning with a view to ordination. The *typicon* of Michael Attaliates provided for the creation of a hospice at Rodesto and for the distribution of alms to the poor of Constantinople. Attached to the monastery of Pantocrator in the capital was an important hospital, containing fifty beds, which reminds us of a modern clinic. It had a medical staff of sixty persons in addition to supervisors or inspectors, accountants, and numerous subordinates. It had a consulting-room and was divided into five sections, each for a different type of illness and under the care of two doctors with two assistants and several orderlies. A special ward was reserved for epileptics. Besides all this it had a hospice for the aged sick, which would accommodate twenty-six old men. Near the monastery of the Kosmosoteira the founder built a hospital containing thirty-six beds and drew up regulations for its proper management. It included baths to which the public was admitted. The hospital belonging to the monastery of Lips was of more modest proportions and had only fifteen beds.

The *typica* do not as a rule confine themselves to a plain statement of precepts and rules, with an occasional supplementary chapter on the property of the monastery. The founder often prefaces them with an account of the lofty motives that have guided him, and introduces in more or less detail some spiritual instruction, generally inspired by a very high ideal. These documents give the most favourable view of the monastic life; but they show only one side of the picture, and we may be allowed to question whether the reality corresponded at all closely with so noble a conception.

To imagine that the institution of monasticism could have persisted through so many centuries and in so many different lands, without any signs of weakness or decline, would be to put too great a confidence in human nature. Only the strict observance, and not the mere framing of rules, however complete and detailed, can prevent abuses or sustain religious fervour, and it would be rash to assert that such regulations generally succeeded in maintaining at a normal level the practice of monastic virtues. On so delicate a matter as this one must not expect to find any precise information in our historical sources; here the gradual decline to laxity and decay is naturally not depicted. Those hagiographers who have described in most intimate detail the inner life of the monasteries, while avoiding its darker features, for the most part only record examples of holy living and noble action. Nevertheless a few contemporary documents have come down to us in which free expression is given to complaints of the faithlessness of monks to their duties, and the consequent decline of coenobitism.

In his novel on religious houses the Emperor Nicephorus Phocas denounced the abuses arising from the accumulation of wealth by monasteries, and spared the monks no unpalatable truth. One of the sharpest criticisms of the monastic life comes from the ranks of the clergy in a treatise by Eustathius, Archbishop of Salonica (*ob.* 1198). The picture he draws of the moral condition of monks was no doubt a true one for his time and diocese. He is careful, however, to note that there were many virtuous monks in the capital of the Empire and its suburbs, but that does not imply that outside Salonica none but regular and devoted houses existed. The causes he alleges for the moral decline of monasteries undoubtedly produced similar effects in other places. The manner of enlisting new recruits to the order left much to be desired, and men entered the monastic life less with the object of serving God than of making sure of their daily bread without working for it. In this way monasteries became filled with the coarse and ignorant, whose one idea was to profit by the material advantages thus provided and to live a life of ease. Their zeal went no further than an attempt to add to the property of the community; but greater wealth was accompanied by greater worldliness. Study was neglected, the most precious books in the library were judged useless and sold. The abbot, whose duty it was to train his subordinates in the paths of virtue, was content to instruct them in the things that concerned material existence and the administration of property. He was the manager of an agricultural estate rather than a spiritual director. Such according to Eustathius was the life of the monks as he knew it. He had seen the failure of his efforts at reform, and gives free rein to his feelings in a satire, in which, though many features are obviously exaggerated, the main causes of the decay of the religious spirit are clearly set forth.

Among pernicious influences was the habit of granting monasteries to laymen. This custom, to which John IV, Patriarch of Antioch (1081–1118), devoted a pamphlet of vigorous protest and which was condemned by the Councils, was widely practised by the Iconoclast Emperors, notably by Constantine V. To these sovereigns it offered a means of rewarding political or military services to the detriment of the monks, their resolute opponents in matters of religious policy. The restoration of orthodoxy caused a temporary lull in a practice so harmful to the institution of monasticism. But it was soon revived in a form that seemed on the face of it completely beneficial. Monasteries with buildings in disrepair and likely to fall into ruin were made over to wealthy laymen or high officials on condition that they should be restored or rebuilt. By degrees this pretext was made to serve for the giving away of religious houses that were in no serious need of repair, then of others still less so, and finally of even the most richly endowed monasteries.

This system proved disastrous for the monasteries. The grantee or *charistikarios* ended by seizing all the goods of the monks, leaving them only a fraction of their revenue. It was impossible for them to celebrate their feasts with the ceremony enjoined by the founder, or to continue their daily distribution of alms or food to the poor, and they were themselves left with only just enough to live upon. They became entirely dependent on the goodwill of the new owner, and the abbot lost all authority over his monks, who were often forced to stoop to any dealings that would bring them the means of subsistence. This state of affairs was even more subversive of discipline in the women's convents. The grantees, with their womenfolk and servants, were in con-

stant contact with the nuns, who had to tax their ingenuity
to the utmost in order to obtain the necessities of life. The
ill effects of the extension of such a practice from which soon
only the most recently founded convents were free may
easily be imagined, and measures to remedy the abuse were
of little avail.[1]

Only by the gradual slackening of traditional observances
can one explain the transformation of coenobitism into the
system known as idiorrhythmicism which to-day may be
studied on Mt. Athos, where it was introduced in the
fifteenth century. Its main effect was to set aside the monastic
rule of poverty. The money brought in by a monk on
entering the monastery, as well as the product of his work
there, remains his own property. If he is a tailor, he may sell
the clothes he makes, if an artist, the works of art for which
he is lucky enough to find a purchaser; and he is free to deal
as he pleases with the sums thus acquired and even to dispose
of them by will. Another feature of idiorrhythmicism consisted in the grouping of the monks within the monastery
into 'families'. These families consist of a president with a
few monks, perhaps five or six, adopted by him in proportion to the resources at his disposal for their upkeep; for,
while bread, wine, oil, and wood are supplied by the monastery, the president has to provide everything else. Each
family occupies quarters with a separate kitchen and refectory, but all assemble for the services, which are celebrated
as in coenobitic monasteries. It has, however, been observed
that the religious rites are much less impressive, since the
system of division into families does not permit of sufficient
attention being given to their preparation, especially to the
adequate training of voices for the choir. Only three times a
year do all the monks take a meal together in the common
refectory. One would expect to find the abbot acting as the
connecting link between the different groups, but idiorrhythmicism has no place for such a dignitary. The central
authority lies with the council of presidents of families, which
itself chooses one of its members to direct its discussions.
So bizarre a system as this can only be regarded as an
obvious sign of the decay of the religious spirit.

[1] Cf. the struggle against the system of Commendam in the West.

The purity of monastic tradition found an enemy of another sort in the mystic doctrines leading to Hesychasm, which deeply troubled the peace of Mt. Athos. The life of solitude and contemplation (*Hesychia*) had long formed part of Byzantine religion, though it will be remembered that St. Basil, while not forbidding eremitism, did not wish to see an increase in the number of hermits, and that Justinian's legislation was inspired by a similar desire. Hermits or hesychasts were regarded as belonging to the highest grade of the monastic life. To become one was a privilege reserved for those coenobites who had given proof of their sanctity and were farthest advanced in perfection. St. Athanasius, the founder of the Lavra, stipulates in his Rule that out of 120 monks only five shall be permitted to live the life of a solitary, that is, to withdraw into separate cells in order to give themselves up to prayer and meditation whilst remaining under the control of the abbot. In the fourteenth century, thanks mainly to Gregory the Sinaite, daring theories, not unlike those of the Indian fakirs, spread among these solitaries and other independent hermits concerning the vision of the Divine Light and the mechanical methods for its attainment. The system may have developed from the mysticism of the celebrated Simeon, the New Theologian (*ob.* 1022), in combination with the extravagant theories of the Massaliani and Bogomils. The Calabrian monk Barlaam vigorously attacked these aberrations, but they found a defender, at least so far as concerns the theological side of the system, in Gregory Palamas. A lengthy controversy followed and much polemical writing. Councils debated the matter. It was Palamas who prevailed, and with him prevailed also Hesychasm, though freed from some of the more grotesque features which had proved attractive to rude and simple natures. But Hesychasm was incompatible with a healthy spirituality or a reasonable asceticism, and it is to this day a running sore in the body of Greek monasticism.

It has been impossible to ignore the harmful germs that in the course of centuries have threatened the existence and lessened the vitality of the great institution of monasticism, though without succeeding in destroying it, but the defects which we have been obliged to record did not prevent it from enjoying long and brilliant periods of prosperity. Amongst a people devoted to religion, in an Empire where the Church was so closely bound to the State, where the sovereign constantly intervened in ecclesiastical affairs, and monks were officially recognized, monasticism was bound to play an important part. In the first place by virtue of their reputation for saintliness famous monks often exercised a personal influence over Emperors and high officers of State. An unlettered man, like Simeon Stylites, was led to intervene in questions of general concern to which his mode of life seemed utterly foreign. 'Never losing interest', said Theodoret, 'in the welfare of the Churches, he led the campaign against Pagan infidelity, denounced the audacity of the Jews and scattered groups of heretics. He sent messages on such subjects to the Emperor, stimulated the zeal of magistrates for the things of God, and even warned the pastors of the churches to give more attention to the welfare of their flocks.'

Daniel, another famous stylite,[1] had frequent dealings with Emperors and ministers of State. The Emperor Leo I often visited him, and on one occasion brought the king of the Lazes in order to get the stylite's decision on a disputed political question. There are many instances of sovereigns asking simple monks for impartial advice and the benefit of their prayers.

It was not only by individual action that monks exerted their influence. In an Empire shaken by heresies continual meddling by the temporal power in matters that should properly be left to theologians inevitably brought about the intervention of religious bodies directly interested in the purity of the Faith. Monks often worked by secret and circumspect methods that can only be guessed at by their effects; but it is rather the solemn demonstrations or prolonged struggles, in which great numbers of monks, if not the whole monastic body, put their prestige and strength at the service of the Church, that have left visible traces on the pages of history. In times of crisis, when religious passions were aroused, when questions of dogma and discipline were bitterly disputed, and the tradition of orthodox doctrine was

[1] Cf. p. 145 *supra*.

threatened by innovators, the monks were willing temporarily to renounce the peace of the cloister. But it would be rash to claim that at all times and in all places their intervention in theological quarrels was happy and praiseworthy, or of service to religion. At a time when the army of monks formed a confused and undisciplined crowd and they had to be forbidden the towns, lest, under pretext of doing good, they should upset the public peace, Theodosius could write to Ambrose: 'Monachi multa scelera faciunt.' It only needed a few bold spirits to launch them upon demonstrations, not only regrettable in themselves, but quite incompatible with the life of prayer and contemplation to which they were vowed.

The role played by the archimandrite Barsumas at the Robber Council of Ephesus, to which he had gone with a thousand monks in support of the doctrine of Eutyches, is only too well known. Bishop Flavian, having appealed to Pope Leo against his condemnation, was violently attacked by Barsumas's band, who handled him so brutally that he died three days later of his wounds. One could give instances of similar interventions on the part of the monks, less violent perhaps, but hardly less regrettable. The great heresies of those times found all too often a favourable soil for their development in the monasteries. In the East, especially in Egypt, the Monophysite party had no keener supporters than the monks, and in Palestine the Origenist monks had to be dispersed. But it would be incorrect to extend the blame to all the monks of the Empire. While bearing in mind exceptional cases such as these, one may say that in general monks have readily ranged themselves on the side of orthodoxy and maintained happy relations with the supporters of the true doctrine. Thus Antony 'the first monk' did not hesitate to quit his desert retreat and appeared in Alexandria to champion orthodoxy and uphold the faith of Nicaea. St. Athanasius greatly befriended the monks. Theodoret, who was, with Flavian, a victim of the Robber Council of Ephesus, at the same time as he appeals to the Pope, writes to the monks of Constantinople, assuring them of his devotion to orthodoxy and of his anxiety to avoid the very appearance of being severed from their communion.

Dalmatius, a monk of Constantinople, answered the appeal of the bishops assembled at the Council of Ephesus: leaving his monastery he led the monks of the capital to the imperial palace and received from Theodosius II the pledge of his adherence to the orthodox faith. When the usurper Basiliscus was favouring the Monophysites, it was to the pillar saint Daniel that the folk of Constantinople resorted: they finally persuaded him to descend from his pillar. His feet were so swollen that he could not walk, but he was carried into the city. In St. Sophia Basiliscus was constrained in the presence of Daniel to abjure his heresy. When in the seventh century the house of Heraclius sought to reconcile the upholders of the doctrine of the Single Nature in Christ by propounding the theory of the Single Will or the Single Energy it was again another monk, Maximus the Confessor, who was the life and soul of the orthodox resistance. Threats, exile, and finally torture all alike failed to break his indomitable resolution.

It was during the period of the Iconoclast Emperors that the energy of the monks was seen at its brightest. Constantine V was fully aware of the influence which the monks enjoyed and tried at first to win them over to his own ideas, but he was met by a determined resistance. Exasperated by his failure, the Emperor persecuted his opponents. In 761 he put to torture the hermit Andrew Calybites. Stephen the Younger saw his monastery sacked, and when thrown into prison he found more than 300 monks locked up for the same cause. At length in 765 he was put to death at the Emperor's order. The populace was incited against the monks, a number of whom were made to file into the hippodrome amid shouts and jeers, each monk holding a nun by the hand. The persecution was not confined to the capital but spread to the provinces: monasteries were sacked and in the public square of Ephesus many monks were given the choice of marriage or death.

In the later stage of the Iconoclast movement it was Theodore the leader of the Studite monks who headed the opposition to the Emperor. Under Leo the Armenian, in an assembly convened by the Emperor, Theodore insisted that the affairs of the Church concerned the clergy only and that the Emperor's authority was limited to secular administration. An imperial decree was forthwith issued which imposed silence on Catholics in matters of faith. To this Theodore refused to submit and organized public resistance. On Palm Sunday a great procession of monks carrying the forbidden images was seen to issue from the monastery. By order of the Emperor Theodore was then sent into exile. During that exile which lasted for twelve years, by his letters, his catechisms, and messages he never ceased to encourage the monastic resistance and continued to be the moving spirit in the opposition to the Emperor. Many of his disciples suffered martyrdom and from his own letters we learn of the sufferings—imprisonment, scourging, and torture—which he and his followers had to endure. On one occasion Theodore was himself condemned to a hundred strokes of the lash; he was left lying on the ground unable to move, eat, or sleep; by the devoted care of his disciple Nicholas he was slowly nursed back to life, taking four months to regain his strength.

The cause of the icons won the day; the heroic efforts of the Studite were apparently crowned with success, but we must not overestimate his triumph. The master idea in the life of Theodore was to win for the Church independence in its own sphere. In this he failed: the tradition of Caesaropapism which dated back from the earliest days of Byzantium emerged from the Iconoclast controversy unshaken. While one must admire Theodore's courage which never yielded under the brutal trials to which it was subjected, it must at the same time be admitted that his temperament was lacking in pliancy and breadth of mind and that his counsels were rarely inspired by moderation. Moreover, by no means all his monks, including even those who shared his views on orthodoxy, approved his intransigent attitude. Those of Mt. Olympus, for instance, led by St. Johannicius, were in favour of a more moderate course. That policy of uncompromising opposition their master Theodore handed on to the Studites with serious results, as in their resistance to the Patriarch Methodius, and the atmosphere they created was perhaps not without influence on the troubles which marked the advent of Photius, or on the events under Michael

Cerularius, with their well-known consequences. But with Theodore's death there disappeared the last of the great monks to intervene decisively in times of crisis.

That monastic intervention in politico-religious disputes was so often crowned with success is due not merely to the influence of a few outstanding personalities, but to the wide popularity of the monastic body as a whole. The monks were loved by the people, from whom indeed their numbers were mostly drawn; the name *kalogeros*, 'good old man', a usual way of addressing them, is evidence of their popularity. They were esteemed for their austerities and for the practice of those essential virtues which were the goal of the religious life. The rule of celibacy earned for them a peculiar respect and placed them far higher in popular regard than the married clergy, who were excluded from the episcopate. The glory of the holiness of the famous men who had come from the monasteries was reflected upon all the members of the order: they were looked upon as men of God. The older monks in particular inspired confidence, and their advice, known to be disinterested, was in constant demand. They were chosen as directors of conscience, and confession was often made to the more saintly of them, even though they were not in priest's orders. Finally they were beloved for their traditional hospitality and their generosity in distributing alms to the utmost limit of their resources.

Nevertheless, the monastic life, as it developed in the Eastern Empire, was not specially organized with a view to the pastoral ministry—monks being for the most part laymen—nor even with a view to charitable works or what we should call social service. The aspirant's intention on entering the monastery is to serve God by working for his own perfection and salvation; it is no burning zeal for the welfare of others that moves him. Whether he wishes to consecrate to God the flower of his youth, seeks in the cloister a peaceful refuge after a life of storm and bitter disillusionment, or shuts himself up in expiation of his sins, the idea of apostleship does not seem to haunt him. Eastern monasticism has known no development parallel to that brought about in the West by the variety of Orders and religious Congregations, each of which responded to a special need and sprang up at

the moment that this need made itself felt. In the West side
by side with the contemplative Orders arose other communities whose members, while working for the salvation of
their own souls, could at the same time engage in the works
of mercy both corporal and spiritual. The great principles
of religion which inspire the monk, whether he be Greek
or Latin, were never in any way hostile to the creation of
monasteries which admitted, alongside of the obligation of
prayer and austerities, practical works of charity for the
world outside, such as popular preaching, instruction,
missions, and service in hospitals. But Greek monasticism
seems to have been arrested in its free development; the
causes of this arrested development are too complex for us
to attempt to unravel. They were perhaps connected in
some way with Justinian's legislation, the effect of which was
to mould all forms of monastic life to a definite and uniform
pattern, subject it to the control of the civil administration,
and discourage in advance any bold initiative. Greek
monasticism never found its place within a powerful organization; it has never been subjected to a rigorous discipline
or controlled by a permanent and unquestioned authority.
And thus, lacking this organization and direction, it has
been unable to make full use of its spiritual forces which are
clearly in large measure wasted.

One is forced to think that here the Schism barred the
way to progress and kept monasticism in a deplorable
stagnation.

The wonderful multiplication of religious Orders in the
West from the twelfth century to this day, with their fresh
blossoming in the sixteenth century, should have made
manifest the happy fruits of a more flexible adaptability; it
should have provoked imitation in the East, or better still
emulation. The Greek Church either could not know of
such developments or affected to ignore them, in the same
way as a man will ignore his next-door neighbour, under the
pretext that the fellow has no business to teach him how to
behave.

In this rapid review we have dealt with the essential
features of the organization and religious action of Byzantine
monasticism. But we would not entirely pass over another

aspect of the monastic life, though there is no need to dwell at length upon so well known a subject. We refer to the intellectual activities of the monks and the traces left by them in the history of art and literature. In the monasteries painters found opportunity for the development of their talent, and it was often the monks themselves who covered the walls of their churches with beautiful frescoes, or guided the hand of the artist in mosaic. But amongst the work that alternated with prayer and psalmody in the monastery, the copying of manuscripts unquestionably occupied the first place. It is needless to recall all that monks have done for the preservation of the works of classical literature, or to dwell upon the famous schools of calligraphy that arose among them. During the great periods of Byzantine history the art of the calligrapher was supplemented by that of the miniaturist, and many beautifully illuminated manuscripts from Byzantine monastic *scriptoria* are reckoned to-day among the greatest treasures of our libraries.

It is not by copies alone that monks have enriched the storehouse of literature. They have produced many original works, ascetical, theological, and historical. A separate place must be reserved for poetry. Greek monks have composed many hymns with which Latin hymnography can but rarely stand comparison. Finally their Lives of the Saints bring before us the great figures of monasticism, and while recording the virtues of these holy men give details of the customs and events of their day that one would seek in vain elsewhere. Here again the Greek can more than hold his own: he has no need to fear the rivalry of the hagiographers of the medieval West.

HIPPOLYTE DELEHAYE

VI

BYZANTINE ART

THE church of St. Sophia in Constantinople is the master-piece of Byzantine art, and it is at the same time one of those monuments where some of the most characteristic features of that art appear most clearly. Thus if one would understand the nature of the Christian art of the East and in what its originality consisted, one must go first of all to this essential building—to this 'Great Church' as it was called throughout the East during the Middle Ages.

When, in 532, the Emperor Justinian decided to rebuild the church which Constantine had formerly erected and dedicated to the Holy Wisdom—for this is the meaning of St. Sophia—he was determined that the new sanctuary should surpass all others in splendour. In the words of a Byzantine chronicler, it was 'a church, the like of which has never been seen since Adam, nor ever will be'. A circular was issued to all the provincial governors, instructing them to send to Constantinople the richest spoils in ancient monuments and the most beautiful marbles from the most famous quarries in the Empire. To add to the magnificence of the building and dazzle the eye of the beholder by a display of unrivalled wealth Justinian determined to make a lavish use of costly materials, gold, silver, ivory, and precious stones. A taste for the sumptuous in all its forms—a passion for splendour—is indeed one of the foremost characteristics of Byzantine art.

For the execution of his design and the realization of his dream the Emperor was fortunate enough to discover two architects of genius, Anthemius of Tralles and Isidore of Miletus, both of whom, it must be borne in mind, came from Asia. Contemporary writers are unanimous in praise of their knowledge, skill, daring, and inventive power; and, since Justinian grudged neither money nor labour, the work progressed at an amazing speed. In less than five years St. Sophia was completed, and on 27 December 537 it was solemnly consecrated by the Emperor.

It has been truly said that the Great Church is 'one of the mightiest creations in all architecture', a statement the truth of which is clearly shown by a close study of this famous monument. The impression given by the exterior is, it is true, by no means striking; a sixth-century Byzantine building, with its bare walls of brick, always presents a somewhat poor and monotonous aspect from without. But before entering the basilica, when one has crossed the space formerly occupied by the great atrium, surrounded by porticoes, and the narthex which opens into the church by nine doors, the effect produced by the interior is in truth incomparable. A vast rectangle, 77 metres by 71·70 in area, forms a broad nave flanked by aisles with galleries above them which pass over the narthex and extend all round the church. At a height of 55 metres from the ground this central nave is crowned by an enormous dome, 31 metres across, which rests upon four great arches supported by four massive piers. Whereas the arches on the north and south sides of the nave are filled by solid walls pierced with windows and carried on two tiers of pillars, those on the east and west are buttressed by two semi-domes, each of which in its turn is supported by two great semicircular niches and in this way strength and balance are given to this astonishing central dome. An apse projects from the middle of the hemicycle which is covered by the eastern semi-dome; *exedrae*, embellished with columns, together with the arcades on the right and left serve to connect the nave with the aisles. But what most impresses the beholder is the dome—henceforth a characteristic feature of Byzantine architecture—which has truly been described by a sixth-century writer as 'a work at once marvellous and terrifying', seeming, so light and airy it was, 'rather to hang by a golden chain from heaven than to be supported on solid masonry'.

There was doubtless nothing new in such a plan. St. Sophia is related to the type of building, familiar in Asia Minor since the fifth century, known as the domed basilica. But, in virtue of its great size, harmony of line, boldness of conception, and constructive skill, it appears none the less as a true creation—'a marvel of stability, daring, fearless logic, and science', as Choisy puts it. When on the day of its inauguration Justinian saw the fulfilment of his dream, one can well imagine that in a transport of enthusiasm he did indeed exclaim: 'Glory be to God who hath deemed me worthy to complete so great a work. I have outdone thee, O Solomon!'

The decoration which covers the interior of St. Sophia is of equal significance in the history of Byzantine art, the splendour of its ornament designed to dazzle the beholder being no less characteristic than its masterly use of architectural forms. Tall columns of porphyry, white marble, and verd antique, crowned by marble capitals, wrought like goldsmith's work and often picked out by touches of blue and gold, rise from the pavement of mosaic and marble, which has been likened to a garden where the rich lawns are strewn with purple flowers. In the spandrels and round the soffits of the arches, delicate decorative carvings of an unmistakably oriental style stand out around disks of porphyry and verd antique, like lacework against a dark ground. The walls are sheeted over with marbles of many colours, their tones blended as if by the most skilful of painters, giving the effect of rich and velvety oriental carpets. And above, on the curves of the vaults, on the pendentives, on the conch of the apse, the crown of the dome, and on the walls that fill the great lateral arches, brilliant mosaics shone out from the dark blue and silver backgrounds that the new art—and this was one of its most essential innovations— was beginning to substitute for the light backgrounds of Alexandrian painting. When St. Sophia had been converted into a mosque the Turks covered every representation of the human figure in these mosaics with a coating of whitewash or paint. Of recent years the process of uncovering the mosaics has been conducted under the authority of the Turkish Government;[1] when the whole work is finished the church will recover still more completely its marvellous splendour. It must, however, be noted that most of the

[1] This work has been under the direction of Professor Whittemore: he has completely cleared the narthex and over the southern door he has disclosed a fine mosaic which appears to date from the tenth century. In the interior of the church in the tribune over the right aisle he has uncovered some curious mosaics of the eleventh and twelfth centuries representing portraits of emperors. For the reports of Professor Whittemore's work see the bibliographical note at p. 405 *infra*.

mosaics in Justinian's church were of a purely ornamental character and that the majority of the figure subjects date from the tenth and eleventh centuries. But from the first the whole decorative scheme showed a wonderful sense of colour, which delighted in skilful combinations of tints and play of light; scorning simplicity, it aimed rather at a dazzling magnificence. To this wonderful decoration, which fortunately still exists, must be added the lost splendours of the pulpit or ambo—the dull gleam of its silver mingling with the glitter of precious stones and the radiance of rare marbles—of the iconostasis in chased silver that enclosed the sanctuary, of the altar in solid gold, shining with rare jewels and enamels; and of the silver canopy or ciborium over the altar, enriched with silk and gold embroideries between its columns. Add to that the beauty of the lighting which at night made the church shine with a fiery splendour and proclaimed to sailors from afar the glory of Justinian and the end of their voyage. Contemporaries, one can well understand, could not sufficiently admire this St. Sophia, 'the marvellous unique building which words are powerless to describe'. Procopius records in moving language its effect upon the visitor. 'On entering the church to pray', he says, 'one feels at once that it is the work, not of man's effort or industry, but in truth the work of the Divine Power; and the spirit, mounting to heaven, realizes that here God is very near and that He delights in this dwelling that He has chosen for Himself.' And one can understand that the popular imagination, which had attached a whole cycle of picturesque legends to the dome of St. Sophia, should, even several centuries later, have easily believed that God in His mercy had received Justinian into Paradise for the sole reason that he had built the Great Church.

Neither the striking success of St. Sophia nor the characteristic features of its style could, however, be understood or explained without presupposing a long period of patient research and resourceful experiment. From the day at the beginning of the fourth century, when by the will of Constantine Christianity became a State religion—and perhaps even before this splendid triumph—a great and

fruitful artistic movement had developed during the course
of two centuries and spread throughout the East, in Egypt,
Syria, Mesopotamia, Asia Minor, Armenia, and elsewhere.
This movement, which was to culminate in the triumph of
the new style in the sixth century, naturally took a different
form in different places; there was a Christian art peculiar to
Egypt, one to Mesopotamia, and another to Asia Minor,
each of which had its own character. But beneath this
diversity of form a few general principles can be traced which
show themselves in certain essential features.

Christian art, as it took form in the East at the beginning
of the fourth century, was faced by a twofold source of
inspiration. On the one hand there was the classical tradition of Hellenistic culture still living and brilliantly fostered
in the large cities, such as Alexandria, Antioch, and Ephesus;
and on the other, there was the oriental tradition, that of the
old Iranian or Semitic East, which in contact with Sassanid
Persia at this time came to life again throughout the interior
of Egypt, Syria, Mesopotamia, and Armenia, and drove
back the Greek influence which had long been triumphant.
Christianity in its hatred of paganism, though unable to cut
itself off completely from the splendour of classic antiquity,
gladly adopted the methods of these indigenous arts which
had suddenly awakened from sleep, and willingly set itself
to learn from the East. Hence was to arise this dualism of
two opposing influences which would endure as long as
Byzantine art itself; indeed it is the combination of these two
influences which gives to Byzantine art its peculiar character.
The debt of the new art to this double tradition we must now
seek to define.

From the beginning of the fourth century triumphant
Christianity had covered the whole East with a wealth of
sumptuous churches, and for these new churches new architectural forms were created. Alongside the Hellenistic
basilica with its timber roof appeared the Eastern barrel-
vaulted basilica (of which the origin, it seems, should be
sought in Mesopotamia); while in addition to the plain
rectilinear basilican form appeared the church of circular,
octagonal, or cruciform plan. In particular, the new architecture acquired from Iran the use of the dome, the model of

which it found in the Persian monuments of Seleucia and Ctesiphon, and crowned with it the new types of building that it invented, such as the domed basilica, or the churches on a centralized or radiate plan. The dome was supported either by squinches (*trompes d'angle*) after the Eastern fashion, or, in the more scientific and more Greek manner, by pendentives.

In the decoration of the churches a like development was taking place. A rich and complicated ornamentation of a somewhat heavy and wholly oriental exuberance covered the walls with luxuriant foliage, in which a host of birds and other creatures disported themselves amongst curving arabesques. From the East came also the technique of this decoration, in which the contrasting blacks and whites alternating on the neutral background supplied by the lightly incised stone gave a charming effect of colour which is absent from the high relief and bold modelling of antique sculptured ornament. On the walls the harmony of classic proportion was replaced by the brilliant effect of polychrome marbles. From Persia came also the arts of enamel and cloisonné work, and the lavish use of sumptuous and coloured fabrics. All this gave to the new art a definitely oriental character.

But the embellishment of the new churches consisted above all in the covering of their walls and vaults with long cycles of frescoes and resplendent mosaics, in which Christian heroes and the events of sacred story stand out against a background of dark blue. In representing them the simple and familiar lines which early Christian art had favoured gave place to majestic and solemn figures of a more individual and realistic type; the primitive symbolism of former times was replaced by the historical and monumental style, and a new iconography arose for the illustration of the sacred themes.

Christian art undoubtedly retained many of the customs and traditions of pagan workshops—the secular motives, rustic themes, and mythological subjects dear to Alexandrian art; and from classical tradition it further inherited a feeling for beauty of design, dignity of pose, elegance in drapery, sobriety, and clearness of treatment. But its chief aim in the decoration of its churches was the instruction and edification of the faithful. The wall-paintings and mosaics were intended to form, as it were, a vast volume open to the view of the illiterate, like a splendidly illuminated Bible in which they could learn with their eyes the great events of Christian history. From the first we find an attempt to illustrate the Sacred Books, and this illustration shows great differences of style in the different places of its origin. For the Gospels there was the version of Alexandria, still entirely under the spell of Hellenistic feeling and grace, and another version of Antioch, more dramatic and more faithful to realism. For the Psalter there was both an 'aristocratic' version, imbued throughout with classic tradition, and a monastic or theological version, remarkable for its realistic style, search for expression, and close observation of nature. Thus can be traced side by side the two opposing traditions, which were by their combination to form Byzantine art.

As instances of the creations of this great artistic movement, we may mention the admirable basilicas still standing in the dead cities of central Syria, namely those of Rouweiha, Mchabbak, Tourmanin, Qalb Louzé, and the monastery of St. Simeon Stylites at Kalat Seman, justly called 'the archaeological gem of Central Syria'; the oldest of the Armenian churches, the originality and influence of which must not, however, be exaggerated; those of Asia Minor, particularly that at Meriamlik in Cilicia, the earliest known example of a domed basilica, which seems to have played an essential part in the transformation of Eastern elements in accordance with the spirit of Greece; at Salonica, the fine basilica of the Virgin (Eski-Djuma), the domed basilica of St. Sophia, and that of St. Demetrius, which with its five naves, lofty columns, and its walls brilliantly decorated with splendid mosaics and marble facing was, before its destruction by fire in 1917, one of the wonders of East Christian art; especially also at Salonica the mosaics of St. George and those of the chapel of Hosios David; and at Ravenna, the Byzantine city where Oriental influences were paramount, the mosaics of the Baptistery of the Orthodox, and, perhaps the most exquisite example that survives of the Christian art of the time, the wonderful decoration of the Mausoleum of Galla Placidia.

It is primarily in the chief Hellenistic centres of the East —in 'the triple constellation' of Alexandria, Antioch, and Ephesus—that we must seek the sources of the great movement from which the new art was to arise. Constantinople, though the capital of the Empire, seems to have played a far smaller part than these three cities in the development of Christian art in the fourth and fifth centuries. But if she created little herself at that time, she has the great honour of having welcomed the varied elements offered by different regions within the Empire, of having co-ordinated, transformed, and hallowed them through the construction of a great masterpiece. It was in Constantinople that an 'imperial art' arose in the sixth century: an official art, the essential aim of which was the glorification of God and the Emperor, an oriental art embodying the lessons both of Greece and of the ancient Asiatic East, an art complex and manifold, secular as well as religious; and it is in Justinian's time that this art, which may henceforth be called Byzantine, has expressed itself fully and in a definitive form.

But St. Sophia is by no means the only creation of what has aptly been called the First Golden Age of Byzantine art. At this time, with unrivalled skill, use was made of every type of architectural construction: the Hellenistic basilica at Ravenna in Sant' Apollinare Nuovo (between 515 and 545) and Sant' Apollinare in Classe (between 534 and 549), and in the beautiful church of Parenzo in Istria (between 532 and 543); the domed churches built on a centralized or radiate plan of Saints Sergius and Bacchus (between 526 and 537) at Constantinople and of San Vitale (between 536 and 547) at Ravenna; the domed basilica type in St. Irene (532) at Constantinople; the five-domed cruciform church in the Holy Apostles (536–45) at Constantinople (destroyed by the Turks shortly after 1453), and in the Church of St. John at Ephesus, the ruins of which have been exposed by the recent excavations. Already we may see in several buildings the plan of the Greek cross soon to become the classic type of Byzantine churches. Never has Christian art been at one and the same time more varied, more creative, scientific, and daring. The characteristic features of St. Sophia appear in a number of other buildings; for example in the cistern of Bin-bir-Direk at Constantinople, which experts are inclined to recognize as the work of Anthemius, or in the aqueduct of Justinian, the work of an unknown master who was undoubtedly an engineer of great ability. In all these buildings we find the same inventive power, the same skill in the solution of the most delicate problems of construction, the same alert activity, and in each of the churches there was, as in St. Sophia, the same wealth of decoration in the form of carved marble capitals, polychrome marble facings—a notable example of which is the apse of the basilica in Parenzo —and above all, in the play of light upon the mosaics.

Of many of these great works there remains, alas, nothing but a memory. In St. Sophia, as we have seen, only some of the mosaics of Justinian's time survive. The magnificent decoration of the Church of the Holy Apostles, one of the masterpieces of sixth-century art, is known to us solely from its description given by Nicholas Mesarites at the beginning of the thirteenth century: events in the life of Christ and in the preaching of Christianity by the Apostles were depicted in chronological order, and far above, in the height of the domes, there were represented the Transfiguration, Crucifixion, Ascension, and Pentecost. This decoration must have been one of the largest and most beautiful compositions of sixth-century Byzantine art, and it would seem that we must recognize in it the handiwork of an artist of genius. A note in the margin of Mesarites' manuscript tells us that the artist's name was Eulalius. From another source we learn that Eulalius, with a just pride in his work, inserted his own portrait into one of the sacred scenes, namely that of the Holy Women at the Tomb, 'in his usual dress and looking exactly as he appeared when he was at work on these paintings'. This curious incident, doubtless unique in the history of Byzantine art, recalls to mind the practice of fifteenth-century Italian artists.

The greater part of the mosaics of St. Demetrius at Salonica have also perished, having been destroyed by the fire of 1917. They formed a series of votive offerings recalling the favours granted by the Saint—the only instance of this theme found in Byzantine art. Three panels alone of this beautiful decoration now remain, hanging, like icons, at the opening of the apse. One of them, which represents St. Demetrius standing between the founders of the church, is a masterpiece of vigorous expression and technical skill. It dates probably from the first third of the seventh century. It is in the West therefore, and above all at Ravenna, that we must look for works of Justinian's century.

Three of the Ravenna churches, namely Sant' Apollinare Nuovo, Sant' Apollinare in Classe, and San Vitale, still retain an important part of their mosaics. In the first of these buildings there are three zones, one over another, representing scenes from the life of Christ, figures of saints and prophets, and two processions, one of male and the other of female saints, advancing towards Christ and the Virgin. In the uppermost of these zones we may note the contrast between the series of miracles, still evidently inspired by the art of the Catacombs, and the cycle of the Passion, which is treated in a definitely historical style, and with obvious anxiety to detract in no way from the Divine Majesty. The two sumptuous processions of saints just referred to are worthy of special attention, for they have no parallel in Byzantine art. Their brilliantly clad figures in their charming poses suggest a distant memory of the Panathenaic frieze. From every point of view these mosaics of Sant' Apollinare Nuovo hold an important place in the evolution of Byzantine iconography. Of no less historic interest is the decoration of Sant' Apollinare in Classe where the curious representation of the Transfiguration appears as a last effort—at once complicated and subtle—of the symbolism of former days. But the most striking of all the compositions in the three churches is undoubtedly that in the choir of San Vitale. Round the altar are grouped episodes foretelling and glorifying the sacrifice of the Divine Lamb, and the whole design is inspired and unified by this sublime idea. Reminiscences of primitive Christian art are still blended with the feeling for realism and the sense of life and nature characteristic of the new style. The mosaics of the apse, a little later in date (about 547), show this style in its perfection. In the conch is the imposing figure of Christ, seated on the globe of the world, accompanied by saints and archangels. But most remarkable of all are the two famous scenes in which Justinian and Theodora appear in all the glory of their imperial pomp, portraits full of life and expression, astonishing visions rising from a dead past. These magnificent decorations, amongst the most precious creations of Byzantine art which we still possess, enable us to form an idea of the nature of profane art at Byzantium, where it held an important place beside religious art. Unfortunately all too few examples of it have survived. We see, too, how powerful an effect could be obtained by employing mosaic, and why this method of decoration persisted in ordinary use for centuries in Eastern churches, whether the aim was solemn grandeur or historical realism.

The same tendencies, the same interests, can be traced in all the artistic remains of the sixth century. Amongst existing fifth- and sixth-century illustrated manuscripts are some that are still throughout inspired by the Hellenistic spirit. In the Genesis MS. in Vienna, which dates from the fifth century, sacred episodes are treated as scenes from everyday life; the characters are placed against a landscape or an architectural background, and many allegorical figures are introduced, such as nymphs of the springs, gods of the mountains, and personifications of cities and virtues. We find a similar treatment in the seventh-century Joshua Roll in the Vatican, which reproduces models of undoubtedly earlier date, and in the Vienna MS. of the Natural History of Dioscorides, illuminated in the sixth century for a princess of the imperial family, in which there appear, among allegorical and mythological figures, portraits of the author himself—a common feature of the illustration of ancient manuscripts. There is, however, already a development in the illustrations of the *Christian Topography* of Cosmas Indicopleustes, which are a creation of sixth-century Alexandrian art, although the earliest extant copy, now in the Vatican, dates from the seventh century. New themes, new types, of a more serious and solemn nature, characteristic of the historical and monumental style, are mingled with picturesque scenes inspired by the Alexandrian tradition. And it is this new spirit which prevails in two sixth-century manuscripts of the Gospels, namely the beautiful Evangelium of Rossano in Calabria, of which the miniatures often seem to be a copy of mosaics, and the Syriac MS. at Florence. In each of these the richness of the ornament testifies to the growing influence of the East.

The same dualism is manifest in the figured textiles, which have been found for the most part in the Egyptian cemeteries of Akhmim and Antinoë. The picturesque subjects which were the favourite motifs of Alexandrian art—mythological figures, genre scenes, dancing girls, and musicians—are followed under Persian influence by compositions in a different style, in which appear horsemen confronting each other, hunters, drivers of chariots, and also religious scenes; here more and more the supple freedom of Hellenistic art is replaced by the solemn realism of the monumental style, while the growing taste for polychromy is revealed in a richer and wider range of colours. The art of the sculptor shows similar tendencies. It is represented chiefly by carved ivories, for monumental sculpture tends to disappear and is reduced to a purely ornamental decoration. The Hellenistic style persists in such works as the Barberini ivory in the Louvre or the diptych of the archangel Michael in the British Museum. But for the most part Oriental influence predominates. A notable example is the celebrated throne of Bishop Maximian preserved at Ravenna, a masterpiece of technical skill and delicate craftsmanship. Here events in the life of Joseph, scenes from the life of Christ, and solemn figures of the Evangelists are placed in a richly decorated setting. In the gold- and silver-work from Antioch—as for example in the silver dishes from Kerynia (Kyrenia) in Cyprus and in the famous Antioch chalice, undoubtedly of the fifth or sixth century—we find the same note of realism, the same quest for truth combined with harmony and elegance.

Thus by the end of the sixth century Christian art in the East seemed to be transformed. More and more under Oriental influence it had gradually abandoned the graces of the picturesque Alexandrian tradition for the solemn and stately grandeur of the historical style. In this development it had often shown novelty, originality, and creative power. It had proved that it could embody the glories and beauties of the Christian faith in great works of art, could invent individual and expressive types for the characters of sacred history, and give living and often dramatic representations of the events of Gospel history. A great religious art had arisen, which, while always retaining something of classic tradition, had yet been strongly marked by Eastern influence. In its application to secular as well as religious subjects this art had produced not only great churches but masterpieces of civil and military architecture. And in spite of the difficult times that followed Justinian's glorious reign, still in the seventh century it shone with unquestioned brilliance, as may be seen in some of the mosaics at Salonica and in the mosaics and frescoes of churches in Rome (St. Agnes, the Oratory of St. Venantius in the Lateran, the Oratory of Pope John VII, and the church of Santa Maria Antiqua). But notwithstanding its great qualities, this art tended to become fixed in those forms which tradition had consecrated. The Iconoclast revolution was, however, soon to reawaken and transform it by the introduction of fresh and living elements.

The Iconoclast Controversy, which disturbed the peace of the Empire from 726 to 843, was fated to have serious results for Byzantine art. The Iconoclast Emperors, though hostile to religious art, were by no means opposed to all display and all beauty. They had no liking for cold, bare churches, or for palaces without splendour, and were careful to put something else in the place of the images they destroyed. They sought the elements of this new decoration in the picturesque motifs dear to Alexandrian art, which, as we have seen, monumental art had progressively abandoned. They had a liking for landscapes full of trees and flowers, circus and hunting scenes, portraits, too, and historical pictures in which their victories were recorded. This was clearly a return to the classical tradition that sixth-century art had gradually eliminated, and thus was foreshadowed the freer and more flexible imperial art of the tenth and eleventh centuries, in which imitation of antique models went side by side with a taste for colour and ornament derived from the East, while its creative power would be revealed through close observation of nature and of life in its search for expressive and picturesque detail.

In spite of persecution, however, religious art had by no means disappeared. On the contrary, it had gained during the struggle an unexpected freshness and vigour, as may be seen in certain manuscripts, such as the Chloudoff Psalter, which were illuminated at this time under the influence of the monastery of Studius and are full of contemporary allusions. Thus arose in the face of imperial art a monastic or popular art, which after the triumph of orthodoxy would more and more set its stamp on the works of Byzantine art. We may infer that at the close of the Iconoclast crisis this art, under the influence of these two opposing currents, was ripe for a new renaissance. This renaissance, which has aptly been called the second golden age of Byzantine art, fills the period from the middle of the ninth to the end of the twelfth century.

What St. Sophia had been for the architecture of the sixth century, that the New Church, the *Nea*, built at Constantinople by order of Basil I, was for the end of the ninth—the characteristic, the typical construction that was to serve as a model for numerous imitators. Like St. Sophia it was approached through a vast and magnificent atrium, but internally all trace of a basilica had disappeared, its plan being that of an equal-armed cross inscribed in a square. It was crowned by five domes which were placed one at the intersection of the arms and the others at the four corners of the building. Doubtless no more than in the case of St. Sophia was this plan a completely new departure, for, from the sixth century and even earlier, it occurs amongst the typical forms of Byzantine architecture. But from the tenth century onwards it became extraordinarily popular, and, although it never entirely supplanted the earlier forms of construction, it appears thenceforth as the habitual, one may say the classic, type of Byzantine architecture. It occurs in Constantinople, where there is an excellent example in the church of the Mother of God (Kilisse Djami), dating apparently from the eleventh century, and also at Salonica in the Kazandjilar Djami (1028) and the church of the Holy Apostles (twelfth century). It is met with in Greece and Asia Minor, in Bulgaria, and Serbia, in Roumania, as well as in Russia. While the plan in its application varies considerably, certain common tendencies appear everywhere of which it is important to underline the characteristic features: (1) an external emphasis on the main lines of the construction by means of four lofty vaults, ending in curved or triangular façades; and (2) the raising to a great height of the central dome by placing it on a lofty polygonal drum. Thus the somewhat heavy cubical mass of the older buildings is replaced by a more elegant and harmonious grouping of a series of diminishing vaults which combine to form a kind of pyramid, culminating in the central dome which completes the graceful outline of the whole. There was a like attempt to give more space and air to the interior of the building by substituting slender columns for the massive piers that formerly supported the dome, while the monotony of straight lines was relieved by hemicycles at the ends of the narthex or by a triapsidal termination of the sanctuary. Thus these Byzantine churches gained something of the grace and vigour of Gothic cathedrals. And, greatest change of all, charming and skilful combinations of colour appeared on the external façades in place of the severe and depressing bareness of the great blank walls of former times. This was effected by alternations of red brick with white rubble, to form geometrical patterns, such as chequers, key-patterns, crosses, lozenges, circles, and stars. Additional brilliance was attained by the use of glazed earthenware vessels and faience tiles. The curve of the apse was decorated with arcades and tall hollow niches, and the whole building was enlivened by the play of the contrasting colours of the decoration. At Constantinople in the churches of Kilisse Djami, Fetiyeh Djami, of the Pantocrator or Zeirek Djami, at Salonica in the church of the Holy Apostles, in Greece at Merbaca, and in Serbia at Kruševats and Kalenič, are preserved charming examples of this style of decoration, which, gradually becoming richer and more complicated, lasted till the thirteenth and fourteenth centuries. All this shows to how great an extent Byzantine architects were able to give expression to their inventive talent and their desire for novelty in spite of the apparent fixity of forms. Their art was by no means clumsy, dry, monotonous, or bound by rigid formulas; it was on the contrary distinguished throughout its history by astonishing diversity of type, by creative power, and by a scientific handling of problems of constructional equilibrium, no less than by the life which inspired it.

If to-day one wishes to form some idea of the magnificence of a Byzantine church during the tenth, eleventh, and twelfth centuries, one should visit St. Mark's at Venice. Doubtless the Venetian basilica, built on the model of the church of the Holy Apostles in Constantinople, differs in plan from that of the equal-armed cross inscribed in a square which was the ordinary type in Byzantine architecture at this time, but with the five domes that form its crown, with its decoration of many-coloured marbles which covers the walls both within and without, in the lofty columns of the nave, and the pierced and delicately carved screens, in the glowing mosaics and the reredos of dazzling enamel set above the altar, in its atmosphere of purple and gold, it realizes the ideal of this art in which colour holds pride of place. By the richness of its mosaics, by the brilliance of its gold, by the splendour of its rare marbles St. Mark's appeared to the Venetians (in the words of an inscription in the basilica) as the glory of the churches of Christendom. For us it stands as the living embodiment of Byzantium during the centuries of her revived magnificence.

Besides these great religious monuments, civil architecture produced its own masterpieces in the shape of the imperial palaces. Nothing remains above ground of the Great Palace,[1] which rose tier upon tier on the slopes which climbed from the sea to the hill upon which now stands the mosque of Sultan Ahmed; nothing remains of the palace of Blachernae at the north-western end of the landward walls whither the residence of the Emperors was moved from the twelfth century onwards; their magnificence is, however, fully attested by the descriptions of contemporary writers. The Great Palace, to which almost every Emperor from Constantine until the tenth century had taken pride in making additions, consisted of a prodigious variety of splendidly decorated structures. We learn that in those of the

---

[1] The Walker Trust of the University of St. Andrews has carried out excavations on the site of the Palace. These excavations were initiated by Professor Baxter in 1935. (See the bibliographical note at pp. 405, 409 infra.)

ninth century the influence of Arabian art was clearly visible. As a whole, the Sacred Palace of Byzantium was not unlike the Kremlin of the Muscovite Czars, or the Old Seraglio of the Ottoman Sultans.

The beauty of the decoration is in keeping with these features of the architecture. To-day on entering one of these twelfth-century churches, such as that of Daphni (near Athens), or that of St. Luke the Stiriote in Phocis, St. Mark's at Venice, or the Palatine Chapel at Palermo, and above all if one enters a church on Mt. Athos, one is at first sight bewildered by the wealth of Gospel scenes and figures of saints with which the walls and vaults are covered. The arrangement of the designs is, however, by no means fortuitous; it was a profound idea which inspired and ordered the disposition of the whole. The successful presentation to the eyes of the faithful of the doctrines of the Church through this new system of decoration was assuredly one of the finest creations of the art of Byzantium during the ninth and tenth centuries. The main object of sixth-century church decoration had been, as we have seen, to record upon the walls of the churches scenes from the Gospel story; now, however, it is dogma and liturgy that are to be expressed in the decoration. Once history had taken the place of symbols, now in its turn history gives way before theology.

Each cycle of scenes occupied in fact a special place in the church in conformity with a profound theological conception. At the crown of the dome the Heavenly Church was represented by the glorious and awe-inspiring image of the Christ Pantocrator surrounded by angels and prophets and dominating the assembly of the faithful. In the apse the Church on Earth appears in its loftiest manifestation, that of the Virgin, praying for humanity, or enthroned between two archangels; and beneath her, over the altar, are other scenes, such as the Communion of the Apostles or the Divine Liturgy, which called to mind the mystery of the Eucharist. In the rest of the building devoted to the Church on Earth the saints and martyrs, heroes and witnesses of the Christian faith, are ranged in hierarchical order; while above them were scenes from the Gospels representing the twelve great feasts of the Church, through which the essentials of Christian dogma are expressed. These are the Annunciation, Nativity, Presentation in the Temple, Baptism, Raising of Lazarus, Transfiguration, Entry into Jerusalem, Crucifixion, Descent into Hell, Ascension, Pentecost, and Death of the Virgin. No attempt was made to arrange these scenes in chronological order, but prominence was given to those of the deepest dogmatic significance, so as to draw to them more forcibly the attention of the faithful: thus at St. Luke the Stiriote's and at Daphni special places are set apart for the Crucifixion and the Resurrection. Again, on the western wall of the church, over the entrance, was the vast composition representing the Last Judgement. Minor episodes, such as the Washing of the Disciples' Feet, and the Doubting of Thomas, complete a great decorative scheme in which, in the words of a theologian, 'all the mysteries of the Incarnation of Christ' were combined. Lastly, scenes from the life of the Virgin were generally represented in the narthex.

At the same time iconography was enriched by the creation of new subjects and of new types, more individual, more expressive, inspired by a greater realism and sincerity. Under the influence of the Apocryphal Gospels scenes from the life of the Virgin took an increasingly prominent part in church decoration. Certain new subjects now make their appearance, such as the Descent into Hell, the Dormition of the Virgin, and the Communion of the Apostles, which are plainly inventions of artists of genius. Here, too, there is creative power which does honour to the Byzantine art of the tenth and eleventh centuries, and it is no small proof of its achievement that these models dominated for centuries the decoration of churches throughout the whole of the Christian East.

The 'New Church' has long vanished. Nothing remains of its mosaics in which the precise formula of the new system of decoration seems for the first time to have reached its full expression, but already some of the later mosaics of St. Sophia have been disclosed, while outside the capital Eastern Christendom can still show several examples of these combinations of theological scenes which are of very real importance and of a living interest. Thus dating from the beginning of the eleventh century there is the church of St. Luke's monastery in Phocis, its mosaics and the marble veneering of its walls almost intact and not marred by any restoration; and from the end of the same century the mosaics of the church of the monastery of Daphni, near Athens, have justly been called 'a masterpiece of Byzantine art'. Between the beginning and the end of the eleventh century the successive stages in the development and progress of the new art are illustrated in a series of other buildings, such as St. Sophia of Kiev (mid-eleventh century), with its mosaics and its curious frescoes representing Byzantine court life and performances in the hippodrome; Nea Moni in the island of Chios, unfortunately seriously damaged; St. Sophia of Salonica, which has a representation of the Ascension in the dome; the church of the Dormition of the Virgin at Nicaea, completely destroyed in the Greco-Turkish war of 1922; the cathedral of Torcello, famous for its great Last Judgement; and in St. Mark's at Venice, which also dates from the end of the eleventh century, the decorations of the three domes of the nave and the cycle of the great feasts of the Church on the curve of the great arches.

It is remarkable how much all these works still owe to ancient tradition. Some, particularly those of Daphni, are almost classic in their feeling for line, sensitive drawing, and delicate modelling. The beauty of the types, the elegant drapery, and harmonious grouping of some of these compositions show to what an extent the influence of antiquity persisted, despite impoverishment, as a living force in Byzantine art. On the other hand, it is from the East that this art acquired its taste for a picturesque and vivid realism, and especially the feeling for colour and its skilful use which constitute one of the chief innovations of the eleventh century. Painting was formerly inspired in great measure by sculpture; sixth-century mosaic figures often resemble statues of marble or of metal. But this sober character now gives way to a variety, a complexity of effects, and a richness that mark the advent of a colourist school. The blue grounds of an earlier period are replaced by gold ones, already at times enlivened by the introduction of decorative landscape or architecture. Against these backgrounds of gold the bright hues of the draperies, the interplay of complementary colours, and the neutral tones of incidental features are all combined; the technical skill of the artist matches the refinement of his work; it is one of the characteristic features of this great artistic movement.

Many of these works and still more the representations of secular subjects drawn from mythology or history which decorated the imperial palace and the houses of the great nobles of this period are derived from this imperial art which was steeped in memories of antiquity, but was freer and more elastic and showed a genuine creative power. But opposed to this official art and very different from it both in spirit and in method there was a monastic and popular art, more realistic and dramatic, which, under the growing influence of the Church, progressively freed itself from the traditions of Hellenism and in the end ousted imperial art imposing its own more rigid and austere programme. The tendencies of this religious art are seen in the newly discovered frescoes of the rock churches of Cappadocia and in those which decorate the chapels of hermits in southern Italy. They appear even more clearly in illuminated manuscripts. It was the ecclesiastic and monastic influences that finally prevailed, fixing the types, stiffening the poses of the figures, and eliminating everything that seemed too much the outcome of individual fantasy, or too suspect of ancient paganism. Nevertheless, for a long time the two opposing schools reacted upon each other; they had many qualities in common, and they shared in one and the same endeavour to inspire with a new spirit the art of Byzantium.

The truth of these observations is borne out by a study of illustrated manuscripts. The epoch of the Macedonian and Comnenian Emperors (from the end of the ninth to the end of the twelfth century) was unquestionably the most brilliant period of Byzantine miniature painting. Many fine manuscripts have come down to us from this time, several of which, illuminated expressly for Emperors, are real masterpieces, revealing the character and the dominating tastes of the age.

What strikes one most in these works is the two opposing tendencies by which they are inspired. Without dwelling on the relatively considerable part played in the art of this time by the illustration of classical works (such as the Nicander in the Bibliothèque Nationale at Paris and the Oppian in the Marcian Library at Venice), in which there is an obvious return to the traditions of Alexandrian art, we notice even in religious manuscripts the same current of antique inspiration. Instances of this may be found in the beautiful psalters of the so-called 'aristocratic' series, a particularly fine example of which is the tenth-century psalter now in the Bibliothèque Nationale at Paris; in illustrated manuscripts of the Gospels, a whole series of which shows the characteristics of the Hellenistic school of Alexandria; and in a whole group of manuscripts of St. Gregory of Nazianzus, in which an essential place is taken by picturesque scenes of everyday life and by episodes borrowed from mythology. The influence of this imperial and secular art is seen also in the very expressive portraits that adorn some of these manuscripts, for instance those of the Emperor Nicephorus Botaniates (in the Bibliothèque Nationale in Paris) who appears in several miniatures with his wife or some of his ministers, and the fine portrait of Basil II in the Venice psalter.

But this imperial art was strongly countered by the monastic tendency. Against the 'aristocratic' psalter stands the psalter with marginal illustrations, in a more popular and realistic style. In contrast to the Alexandrian version of Gospel illustration, we find the Eastern version from Antioch; and side by side with the literary and secular type of the miniatures of the manuscript of Gregory of Nazianzus there is the theological type, a fine example of which is the beautiful manuscript executed for Basil I in the Bibliothèque Nationale of Paris. This monastic art had assuredly no less creative power than its imperial rival: witness the illustrations of the Octateuch, where at times a distinctly novel effect is produced by the turn for realist observation which has made contemporary dress and manners live again for us; witness also the beautiful ornament, inspired by the East, that covers with a profusion of brightly coloured motifs the initial pages of many Gospel manuscripts. But in these miniature paintings, as in the larger works of Byzantine painting, one notes the progressive weakening of classical tradition and the increasing ascendancy of religious influences. The sumptuous Menologium in the Vatican Library, illuminated for Basil II, is somewhat monotonous and shows an obvious anxiety to conform to the traditional 'canon', notwithstanding the apparent variety of subject and the skill of the eight artists who illustrated it. And the triumph of the monastic spirit is still more evident in twelfth-century manuscripts, such as that containing the Homilies of James the Monk. Art became more and more subject to the rule laid down by the Council of Nicaea in 787; 'it is for painters to execute, for the Fathers to order and to prescribe'. In the end the Church succeeded in making her doctrinal and liturgical tendencies prevail. But it is none the less a fact that the miniature painting of the Second Golden Age, as conceived by the artists of the imperial school, with their love of incident, landscape, and the picturesque, contributed largely to prepare the development from which the last renaissance of Byzantine art arose.

A further noteworthy characteristic of all the works of this period is the taste for magnificence and display. With its love of luxury and passion for colour, the art of this age delighted in the production of masterpieces that spread the fame of Byzantium in the Middle Ages throughout the whole of the Christian world.

Amongst these were the beautiful silks from the workshops of Constantinople, triumphs of Byzantine industry, portraying in dazzling colour animals—lions, elephants, eagles, and griffins—confronting each other, or representing Emperors gorgeously arrayed on horseback or engaged in the chase. There were also carvings in ivory, precious caskets adorned with classical or secular motifs, or, as on the casket at Troyes, with figures of Emperors, together with diptychs, such as the tenth-century plaque in the Cabinet of Medals at Paris, on which Christ is shown crowning Romanus II and Eudocia (tenth century). This is one of the finest achievements which Byzantine art has bequeathed to us. There were ivories carved with religious subjects, such as the Harbaville triptych in the Louvre (tenth century), the Sens casket, the Virgin from the former Stroganoff collection in Rome, now in the Cleveland (U.S.A.) Museum, and many others in which the lessons of classical tradition are combined with the inspiration of the East and with an observation of nature: there were bronze doors executed in a skilful combination of damascening with niello work, and the craftsmanship of goldsmiths and silversmiths, a fine example of which is the beautiful repoussé silver-gilt plaque in the Louvre, representing the Holy Women at the Sepulchre; and, above all, enamel-work, which Byzantium had borrowed from Persia, was specially popular in the tenth and eleventh centuries on account of its brilliant and gorgeous colouring. With a wealth of enamel the Byzantines adorned crosses, reliquaries, reredoses, icons, caskets and even crowns, rich bookbindings, and dresses for state occasions. Enamels, in fact, together with figured textiles represented the height of Byzantine luxury. A few beautiful examples which bear witness to the fine qualities of this art have happily survived: the reliquary at Limburg, which belonged to an Emperor of the tenth century; the twelfth-century Esztergon reliquary; the admirable figure of St. Michael in the Treasury of St. Mark's at Venice (tenth or eleventh century); the crowns of Constantine Monomachus and St. Stephen at Budapest; the cross of Cosenza; and the dazzling Pala d'Oro over the high altar of the basilica of Venice. As Kondakov has truly said, 'nothing shows more clearly than these enamels the gross error of those who talk of the stiffness and poverty of Byzantine art', and nothing else can so well account for its far-reaching influence.

From the tenth to the twelfth centuries Byzantine Constantinople appeared to the whole civilized world to be a city of marvels: in the words of Villehardouin, 'the city sovereign above all others'. In the cold fogs of Scandinavia and beside icy Russian rivers, in Venetian counting-houses or Western castles, in Christian France and Italy as well as in the Mussulman East, all through the Middle Ages folk dreamed of Byzantium, the incomparable city, radiant in a blaze of gold. As early as the sixth century the range of its influence was already astonishing, and its art had exercised a potent influence in North Africa, in Italy, and even in

Spain. From the tenth to the twelfth centuries this influence became yet greater; Byzantine art was at that time 'the art which set the standard for Europe', and its supremacy can be compared only with that of French art in the thirteenth century. For any choice work, if it were difficult of execution or of rare quality, recourse was had to Constantinople. Russian princes of Kiev, Venetian doges, abbots of Monte Cassino, merchants of Amalfi, or Norman kings of Sicily—if a church had to be built, decorated with mosaics, or enriched with costly work in gold and silver, it was to the great city on the Bosphorus that they resorted for artists or works of art. Russia, Venice, southern Italy, and Sicily were at that time virtually provincial centres of East Christian art. The twelfth-century frescoes of the churches of Nereditza, near Novgorod, Pskov and Staraya Ladoga, and especially those lately discovered in St. Demetrius at Vladimir, repeat the creations of the masters of the Byzantine capital. The same may be said of the eleventh-century mosaics at Kiev in the churches of St. Sophia and St. Michael of the Golden Heads. The bronze doors preserved in the churches of Amalfi, Salerno, at Monte Sant' Angelo, and San Paolo Without the Walls are Byzantine works, as is likewise the beautiful fresco over the entrance to Sant' Angelo in Formis. The art which arose in the eleventh century at the great Abbey of Monte Cassino and that which in the twelfth and thirteenth centuries decorated with mosaics the churches of Rome are profoundly marked by Oriental influence. By their style, arrangement, and iconography the mosaics of St. Mark's at Venice and of the cathedral at Torcello clearly reveal their Byzantine origin. Similarly those of the Palatine Chapel, the Martorana at Palermo, and the cathedral of Cefalù, together with the vast decoration of the cathedral at Monreale, demonstrate the influence of Byzantium on the Norman Court of Sicily in the twelfth century. Hispano-Moorish art was unquestionably derived from the Byzantine. Romanesque art owes much to the East, from which it borrowed not only its decorative forms but the plan of some of its buildings, as is proved, for instance, by the domed churches of south-western France. The Ottonian renaissance in Germany in the tenth and eleventh centuries was likewise strongly affected by Byzantine influence which lasted on into the twelfth century. Certainly one must not exaggerate either the range or the duration of the effect of the East on the arts of the West. The artists who sat at the feet of Byzantine masters were not entirely forgetful of their national traditions, and Byzantine models tended rather, as has been said, 'to awaken in them a consciousness of their own qualities'. From the school of the Greeks they learned a feeling for colour, a higher technical accomplishment, and a greater mastery over their materials, and profiting by these lessons they were enabled to attempt works of a more individual character. It is none the less true that from the tenth to the twelfth century Byzantium was the main source of inspiration for the West. The marvellous expansion of her art during this period is one of the most remarkable facts in her history.

At about the same time Byzantium exercised a similar influence in Asia. The churches of Armenia and Georgia, though highly original, are linked by many features to the Byzantine tradition, and there is doubtless some exaggeration in attributing to Armenia, as has lately been done, a paramount influence in the formation of Byzantine art. Eastern Europe certainly received much from Armenia, but in this exchange of influences Byzantium gave at least as much as she received. Arabian art also profited greatly by her teaching. Though Byzantium undoubtedly learnt much from the art of Arabia, in return she made the influence of her civilization felt there, as she did in the twelfth century in Latin Syria.

From the end of the twelfth century one can observe a development in Byzantine art that was to have important consequences. In the frescoes of the church of Nerez (near Skoplie in Serbia), which are dated to 1165, there appears an unexpected tendency towards dramatic or pathetic feeling in the representations of the Threnos, or the Descent from the Cross. The frescoes of the Serbian churches of Mileševo (1236) and Sopočani (about 1250), and of Boiana in Bulgaria (1259), show in the expression of the faces a remarkable sense of realism and life; and in the thirteenth-century

Genesis mosaics which decorate the narthex of St. Mark's at Venice we find landscape, architectural features, and an equally novel taste for the picturesque. These characteristic tendencies mark the beginning of a transformation in Byzantine art. Moreover the well-known intellectual movement in Constantinople of the fourteenth century brought about a revival of the classical tradition and a return to the ideas and models of Greek antiquity. These facts might lead us to expect, and do indeed explain, the new aspect which Byzantine art was to assume in the fourteenth and fifteenth centuries and that last brilliant renaissance in which it found its expression.

When fifty years ago mosaics dating from the beginning of the fourteenth century were discovered in the mosque of Kahrieh Djami at Constantinople, they revealed an art so different from that of the Byzantine monuments which were then known that they gave rise to much perplexity. They were at first taken for Italian work; it was proposed to credit them to some pupil of Giotto, who about this time was designing the frescoes of the chapel of the Arena at Padua in much the same style. Discoveries made in the East during the last thirty years have, however, demonstrated the falsity of this hypothesis and proved that the Kahrieh mosaics were by no means a solitary creation but one of a great series of works scattered over the whole of the Christian East. This powerful artistic movement can be traced in the frescoes which decorate the churches of Mistra in the Morea, as well as in the churches of Macedonia and Serbia: it appears in the churches of Roumania as at Curtea de Argès and in the Russian churches at Novgorod; it is even visible in the mosaics of the baptistery of St. Mark's at Venice. Of the Mt. Athos paintings, while the earliest date from the fourteenth century, those of the sixteenth show the last flowering of this great artistic revival. In all these closely allied works the art is the same; everywhere we find the same love of life, of movement, and the picturesque, together with a passion for the dramatic, the tender, and the pathetic. It was a realistic art, in which a masterly power of composition was combined with a wonderful sense of colour, and thus in the history of Byzantine art it appears as both original and creative.

One must admit that this art was influenced to some extent by the Italian masters of Siena, Florence, and Venice; from them it learned some lessons. And in the same way it may be admitted that, as has been said, the fourteenth-century Byzantine painters sought at times to revive their impoverished art by imitating the narrative style of their own sixth-century models. Nevertheless imitation of Italy was always cautious and restrained, and it cannot be doubted that this art remained essentially Byzantine alike in arrangement, in style, and in iconography. Its incontestable originality and creative power are evidenced by the altered character of its iconography, which has become richer and more complex, reviving ancient motifs and at the same time inventing new subjects; it is manifested in its incomparable colour sense, which at times suggests modern impressionist art. These new qualities are in themselves the expression of a new aesthetic by virtue of which a particular value is attached to beauty of form, to technical skill, to graceful attitudes, and to the portrayal of facial emotions. One can therefore no longer dispute either the definitely Byzantine character or the originality of this last renaissance (from the fourteenth to the sixteenth century) which may be called a Third Golden Age of Byzantine Art.

The architectural creations of this period need not long detain us. There are, however, some buildings worthy of note, such as the charming church of the Pantanassa at Mistra (first half of the fifteenth century) or that of the Serbian monastery at Dečani (first half of the fourteenth century), both interesting examples of the combination of Western influence with Byzantine tradition. Their exterior decoration is also very picturesque, as is that of the Serbian churches of the Morava school (end of the fourteenth century). On the whole the Byzantine buildings of this time do little more than carry on the traditions of the preceding period, and though we find in them great variety and can even distinguish different schools of architecture, such as the Greek and Serbian schools, there are few really original creations. Beautiful churches were still being built, such as the Fetiyeh Djami at Constantinople, the church of the

Holy Apostles at Salonica, the Peribleptos at Mistra, or the church of Our Lady of Consolation at Arta, and many others; but though their architects made ingenious use of traditional forms, they seldom added anything new or individual.

Further, in the impoverished state of the Empire, the arts of luxury began to decline. The production of works in costly material—gold and silver—or of those which needed patient or difficult technical proficiency, such as ivories and enamels, seems to have been almost abandoned. Fresco painting, on the other hand, which more and more took the place of the too costly mosaic, was of extreme importance in the art of this period. The flexibility and the wider possibilities of this medium responded better to the new tendencies of an art that aimed at refinement of execution and delicacy of colouring in its rendering of movement, expression, and the picturesque. For this reason the period from the beginning of the fourteenth century to the middle of the sixteenth, remarkable works of which are still extant, is perhaps the finest epoch in the history of Byzantine painting.

Between 1310 and 1320 the Great Logothete, Theodore Metochites, caused the church of the monastery of Chora in Constantinople (now the Kahrieh Djami) to be decorated with the beautiful mosaics still to be seen there. It is the masterpiece of the school that flourished in the capital at that time. In the series of scenes taken from the life of the Virgin and from the life of Christ which decorate the walls of the church we find a masterly power of composition, as, for instance, in the Distribution of the Purple, or the Taking of the Census before Quirinius; a close observation, and often a singularly realistic rendering of life, as in figures of the scene where the Christ is healing the sick; a taste for the picturesque which finds expression in the landscapes and architectural features introduced in the backgrounds of the compositions, and in the tendency to transform sacred episodes into veritable genre scenes, as in the tenderness of the St. Anne at prayer in a flowery garden. The effect of the whole series was greatly enhanced by the brilliant and harmonious colouring with its deep rich tones and the lively play of its lighting. This church, which, in its founder's words, had assured him eternal glory amongst those who should come after him, is indeed a superb creation.

Similar qualities are found in the paintings in the churches of Mistra. The unknown master who painted the frescoes of the Peribleptos (mid-fourteenth century) has shown more than once, it has been truly said, the expressive power of Giotto himself, as for instance in his admirable rendering of the Divine Liturgy. One feels that these works are the product of an art of the utmost erudition and refinement, penetrated through and through by the influence of humanism and strongly attracted by the worldly graces that were always in the ascendant at Constantinople. The Mistra frescoes are also distinguished by a rare colour sense. From every point of view they may be regarded as the finest embodiment of the new style that arose in the first half of the fourteenth century.

The artists, certainly of Greek origin and probably summoned from Constantinople, who decorated for the Serbian princes the churches of Studenitza (1314), Nagoričino (1317), Gračanica, and a little later that of Lesnovo (1349), show the same high qualities in their work. Some of their compositions, such as the Presentation of the Virgin at Studenitza and the Dormition of the Virgin at Nagoričino have a peculiar charm, and the portraits of their founders in most of these churches are no less remarkable. Equally worthy of attention are the Serbian frescoes of the end of the fourteenth century and the beginning of the fifteenth, such as those at Ravanitza, Ljubostinja, Manassija, and Kalenić.

But the influence of Byzantine art in the time of the Palaeologi extended even beyond Serbia and its neighbour Bulgaria. In the church of St. Nicholas Domnese at Curtea de Argès in Roumania there are some admirable mid-fourteenth-century frescoes—a masterpiece of composition and tender feeling. And even after the fall of Constantinople the picturesque churches of Northern Moldavia, so curiously decorated with paintings even on the outside walls, carried on the remote tradition of the wonders of Byzantium until the end of the sixteenth century. In Russia the churches in and around Novgorod were decorated towards the end of the fourteenth century with remarkable frescoes, attributed to an artist known as Theophanes the Greek. Here, too, the Byzantine origin of these paintings is unquestionable; they afford another instance of the astonishing vitality and prestige of Byzantine art in its last phase.

Once again it was in the capital of the Empire that this last great movement in Byzantine art seems to have originated. At that time there was a brilliant school of art in Constantinople; many of its works have survived to testify to its excellence. From it, doubtless, were derived the two great currents into which the movement diverged, which have been called the Macedonian and the Cretan schools. Each of them had its own distinctive character. The former, open to both Eastern and Italian influence, owes to the East its realistic and dramatic style and the arrangement of the composition in long unbroken friezes, while from Italy came the tender feeling shown in certain gestures and the emotion expressed by certain attitudes, such as those of the Virgin Mother caressing the Holy Child or fainting at the foot of the Cross, or in the details of the grievous story of the Passion. Yet beneath this discreet borrowing the Byzantine foundation is always apparent. In the origin of its master artists as well as by the nature of its themes this Macedonian school descends from Byzantium. It is marked by a broad and spirited technique, definitely characteristic of fresco painting.

By contrast the Cretan school was truer to Byzantine idealism. While not despising the graceful or the picturesque, it was remarkable rather for its lucidity, restraint, and aristocratic quality, which bear witness to its high ideal of distinction. It was characterized also by great technical skill. Its art was the refined and scholarly art of painters of easel pieces and subtle icons. Like the Macedonian school it had a profound knowledge of colour, which it applied with even greater skill and refinement, playing on the scale of tones and combining tone-values into exquisite harmonies. It would seem probable that it sprang directly from the school that flourished at Constantinople and that it learned there the traditions of the imperial city.

During nearly three centuries these two great schools shared in guiding the course of art throughout Eastern

Christendom. The Macedonian School flourished especially
in the fourteenth century. To this school we owe the paintings in the Macedonian and Serbian churches, which constitute one of the richest legacies which Byzantine art has
bequeathed to us. From this school come the masterly
frescoes of Curtea de Argès, the decorations of the Metropolitan Church at Mistra, and those of several churches in
and around Novgorod. At about the same time the influence
of the Cretan school made itself felt at Mistra in the frescoes
of the Peribleptos, which are doubtless its great masterpiece.
From the end of the fourteenth century it ousted its rival in
Serbia and in Russia, where the great master Theophanes
the Greek was working; similarly in the sixteenth century it
was to supplant it also in the monasteries of Mt. Athos, where
the two opposing schools met for the last time.

On Mt. Athos in the fourteenth century the Macedonian
school had been at first predominant. It had decorated the
churches of Vatopedi, Chilandari, and notably that of the
Protaton at Karyes, where the paintings which survive are
perhaps the most remarkable of all those on the Holy
Mountain. Then, in the sixteenth century, the Cretan
school triumphed. We owe to it the decorations of the
Catholicon of the Lavra (1535), of Dionysiou (1547),
Dochiariou (1568), and many others. But at the same time
the Macedonian school still retained its influence, and its
work is seen in the refectories of the Lavra (1512) and of
Dionysiou (1545). The two schools were represented by two
great rival painters, namely Manuel Panselinus of Salonica,
and Theophanes of Crete. To the former, a somewhat
mysterious artist who has in turn been called the Giotto and
the Raphael of Byzantine painting, the monks of Mt. Athos
are ready to attribute every outstanding piece of work
preserved in their monasteries. *The Painters' Manual* says
that 'he towered above all painters, ancient or modern, as is
abundantly proved by his frescoes and panel pictures'. He
was the last and most illustrious representative of the Macedonian school. With no less distinction Theophanes of
Crete, with his sons and pupils, represented the Cretan
school, as may be seen in the paintings bearing his signature
which survive in the monasteries of Mt. Athos and the

Meteora. The admiration of contemporaries was divided between these two great artists. And it is a remarkable testimony to the versatility of this art that alongside of these clearly distinct schools one can also recognize powerful personalities, each having his own individual style and manner.

There are other works from this last period of Byzantine art which still survive. First, there are the illuminated manuscripts. It is true that these miniature paintings seldom have the outstanding qualities characteristic of the preceding period. A poverty of ideas, and these often rendered by childish daubs—such is the scornful judgement which has been passed on them. Several works, however, such as the manuscript of John Cantacuzenus in the Bibliothèque Nationale at Paris, or the Serbian Psalter at Munich, lack neither beauty nor interest, and the vigorous and glowing colour of the latter has justly received high praise. The manuscript of the Chronicle of Skylitzes (preserved at Madrid) in its six hundred curious miniatures seems to reflect the historical wall-paintings which decorated Byzantine palaces. In all these works one finds the same taste for the picturesque, power of realistic observation, and sense of colour which are found in the frescoes of that time. But apart from paintings on a large scale it is icons and embroideries that appear to have been the favourite forms of artistic production from the fourteenth to the sixteenth century. In particular the masters of the Cretan school seem to have been great painters of icons, and indeed this form of art accorded even better than fresco painting with the new aesthetic of the age. There have survived also from the time of the Palaeologi a large number of works in mosaic and tempera. In more than one instance there can be traced in these compositions the life and freedom, the love of the picturesque, and the tender feeling characteristic of fourteenth-century painting. The same may be said of certain masterpieces of embroidery, such as the so-called 'Dalmatic of Charlemagne' to be seen in the sacristy of St. Peter's at Rome, or the beautiful Epitaphios of Salonica now in the Byzantine Museum at Athens, which are both undoubtedly works of the school of Constantinople. In harmony of colour and beauty of design they both attain a very high level, and they display the same qualities that can be seen in the mosaics of Kahrieh Djami, in the frescoes of Mistra, and the paintings of Serbian churches. Thus all the qualities of Byzantine art are preserved in these works of the fourteenth century; everywhere in the picturesque or pathetic elements of their compositions, and in the matchless skill of their colouring, we find the same observation of nature and life, the same contrast between elegance and realism, and the same creative impulse. If moreover due account is taken of the great inventive power of the new iconography which made its appearance at that time, it is not possible to deny the originality of this last phase of Byzantine art, whatever its remoter origins may have been.

At this time once more, as in the sixth and as in the eleventh and twelfth centuries, the influence of Byzantine art spread far and wide. We have seen how great it was throughout the Christian East, and how Russian icon painting in the fourteenth and fifteenth centuries followed the teaching of Byzantium. In the West, especially in Italy in the twelfth and fourteenth centuries, it was no less significant; and it has aptly been said that 'the two worlds, so widely separated in language, religion, customs and ideas, seem to be in communion with each other through their art'. We have mentioned some of the resemblances—gestures and poses, for instance—that seem to have been copied from Italian models. But Byzantium in fact gave more to Italy than she received from her. A study of the mosaics of the Baptistery at Florence and the frescoes of the Baptistery of Parma, both of the thirteenth century, or of the remarkable paintings lately found in the church of St. Mary in Vescovio reveals the unmistakable imprint of Byzantine art. Duccio, in his famous reredos of the Maestà, and Giotto, in his frescoes of the Arena Chapel, have drawn freely from the treasury of Byzantine iconography, and in spite of all that is individual in their work it is evident that they owe much to the lessons and traditions of Byzantium. It is indeed hardly a paradox to maintain, as has been done, that Giotto was simply a Byzantine of genius.

Thus in the Christian East there arose between the thirteenth and the middle of the sixteenth century a great artistic movement which displayed its real originality in many remarkable creations. It was the final effort of this Byzantine art which after the middle of the sixteenth century was gradually to become fixed in what has been called a 'hieratic' immobility, in a lifeless repetition, from which there was no escape. The technical handbook known as *The Painters' Manual* clearly shows the importance of the place that workshop formulae were henceforth to take in the creation of works of art. Such manuals, dignified by the famous names of Panselinus and Theophanes of Crete, existed from the sixteenth century. But before it reached this decadence Byzantine art had had a glorious existence for many centuries. It was by no means, as has often been said of it, a stagnant art, incapable of self-renewal, nothing more than the imitation during a thousand years of the works of those artists of genius who in the fifth and sixth centuries had given it a new form. It was a living art and, like every living organism, it had known development and transformation. At first in Justinian's century, then under the Macedonian and Comnenian Emperors, and again in the time of the Palaeologi, it knew successive periods of incomparable brilliance, each with its own characteristic differences. Not only so, but throughout every phase of its history it exercised a profound influence upon the world without. Such was Byzantine art, and for this reason it must always remain one of the most remarkable aspects of Byzantine civilization and one of its lasting glories.

CHARLES DIEHL

VII

BYZANTINE EDUCATION

To write about education in the Byzantine Empire is no easy task. The time embraced from Constantine to 1453 is eleven centuries, and the area covered, at least in the early days, is enormous, for a subject of the Emperor of Constantinople might be born and educated in Athens, Alexandria, or Antioch. Furthermore, information is hard to collect because, though scholars abound as the finished product, education is so rarely described at length and the allusions to its methods are often regrettably vague.

With this proviso we shall attempt to ascertain (1) who were taught in the Byzantine Empire and what they learnt, (2) who gave the teaching and where.

1. St. Gregory Nazianzen confidently states: 'I think that all those who have sense will acknowledge that education is the first of the goods we possess', and J. B. Bury was doubtless right in saying that in the Eastern Empire 'every boy and girl whose parents could afford to pay was educated', in contrast to the West where in the Dark Ages book learning was drawn from monastic sources. Princes and princesses might of course command the services of instructors in public positions. St. Arsenius, 'admired for Hellenic and Latin learning', was summoned from Rome by Theodosius I to teach his two sons, and a daughter of Leo I studied with Dioscurius, afterwards City Prefect. The ex-Patriarch Photius taught in the family of Basil I; young Michael VII learnt from Psellus, 'chief of the philosophers', and his son Constantine Ducas was the ornament of a School kept by Archbishop Theophylact. John of Euchaïta tells us that St. Dorotheus the Younger, sprung from a noble family of Trebizond, spent the first twelve years of his life 'as was natural to one well-born' under the rule of 'teachers and pedagogues'. But middle-class children also, like St. Theodore the Studite or Psellus, might be well educated. Even the Scythian slave St. Andreas Salos was taught Greek and the 'sacred writings' by his master's orders, and St.

Theodore the Syceote, son of a prostitute in a Galatian inn, went to the village school. The fourth-century philosopher Themistius, indeed, said that one could learn as well in a small town as a large; Bréhier has, however, shown that rural education was by no means completely organized.[1] The parents of St. Simeon Stylites only had him taught to mind sheep; St. Joannicius was too busy tending his father's pigs to acquire even the rudiments till at forty-seven he became a monk; St. Euthymius when he entered a monastery could neither read nor write.

Naturally it is chiefly from the biographies of famous men that we can learn some details of educational practice. About obscurer boys we know next to nothing, and in the case of women we can only infer, from scattered hints, that handicrafts and a knowledge of the 'sacred writings' learnt at home were usually, even for a scholar's child like Styliane, daughter of Psellus, considered education enough. East Roman girls apparently went neither to school nor to university. Attention must therefore perforce be concentrated upon the education of a few outstanding personalities.

Although the Byzantines were eager to call themselves *Romaioi* and to claim for their own a Roman tradition, their training was purely Greek. Libanius in the fourth century neither studied nor taught 'barbarian' Latin, and though Theodosius II in A.D. 425 appointed to his University in Constantinople both Latin and Greek teachers, the latter outnumbered the former. Justinian, who published in Latin his Code, Digest, and Institutes of Roman law, yet issued his later constitutions in the Greek language that they might more readily be understood. In 1045 Constantine IX had to stipulate that the head of his new Law School must know Latin, and this knowledge was probably purely academic, as we have no evidence of *spoken* Latin in eleventh-century Byzantium. From the fourth century the language and the substance of education in the Eastern provinces of the Empire was Greek. Only in the last two centuries of the Empire's history the attempts to unite the Churches of West and East necessitated a knowledge of Latin. There

---

[1] L. Bréhier, 'Les Populations rurales au IXe siècle d'après l'hagiographie byzantine', *Byzantion*, vol. i (1924), pp. 177-90, at p. 182.

was, as Professor Maas has said, 'a perhaps unexpressed but none the less binding law' to exclude Latin words from the 'Hochsprache'.

Within the Eastern provinces of the Empire, indeed, the Latin language never took root. Berytus, with its famous school of Roman law, must have long remained a Latin island in a Greek sea. Latinisms, it is true, survived in the legends upon the coinage, in the technical, legal, and military terms, and in Court titles. Many Latin words found their way into popular speech and are used by the writers of chronicles and of biographies of the saints. Not a few of these Latinisms have persisted right through the Middle Ages and are still present in modern Greek. Psellus in his *Chronographia* praises Romanus III for having shared in the culture connected with Italian (i.e. Roman) letters, but it may well be doubted whether the Emperor could in fact even read Latin texts.

Further, it must not be forgotten that the distinction was sharply drawn between 'our', that is, Christian, learning and the kind described as 'outside', 'foreign', or 'Hellene', i.e. classical pagan culture. When Christianity had become the State religion, if 'Orthography' and 'Grammar' were to be taught at all, Christian children must of necessity still use pagan text-books and read pagan works. St. Basil, instancing Moses and Daniel as men who had profited by profane learning, advised the young to study classical history and literature, but purely for the moral conveyed. They were, like Ulysses with the Sirens, to close their ears against any poetry that told of bad men or evil gods, and in all literature they were to pick out the good as bees draw their honey from the flowers. In the Lives of the Saints we are frequently assured that, though the holy men studied astronomy, they piously referred all phenomena to God and not to the stars, and though they learnt the practice and copied the grace of Greek rhetoric, they avoided its 'babble' and 'falsities' no less than 'the sophistical part' of philosophy. It was his 'virtue' quite as much as his 'Hellenic culture' that entitled John of Euchaïta, as the Menaion of 30 January tells us, to pronounce on the intellectual merits of the three great Fathers of the Church, St. Basil, St. John Chrysostom, and

St. Gregory Nazianzen. The hymn-writer Romanus sent all pagan authors to hell. Though the Greek poets were largely studied, they were theoretically under suspicion as seductive liars, unless an ingenious teacher (like Psellus's friend Nicetas) could discover some Christian allegory in their verse. If Homer was as a matter of fact read by all, it was partly as fairy-tales are by us, partly because men believed with St. Basil that 'all the poetry of Homer is a praise of virtue' disguised in a story.

It is therefore small wonder that careful parents had their children grounded in 'our' doctrines first of all. In early childhood boys and girls, unless sent like St. Euphrosyne to a cloister, or handed over to some cleric at six years old like St. Lazarus the Stylite or even at the age of three like St. Michael Syncellus, were usually brought up by their own parents in the 'nurture and admonition of the Lord', being made to listen to the 'Divine Scriptures' and other 'sacred writings', and above all to learn the Psalter by heart. The training of the small child's memory and pronunciation was the aim of the educators, and the Bible was their instrument ready to hand. St. Eutychius was taught until the age of twelve by a clerical grandfather; the father of St. John the Psichaïte 'trained the mind of his children'. The parents of St. Domnica made her read the 'sacred writings'; the mother of St. Theodore the Studite (ninth century) did the same by his sister; Psellus's mother (eleventh century) told him Bible stories at night. The influence of the mother on the child's education and her power to coerce or punish, even by flogging, comes out in many biographies; thus Xiphilinus, a patriarch of Constantinople in the eleventh century, owed much to maternal upbringing.

But we also find 'Grammarians' giving instruction in the 'sacred writings' to tiny children, to St. Neophytus, for example, as soon as he had been baptized and weaned, to St. Agathonicus and Psellus at the age of five or to St. Stephen the Younger at six years old (when he already 'ought to have been working at profane studies'); St. Christodulus and the fourteenth-century monk Macarius also got their early teaching in 'the art of the divine writings' from masters and not from their parents.

Secular education began between the ages of six and eight, and the child studied with teachers in the elementary school of his native place the all-important 'Orthography', i.e. reading and writing, for in view of the change in current pronunciation it was essential to learn with toil and pains the old classical spelling. Libanius was allowed by his widowed mother to idle in the country till he was fourteen, and he left the Antioch School when he was sixteen, so he was mainly self-taught, but this was exceptional. So also was the early age of eight at which the soldier Germanus and the Patriarch St. Nicephorus left their homes in Illyria and Galatia for the capital, the one entering the 'Schools of the grammarians' there, and the other the religious 'Museum' of Mosellus or Mosele.[1]

At ten or twelve years of age the boy turned from this 'preliminary education' to 'Grammar' which aimed at a complete 'Hellenizing' of the speech and mind, and strove to defend classical Greek against the inroads of the popular language. From papyri, from the biographies of St. John of Damascus and of St. Theodore the Studite, from Psellus's autobiographical statements and Zonaras's remarks about Anna Comnena, we gather that this process, in spite of any old prejudice against 'pagan' writers, involved a thorough study of the matter as well as the form of classical poetry, Homer especially being learnt by heart and explained word by word. This secondary education was sometimes described as the 'beginning of learning' (*ta prōta mathēmata*).

Finally, unless the call to 'more perfect knowledge' had already led to the monastic life—St. Nicolas the Studite entered a school for monks when he had 'ended his first decade'—the boy would go, like George Acropolites at sixteen, or, like Libanius and St. Basil, not until he was twenty years of age or over, to some university to acquire 'higher learning' by studying rhetoric and philosophy on strictly classical lines. For rhetoric, 'the power of artistic persuasive speech', he would read and memorize Greek historians and orators, and write compositions or make speeches according to classical rules and in imitation of classical styles. In philosophy, like St. John of Damascus,

[1] Cf. *Analecta Bollandiana*, vol. xiv (1895), pp. 161-5.

he would 'mount' from logic to speculation, and in argument would try to entangle his opponent in a 'Cretan labyrinth' of perplexity. In reading he would pass from Aristotle to Plato and the works of the Neoplatonists, Plotinus, and Proclus, and would apply to his understanding of Platonic doctrines all his previously gained knowledge of the natural and mathematical sciences. One of these, astronomy, might lead on in certain cases to theology, the contemplation of Him Who created the stars, the 'philosophy among ourselves', 'divine learning', the 'science of more perfect things'.

Of these higher studies rhetoric is pronounced by Synesius to be indispensable for serving one's city, but 'philosophy in itself is worth more'. Psellus tells us that few are proficient in both, but he himself claims to have mastered philosophy, rhetoric, geometry, music, astronomy, and even theology, in short, 'every branch of knowledge, not Greek and Latin philosophy only, but also Chaldaean, Egyptian, and Jewish'.

We must pause a moment to consider the disconcerting looseness in the Byzantine use of educational terms. Thus the adjective *encyclios* applied to education (*paideia* or *paideusis*), which to Quintilian had meant 'all-embracing', was gradually degraded to signify 'preliminary'. This change of sense came about in a curious fashion. The twelfth-century Tzetzes, following the etymology, seems at first sight to have kept the old wide meaning, for his 'circle of learning' comprises the *quadrivium* of arithmetic, music, geometry, and astronomy, and also grammar, rhetoric, and philosophy. But when we realize that philosophy to him is merely the pagan philosophy which ever since the days of the Greek Fathers had been the step *below* theology, we see how in his view the 'circle' has become 'preliminary' to this highest of studies. But this is not all. *Encyclios paideia* in Byzantine literature usually means something lower still. It denotes 'school learning' as preliminary to all higher studies (e.g. in Anna Comnena's *Alexiad*) or it may mean simply 'the rudiments' as the 'foundation' for study of any kind (e.g. to the eighth-century monk Cosmas). It is thus equivalent to purely elementary instruction in language and the outlines of *Grammatike* to which it served as an introduction. Psellus (eleventh century) gives as the three stages of education

(1) *encyclios paideusis*, (2) 'grammar', and (3) 'higher learning', i.e. rhetoric and philosophy.

Again 'grammar' by which 'Hellenic speech is regulated' commonly means the second stage in a boy's education, 'orthography' or *encyclios paideusis* in the sense of 'rudiments' being the first. But as taught by Nicetas and described by Psellus 'orthography' is synonymous with *Grammatike*, or again 'grammar' is treated by the biographer of the seventh-century Maximus the Confessor as part of *encyclios paideusis*, and by the thirteenth-century George Acropolites as its equivalent. Sometimes 'grammar' covers all subjects that might be taught in a secondary school—literature, history, metre, geometry, and geography—and thus precedes rhetoric; sometimes, together with rhetoric, it forms a part of more advanced education. Finally 'philosophy', generally regarded as 'the art of arts and science of sciences'—the 'heights', towering above *encyclios paideusis*, grammar and rhetoric alike—is found in certain passages to include the *quadrivium*, elsewhere differentiated as 'the four servants of true knowledge' with philosophy as their mistress. The letters of Synesius show that under Hypatia at Alexandria the 'mysteries of philosophy' comprised mathematics and physics. In common parlance 'philosophy' covered not only ethics and speculative ideas, but also logic and dialectic; being, as we have just said, essentially 'Hellenic' and 'foreign' it was not without danger, and the clergy especially needed to handle it judiciously or they might fall from orthodoxy.

We have then to admit that neither the names nor the sequence of the different branches of Byzantine education are very clear to us. School and university subjects seem to have overlapped. St. Gregory Nazianzen and St. Basil, full-grown men who had passed through their *encyclios paideusis* while in Cappadocia and had later studied in other schools, worked in the University of Athens at grammar, metres, politics, and history, as well as at rhetoric, philosophy, and medicine. The study of medicine up to a certain point figured in general education. Professionals like Caesarius who was given 'first rank among the doctors' in Constantinople, doubtless had a full practical training, but educated people generally, like St. Basil, Photius, Psellus, and Anna

Comnena, would diagnose the 'causes of diseases' and pronounce views on their treatment. Similarly legal knowledge of an elementary kind was not uncommon, but embryo lawyers or civil servants had to follow a special advanced course. Thus an official in fourth-century Egypt went to Elementary School, Latin School, and Law School, which he left, like the graduates from Berytus and later on from the law school of Constantine IX at Constantinople, as a certificated advocate, qualified to take up his profession. Law students were early set apart from others; the Trullan Council (692) enacts: 'Those who are taught the civil laws may not go to the theatre or indulge in athletic exercises or wear peculiar clothes.' Finally theology was a separate branch of learning which was probably confined to the patriarchal school and to monasteries; it was studied by few laymen. The edict of Theodosius II (A.D. 425) reorganizing the university at Constantinople is included in the section of the Theodosian Code headed 'De Studiis liberalibus', i.e. the studies concerned with profane as opposed to sacred knowledge. For though it is true that all classical literature tended, as in the case of Nicetas' teaching, to be interpreted theologically, yet in a form of education so wholly determined by classical tradition theology as a separate discipline had no specific place. It was this state of things which Alexius I (1081–1118) strove to remedy by precept and example.

It may, indeed, be concluded that boys of all classes might, and frequently did, receive instruction from their babyhood to their twenties. The parents of St. John Calybita hoped that 'science and letters' would ensure him a good post, and in all the circles of trade and commerce the same motive and practice probably prevailed. The law in all its branches had its own requirements, imperial secretaries needed training in 'speed-writing', monks learnt fine calligraphy and brushwork, and soldiers would turn early to 'military matters'. But for the mass of the population the routine was: first, oral religious teaching at home, next, 'orthography' in the local elementary school. Beyond this primary education many children never went, but for those who continued their studies there was 'grammar'—a comprehensive term—to be learnt in the middle school, and the course would be completed in some university by rhetoric and philosophy, the two broad classifications into which Psellus divides true learning.

The thoroughness of the education can be judged from the reputation and the writings of those educated. Krumbacher's *History of Byzantine Literature* tabulates the enormous output of those eleven centuries in poetry and prose; here a few examples must suffice.

Beginning with the Emperors, we must take it on trust that Theophilus studied Greek, Latin, astronomy, natural history, and painting, copied manuscripts, invented a lamp, and argued with theologians, but we know positively that he had a learned wife, for some of her verses survive. Leo III revised the laws. So did Basil I and his son Leo VI, 'most philosophical of Emperors', who also composed poems, sermons, and a Life of his father. Constantine VII wrote and caused others to write volumes of encyclopaedic learning, while his daughter Agatha acted as his private secretary. Michael VII pored over books, neglecting his imperial duties. But the most numerous literary achievements come from the Comneni. Alexius I, though he wrote some verse, was essentially a controversialist, and he and his wife Irene put theology above all other study. But his son Isaac has been held to be a minor poet, his grandson Manuel I was an authority on dogma and had a 'most Homeric' wife, and his daughter Anna Comnena has given us in her *Alexiad* not only one of the finest products of Byzantine literature, but also a proof of her own wide education, though how that education was acquired we are not told. After the Restoration of 1261 Michael VIII (Palaeologus) appears as a patron of education and also as his own biographer. Finally John VI and Manuel II have left us, from the death-bed as it were of the Empire, remarkable specimens of letters, history, and polemics.

In less exalted stations we find writers of every kind constantly imitating and citing the classical masterpieces on the study of which their education had been based. To the minds of ecclesiastical writers the Bible is always present; thus St. John Chrysostom, holding that 'ignorance of the

Scriptures is the cause of all evils', makes 7,000 quotations from the Old Testament and 11,000 from the New. Photius is said even by an enemy to have rivalled the ancients and excelled all moderns in 'almost every branch of profane learning'. He composed a dictionary, school-books, and treatises; in his letters he corrected his friends' grammar and prescribed for their ailments; he helped Basil I to revise the laws, and held in his house a debating society and study circle. His *Bibliotheca*, summarizing for an absent brother the 270 books read by this circle, shows a marvellous range; poetry only is excluded. Another encyclopaedic scholar, Psellus, has left poetical and prose works on philosophy, history, law, medicine, theology, and occult science, while his study of and love for Plato and his enthusiasm for all learning helped to pave the way for the fifteenth-century Humanists. John of Euchaïta begins a religious poem with an obvious reminiscence of Euripides' *Hippolytus*. The letters of Michael Italicus show familiarity with a remarkable range of subjects, exclusive, however, of Latin and legal science. And shortly before the catastrophe of 1453 we have one last great scholar in Joseph Bryennius, who after mastering grammar, rhetoric, dialectic, and the *quadrivium* proceeded to philosophy. He is well read in the Bible and the Greek Fathers, and even quotes Augustine and Thomas Aquinas; the Renaissance, with the mutual interpenetration of East and West, is near at hand.

2. Passing to Byzantine teachers we are struck with the importance of their position. Private masters might complain of poverty, like Palladas or Prodromus or the Antioch guilds of rhetoricians who sold their wives' jewellery to satisfy their bakers, but public professors, paid by the State or municipality primarily to train efficient civil servants, lived, in Synesius's words, 'magnificently'. Under the thirteenth-century Emperors of Nicaea teachers of rhetoric, medicine, and mathematics were financed by the municipalities; teachers of law and philosophy had to be content with the pupils' fees. Teachers were a necessity; Anna Comnena hints that only the crazily conceited try to study alone. Parents made real sacrifices, sometimes surrendering mules or asses to be sold for their sons' tuition fees; to pay

his own, one youth worked as a stoker in the bath. Libanius
has depicted fourth-century student life. The masters were
in loco parentis and could flog or even dismiss their pupils if
'the whip' failed, as Psellus would say, to 'draw them to
learning'; but, as private teachers lived on the precarious
fees settled by individual contracts, they wished to keep old
students and acquire new. The 'choruses' of these young
men acted as their professors' press-gangs; Libanius on
reaching Athens was coerced into becoming the 'listener' of
an Arabian, and was initiated with bath and banquet. In
Constantinople at a later date his popularity and the increased
number of his pupils made other teachers jealous. The
personal element was strong: Photius boasts of his adoring
'wise chorus' of scholars; Psellus claimed to attract as
followers Celts, Arabs, Egyptians, Persians, Ethiopians, and
Babylonians; in religious controversies Nicephorus Gregoras
counted on his pupils as his army. Grateful addresses to or
funeral eulogies on teachers are common, and presentation
portraits or busts are not unknown.

The responsibility of professors for their scholars makes
St. Gregory of Nyssa implore the pupils of his brother St.
Basil to be worthy of their master; men judge teachers by the
results of their teaching. Mosellus (Mosele) taught St.
Nicephorus 'sacred Scripture only', fearing that profane
studies might indelibly stamp evil on his young mind. The
father of St. John of Damascus searched all Persia for a
master who would not inspire in his son a passion for
archery, soldiering, hunting, or athletics. There is a
paternal tone in the 'Princely Education' addressed by
Theophylact to Constantine Ducas, and in Psellus's entreaties
to his university pupils not to be kept away by bad weather
or the usual seductions of student life, the theatre, dice,
sports, or banquets. These are similarly deprecated by
Libanius, by the biographers of St. Gregory Nazianzen and
St. Theodore the Studite, and by Anna Comnena and
Theodore Hyrtacenus (fourteenth century). Again, Psellus
implores his hearers not to come to the classes late and half-
asleep, and not to ask stupid perfunctory questions when he
strives so hard to arouse their interest, often working over
his lectures all night.

Byzantine youth came under various instructors. In the early home years the 'pedagogue' slaves heard lessons recited, or a mother, Theodote, helped her child Psellus. St. John Chrysostom speaks of the troubles of small scholars, labouring with *stylus* and wax tablet. Though university professors were not allowed to teach private pupils, an ordinary teacher, even if he might not teach in public, might open a private school anywhere; John of Euchaïta and Michael Italicus taught in their houses, Libanius in a former shop. Public teachers officiated in a basilica, church, or municipal building. Private and public teachers alike taught a variety of subjects; the 'School' might also be termed *museum*, *auditorium*, or *didascaleion*. The boys stood in line or sat on benches or on the floor round the teacher's 'throne', holding on their knees copies of the texts to be expounded. Teaching at Antioch was in the forenoon. At Berytus in the fifth century and down to 533 classes were held every afternoon except Saturday and Sunday, while the mornings were devoted to preparation by the scholars. In St. Theodore the Syceote's village the boys had morning and afternoon lessons and, unless kept in for bad work, went home to a midday meal, an arrangement later advocated by Michael Apostolius (fifteenth century). Sometimes they brought food, which young ascetics, like St. Neophytus, would give away to poorer companions. 'Pedagogues' from home escorted the richer boys and carried their books; when St. Nicephorus's mother performed this office it was probably because his way lay 'through the market' with its questionable attractions. The pupils read aloud or recited or held discussions or wrote, as the master might order; some of their lecture-notes still survive. They had to answer questions and might also ask them. Teachers composed verses to help their scholars' memories; Psellus has left several, and a contemporary of his fitted grammatical rules into the metre of a hymn. One School Catechism of the eleventh century is presumably not typical, as the pupil is throughout scolded for ignorance. The teacher here supplies both questions and answers on grammar, rhetoric, philosophy including physics, the *quadrivium*, Platonism, Neoplatonism, and law.

The boy studying away from home lived in lodgings.

St. Gregory Nazianzen and St. Basil shared rooms in Athens; St. Marcellus boarded with a pious household in Ephesus. Often students visited successively three seats of learning, or occasionally even four as did Nicephorus Blemmydes. Private masters might be followed from one place to another, for they were always liable, like Libanius, Stephen of Alexandria, and Leo the Mathematician, to be called into the more honourable service of public education. The Emperors supported professors throughout the Empire; when Justinian ceased to pay salaries at Athens he virtually killed the Platonist School. Teachers received no special training; the great masters, St. Gregory Nazianzen, Photius, Psellus, John of Euchaïta, and Michael Italicus seem to have taught directly their own student course was finished. All could draw from the supreme source of education, namely, books. Manuscripts of the Classics, many of them unknown for several centuries in the West, were transcribed by experts in the Palace from the fourth century onwards and by many other laymen, the number of surviving copies proving the prevalence of private reading. Furthermore, right down to the fall of the Empire, the Byzantines wrote text-books for every conceivable study, from syntax to high philosophy; very many are still extant, though unpublished. Universities, schools, churches, monasteries, palaces, and private houses had their collections of books. The noble Caesaria spent all night reading her 700 volumes of the Fathers; it was with books in a neighbouring church that St. Lazarus the Stylite consoled himself after a flogging. Constantine VII thought campaigning Emperors should carry a travelling library; Cecaumenus urged generals on leave to study 'histories and the Church's books', culling tactics from the Old Testament and moral maxims from the New. The charge of the law library in the renewed university was committed by Constantine IX to the chief law officer of the Crown. From the Patmos monastery, where 260 manuscripts still exist, we have three catalogues (1201, 1355, and 1382); the wealth of Mt. Athos in original documents is proverbial. A twelfth-century Archbishop reproved the monks in his diocese for selling their literary treasures and leaving their shelves as bare as their souls. Tzetzes boasts of his library, and only poverty keeps Prodromus from buying books.

We must now enumerate the Byzantine centres of learning, almost all destroyed by the Arab conquest. The first is Athens, 'mother of learning', especially pagan philosophy. According to Synesius her scholars despised all others, and behaved 'as demi-gods among mules'. Even after Justinian closed her schools Theodore of Tarsus studied here before becoming an English bishop. But the palmy days were over, and in the twelfth century an Archbishop of Athens bewails her desolate condition, though even his gloomy letters show that culture had not completely deserted the city. Next comes Alexandria, 'workshop of varied education'. Before Hypatia's day it was visited by St. Gregory Nazianzen for the sake of its library and by his brother Caesarius for its medical school. In 484 Severus of Sozopolis attended its 'museum', learning grammar, rhetoric, philosophy, Latin, and law, in preparation for a legal training at Berytus. Both Caesarea, with its library of 30,000 Christian books, and Gaza had renowned schools of rhetoric. Antioch in Syria was the birthplace of Libanius, who taught there most of his life, keeping a day school with assistants under him; here, too, was born St. John Chrysostom, who completed his education by attending the local law-courts. The city never recovered from the 300 years of Saracen rule (635–969), though the Antiochene second wife of Manuel I is described as highly educated. At Ephesus St. Marcellus studied theology; nearer the capital we find great culture at Nicaea, which after the capture of Constantinople by the Latins became the seat of Empire (1204–61). The theological school of Edessa played an important part during the fifth century in the Christological controversy. For this a knowledge of Greek was essential, and the Syrian scholars both spoke and wrote Greek. Later Syria became Monophysite. It is to Edessa of the sixth century that we owe the Chronicle of Joshua the Stylite (which gives a contemporary's account of the events of the years 495–506) and also the Edessene Chronicle (written about 540).[1] In the ninth century

---

[1] For Edessa in the fifth and sixth centuries see R. Duval, *Histoire politique, religieuse et littéraire d'Édesse jusqu'à la première Croisade* (Paris, Leroux, 1892), chs. x and xi.

Edessa supported a public teacher under whom Theodore of
Edessa learnt grammar, rhetoric, and philosophy.

But the most interesting provincial institution is the
School of Law in Berytus, the principal training ground of
lawyers and civil servants until the earthquake of 551
shattered the city. Justinian's Constitution recognizing
Berytus, 'nurse of laws', as one of the three sanctioned legal
schools (the other two being Rome and Constantinople)
enacts that its students, whose 'associations' were addicted
to riotous living and (as we learn elsewhere) to magic, were
to be controlled by the Governor of Phoenicia, the Bishop,
and the professors. So great were the temptations of the
place that young Christians, for fear of falling away, would
wait to be baptized till their studies were over. The School
under its rectors (bearing the title of 'oecumenical masters')
was at its zenith in the fifth century. The usual course of
study lasted four years, with an optional fifth, and drew
pupils from all parts of the Empire.

Since the discovery of the *Scholia Sinaitica* we have gained
a clearer conception of the methods adopted in teaching by
the professors of the Law School. In the fifth century the
teaching was in Greek, but students had in their hands copies
of the Latin texts. Parallel passages would be cited and the
opinions of different jurisconsults compared. Teachers
would report their own opinions on disputed points as given
to their clients. Students would be advised to 'skip' certain
chapters of works, while important sections would be com-
mented upon at length. To a modern teacher these Scholia
bring a curious sense of actuality: the Byzantine professor of
law seems much less remote.

It is surprising how little we know of Byzantine literary
education in the provincial centres of the Empire. It is of
the culture of Salonica in the fourteenth century that we
can gain the clearest idea. The city at this time was full of
intellectual activity, thus carrying on the tradition which
Eustathius's commentaries on Homer had inaugurated in the
twelfth century. Here thought was freer than in the capital:
the control exercised by the Patriarch was not so rigorous.
Cabasilas could contend that the saints themselves were
incomplete personalities if they had not received sufficient

instruction in this world. Plethon overstepped even the liberty admitted in Salonica and urged a return to classical paganism. Here Hellenic feeling is so strong that the term 'Hellenes' need no longer be used as synonymous with 'pagans': it can revert to its older sense: the Byzantine monarch is not 'Emperor of the Romans', he becomes the 'Emperor of the Greeks'. A correspondence was maintained between the scholars of Constantinople and those of Salonica; writers exchanged their works and visited each other. There was much interest in education: parents were urged to send their children to school—they should postpone the teaching of a trade until adolescence. Higher education was in the hands both of lay teachers and of the clergy. In the city budget salaries were included for professors of medicine, mathematics, and rhetoric, while professors of philosophy and of law, since they 'despised money', received no salary.[1]

In the Byzantine Empire three types of educational institution must be distinguished: the secular university in Constantinople, the Patriarchal School, also in the capital, and the schools attached to the monasteries. (i) To these monastic schools St. Basil was prepared to admit the children of laymen—the children belonging to the world outside the walls of the monastery. But this practice was forbidden by a canon of the Council of Chalcedon which was later reaffirmed and was consistently observed. The monastic schools were confined to those who in early years had been dedicated by their parents to the life of the monk. Here there is a striking difference from the monastic schools of western Europe, which were freely attended by children who were not being trained for monastic asceticism. In the Eastern Empire it was only in the thirteenth century that the traditional rule was violated, when Planudes trained students for a public career in the civil service, the army, or in medicine. The teaching in the monastic schools was narrowly confined in its range: thus of the school of Mosellus or Mosele in the tenth century we are told that instruction was limited to the scriptures. The monastic libraries were composed in the main of the works of the Fathers of the Church: there was little opportunity for

[1] See an interesting chapter on the scientific, literary, and artistic movement in O. Tafrali, *Thessalonique au quatorzième siècle* (Paris, Geuthner, 1913), pp. 149–69.

any wide learning and the preservation of the literature of classical Greece was, it would seem, due for the most part to lay scriptoria. Monks would copy and illuminate theological works and would paint the icons which held so outstanding a place in the devotion of the East Romans. In the monasteries were written those chronicles which for some periods are our only sources for the history of the Empire, and it is to the monasteries that we owe the works of the Byzantine mystics which to-day are being studied with a new interest and a fuller understanding.

(ii) The University of Constantinople—unfortunately omitted by Rashdall from his study of medieval universities —depended directly upon imperial initiative and the support of the State. It is probable that Constantine founded in his capital the school where Libanius and Themistius subsequently taught: it is certain that in A.D. 425 Theodosius II appointed thirty-one professors paid by the State, freed from taxation, and strictly distinguished from private teachers. While Alexandria was famed for its school of medicine, Constantinople, together with Rome and Berytus, was a centre for legal study. The Eastern capital often drew its professors of Latin from Africa. In the fifth century the teachers of philosophy were frequently pagans: it was only with Justinian that pagan teachers were finally banished from the university.

Under Phocas (A.D. 602–10) all culture suffered, but with Heraclius there was a renewed interest in learning. It was in the metropolitan university that Cosmas a century later acquired that vast learning which he imparted to St. John of Damascus. Here, too, St. John the Psichaïte 'despised' the curriculum which his biographer gives in full: grammar, classical literature, rhetoric, secular philosophy, dialectics, astronomy, geometry, and arithmetic.

Of the fortunes of the university under the Iconoclasts we have no certain knowledge. The statement, made by late writers who sought to blacken the memory of the Iconoclasts, that Leo III closed an institute of higher studies and burnt alive its professors is now generally regarded as a legend without historic foundation. We cannot use this report in any attempt to reconstruct the history of the university in

Constantinople, though it may truly reflect the policy of Leo III to favour the military class at the expense of the teachers of the university.

After the restoration of the icons Bardas, the uncle of Michael III, wishing perhaps to emulate Bagdad, reorganized the university in the Magnaura Palace. He did so on strictly secular lines, though the head of the school, Leo the Mathematician, had previously lectured on philosophy in a church and had then become an Archbishop. Here Photius and others taught, and Cyril, the Apostle of the Slavs, learned all 'profane' branches of science but no theology. Under Constantine VII, with his passion for encyclopaedic knowledge, we hear of four chairs—those for philosophy, geometry, astronomy, and rhetoric, with supplementary teaching in arithmetic, music, grammar, law, and medicine. From the professors and students the Government, the Church, and the Courts of Law drew their highest officials.

The reigns of the military Emperors Nicephorus II, John Tzimisces, and Basil II seem to have brought education to a low ebb. It is true that Simeon the Younger found teachers about A.D. 1000, and Psellus learned from Nicetas and John of Euchaïta, but unless the latter's complaints are purely rhetorical he and his fellow student Xiphilinus had to teach each other law and philosophy. In 1045 Constantine IX, wishing to create a body of intelligent public servants, re-founded the university and laid down the conditions under which the professors and students should work. The university was divided into two Schools—one a school of philosophy with Psellus at its head, the other a school of law with John Xiphilinus as its director (*nomophylax*). Admission to the university was to be open to capacity without payment of fees and here future judges and administrators would receive their training. It would seem that from about A.D. 1150 the important post of director of the law school was generally held by one of the clergy attached to the church of St. Sophia. The last outstanding nomophylax was Harmenopulus (fourteenth century), who began to learn law at sixteen and to teach it at twenty-two years of age.

The position of 'Chief of the Philosophers' was both

arduous and dangerous. Psellus taught, besides philosophy, eleven subjects, including geography, music, and astrology, and was 'the soul of the university'[1] as well as one of the imperial counsellors, yet he was compelled to make a public profession of the orthodox faith, while his successor John Italus fell into disgrace with his Emperor for teaching heresy. At one period of acute dogmatic dissension the office was vacant for fifty years, till Manuel I filled it with a deacon of St. Sophia. In 1204 all that was left of the university moved to Nicaea, and the application of Baldwin I to the Pope for leave to found a 'Latin' School in Constantinople was frustrated by the jealous Faculty of Paris. Michael VIII restored the School of Philosophy under the Court official George Acropolites, who lectured in St. Sophia on mathematics and Aristotle, but not on Platonism, which the Emperor considered 'unsound'. The next head, Manuel Holobolus, once an imperial secretary, was proposed by the Patriarch and called 'Rhetor of the Great Church'. It was desired that provision should be made so as to allow the clergy to share in the lay education. The letters of the schoolmaster Theodore Hyrtacenus show that by A.D. 1300 State-paid teachers were regular Government officials, but private education had become popular, and the erudition of Nicephorus Gregoras and Theodore Metochites was both acquired and imparted in private houses. In 1445 John VIII transferred the School of Philosophy to another building because Argyropulus reported that schools in Italy were better housed. But Pope Pius II (1405–64) could still write of Constantinople as the 'home of letters and citadel of high philosophy' and the end came only with the Turkish conquest in 1453.

(iii) Of the School of the Patriarch no history can be written, for our sources are totally inadequate, but it would seem probable that this school existed side by side with the university throughout the history of the Empire. While the regular subjects of instruction were taught in the school, these subjects were all designed to lead up to the study of theology. The Rector of the School—the 'oecumenical teacher'—was

[1] Cf. F. Fuchs, *Die höheren Schulen von Konstantinopel im Mittelalter* (= *Byzantinisches Archiv*, ed. A. Heisenberg, Heft 8), Leipzig & Berlin, Teubner, 1926, p. 31.

entrusted with the exposition of the Gospels, while there was
a special teacher for the Epistles. There may have been
several schools under the control of the Church. Thus under
Constantine VII we find schools in two of the churches of
Constantinople, though practically nothing is known of their
teaching. An eleventh-century teacher begs the Patriarch
to transfer him from a small school to a larger one. The
institution where Alexius I educated his soldiers' orphans
was attached to St. Paul's Church, but though Anna
Comnena mentions the subjects of study it is not clear
whether it was under Church or State; certainly Michael
VIII reopened it after 1261 as a 'School for learning
Grammar', and honoured both teachers and pupils with his
personal favour. Bréhier believes that it gave secondary
education in connexion with, yet distinct from, the university. Near the present Fetiyeh Mosque,[1] once the Church
of the Holy Apostles, stood a school described about 1200
by Nicolas Mesarites, and it is open to question whether this
was the old university under new patriarchal supervision, or
merely a patriarchal school of special eminence. Ordinary
elementary education was given in the halls around, but in
the centre the higher branches were handled by the students
themselves, who met in small groups—seminars—for (often
noisy) discussion, when no Professor presided. The
Patriarch John Camaterus went daily to settle disputes and
answer questions. Finally, as the 'oecumenical palace
School', where Bessarion and Gennadius studied in the first
half of the fifteenth century, was directed by a celebrated
'Rhetor', a deacon of St. Sophia, we may fairly conclude that,
from the time of the dogmatic controversies under the
Comnenian Emperors till the fall of the Empire, public
education even when provided by the State was largely controlled by the Church and its Patriarch. And after the fall of
Constantinople (1453) it was the Church which kept the
Hellenic consciousness alive: it was in the schools maintained
by the Church that was fostered the spirit which led to the
War of Independence. A German scholar has written: the
'desire for schooling is implanted in the Greek nature from
the times of late antiquity and . . . it has prevented the Greeks

[1] See p. 192.

from losing their national consciousness. Even the Church is
held so sacred by the Greeks only because she has been the
bearer of national ideals in the times of slavery.'[1] Such was
the persistence of the Byzantine educational tradition.

GEORGINA BUCKLER

[1] Karl Dieterich, *Hellenism in Asia Minor* (Oxford University Press, New York,
1918), p. 44.

VIII

BYZANTINE LITERATURE

BYZANTINE literature as a whole is not a great literature; few would study it for pleasure unless they were already interested in the culture of the East Roman Empire. Yet as a mirror of Byzantine civilization this literature can claim permanent significance. It is not on purely aesthetic or literary standards that it must be judged; in form and in language the works may be traditional, but the men who wrote them are representative of the vigorous life which sustained the Empire and it is they whom the reader seeks to know through the traditional medium. The Byzantine writers can never forget that they are the heirs of a great past which has created the literary moulds to which they must to the best of their ability loyally adhere. The form is determined: it is the task of a sympathetic scholarship to recover the individuality of the writer as it is expressed through that inherited form.

Throughout the long history of Byzantine literature there is continuity; here there is no break with the ancient world as there is in western Europe. But in that continuous history it is possible to distinguish certain periods which have their own characteristic features. And the first of these is clearly marked: it stretches from the early years of the fourth century to the beginning of the seventh century—from the reign of Constantine the Great to that of the Emperor Heraclius. It is essentially the period of transition from the culture of the ancient world to the distinctively Christian civilization of the Byzantine Empire. This period saw the decline and extinction of pagan literature, while in nearly every sphere of literary composition it created the new forms which were to serve as models for later Christian writers. Thus the literature of these centuries can naturally be considered from two very different standpoints. The student of classical literature regards it as the melancholy close of a glorious achievement: he stands at the patient's death-bed; to the historian of Christian literature the fourth and fifth centuries will appear as the climax of the patristic age, the period when the Church entered into and in large measure appropriated the classical inheritance of ancient Greece, abandoning in fact, despite many protestations to the contrary effect, its earlier hostility to the culture of the pagan world. It was not for nothing that the Christian scholars of Alexandria had become the disciples of the Greeks: the views of Origen might be condemned as heretical, but Origen's influence remained of paramount significance. The leaders of the Eastern Church in the fourth century had studied at the same universities as their pagan contemporaries, and the rhetoric which all alike had learnt did not fashion pagan eloquence alone, it moulded also the form of Christian literature. The Church had allied itself with the imperial Court: with Eusebius in the reign of Constantine the Great a new courtly style arose to fit the changed conditions. The curiosity and subtlety of the Greek intellect were not dead: they did but take fresh spheres for their exercise: they deserted pagan philosophy for Christian theology and on this ground fought their old battles. The creeds of Christianity stand as permanent witness to the debt of the Church to Greek thought. Thus, as pagan writers wearied and gave up the unequal struggle, Christian authors pressed into the new land, fired by the very novelty of their effort to a truly creative activity. Zosimus (fifth century) is the last of the pagan historians of the Empire, but the sixth century saw in Procopius, who recounted the triumphs of Justinian, a Christian successor in no way inferior to the champion of the older faith. In this period ecclesiastical history, which begins with Eusebius, comes to a close with Evagrius: only the monastic chronicler remains to record the history of the East Roman Church. Eunapius, the pagan, wrote the biographies of the Neoplatonist philosophers of the fourth century, but these are the memoirs of a narrow circle of enthusiasts: their disciple, Julian the Apostate, in his *Misopogon* acknowledged that their credo could win but little response from the citizens of Antioch, the capital of Roman Asia. But in Egypt a new 'philosophy' had been born, the asceticism of the Christian monk, and the greatest literary work of Athanasius, the *Life of Antony* the Egyptian solitary, is a religious classic which was read alike in the East and, through the medium of a Latin translation, in western Europe. This

Christian 'philosophy' peopled the deserts which bordered the valley of the Nile and spread monasticism through the Western provinces of the Empire. The *Life of Antony* became the model which was followed by later Greek hagiographers. Neoplatonism itself profoundly influenced the theology of the Cappadocian Fathers, Gregory of Nazianzus and Gregory of Nyssa, while somewhere, it would seem, about the year A.D. 500 the unknown author who issued his writings under the name of Dionysius the Areopagite, the contemporary of the Apostle Paul, borrowed largely from the work of the Neoplatonist Proclus. When those writings had once been accepted as the product of the Apostolic age, Neoplatonic thought became part of the orthodox theology of the Eastern Church. Proclus wrote Neoplatonic hymns, but in the first decade of the fifth century the pagan Synesius became a Christian bishop and on the model of the poetry of the classical world gave to the Greek Church some of the earliest of its Christian hymns. In the sixth century Greek religious poetry reached its climax in the hymns of the converted Jew Romanus, but these were no longer written in the quantitative metre of classical poetry, but in the accentual rhythm which was natural to the Christian congregations which thronged the churches of Constantinople. Under the early Empire the Stoic and Cynic missionaries had journeyed through the Roman world carrying their message to the common folk through the medium of the sermon (diatribē): the intellectualism of the Neoplatonist had no such popular message, but in Antioch, the city which had remained unresponsive to the religious zeal of Julian the Apostate, Chrysostom filled the Christian churches, and to a populace attracted by the spell of his oratory proclaimed alike on Sundays and on weekdays the moral demands of the new faith. The Neoplatonist could appeal to the lettered aristocracy of the Greek world: the Christian preacher could hold a wider audience. The same transformation can be traced in other branches of literature: the pagan epigram dies but the Christian epigrammatist follows only too closely the ancient models. In the fifth century Nonnus produces his *Dionysiaca*—the last pagan epic; in the seventh century George of Pisidia as poet laureate of the East Roman Court writes his Christian epics, in which he celebrates the victory of the Emperor Heraclius over Rome's hereditary enemy, the Persian: the altars of the fire-worshippers are overthrown and the True Cross, rescued from Persian captivity, is restored to the Holy City, Jerusalem. But this Christian epic is no longer written in hexameters: it preserves with faultless accuracy the quantitative iambic metre of the classical age, but in feeling it is already a twelve-syllabled line of accentual verse with an accent on the last syllable but one.

These examples may serve to illustrate the character of this first period of transition and re-creation. It is followed by a gap in literary history of some 200 years (A.D. 650–850). The Empire was fighting its life and death struggle with the Arab invaders and the early Caliphate: Africa, Egypt, and Syria were lost to the infidel: new foes—the Slav and the Bulgar—were threatening Rome's hold upon the Balkan peninsula. Men wielded the sword and not the pen. The literature of the Iconoclasts has perished, and even from the side of the defenders of the icons, apart from theological writings, we have only the world chronicles which were produced within the shelter of the monasteries. It is in the seventh century, however, that Maximus the Confessor carried on the mystical tradition of Dionysius the Areopagite, while in the eighth John of Damascus restated in classical form the orthodox faith of the East Roman Church.

The third period begins with the literary revival of the ninth century, which is associated with the name of the Patriarch of Constantinople, Photius. The University of the capital is re-founded. After the victories of the Macedonian house men have time to study once more their inheritance from the past, and in the tenth century the imperial traditions are renewed by the scholar Emperor Constantine Porphyrogenitus: the preservation of those traditions was in his view a service rendered to the commonwealth. Towards the middle of the eleventh century the popular songs which had celebrated the military triumphs of the Amorian and Basilian emperors are taken up and woven into the earliest form of the epic of Digenes Akritas, the defender of the Asiatic march against the Saracen emirs.[1]

[1] See p. 245 *infra*.

In the literary revival of the eleventh century Psellus is the outstanding figure. Philosophy is studied and Neoplatonism challenges the supremacy of Aristotle. Byzantine mysticism reaches its height in the hymns of Simeon the Young, and Anna Comnena, the Byzantine princess, writes her history of her own times.

In A.D. 1204 the Fourth Crusade, by the capture and sack of Constantinople, strikes the felon blow from which the Empire never recovered. But some sixty years later, with the restoration of a Greek sovereign to the city of Constantine, literary activity revived and there follows the age of the Byzantine encyclopaedists—scholars such as Nicephorus Gregoras and Pachymeres. The continuity of tradition is reasserted with renewed enthusiasm, and the legacy of the past is studied afresh, though that study is not marked by any outstanding originality.

Throughout the literary history of East Rome the centres of production are the Court and the monastery. Popular literature received little encouragement, and the centralization of the Empire's life in the capital did not favour the growth of any literary activity in the provincial cities. Thus it is only from popular hagiography that we can hope to recover in any detail the daily life of the middle classes or that of the people. Byzantine literature is limited in its interests. East Roman writers either hold official positions or they are ecclesiastics, and many of the problems which perplex a student must perforce remain unsolved. In the present survey it will be unnecessary to consider technical works such as the military handbooks, while there is little to detain us in the fields of drama, of lyric poetry, or of secular oratory. It will be best to select a comparatively few writers as representatives of different types of literary composition: a mere enumeration of names would be at once futile and wearisome.

The main division is naturally into Prose and Poetry. Prose may be subdivided into Theology; History and Chronicles; Hagiography, Biography, Letters, and Funeral Orations; the Novel; Satire and Miscellanea, Poetry into Hymns; the Epigram; the solitary 'Drama', the *Christus patiens*; Romantic and epic poems; Lyric poetry as revived under Western influence; and Miscellanea, including satiric, begging, and didactic poems.

PROSE

Theology. If its bulk were the criterion, Byzantine theological literature would occupy a considerable part of this sketch. But it is convenient to regard it, broadly speaking, as a technical part of Byzantine writing, parallel in a sense to the technical treatises on military and naval tactics which it has been decided to exclude. Moreover, after the sixth century, apart from the revival associated with the Iconoclast controversy, it is only in the development of mysticism that Byzantine theological literature shows any marked originality. It is noteworthy that the three great theologians of the fourth century, Basil of Caesarea, his younger brother Gregory of Nyssa, and Gregory of Nazianzus, all come from Cappadocia, and it is perhaps to Eastern influences that their asceticism may be attributed. At the same time they show kinship with Hellenism in their leaning towards rhetoric and speculation; most of their writings, unlike those of Chrysostom, are learned and in no sense addressed to the masses. They are all under the influence of the Arian controversy of their time. Basil, in addition to drawing up rulings for reformed monasticism, wrote against the extreme Arian Eunomius. His expository side is illustrated by his homilies and commentaries. In his reform of Eastern monasticism common-sense labour was to accompany ascetic abstinence. 'The ascetic', he says, 'should pursue fitting occupations, provided that they are free from all trading, overlong attention and base gain.' In the face of the Arian peril Basil the statesman sought unremittingly to establish an alliance between the Western and Eastern Churches in defence of orthodoxy; despite successive rebuffs he persisted in his efforts to win Pope Damasus to his views. In the organization of asceticism on the basis of the common life that same statesmanship was crowned with success. The Byzantine monk as distinguished from the Christian solitary continued through the centuries to look to Basil as his teacher and guide. The sobriety of Basil's literary style represented a return to Atticism, so far as that was possible without pedantry, and that style reveals a familiarity with the masters of Greek prose, especially with Demosthenes and Plato.

Basil's brother Gregory was also an ardent foe of the Arians and Eunomius, against whom he wrote polemical treatises. Like his brother he composed homiletic works on various parts of the Bible, and his ascetic side is illustrated by his tract 'On the true aim of the ascetic life', the motto of which may be said to be: 'It is the will of God that the soul be cleansed by grace.' His eloquence and richness of style are manifested in his funeral orations and letters.

Gregory of Nazianzus became at Constantinople the champion of the Orthodox against the Arians, but his polemics were relieved by the inculcation of a true Christian spirit, as shown in his speech 'On the love of the poor'. He earned his title of 'Theologus' by his discourses on the Trinity. If his invectives against the Emperor Julian the Apostate repel the modern student by their unmeasured violence, they are yet of the greatest value as a historical source for the Emperor's conception of a reformed paganism, while his letters are marked by naturalness and wit. His poems are of the greatest literary importance: in two of these—the Evening Hymn and the Exhortation to Virgins —we have the first examples of the use of the new accentual metre as distinguished from the quantitative poetry of the ancient world. Gregory's autobiographical poems have often been compared with Augustine's *Confessions*.

Evagrius, a contemporary of the great Cappadocians, is of significance as reviving in the fourth century the thought of Origen. With Evagrius the monk takes his place in literature. He first outlines the aims of Byzantine mysticism, and though his writings were condemned as heretical under Justinian, they formed the source of the ascetic works of the orthodox Maximus the Confessor in the seventh century, and thus permanently influenced the later development of Byzantine theological thought. The other primary source of East Roman mysticism is Dionysius the Areopagite (*c.* A.D. 500), on whose works commentaries continued to be written until the thirteenth century. The aim of devotion for Dionysius is the ecstatic vision of God, when the soul in complete passivity after long purification is enlightened from above and is united with God. Purification, illumination, union with God are thus the stages of man's mystical ascent.

The triumvirate of Basil and the two Gregories marks the acme of cultured Byzantine orthodox literature; there follow the morasses of Monophysite and Monothelete controversy. But the Iconoclast struggle, which began in 726 and continued at intervals until 842, created a kind of revival in religious literature. The writings of the Iconoclasts are not preserved, but the works of the defenders of the icons may be represented for us by those of John of Damascus and Theodore the Studite. John of Damascus, whose literary activity was prosecuted in the famous Sabas Cloister in Palestine in the time of Leo III, stoutly maintains in three treatises that the adoration of images rests upon ecclesiastical tradition, and that 'it is not the part of Emperors to legislate for the Church'. His great work, *The Fountain of Knowledge*, has been called the Dogmatic Handbook of the Middle Ages. It is a compilation, starting with Aristotelian definitions of Being, going on to inveigh against heresies, and ending with an exposition of dogmatic theology. We shall meet with another side of this remarkable man's activities when we consider Byzantine Hymnology.

Iconoclast controversy occupied a relatively small part of the writings of that noble figure, Theodore, abbot of the monastery of Studius at Constantinople from the year 798, who exercised so great an influence on the reform of monastic life. In him we find a link with Basil the Great, for it was that father's ascetic teaching and his views on the duty of common labour within the monastery which inspired the abbot's reforms. Theodore held that Iconoclasm was a kind of heresy. His arguments against it are contained in three formal tracts, as well as in his letters. They are based on the principles that there was a human side of Christ's nature and that symbolism in religious worship is a necessity. The defenders of the sacred icons admitted that God the Father could not be depicted in art, but since man could be thus represented, to deny the legitimacy of icons of Christ was in fact to deny the Incarnation. It was false to maintain as did the Iconoclasts that the symbol must be of the same essence as that which it symbolized. Had that been true, the defender of images must have agreed with the Iconoclast that the only legitimate icon of Christ was the sacred elements after the prayer of consecration.

In the eleventh century Byzantine mysticism reaches its climax in the work of Simeon the Young. The Greek text of most of his writings is still unpublished, but even through the Latin translation of Pontanus the passion with which he sought the ecstasy of the vision of the Divine Light—that 'deification' which is the supreme goal of Byzantine piety—is profoundly impressive. Here is the immediacy of spiritual experience.

Theological writing was continued under Alexius Comnenus (1081–1118). A representative figure is that of Euthymius Zigabenus, a monk in the monastery of Our Lady the Peribleptos (the 'Celebrated') at Constantinople. It was at the order of the Emperor, who himself had entered the arena against heretics, that Zigabenus—so Alexius's daughter Anna Comnena tells us—compiled his *Dogmatic Panoply*, an armoury for the Orthodox theologian. It consists of dogmatic statements of Orthodox views on the Trinity, and attacks all kinds of heretics, among whom Zigabenus included Iconoclasts, Armenians, Paulicians, Bogomils, and Saracens. The author relies much on the three great Cappadocians, and thus Byzantine theological prose ends, as it had begun, on a note of dogma.

History and Chronicles. In profane Byzantine literature the writing of history undoubtedly stands out most prominently. The educated classes, owing to their employment in the bureaucracy, were compelled to take an interest in foreign affairs, whilst the man in the street was daily brought into contact with folk from other countries, and was often alarmed by threats to the city from Persian, Arab, Slavonic, and, later, from Turkish invaders. Under these circumstances it is not surprising that Byzantine historical writing falls into two well-marked classes—history proper, written by men of high education in a style reminiscent of the ancient Greek historians and intended for the intelligent reader, and popular chronicles designed for the consumption of the masses.

These last were as a rule the work of half-educated monks, and consequently redolent of the cloister.

As representatives of historical writing proper may be selected Procopius (sixth century), Constantine Porphyrogenitus and Leo Diaconus (tenth), Anna Comnena and Nicetas Acominatus (twelfth), and the four historians of the fall of Constantinople—Laonicus Chalcocondyles, George Phrantzes, Ducas, and Critobulus of Imbros (fifteenth). Of the long line of Byzantine chroniclers, we may choose John Malalas (sixth century), George the Monk (ninth), and John Zonaras (twelfth).

Procopius, who heads our list, is a good representative of the highly educated Byzantine historian. Trained as a jurist, he became secretary to Justinian's famous general Belisarius, whom he accompanied on his campaigns. His great historical work is his description of Justinian's wars against the Persians, Vandals, and Goths, based mainly on his own personal experiences. In style he is a follower of Herodotus and Thucydides. The work is of high merit and historical value, especially for the information it gives on geography and the peoples lying outside the Byzantine Empire. Apart from the panegyrics on Justinian the histories of Procopius are marked by a love of truth. As a supplement, he wrote later the famous *Anecdota*, the *Secret History*, which purports to set out facts formerly suppressed out of fear of Justinian and Theodora, who are now unsparingly attacked. 'It was not possible', he says in the Preface, 'to record in a fitting manner events while the actors in them were still alive. It would have been impossible to escape the attentions of the swarms of spies, or avoid being detected and perishing most miserably.' Though this outburst may lower our opinion of Procopius as a man, it does not shake his credit as a historian. It well illustrates the difficulties which beset a Court-historian, and the duty of writing his master's panegyric finds an outlet in a third work of Procopius, *On the buildings of Justinian*. As a whole Procopius is characterized rather by accuracy in fact than by a wide philosophic outlook.

In Constantine VII Porphyrogenitus[1] of the tenth century

[1] For Constantine's literary activities, see A. Rambaud, *L'Empire grec au dixième siècle* (Paris, Franck, 1870), pp. 51-174.

we reach the imperial historian and master of compilation,
the fashion of which had been set in the previous century by
the Patriarch Photius with his *Myriobiblion*. We may pass
over with a bare mention the great historical compilations
inspired by this monarch—*The History of the Emperors* by
Genesius, the Continuation of the Chronicle of Theophanes
(Constantine's uncle), and the great Historical Collection in
fifty-three books (only fragments of which are extant), and
give a very brief account of the works in which Constantine
seems to have taken a considerable personal share. The book
On the Themes may be dismissed shortly as a youthful work
based almost entirely on out-of-date library information of
the sixth century. The *Ceremonies* is a patchwork, dealing
with Emperors who preceded and followed Constantine—
it thus embodies later additions—and containing catalogues
of tombs, robes, and valuables, as well as descriptions of the
ceremonies which justify the title. But these descriptions are
of great value, as they give us much information about the
Byzantine bureaucracy and the elaborate Court and religious
ceremonial. Probably nearly contemporary with the earlier
chapters of the *Ceremonies* is the handbook drawn up for the
guidance of Constantine's young son Romanus, afterwards
·Romanus II; this work, generally known as the *De admini-
strando Imperio*, may be dated between 949 and 953. The
style is somewhat bombastic, but the writer betrays a real
pride in and affection for his son, and the book is a storehouse of information concerning the peoples bordering on
the Byzantine Empire. The *Life of Basil*, Constantine's
latest work, is a defence of his grandfather, and is chiefly
remarkable for its skilful slurring over of the worst features
of Basil I's career, the murders of the Caesar Bardas and
Michael III.

Leo the Deacon was born about 950. His history
describes in ten books the events of his own times (959–75),
and embraces the important wars waged by Nicephorus
Phocas and John Tzimisces against the Arabs in Crete and
Asia, and against Bulgarians and Russians. His information
is good, based partly on his own observation and partly on the
authority of contemporaries, but compared with Procopius
he is deficient in literary education, and his endeavours to

imitate Procopian style result in heaviness, affectation, and monotony. He is honest, but not free from the superstitions of his age.

The historians of the twelfth century are marked by a great increase of learning, a continuation of the revival of literary studies ushered in by the polymath Michael Psellus (eleventh century), who included history-writing in his multifarious activities. This tendency is well illustrated by the work of the princess Anna Comnena, daughter of the Emperor Alexius I, who wrote a history of her father's achievements under the epic title of the *Alexiad*. Though an easy mark for ridicule on account of her pride in learning and horror of the vulgar, Anna is for all that an outstanding figure among Byzantine historians. In contrast to the ecclesiastic Leo she is a humanist, steeped in classical reading as well as in that of the Bible. She says in her Preface: 'I was not without share in letters, but had brought my study of Greek to the highest pitch; I had not neglected rhetoric, but had read thoroughly the works of Aristotle and the dialogues of Plato.' The *Alexiad* is really a continuation of the history written by her husband, the Caesar Nicephorus Bryennius, whom she lauds in her work, but subsequently accused of weakness for failing to support her attempt to win the Byzantine crown; the frustration of her hopes led to her retirement into a convent, where she had leisure to complete her task. There is no reason to suppose that Anna deliberately departed from the high standard of truth which she set herself, but she obviously tries to place the career of her father in the best light. Yet even so her history, based on personal and contemporary information, is a remarkable account of a remarkable man. Its deficiencies spring from an imperfect mastery of chronology and a feminine tendency to be led away by externals. Anna shares to the full, and not without some justification, the normal Byzantine prejudice against the Western Crusaders.

Nicetas Acominatus, the historian of the capture of Constantinople by the Latins in 1204, is a contrast to Anna in more ways than one. Born at Chonae in Phrygia about 1150, he received his education at Constantinople, and rose high in the imperial service. He lacks the classical leanings of the authoress of the *Alexiad*: he shares her weakness in chrono-logy, but is less carried away by personal feeling. He begins with the reign of John Comnenus in order to link his history with the times of Alexius, but he pays chief attention to the period 1180 to 1206 as lying within his own experience, and in his Preface he claims the reader's indulgence on the plea that he is making a track through virgin soil. His sources, personal and contemporary, are good, and, though hostile to the Crusaders, he is on the whole fair and unprejudiced. A noteworthy feature is his interest in works of art; he gives a detailed description of the destruction of a bronze Athena in the Forum of Constantine, perhaps the Athena Promachos of Pheidias, by a drunken mob in 1203, and also wrote a valuable appendix on the artistic treasures destroyed by the Latins.

A brightness is shed on historical prose at the close of the Byzantine Empire by the comparative excellence of four historians who recorded its overthrow. In the second half of the fifteenth century Laonicus Chalcocondyles of Athens, a man of good family, composed a history of the period 1298–1463, narrating the rise and progress of the Turkish Empire, and the momentous events, particularly the overthrow of the Byzantine Empire, brought about by that rise, a theme, which, as he asserts with some truth, is second in importance to none. Ducas writes of the progress of the Turks after the battle of Kossovo (1389). He was deeply religious, an advocate of the union of the Eastern and Western Churches, a patriotic Greek, and an ardent foe of Mahomet II. Though not an attractive stylist, he can occasionally rise to eloquence; he is honest, and valuable for his first-hand knowledge of the conditions of the western coast of Asia Minor and the adjacent islands. George Phrantzes records in detail events between 1402 and 1478. He again was a man of action and a trusted servant of the imperial family, particularly of Constantine Dragases, last of the Byzantine Emperors. His account of the siege and capture of Con-stantinople is especially valuable, since he was an eyewitness. He is also interesting for the strange vicissitudes of his own career. His style, unlike that of Ducas, is attractive. Crito-bulus of Imbros is the panegyrist of Mahomet II. He is an avowed imitator of Thucydides, and changes contemporary place-names into classical forms. His history is dedicated to the Conqueror, and is an account of his exploits. As a Greek he apologizes for this attitude, declaring that he is not deficient in sympathy for the misfortunes of his own nation. His account of the siege is good and reliable, and the history of Mahomet is of great value as written by an educated Greek from the Turkish standpoint.

If in the writing of history the Byzantine owed his inspiration primarily to the writers of classical Greece, it would seem that the Jew of the Hellenistic period first fashioned the type of popular chronicle of world-history later adopted by the Christians of the Eastern Empire. Here the Old Testament story was the common basis.

The series of Byzantine world-chronicles is opened by John Malalas in the sixth century. He provided the model for many successors. He was a Syrian, born at Antioch, and his view of world-history is dominated by Antioch and Constantinople. His work extends from legendary Egypt to the end of Justinian's reign. It is a monkish production, utterly uncritical; snippets of undigested and often erroneous 'facts' are offered to the reader in the manner of popular journalism. Sallust, for example, is a distinguished poet. Chronology is mixed with complete insouciance: 'And then twenty-three other (Macedonian) kings reigned up to Philip. At that time there were teaching Greek affairs, as philosophers and poets, Sophocles and Heracleides and Euripides and Herodotus and the great Pythagoras.' Items culled from the lives of the saints bulk large, but are presented in the coarsest fashion. The curious and the miraculous especially appeal to Malalas: we have the itinerant Italian's dog of the time of Justinian, which picked out buried rings and returned them to their owners, distinguished coins of different Emperors, and in addition showed an embarrassing knowledge of human character. But the whole is rendered amusing by its unconscious humour, and the style, evidently well preserved in the single surviving manuscript at Oxford, is instructive as an example of the popular Greek of Malalas's day.

Our next typical chronicler is George the Monk, known also as Hamartōlus or The Sinner. His work was written under Michael III (842–67), and claims modestly to be nothing but a compilation put together from the products of various chronographers. In time it stretches from Adam to the death of the Emperor Theophilus in 842, though there is a continuation to 948 by later hands. It has not the naïve amusingness of Malalas, some use of whom is, however, discernible; its principal source is Theophanes Confessor (died 817). It is a typical monkish production, its author showing a preference for Greek mythology and monasticism. 'It is better', says George, 'to stammer in company with truth than to platonize with falsehood.' So we are not surprised to find fanatical attacks on the Iconoclasts like this: 'Leo the Isaurian, that swinish man, hearkened to the counsel of the deceivers and turned all the churches of the East in his Empire upside down.' The work, which throws much light on monasticism at the writer's period, was borrowed from by the excerptors employed by Constantine Porphyrogenitus and by later chroniclers; as in the case of Malalas, George the Monk was used by the compilers of the Slav chronicles.

John Zonaras, who completed his chronicle towards the middle of the twelfth century, produced a work of a rather different type. He was a man of superior education, who rose high in the imperial service, but subsequently withdrew to a monastery on one of the Princes' Islands, where he compiled his *Epitome of Histories*. He describes how he was urged to the work by his friends who said: 'Use your leisure to produce a work of common benefit, and you will have recompense from God laid up for you from this also.' The Chronicle begins with the Creation and ends with the accession of John II Comnenus in 1118. Zonaras takes a higher rank than his predecessors in the same field. He uses better sources while thinking it necessary to apologize for his interest in profane history. He draws upon Herodotus, Xenophon, Josephus, Plutarch, and Dio Cassius, as well as Procopius, George the Monk, and Psellus for later times. In style he is fairly fluent, but not uniform, being influenced by that of his sources.

It is easy to criticize the manifold deficiencies of these popular historians. But the world owes a debt to the long line of monks, since they at least provided some intellectual food for the masses, who would otherwise have been in danger of mental starvation, while for some periods they are our only historical sources.

Hagiography, Biography, &c. The lives of the saints stand in close relationship to the chronicles, for which, as we have seen, they supplied material; like the chronicles, they were intended to interest and edify the masses, and were usually written in the popular language. When the period of the persecutions ceased, the saint took the place which the martyr had held in the early Church. It was to his mediation that the folk of East Rome trusted; it was the Virgin or the saint who was the most powerful defender of the cities of the Empire; the relics of the saints were eagerly sought for and highly prized. The *Life of Antony*, written by Athanasius, formed, as was noted above, the model for subsequent biographies. It is in the sixth and seventh centuries that Greek hagiography is seen at its best in the work of Cyril of Scythopolis and Leontius of Neapolis (in Cyprus). The former wrote, as a contemporary, memoirs of the great solitaries of Palestine, while Leontius in his life of John the Almsgiver, Patriarch of Alexandria, paints vivid pictures of life in the Egyptian capital. In the biography of John the Almsgiver we see the Patriarch, 'like a second Nile', pouring forth a rich stream of charity—helping refugees from the Persian invasion of Syria, founding poor-houses and hospitals, and not disdaining to secure the employment of just weights. It is these earlier biographies that are of most value. Simeon Metaphrastes, who in the eleventh century (as recent researches seem to show) collected and rewrote in the rhetorical style of his day the older and simpler documents, has thus often destroyed the element which gives to them their freshness and their charm, though he affords us an indication of the extent of the material we have lost.

Another life full of interest is that of Nicon Metanoites[1] (died 998), who was the apostle of Crete after its recovery from the Saracens by Nicephorus Phocas. Nicon reconverted the islamized inhabitants to Christianity, and subse-

[1] See Schlumberger, *Un Empereur byzantin au dixième siècle* (Paris, Firmin-Didot, 1890), p. 96.

quently transferred his beneficent activities to Sparta. The biography of Nilus of Rossano[1] (died 1005), founder of the monastery of Grottaferrata, is instructive for lay and ecclesiastical conditions in Italy in the tenth century. The saint's life was full of varied activity; he lived as an ascetic in caves, held diplomatic interviews with marauding Saracens, resisted extortionate Byzantine officials, and introduced Basilian rulings into Italian monasteries.

Funeral orations are also a valuable source of biography. Striking examples are those pronounced by Theodore of the monastery of Studius (759–826) over his mother Theoctista, who stands out as the type of pious but practical Byzantine lady, and over his uncle Plato, abbot of the Saccudion monastery, whose rules supplied a pattern to Theodore for his own monastic reform. Michael Psellus (1018–78?) delivered funeral speeches over the famous Patriarchs of his own time—Michael Cerularius, Constantine Leichudes, and John Xiphilinus. The letters of both Theodore and Psellus also throw light on contemporary conditions, while those of Michael Acominatus (c. 1140–1220), which he wrote when Archbishop of Athens, depict the plight of the city, whose inhabitants were clothed in rags and fed mainly on barley-bread.

Two special monographs of a historical character deserve mention on account of their intrinsic interest. In 904 the Byzantine world was stirred at the news of the terrible sack of Salonica by Saracen corsairs under their renegade leader Leo of Tripolis. We have a graphic account of this event from the pen of John Cameniates, a priest of the city, who with other members of his family was carried off into captivity. The account was written at Tarsus, where Cameniates was awaiting exchange. The picture of the prosperity of Salonica, with its surrounding non-Greek population, is well drawn. The sufferings of the 22,000 young of both sexes in the heat and confinement of the galleys are described with unsparing realism, as are the circumstances of their sale into slavery at Chandax in Crete. Though not a man of very high education, Cameniates writes in a tolerable style.

[1] See J. Gay, *L'Italie méridionale et l'Empire byzantin* (Paris, Fontemoing, 1904), pp. 268–86.

The second monograph is the *Strategicon* of Cecaumenus, a Byzantine aristocrat, composed in the eleventh century. The work cannot be dismissed as purely technical, for besides the remarks on the art of war, it contains rules for good morals, Court-behaviour, and housekeeping. Its most valuable feature is the information it gives about the various peoples brought into contact with the Byzantine Empire. There are besides passages containing miscellaneous historical items from the time of Basil II to Romanus IV Diogenes. Cecaumenus considered that Constantine IX Monomachus ruined the Empire by paying tribute to frontier enemies instead of maintaining troops to repel them.

The Novel. This is represented by a single work, an 'edifying' tale of high merit, *Barlaam and Ioasaph.* It is of Indian origin, and is a life of Buddha turned into Christian Greek form. The Greek adapter, John the Monk of the cloister of St. Sabas, wrote it probably in the first half of the seventh century.[1] 'It is a tale', he says, 'told me by pious men of the interior country of the Ethiopians, whom report calls Indians, having translated it from trustworthy memoranda.' It is noteworthy that the second century *Apology* of Aristeides, discovered in a Syriac version in 1889, has been incorporated in the Greek tale. The story relates how Abenner, a king 'of the Hellenic faction' in India, learned by astrology that his son Ioasaph would be converted to Christianity. To avert this he built his son a splendid palace in a remote spot. But his design failed, for even in his isolation Ioasaph could not be kept from the sight of the sick, the blind, and the dead. Under stress of feelings thus inspired, he met the ascetic Barlaam, disguised as a merchant and feigning to carry a stone of great price. Barlaam turned him to Christianity, whereupon the prince renounced the half of the kingdom bestowed on him by Abenner, converted his father, and ended his days as a pious hermit. His church-tomb became a place of miracles.

This medieval Greek novel is written in a fluent and rhetorical style, and the character-drawing is good. The

[1] The adaptation has been attributed to John of Damascus. Cf. the English translation by G. R. Woodward and H. Mattingly, St. John Damascene, *Barlaam and Ioasaph*, in the Loeb Classical Library, London, Heinemann, 1914.

tale has spread far and wide; the Western versions begin in the twelfth century, and it is also diffused in Slavonic and Armenian editions.

Satire and Miscellanea. There are three remarkable Byzantine prose-pieces which can be placed under the head of Satire, though this classification is least applicable to the earliest, the *Philopatris*. The situation revealed by it fits the reign of Nicephorus Phocas (963–9); there are discontents in the capital which threaten the security of the Emperor, such as those brought about by this monarch's heavy taxation and limitation of church property, while on the other hand there are victories over the Persians (Arabs) and Scythians (Russians). In the first part of the work the author attacks the 'pagans' of Constantinople—the humanists who by their enthusiasm for the literature of classical Greece were once more introducing the gods of the ancient faith; in the second part he is more serious: here he turns against those who are plotting against the State. The true Patriot (Philopatris) will free himself from both. Religious orthodoxy mated with unquestioning loyalty to the commonwealth is the writer's faith. The two other Byzantine satires—the *Timarion* and the *Mazaris*—are frank imitations of Lucian's *Nekyomanteia*; they belong to the twelfth and fifteenth centuries respectively.[1] The *Timarion* has much the greater literary merit, and satirizes types, such as physicians, rhetoricians, and sophists, in an amusing way.

A brief mention of one curious work may here find a place. The *Christian Topography* of Cosmas was written in the sixth century and in it the author, a merchant who had traded with India and on his retirement had withdrawn into a monastery, sought to prove from the Scriptures that the earth was flat and not spherical. Geographers have always made use of the accounts given by Cosmas of Ceylon, of the ports, commerce, and animals of India, and of the Kingdom of Axum in Ethiopia. But his work has a further interest, for Cosmas can ask unusual questions, e.g., why did God take six days to create the world? And the answer which he gives to that question is unexpected: it was that the angels might

---

[1] For a full analysis of both these works cf. H. F. Tozer's article in the *Journal of Hellenic Studies*, vol. ii (1881), pp. 233–70, on 'Byzantine Satire'.

gain a full understanding of God's purpose so that they
might not fail in their service of man despite constant
disappointments due to man's sin and perversity. Having
been led gradually into a comprehension of God's ultimate
aim they could take fresh heart and persevere. While
Cosmas's study of Gospel texts is remarkable, his account of
the widespread expansion of Christianity forms a striking
picture. His curiosity is alert and eager; in Ethiopia he
copied inscriptions and incorporated them into his book.
It is thus to him that we owe our only record of the expedition which Ptolemy Euergetes made into Asia soon after
247 B.C. Cosmas is one of the comparatively few Byzantine
authors who have been translated into English: his work, if
one has learned the art of 'skipping', is well worth reading.

POETRY

Hymns. Antiphonal hymns were very early in use amongst
the Christians, as we know from Pliny's famous letter to
Trajan. The first Greek hymns were in classical metres—
hexameter, elegiac, iambic, anacreontic, and anapaestic;
such were those composed by Gregory of Nazianzus and
Synesius in the fourth and fifth centuries. The gradual
transition of Greek from a quantitative to an accented
language brought about the great change associated with the
name of Romanus, whereby the character of Greek hymnology was finally established. The discoveries of Cardinal
Pitra confirmed the reputation of Romanus as the most
forceful and original of Greek hymn-writers. Of his life
little is known, save that he was born in Syria and became a
deacon of the church at Berytus. He migrated to Constantinople in the reign of Anastasius I, and it was under Justinian
that the greater number of his hymns were composed.
Romanus was, it would seem, influenced by the poetry of
Syria, the land of his birth, though the origin of the elaborate
metrical scheme of his hymns is still obscure. Ephraem the
Syrian in his hymns had dramatized Bible stories and introduced into them vivid dialogues which reappear in the poems
of Romanus. The hymns of Romanus are sermons in poetic
form, and they have much in common with such rhythmic

prose as that of the sermons of Basil of Seleucia. The music to which they were sung is lost; their content would suggest that they were rendered in a kind of recitative, the congregation joining in the refrain. With Romanus the Greek hymn[1] took on its specific form, consisting of a *heirmos*, which fixed the rhythm of the succeeding *troparia*, or stanzas; these correspond to the *heirmos* in the number of syllables, in caesura and accents. Some idea of the caesura can be gained from the pointing of the Psalms in our own Prayer Book version. A number of stanzas—from three to thirty-three —make up the Ode or Hymn. Romanus is said to have written a thousand hymns, some eighty of which are preserved. The subjects range widely, and include Old Testament stories such as that of Joseph, New Testament episodes like those of Judas's Betrayal, Peter's Denial, Mary at the Cross, and activities of Saints and Prophets; there are also hymns for festivals, e.g. Easter and Christmas. The hymns are characterized by their dramatic qualities, and bear some resemblance to oratorios, being of considerable length. This length and a certain dogmatic discursiveness tend to obscure for Western taste Romanus's undoubted poetic qualities. In the Christmas hymn the Magi discourse on the moral condition of the East, and the Virgin instructs them in Jewish history; on the other hand, in the Easter hymn the women's announcement of the risen Lord is full of poetic fire.

A famous hymn, perhaps composed by the Patriarch Sergius, is the 'Acathistus', still sung in Greek churches in the fifth week in Lent. As its name implies, it is sung with the congregation standing. It consists of twenty-four stanzas in honour of the Virgin Mary, whose protection delivered Constantinople from the Avars and Persians in 626.

As time went on, Greek hymns increased in elaboration of form, a change illustrated by the Canons, which consist nominally of nine Odes, but practically of eight.[2] They were mainly composed during the period of the Iconoclast

---

[1] See the introduction to J. M. Neale's *Hymns of the Eastern Church*, 4th ed., 1882 (Neale, however, had not the advantage of Pitra's discoveries); Alice Gardner, *Theodore of Studium*, pp. 236–52. See, further, the Bibliographical Appendix at p. 412 *infra*.

[2] Some idea of their content can be gained from the translations of portions given by J. M. Neale, op. cit., though the metres are admittedly changed.

controversy. The principal names associated with the
writing of the Canons are those of Andrew, Bishop of Crete,
author of the Great mid-Lent Canon, John of Damascus, and
Theodore of the monastery of Studius, all of the eighth and
ninth centuries. The main characteristic of these long hymns
is an advance in refinement and elaboration, accompanied by
some loss of spontaneity. This tendency grew in the ninth
century and led to a progressive loss of feeling and vitality,
with the result that Byzantine hymn-writing practically died
out by the eleventh century.

The Epigram. The Byzantine fondness for the epigram is
an example of the links which unite Byzantine to Alexandrian civilization. The epigram was alive from the fourth to
the eleventh century. From the fourth to the sixth the
classical tone predominates. Representatives of this period
are the purely pagan Palladas of Alexandria, whose gloomy
spirit is summed up in the pessimistic couplet:

> Thou talkest much, but soon art reft of breath;
> Be silent, and yet living study death,

and Agathias and Paul the Silentiary, who illustrate the
revival of the epigram in the reign of Justinian. Some Attic
grace still clings to them, as in Paul's verse inscription for a
drinking-cup:

> From me Aniceteia wets her golden lip;
> Be mine to give her bridal draught to sip.

In the eighth and ninth centuries the tone is chiefly Christian.
Theodore the Studite generally uses the iambic trimeter, and
his epigrams deal with saints, images, churches, and all sides
of monastic life. The most interesting are those addressed
to the humbler servants of the monastery, such as the shoemaker or the cook. The shoemaker is bidden to remember
that his work is the same [*sic*] as that of the Apostle Paul, and
in general 'making drudgery divine' is the prevailing idea of
these epigrams. They are a welcome change from the elegant
trifles of an Agathias.

John Geometres, who attained high rank in the tenth
century, is typical of the mixture of the pagan and Christian
elements which appear in the epigrams of this and the
following century. He writes on Nicephorus Phocas and

John Tzimisces as well as on Plato and Aristotle, but does not neglect the Fathers of the Church, saints, and hymn-writers. A similar mingling of the sacred and profane characterizes the graceful epigrams of Christophorus of Mytilene in the eleventh century; with him and his contemporary John Mauropous the Byzantine epigram dies out.

A word, however, should be said on the two great collections of Greek epigrams made respectively by Cephalas, probably under Constantine Porphyrogenitus in the tenth century (the *Anthologia Palatina*), and by Maximus Planudes in the fourteenth. The latter is based on Cephalas's collection, but contains nearly four hundred additional epigrams. These anthologies are good examples of the Byzantine love of collecting to which the world is considerably indebted.

The Drama. There has been of late much discussion of the question whether there was in the Byzantine Empire any acted religious drama corresponding to the mystery-plays of Western Europe. It was formerly thought that Liutprand of Cremona had reported 'the taking up of the prophet Elijah in a stage play' as happening during his visit to Constantinople, but it would now appear that this view is based upon a mistranslation: Liutprand was objecting to the performance of scenic games upon a religious festival commemorating the ascension of the prophet Elijah. The evidence for the performance in tenth-century Constantinople of something in the nature of a mystery-play thus disappears. There is one literary religious drama—the *Christus Patiens*—which has been preserved, but this is a learned work and it is unlikely that it was ever acted. In it the central figure is the Virgin as the author himself indicates in the lines:

> Her first my story will to you present
> Mourning, as mother should, in hour of woe.

The date of the work is probably the eleventh or twelfth century; the language is an almost comic mixture of Euripides, Sophocles, Aeschylus, and the Bible. The author starts by saying:

> Now in the manner of Euripides
> I will the Passion tell which saved the world.

The commingling of pagan and Christian elements in the
play is very characteristic of the period.

In 1931 Vogt published the text of a Greek mystery-play
on the Passion. The manuscript which contains this text
comes from Cyprus and the play, it appears, must have been
composed under the Lusignan rule of the island. It is to be
regarded, writes Samuel Baud-Bovy, as an effort to acclima-
tize on Greek territory the mystery-plays which were then
flourishing in the West. It is probable that the attempt was a
failure. This is the sole text which gives clear evidence of an
acted religious drama amongst the Greeks of the Middle
Age, and Baud-Bovy has no hesitation in asserting that
'Byzance n'a pas connu de théâtre religieux'.

The Byzantine theatre knew only mime and pantomime,
revues and music-hall sketches, dances and satiric interludes.
Cultured students read the classic tragedies and comedies,
but they were not acted. Of the ephemeral mimes no texts
have been preserved, and thus, in a chapter on Byzantine
literature, a discussion of the evidence for the influence of
the Byzantine theatre would be out of place.

Romantic and Epic Poems. The writers of the East Roman
capital produced no genuine epics and we have only the most
miserable specimens of Byzantine romantic poems. But in
the provinces an important epic could be produced, as well
as poems of real romanticism, when Greek imagination was,
as it were, revivified by the fresher breezes blowing in from
the West.

The Byzantine 'romantic' poem is represented by two
names—Theodore Prodromus, with whom we shall meet
again, and Nicetas Eugenianus, both of the twelfth century.
Their iambic trimeter productions are respectively *Rhodanthe
and Dosicles* (based on Heliodorus), and *Drosilla and
Charicles* (derived from Achilles Tatius and Longus). To
the same class belongs the prose romance of Eustathius
Macrembolites called *Hysminias and Hysmine*, also of the
twelfth century. The machinery of all three is similar—
capture of the beloved one, parting of the loving pair by
pirates, and their miraculous reunion, or, as the argument
prefixed to Eugenianus's work puts it: 'Flight, wander-
ings, waves, captures, violence of brigands, imprisonment,

pirates.' They are centos of the worst variety, marked by extreme coarseness. On the other hand, the romantic poems which appear in the next century reach, under Western influence, a higher plane. Such are *Callimachus and Chrysorrhoe* (thirteenth century), whose theme is the rescuing of a princess from a dragon by a prince and includes a wealth of magical apparatus, and *Lybistrus and Rhodamne* (? fourteenth century), in which a princess is won by a Latin prince from a Frankish rival at a tournament. Equally touched by Frankish influence is the interesting romance of *Belthandrus and Chrysantza*.[1] The three poems mentioned are all in the popular fifteen-syllable 'political' metre, as is an attractive poem of a rather later date (fifteenth century), *Imberius and Margarona*, which is entirely based on a French romance, though this has been modified to suit Greek taste. The poem describes the winning of the Neapolitan princess Margarona by the Provençal prince Imberius, and the remarkable adventures of the pair. It is worth noting that this poem influenced the author of the great seventeenth-century Cretan romance, the *Erotocritus*.

[At my request Professor Mavrogordato has generously contributed this section on the *Digenes Akritas Epic*: it is to be hoped that he will publish an annotated English translation of the poem. N.H.B.]

The Epic. The Epic of Digenes Akritas occupies a place of peculiar importance in Byzantine literature. It is not, as is sometimes said, the picture of a secular conflict between East and West. Such a notion would have been meaningless in the Byzantine world. The hero of the epic who gives to it the name of his origin and occupation brings peace to the borders of the Empire. It marks with its associated tales and ballads a transition between medieval and modern Greek literature. It draws not only on Byzantine histories and on local chronicles, but also, to an extent hitherto unrecognized, on Hellenistic writings and on a mass of folk-lore much of which is still current in the Greek world, and being untouched by Western influence it may be said to transmit through romance and ballad a faint folk memory of the ancient world.

---

[1] This and *Lybistrus and Rhodamne* have been translated into French by Gidel in his *Études sur la littérature grecque moderne* (Paris, 1866).

The epic tells how there was once an Arabian Emir who was a prince in Syria. One day he came raiding over the frontier into Cappadocia and carried off the daughter of a Roman general of the Doukas family who had been banished from his estates. Her five brothers ride in pursuit and overtake the Emir who, having been outfought, reveals that the girl, sometimes named Eirene, is unharmed; if he may marry her he will come over with all his followers into Romania (the Roman Empire). His name is Mousour, and he tells them that he is a son of Chrysocherpes, a nephew of Karoës, and a grandson of the great Emir Ambron. His father is dead and he was brought up by his Arabian uncles as a Muhammadan. So they all returned rejoicing to Roman territory, where he was baptized and married to Eirene. A son was born to them called Basil, afterwards known as Digenes, because he was born of two races, and Akritas, because he chose to live alone on the frontiers. The Emir's mother writes to him reproachfully from Edessa, and after some disagreement with his brothers-in-law he rides off to visit her and soon converts her, too, with all her household and brings them back with him rejoicing. The fourth book turns to the hero of the poem, the young Basil, and describes his first acquaintance with wild beasts and robbers and his courtship of Evdokia, daughter of another general of the Doukas family. He carries her off by night, forces her father and brothers to consent, and takes her back to his own father's castle for the wedding. The presents from the bride's father included embroidered tents, golden icons, hawks, leopards, the sword of Chosroës, and a tame lion. Afterwards Digenes and his bride rode out to live alone; he destroyed many robbers and kept the peace on all the frontiers of the Empire. His fame reached the ears of the Emperor who rode down to the Euphrates (mentioned here for the first time) to congratulate and honour him while Digenes lectured the Emperor on his imperial duties. The next two books contain a collection of disconnected episodes. In the month of May he defends his bride against brigands and wild beasts. He describes some of his past adventures in love and fighting; these culminated in a meeting with the Amazon Maximo. The picture of Maximo, appearing on her black horse before daybreak on the river bank, has a poetical quality not attained elsewhere in the epic. Digenes built a palace on the Euphrates and made a garden, and here he lived devoting his wealth to good works and to the maintenance of peace. Here he fell ill and died after recalling to Evdokia the lovely adventures of their life in the wilderness, and she, seeing him die, fell dead in the middle of her prayer; so ends all earthly glory.

Of this epic there are seven versions extant and there are also Ballads of the so-called Akritic Cycle: these picture a different world of supernatural exploits, magic weapons, and talking animals in which Digenes is only one among a number of half-effaced heroes. They represent a different level of interest in the same community: they are not to be regarded as the direct sources of the epic.

Some of the characters of the epic have been identified: Chrysocherpes, father of the Emir Mousour, is Chrysocheir, a leader of the Paulician heretics who was defeated by the Byzantine forces in A.D. 873. Karoës, uncle of the Emir, reflects Karbeas, another Paulician leader, and Ambron, grandfather of the Emir Mousour, represents the Syrian Emir, Omar of Melitene, who became the ally of the Paulician Christians in the revolt against the Empire. The supposed period of the Digenes Epic is the century A.D. 860–960; its scene is laid in the parts of Mesopotamia between Samosata and Melitene, and also in Cappadocia where the Paulicians were persecuted. But the writer of the epic never mentions the Paulician heresy. He names the Paulician leaders only as brave enemies hardly distinguishable from the Arabs. The hero is set in a Paulician environment, but the resistance of the heretics is only a faded backcloth to the poem: its interest is not religious.

The poem must have been written at a time when tranquillity had been restored on the Euphrates frontier, which would point to the reign of Constantine IX Monomachus (1042–54): its composition may thus be placed about the middle of the eleventh century.

Romantic histories like that of Alexander the Great, romantic biographies like those of *Barlaam* or of *Apollonius of Tyana*, biblical romances like the story of Joseph as told by Josephus, novels containing one or two historical names like Chariton's *Chaireas and Callirrhoe* (in which the heroine is a daughter of the Syracusan general Hermocrates) had established in Hellenistic literature a firm tradition of more or less historical romance. The writer of *Digenes* was well in the line of this tradition. Of the Alexander Romance he has many clear reminiscences. The figure of the Lonely Sage with the privilege of outspokenness in the King's presence was authorized by Barlaam and by Apollonius and also by any number of Byzantine saints. For descriptive passages he borrowed freely and verbally from the pure novels of adventure, from Heliodorus and Achilles Tatius. The idea of the double descent of Alexander and other great men is a commonplace of Greco-Oriental romance. Kyriakides has shown that Byzantine historians emphasized the double descent of Leo V (813–20)—of whom the very word *digenes* is used—and of Basil I (867–86). Our poet may have had local chronicles of places like Edessa and Samosata. He may have had some folk-chronicles in verse like those produced in Crete after the insurrection of 1770. He would have found in Mesopotamia a reservoir of legend drawn from all the countries of the Near East and rediffused in all the languages that there overlapped. He clearly had access to both literary and popular sources and he had, further, the intellectual grasp to blend both in the popular medium of the fifteen-syllable 'political' verse.

Although the poet lacked emotional depth, he had enough originality to give his romance a purpose—its theme good government and the guarantee of peace by a union of Christian and Arab. The first three books are entirely concerned with the hero's father, the Emir Mousour: he, as son of Chrysocheir-Chrysocherpes the Paulician Christian who married Omar's daughter, was himself a *digenes*, the son of a mixed marriage uniting two creeds and two races. Thus the poem is a duplication of the same story, two complementary versions, the first about the father and the second about the son, both father and son being heroes who were neither pure Christian nor pure Arab, but the best of both. In *Digenes Akritas* we have a double story of double descent, a romance reflecting old alliances between Syrian Arabs and Paulician

Christians from Commagene and Cappadocia presented as a message of peace upon the troubled eastern frontiers of the Byzantine Empire.

JOHN MAVROGORDATO

Lyric Poetry. Of genuine lyric poetry, before the influence of Western chivalry made itself felt, Byzantine literature had nothing. In a fifteenth-century manuscript, preserved in the British Museum, is contained an attractive group of love-songs, known, without much justification, as Rhodian.[1] They form a kind of lover's handbook. The lyrics include a dialogue between a youth and a maiden, arranged in alpha-betical stanzas, complaints of a lover, also arranged alpha-betically, and a love-test for a short and bashful youth, in which he has to compose a hundred stanzas beginning with the numbers one to a hundred, a sentence which is subse-quently reduced. The girl says:

> Young one, upon a hundred words I will now question thee;
> If thou resolvest these aright, kisses in full there'll be.

In reality these so-called Rhodian love-songs are popular songs belonging to the Archipelago, reminiscences of which can still be heard, though the freedom accorded to women is perhaps a Frankish trait. There seems little doubt that they go back to a date earlier than the fifteenth century.

Miscellanea. In late Byzantine literature there is a large class of miscellaneous poetry in the popular fifteen-syllable 'political' metre, at first unrhymed, then rhymed. Verses of a popular character emerge here and there at an early period, and they appear to have been used to give vent to the satiric strain inherent in the populace. Such were those shouted by the crowd to the Emperor Maurice at the end of the sixth century with allusion to his numerous illegitimate offspring, or to Alexius Comnenus in recognition of his cleverness in counteracting a plot against his family. A popular song of a different type is the spring-song quoted by Constantine Porphyrogenitus. Satiric poems were composed by the ever-fertile Theodore Prodromus in the twelfth century in the form of beast and bird fables; those of Archilochus and Semonides of Amorgos remind us how long a tradition lies

[1] See Hesseling and Pernot, *Chansons d'Amour* (Paris, 1913).

behind this form of composition. Others embodied a lamentation over his married life and a complaint against two abbots who presided over a monastery in which he was a monk. By other writers even religion is parodied after a fashion set by Michael Psellus in the eleventh century, when he attacked the drunken habits of a fellow monk in verses which are a parody of the Mass. This tendency to parody sacred things reaches its extreme form in the prose satire 'On a Beardless Man', which consists of a series of curse-formulae arranged on the lines of the Mass.

In the twelfth and following centuries flourishes the 'Begging' poem, and here again Prodromus is forward with his grovelling, but not unamusing, complaints to the Emperor Manuel Comnenus. The concluding lines give the key to the whole production:

> Deliver me from poverty, save me from hunger's pains;
> Drive off my creditors' assaults and all the world's disdains.

An even lower pitch of grovelling is reached by Manuel Philes in his begging requests to the Palaeologi; his ambitions seem never to rise above the acquisition of food and clothing.

A fondness for the moral didactic poem is characteristic of later Byzantine times, perhaps because the period was by no means distinguished for a high standard of morality. Such poems mainly advocate worldly wisdom as a means to attaining practical success in life. The most prominent of these poems is the *Spaneas*, which takes the form of an admonition by Alexius, son of John Comnenus, to his nephew (twelfth century). It is written in popular Greek, and the advice, though platitudinous, is on the high plane of 'Love thy neighbour'. The poem was freely imitated in later versions, and in these the moral standard shows a decided change for the worse.

Special mention may perhaps be made of the descriptive poem in Byzantine literature. The tradition here is unmistakably Greek. It is as old as Homer's portrayal of the Shield of Achilles, and the treatment of such themes, constantly imitated and improved upon during the whole classical period, had attained a notable standard of excellence.

The best-known Byzantine example is, perhaps, Paul the Silentiary's contemporary description, in hexameters, of Justinian's reopening (probably in 563) of his great Church of the Holy Wisdom, which had been damaged by an earthquake. Its main interest for modern readers lies in its accurate and scholarly delineation of the architectural features of St. Sophia. But the author, despite derivative mannerisms and occasional frigidity of treatment, was a true poet. In a memorable passage he pictures the great dome at night, with its illuminated windows shining reassuringly over city and harbour, and welcoming the sailor as he leaves the storm-tossed Euxine or the Aegean and faces the last perils of his homeward voyage. 'He does not guide his laden vessel by the light of Cynosura or the circling Bear, but by the divine light of the church itself. Yet not only does it guide the merchant at night, like the rays of the Pharos on the African shore; it also points the way to the living God.'

Many features in the epic of *Digenes Akritas*, in the Romantic poems, the 'Rhodian' lover's handbook, and in satiric verse point forward to modern Greek literature, where the love-song is prominent, the satiric element is common, and a high standard of morality and family life is inculcated. The centralization of life in Constantinople, which, it was noted, did not favour literary activity in the provinces in the earlier Byzantine period, gave way before Western influences. Thus it is that after the period of the Crusades a link is established between Byzantine and modern Greek literature.

F. H. MARSHALL

IX

THE GREEK LANGUAGE IN THE
BYZANTINE PERIOD

THE political results of the conquests of Alexander the Great could not but exercise a vast influence upon the language of Greece. The congeries of dialects, local and literary, which had hitherto constituted the Greek language, was now called upon to produce from its own resources a medium of intercourse fitted for the use of an immense area of the world, in much of which other and quite alien languages had hitherto flourished. A certain simplification of the inflexions was natural, and a loss of the peculiar delicacies of Attic syntax was inevitable; the non-Greek world could hardly wield the idiom of Plato and of the orators and poets of the older Hellas. To this need the response of the Greek was the formation of the Hellenistic *koine*, ἡ κοινὴ διάλεκτος, the 'common language'. The very existence of such a generally accepted form of the language, whatever local differences it may have had within itself, was sooner or later fatal to the old dialects: the basis of modern Greek is quite naturally the *koine*.

To this clean sweep of the ancient dialects we have one interesting exception: the dialect still spoken by the Tsakonians in the Peloponnese does undoubtedly, in spite of recent objections to this view, retain among much that has come to it from the surrounding districts large elements from some ancient Laconian dialect.[1] Beyond this the remains of the ancient dialects are very scanty.[2]

---

[1] There is a list of the Dorisms in Tsakonian in Hatzidakis's *Einleitung in die neugriechische Grammatik* (Leipzig, 1892), pp. 8, 9. The anti-Doric view is expounded by H. Pernot in *Revue phonétique*, vol. iv (1917), pp. 153–88. This opinion Pernot has revised in his *Introduction à l'étude du dialecte tsakonien* (Paris, 1934), p. 102. He now thinks that Tsakonian is based on a local *koine* with a strongly Dorian tinge.

[2] Hatzidakis, *Einleitung*, p. 165. There is also a list of Dorisms in Hatzidakis's Μικρὰ συμβολή (*Comptes rendus de l'Acad. d'Athènes*, vol. iii (1926), p. 214). These have been disputed by Pernot in *Bibl. de l'École des Hautes Études*, vol. xcii, pp. 52–66, where he again deals with Tsakonian.

This disappearance of the old dialects worked towards a certain uniformity in the language, but before it could be complete—and how far the old dialects may have lingered in out-of-the-way places, no one can say—the changes which were leading to the formation of modern Greek were well on their way, and with them came the entirely fresh dialect divisions which mark the new language. To assign dates is not easy, but Hatzidakis shows reasons for believing that these processes belong to the long period between Alexander the Great and the reign of Justinian in the sixth century A.D., and that in any case the modern language was in its main features formed long before the tenth century.[1] The changes involved were naturally carried out more rapidly in some places than in others, and of this we have very strong evidence in the conservative character of some of the contemporary spoken dialects.[2] These dialectic differences throw, as we shall see presently, much light on the character of the spoken language of Byzantine times.

But the victory of the *koine* and its progeny was not at first complete. To men with a scholarly or antiquarian turn of mind it seemed an inelegant declension from the ancient standards of literature: hence began the atticizing school, represented most typically by Lucian, and all through the Byzantine period writers were imbued with this same purist spirit, though their standard was no longer Attic but the *koine* itself. And as this was also the language of the Church, fixed and liturgical, it was possible to check the processes of linguistic change to a really very remarkable degree. This standardizing of Greek was not without its good effects, but it inevitably produced a certain deadness, as learning and literature became the close preserve of trained scholars rather than a field open to all comers. A crabbed obscurity was admired, and writers forgot the truth embodied in the dictum

---

[1] Μεσαιωνικὰ καὶ νέα Ἑλληνικά (Athens, Βιβλιοθήκη Μαρασλῆ, 1905), vol. i, pp. 406, 480.

[2] Notably in the dialects of Asia Minor—I speak of the time before the catastrophe of 1923—Cyprus, south Italy, and certain oases, such as Chios, Rhodes, and Thrace: for which see Psaltis in Λεξικογραφικὸν Ἀρχεῖον (published by the National Dictionary now being compiled in Athens), vol. v, p. 258. For a summary account of the dialects, see 'The Dialects of Modern Greece', in the *Trans. of the Philological Society*, 1940.

of Koraes, that it is not enough for a writer to be learned and clever (σοφός); he must be clear (σαφής) as well.

In the development of Greek we have therefore to follow up two parallel but interacting currents: one is of the spoken language and the other is of the Greek of the written, classical tradition. For the second our task is plain; we have only to examine the voluminous literature of Byzantium, nearly all of which is in this form of the language. But this very fact has inevitably concealed from us a great many steps in the shaping of spoken Greek; of its local developments earlier than the thirteenth century we in fact know very little more than nothing. For what happened earlier than this date we have to depend upon contemporary documents—papyri and inscriptions—and still more upon the prohibitions of grammarians and their distinctions between classical and vulgar words and expressions, and upon the slips and errors of writers who were all the time aiming at writing anything but the popular Greek whose course we are trying to trace. It is fortunate that by the side of the learned historians we have the more popular chroniclers, such as Malalas of the sixth and Theophanes of the eighth century, and the writers of lives of the Greek saints, all of whom allow themselves to use a less classical style. Here, of course, a knowledge of the modern language is indispensable; it alone enables us to read the evidence correctly by letting us see the end towards which the language of the Byzantine period was tending.

For the twelfth century and onwards we have a series of texts, beginning with the satiric poems of Theodore Ptocho-Prodromus, written with more or less consistency in the spoken language: in all these writings we find a mixture of old and new forms, the latter steadily advancing at the expense of the former. Much obviously depends on the method of interpretation applied to these texts, and their evidence has, in fact, been read in two very different ways. Hatzidakis held that the inconsistency of their language arises from the writers using sometimes the ancient forms of the written tradition, and sometimes the forms with which they were themselves familiar as a part of the ordinary spoken Greek of the day, and that therefore what we are to see in these texts is the already formed modern language gradually forcing itself into literary use. By the side of these texts in popular Greek there are always the learned texts in which the authors as consistently as they could steadily followed the written, classical tradition.

To this view of the matter Psychari was fundamentally opposed. He rejected Hatzidakis's view of the mixed language, and therefore elaborately tabulated the increase in the texts of certain modern formations, and held that this reflects not their gradual adoption into written Greek, but their actual creation and spread in the spoken language.[1] From this it results that he put the formation of the modern language centuries later than Hatzidakis, and held that the most we can say of the period before the tenth century is that the *koine* was then weakening; that from then to about the year 1600 modern Greek was shaping itself, and that this process was only complete in the seventeenth century. Hatzidakis's evidence for the earlier centuries is largely drawn from the formation of new types of nouns and verbs regarded as involving the deep change in the language by which modern Greek was formed. All this very cogent evidence Psychari was able to set aside by a simple assertion that morphology, word-formation, and phonetic changes, being three different and separate things, may occur quite independently one of the other. I have no hesitation in following Hatzidakis in this matter.

In discussing the double current of all later Greek it will be convenient to begin with the language of the written tradition, the parent of the 'purifying speech', the *katharévousa*, of our own day.

In no department of life is the innate conservatism of the Byzantines more marked than in their adhesion to the old written tradition of literary Greek. Pride in their nationality, in their culture, and in their past; the haughty distinction between themselves and the outside barbarian peoples; all

---

[1] Psychari's views are expressed in his *Essais de grammaire historique néo-grecque*, part i (Paris, 1886), especially pp. 164–88. Hatzidakis criticized this paper very severely, both the method and the way in which it was applied, in the *Zeitschrift für vergleichende Sprachforschung*, vol. xxxi (1892), pp. 103–56, and gave his views on the early development of the modern language in his *Einleitung in die neugr. Grammatik* (1892), pp. 172–229, repeated in Μεσαιωνικὰ καὶ νέα Ἑλληνικά, vol. i, pp. 406–81, with a further criticism of Psychari, ibid., pp. 482–536.

these tended to confer on the language as handed down to them by a long chain of writers, always scholars and often saints as well, an almost sacred character, and produced from time to time revivals of classical style, when the written language was in the natural course of events showing signs of yielding to the pressure of the vernacular and following the new developments of the spoken Greek. Hence it is that later authors often write more classically than their predecessors: Photius in the ninth century is more classical than Theophanes in the eighth; Psellus in the eleventh and Eustathius of Thessalonica in the twelfth than the Emperor Constantine Porphyrogenitus in the tenth.[1] Such a revival was indeed very marked in·the period of the Comneni, and Anna Comnena conspicuously uses a purer style than some of the earlier writers. These backward movements present us with the extraordinary result that in point of classical correctness there is not very much to choose between, say, Procopius, writing at the beginning of our period, and Critobulus, recording the conquests of the Turks and the end of the Greek Empire in the fifteenth century. The same tendency towards an artificial purism, again with the same patriotic motive behind it, was very apparent in the literary movement associated with the regained freedom of Greece in the early years of the nineteenth century. The Orthodox Church with its long, complicated, and much-loved liturgies and services disposed people in the same direction. Membership of the Church was a mark of nationality, and it is due to the use of the liturgical language that a great many words not used in ordinary speech are for all that perfectly intelligible to almost any Greek.[2]

Psellus was the great literary figure of the eleventh century. He uses the purest written Byzantine style, which he himself calls the *koine*, a Greek which is in the direct line of ascent from the 'purifying speech' of the present day. This Greek may be briefly described as being as classical as the writer could make it.[3] In accidence Psellus keeps in the

---

[1] So Hatzidakis in *Zeitschrift für vergleichende Sprachforschung*, vol. xxxi, p. 108.

[2] See Hatzidakis's pamphlet Περὶ τῆς ἑνότητος τῆς Ἑλληνικῆς Γλώσσης (Ἐπετηρὶς τοῦ Ἐθνικοῦ Πανεπιστημίου, Athens, 1909), p. 141.

[3] Here I follow Émile Renauld, *Étude de la langue et du style de Michel Psellos* (Paris, 1920).

main to the old rules, yet, when he comes to employ exactly those forms which we are most certain had been for a long time out of spoken use, there are distinct signs that he found himself in the difficulties natural to a man writing a language which he does not speak. Notably the verbs in μι are very much broken down, and the pluperfect has very often dropped its augment. In syntax we have the same story: by the side of classical constructions we find what we can only call 'Byzantinisms', cases in which Psellus's lack of familiarity with ancient idiom caused him to make what, considering his aims, it is not unfair to call blunders. And another mark of artificiality is his predilection for precisely the forms which in the spoken language were most dead. Thus he has a particular liking for the dual and a strong tendency to over-work the optative, both being marks of forced purism, and to be seen as such when we remember that in the natural Greek of the New Testament the dual is not used at all and the optative is extremely rare. The perfect too is handled in a way that suggests that it is a dead and not a living form. Equally significant is the tendency to confuse the present and aorist imperative, a confusion which is at the back of the modern Cappadocian rule by which the contracted verbs use only the present, and all the other verbs only the aorist of the imperative, without any distinction of meaning.[1]

Rather more than a century later comes Anna Comnena.[2] Her purist ideals are the same as those of Psellus, and she dislikes to record even the names of barbarians, for fear that they may defile the pages of her history. But she is less successful than Psellus in her imitation of the ancient models. We may even find a sentence in which she uses in successive principal clauses a future indicative, an aorist subjunctive, and an aorist optative, without any distinction of meaning. The prologue of the *Alexias*, her history of her father's achievements, gives us her notion of the proper equipment for an historian. After remarking that history alone can save the memory of events from being swept away by the

---

[1] R. M. Dawkins, *Modern Greek in Asia Minor* (Cambridge, 1916), p. 139.
[2] Georgina Buckler, *Anna Comnena, a Study* (Oxford, 1929, p. 483). The sentence I refer to is in *Alexias*, xiii, p. 410 D. For her horror of 'barbarian' names cf. *ibid.*, vi. 14, p. 182 B; x. 8, p. 289 D; xiii. 6, p. 393 C.

X

stream of time, she announces herself proudly as 'nurtured and born in the purple, not without my full share of letters, for I carried to its highest point the art of writing Greek, nor did I neglect the study of rhetoric: I read with care the system of Aristotle and the dialogues of Plato, and fortified my mind with the *quadrivium* of sciences.' The ideals of the writer of a traditional style could hardly be put more clearly.

At the very end of the Empire we find the same ideals: Critobulus writes in the same purist style, and his opening words set the key to his book as a whole.[1] Just as Thucydides the Athenian announced himself as the author of his history, so nearly two thousand years later Critobulus of Imbros begins his book with the words: '*Critobulus the Islander, who traces his origin to the men of Imbros, wrote this history, judging it not right that matters so great and marvellous, happening in our own time, should remain unheard, but that he should write them down, and so hand them on to the generations which will follow us.*'

But all the world does not go to school. No doubt the level of education in Byzantium was high, nor was there any lack of successors to the pedantic Ulpian, the orator of Tyre, who would never sit down to a meal without first making sure that every word on the bill of fare was to be found (κεῖται) in the classical authors, for which he earned the nickname Keitoukeitos, a man who asked always 'Is the word classical or not?' (κεῖται; οὐ κεῖται;)[2] We may be sure too that pains were not spared to keep the language spoken at the imperial Court and in official circles at least very much nearer to the classical norm than the Greek of the streets and of the market-place.[3] But at the same time no efforts can keep a spoken language entirely stable. Beneath the language of the written tradition the conversational idiom of everyday life was continually developing fresh forms, and

[1] Published in Carl Müller's *Fragmenta historicorum graecorum*, vol. v (Paris, 1873). The prologue (p. 54) runs in the original: Κριτόβουλος ὁ νησιώτης, τὰ πρῶτα τῶν Ἰμβριωτῶν, τὴν ξυγγραφὴν τήνδε ξυνέγραψε, δικαιώσας μὴ πράγματα οὕτω μεγάλα καὶ θαυμαστὰ ἐφ' ἡμῶν γεγονότα μεῖναι ἀνήκουστα, ἀλλὰ ξυγγραψάμενος παραδοῦναι ταῖς μεθ' ἡμᾶς γενεαῖς, κ.τ.λ.

[2] Athenaeus, Book I, ch. 1. In the Loeb edition, vol. i, p. 6, line 5.

[3] Evidence for the purity of the Greek spoken by the much secluded ladies of the Byzantine aristocracy is to be found in a letter of 1451 from Filelfo to Sforza. The passage is on p. 183 of the 1478 edition of Filelfo's letters.

perhaps all the more easily as its work was untouched by the efforts of scholars, who were devoting themselves primarily to the preservation of their treasured inheritance, the written language, to the avoidance of solecisms and of such incursions of the spoken language into it as would seem from their point of view to be simply barbarisms.

Here the question arises: what do we legitimately mean by the very frequently used word 'barbarism'?[1] If we look impartially at the formation of the modern language, we cannot call everything non-classical a barbarism; to call the use of ἀπό with the accusative a barbarism is patently absurd. Yet the word has a real meaning. What may properly be called a barbarism is an error made in speech or writing by a man trying to use a language of which he has no real knowledge, or aiming at using an obsolete type of his own language; of barbarisms of this latter sort the medieval Greek texts are full. Such errors are very instructive, for they tell us at once that the word or form so used was no longer a part of the living language; it was a thing for the use of which there was no longer a genuine linguistic consciousness. I give some examples. In ancient Greek εἰς with the accusative and ἐν with the dative are kept distinct: in modern Greek both senses are rendered by εἰς with the accusative, and this began very early. So when Byzantine authors use ἐν with the dative it is a purist archaism, and when they carry it so far as to use their ἐν to express 'motion towards', they are committing a barbarism, and one that tells us that, in fact, ἐν with the dative must at that time have been a dead form. This barbarous use of the preposition is, indeed, very common. Again, in the *Chronicle of the Morea* we find an aorist participle ἀκούσων, and this is used for both the singular and the plural:[2] from this we can deduce that the writer was not really familiar with aorist participles, certainly not in their classical form. The present participle, on the other hand, supplies us with a set of examples which cannot properly be called barbarisms. Already in the papyri the

[1] The subject of 'barbarisms' I have treated at some length in a paper called 'Graeco-barbara', in the *Trans. of the Philological Society* for 1939.

[2] John Schmitt's edition (London, 1904), line 701, where the *codex hafniensis* reads Ἀκούσων ταῦτα οἱ ἄρχοντες τοῦ φραγκικοῦ φοσσάτου, and the *parisinus*, not much better, ἠκούσας, κ.τ.λ. There is another example in line 744.

masculine terminations of the present participle active are used for the feminine: an example is (the nominative) γυναῖκες ὀμνύοντας, *women swearing*. Then later the accusative singular masculine is used without distinction of gender or number or case. These uses have been called barbarous, but when we find in modern Greek the indeclinable participle in -οντα and the more developed form in -οντας, we shall be likely to think that all these seemingly barbarous forms were in actual use: they are not real barbarisms, but rather they prove that in actual usage the linguistic sense for the declined participle was breaking down, and that the undeclined participle of the modern language, with its special use, was gradually taking its place.[1] A real barbarism is a sort of linguistic Melchisedek, 'without father, without mother, without descent': these masculine for feminine forms are a part of the history of the language.

The use of the third person of the reflexive pronoun for the first and second persons is found already in Hellenistic Greek, and continues to be common: thus the eleventh-century text *Barlaam and Ioasaph* contains a number of examples.[2] This again we cannot call a barbarism, because in modern Greek ἑαυτό(ν, and even though less commonly ἐμαυτό(ν, is used for all three persons: an example is κύτταξα τὸν ἑαυτό μου, *I took a look at myself*.[3]

Modern Greek usage can therefore help us towards a knowledge of the spoken language of the Byzantine period. Sometimes, however, in the medieval texts we meet with forms that belong neither to the classical nor to the modern language. Such forms, if well established, are not to be rejected as mere barbarisms, but are to be regarded as inter-

---

[1] For this see Hatzidakis, *Einleitung in die neugriechische Grammatik*, p. 144, with many examples, from which I take the one in the text.

[2] e.g. on p. 270 in the Loeb edition (*St. John Damascene, Barlaam and Ioasaph*, London, 1914) we find Θησαυρὸν ἑαυτῷ εἰς τὸ μέλλον ἄσυλον θησαύρισον, and on p. 290: ταῖς ἀρεταῖς ἔθιζε ἑαυτόν. I accept Peeters's argument that this text is not by John of Damascus, but by Euthymius, Abbot of Iviron on Athos. For further discussion see *Analecta bollandiana*, vol. xlix (1931), pp. 276–312; and *Byzantion*, vol. vii, p. 692.

[3] For this and many other examples see Louis Roussel, *Grammaire descriptive du Roméique littéraire* (Paris, n.d. [1922?]), p. 125. For instances of the usage in *Barlaam and Ioasaph* see Loeb edition (cited note 2 *supra*) at pp. 40, 270, 284, &c.

mediate between the old and the new.[1] Thus the instru-
mental dative went out of use very early, and gave place
successively to ἐν with the dative, διά with the genitive, μετά
with the genitive, and finally to what is in use to-day, μετά or
μέ with the accusative.[2] Here is a whole series of inter-
mediate forms. Again, between the old synthetic future and
the modern future made with θά and the subjunctive we have
the medieval form made with ἔχω and the aorist infinitive;
a form which still exists in the modern language, but
expresses not the future but the perfect.[3] A study of popular
Greek will yield many more such instances. Thus we have
already seen that the present participle has now been reduced
to an indeclinable fragment of its old self. Yet there was in
Byzantine Greek a tendency to extend its use by combining
it, and other participles as well, with the verb *to be*, and
in this way forming analytical tenses. We find plenty
of examples in *Barlaam and Ioasaph*: thus συναθροίζων ἦν
and ἦν ἀποστείλας are equivalent to an imperfect and a
pluperfect, whilst συνδιαιωνίζων ἔσῃ is a durative future.[4]
For this idiom there is no room in modern Greek with its
loss of the participles, and it is a feature of the medieval
language which led to nothing, but before it perished its
extension was considerable. In the eighteenth-century
translation into popular Greek of the Lausiac History[5] this
usage is so frequent as to be a real mark of the style of the
book; it has been preserved, too, in Tsakonian. Here the
present and imperfect of the indicative have been lost—
though not the subjunctive present—and in their place the
present participle is used with the present and imperfect of
the verb *to be*. Thus *I see* is for the masculine ὁροὺρ ἔνι
(= ὁρῶν εἶμαι) and for the feminine ὁροῦαρ ἔνι (= ὁρῶσα

---

[1] For these forms see Hatzidakis, *Einleitung in die neugriechische Grammatik*,
p. 15, and also his Μεσαιωνικὰ καὶ νέα Ἑλληνικά, vol. i, p. 373.

[2] From Jean Humbert, *La Disparition du datif en Grec* (Paris, 1930), pp. 99–160
and p. 199.

[3] This form and the change in its meaning are discussed by Hatzidakis in
Μεσαιωνικὰ καὶ νέα Ἑλληνικά, pp. 598–609.

[4] The references to the Loeb edition (see p. 260, n. 2) are pp. 518, 458, and 602.
Renauld finds examples in Psellus, though he takes occasion to remark that they
are not quite equivalent to the corresponding tenses of the verb whose participle
is used in this way; see *Étude de la langue et du style de Michel Psellos*, p. 378.

[5] Λαυσιακόν. ἔκδοσις νέα. Ἀθῆναι, 1913, βιβλιοπωλεῖον Β. Κομπογιᾶ.

εἶμαι), and *we see* is ὁροῦντερ ἔμε for both genders, the specifically feminine participle having been lost in the way already described.[1]

On these two lines the language developed, and it is not an exaggeration to say that these two currents of Greek, classical and popular, have existed side by side from the very beginning of our period, and very probably even a great deal earlier, right down to the present day with its disputes on the 'language question'. What is particularly obnoxious to the modern champions of popular Greek is any coexistence of different forms of a language: any such 'doubleness of language' (διγλωσσία) they regard as harmful and absurd.[2]

From the fifteenth century we have an interesting piece of testimony that the Greeks themselves were very well aware of this state of affairs. The Cypriot chronicler Makhairas says that before the Frankish crusaders had seized the island the people had been capable of writing 'good Greek', ῥωμαῖκα καθολικά, and had used it for correspondence with the Emperor, but that when French was brought into the island and they were cut off from their cultural headquarters, then their Greek became barbarous. He puts it in this way: 'we write both French and Greek, in such a way that no one in the world can say what our language is'.[3] The traditional written Greek kept up by their connexion with the capital was lost, and the islanders were left with their uncultivated vernacular to which was added, as a further element of corruption, the influence of the language of their French conquerors.

The Hellenistic 'common language' began very early to split up into dialects, of which the descendants are being spoken to-day. Evidence for the age of these fresh divisions may be seen in the preservation in certain districts of features of the ancient language which began very early to change in the direction of the norm of modern Greek. An example is the ending -as of the accusative plural; this began to dis-

[1] Forms quoted from C. A. Scutt, *Annual of the British School at Athens*, vol. xix (1942–3), p. 168.
[2] Representative here is *Greek Bilingualism and some Parallel Cases*, by Peter Vlasto; Athens, at the 'Hestia' Press, 1933.
[3] *The Chronicle of Makhairas*, ed. Dawkins, 1932, vol. i, p. 143.

appear in favour of -ες as early as the reign of Nero. But it is still preserved in Pontus as well as in Ikaria, and sometimes in Chios and Rhodes: in these islands it is still distinguished from the -ες of the nominative.[1] To take another example; the velar consonants κ and χ began very early to acquire a palatal sound before ε and ι, and the earliness of this change is attested by its spread over the whole area of modern Greek excepting the island of Therasia and certain villages in Karpathos. In these places there has never been any palatalization, and the old velar sounds of κ and χ are preserved throughout, so that the κ in, for example, καί, has the same sound as the κ in κάνω.[2] Again, at least as early as the eleventh century, the feminine plural of the article followed the masculine, and for οἱ, αἱ we have οἱ, οἱ, pronounced ι; but in the Terra d'Otranto villages the αι has been kept and the plural runs masculine ι; feminine ε, and the only difference from ancient Greek is that the neuter is not τά but a.[3] It is interesting to note that in Kastellorrhizo there has been a levelling change in the opposite direction and αι, so far from disappearing, now serves for both masculine and feminine and for both numbers.[4] As a last example, an accented ι before another vowel now, as a rule, throws the accent on to the second vowel, so that, for example, παιδία is pronounced παιδιά. But in Terra d'Otranto, in Pontus, and in certain districts which fringe mainland Greece—Athens in its old dialect, Megara, Aegina, Mani, and in some of the Ionian islands—we still have the old accentuation παιδία preserved.[5] This shift of accent cannot, so far as I know, be dated, but it is certainly old enough to have formed a distinction between dialects in the Byzantine age. And these 'fringe' dialects still resist to some extent the *itacism* which marks modern Greek, for in

[1] For the significance of several of these dialectical variations see Hatzidakis in Μεσ. κ. νέα Ἑλλ., vol. i, p. 381; vol. ii, p. 438.

[2] Μιχαηλίδης–Νουάρος, Δημοτικὰ τραγούδια Καρπάθου (Athens, 1928), pp. 13, 14, with a review in the *Journal of Hellenic Studies*, vol. xlviii, p. 249.

[3] Hatzidakis, *Einl. in d. neugr. Grammatik*, p. 14, and for actual forms see Morosi, *Studi sui dialetti Greci della Terra d'Otranto* (Lecce, 1870), p. 118.

[4] Forms are to be found in Diamantaras's collections in Ζωγραφεῖος Ἀγών in Φιλολ. Σύλλογος Κ/πόλεως, vol. xxi (1892), pp. 315–66. Examples are ἐ οὐρανός, ἐ θάλασσα, ἐ Φράντσοι, the Franks.

[5] Thumb, *Handbuch d. neugr. Volkssprache*, 2nd ed. (Strassburg, 1910), p. 9. There is an English translation of this edition, Edinburgh, Clark, 1912.

them *v* still retains its old pronunciation *ü* or *u*, and has not as elsewhere become *i*.[1]

Similar evidence is provided by a study of the vocabulary of the spoken peasant dialects.[2] In them many words are preserved that have either entirely disappeared from the language as a whole—excepting of course the high written style—or else are represented in it merely by a few compounds, while at the same time the commonly used equivalents are sufficiently old to show that all through the Byzantine age the pairs of words existed side by side in the spoken language though in different areas. Thus ὀφθαλμός has everywhere given place to μάτι (= ὀμμάτιον), except that at Pharasa in the Taurus they used φτάρμι: elsewhere ὀφθαλμός survives only, so far as I know, in the island verb φταρμίζω, *to give the evil eye*. *Door* is everywhere πόρτα, just as οἶκος has given way to the equally Latin σπίτι (*hospitium*), but in Cappadocia θύρα was in use. In the Terra d'Otranto we have *phrea* and *liri* for *well* and *rainbow*, instead of πηγάδι and δοξάρι. The word for *bone* is now κόκκαλον, but in Terra d'Otranto we find *steo*, at Pharasa στό, and at Sinasos in Cappadocia στούδι; all from ὀστοῦν. The rarer word sometimes has a very much larger area. Thus for *sick*, ἄρρωστος is usual; in the Greek of Cyprus and Asia ἀστενής is preferred.[3] Of πῦρ only a few derivative compounds are left; the common word for *fire* is φωτιά. But in a song from Pharasa (unpublished) I find μπύρ' τὸ φοῦρνο for *put* (imperative) *fire into the oven*, and in Cappadocia forms from ἑστία were used; in Pontus ἄψιμο from ἄπτω; in Cyprus λαμπρόν; all of them are ancient words and, except λαμπρός, not usual in any sense outside these special areas. Such variations must go back to the very beginning of modern dialect division if they do not go further and point to

---

[1] Hatzidakis, Μεσ. κ. νέα Ἑλλ., vol. i, p. 53.

[2] It is in household and country words that these survivals are for the most part to be sought. In Karpathos I note τὸ τουττάρι, *afterbirth*, a diminutive of κύτταρος (Μιχαηλίδης, Λαογραφικὰ σύμμεικτα Καρπάθου p. 98); λεμιθόχορτον, λεβιθόχορτο (in which ἕλμινς is preserved), a *seaweed used as a vermifuge*; and many others.

[3] Other such 'easternisms' are ἀνοιχτάρι for κλειδί, ἀντάμα for μαζῆ, θωρῶ for βλέπω, μάτι for ὑποκάμισο (*shirt*). A list of these words is in Dawkins, *Philological Society's Transactions*, 1925–30, p. 318. For local differences in the *koine* itself and especially the question of an 'eastern *koine*', see Thumb's *Die Griechische Sprache im Zeitalter des Hellenismus* (Strassburg, 1901).

differences in the *koine* itself. Medieval Greek was, as Hatzidakis has said, anything but the plain and uniform successor to the *koine* which we find in the Byzantine authors of the written tradition.[1] To show its possible variations I give a piece from the story of the Cross; first as it appears in a version written probably somewhere in northern Greece and then as it is rendered into fifteenth-century Cypriot by Makhairas.

Καὶ εἶδεν ὄνειρον θεϊκόν, ὅτι ἔνας νέος ἄνθρωπος τὴν ἔλεγεν· Κυρία Ἑλένη, καθὼς ἔκαμες εἰς τὴν Ἱ(ερουσα)λὴμ καὶ ᾠκοδόμησες πολλοὺς ναούς, ἔτζι νὰ ,κάμῃς καὶ ἐδῶ.

In Cypriot we have:

Καὶ εἶδεν ἕναν ὅρωμαν, ὅτι ἔνας παιδίος ἄνθρωπος εἶπεν της· Κυρία μου Ἑλένη, ὡς γοιὸν ἐποίκες εἰς τὴν Ἱερουσαλὴμ καὶ ἔκτισες πολλοὺς ναούς, ἤτζου ποῖσε καὶ ὧδε.[2]

These local dialects no doubt seemed very rough and rustic to educated persons. Thus the fifteenth-century satirist Mazaris, professing to give a few words from the Tsakonian dialect, in fact heaps together a few colloquial and dialectic forms, which would seem so uncouth and provincial that they might well be from the incomprehensible speech of the Tsakonian peasants. Among the words he gives are two third plurals of the imperfect middle, ἐρχόντησαν and καθεζόντησαν, which in fact belong to the Peloponnesian speech of to-day, and some imperatives in -ον, which belong to-day, and probably then also, only to the Greek of Pontus and of south Italy. The forms are πιάσον τα, δῶσον τα, σφίξον τα.[3]

In the tenth century, too, the speech of Old Greece seemed barbarous to the educated. We have an epigram of this date: 'It was in no barbarous land but in Hellas that you became a barbarian both in speech and manners.'[4] Again, at the beginning of the thirteenth century we find Michael Acominatus, the Bishop of Athens, writing that long residence at Athens

---

[1] Hatzidakis, Μικρὰ συμβολὴ εἰς τ. ἱστορίαν τ. ἑλληνικῆς γλώσσης; *Comptes rendus de l'Académie d'Athènes*, vol. iii (1926), p. 214.

[2] Dawkins, *The Chronicle of Makhairas*, vol. i, p. 6; vol. ii, p. 14; see also Κυπριακὰ Χρονικά, vol. xi (1935), p. 10.

[3] Ellissen's *Analekten* (Leipzig, 1860), vol. iv, p. 230.

[4] Οὐ βαρβάρων γῆν, ἀλλ' ἰδὼν τὴν Ἑλλάδα,
ἐβαρβαρώθης καὶ λόγον καὶ τὸν τρόπον.
Printed in G. Soyter's *Byzantinische Dichtung* (Athens, 1938), p. 24, and also in Gregorovius, *Geschichte der Stadt Athen im Mittelalter*, Bk. I, ch. vii.

had made him a barbarian: βεβαρβάρωμαι χρόνιος ὢν ἐν ᾿Αθήναις.[1]

The Turkish conquest could not put an end to these tendencies in the language. The popular style, which had already appeared in writers of the period of the Comneni, came more and more to the fore, and Greek began to be written in a form closely resembling the common speech of everyday life. Good examples of this style are the books of the eighteenth-century geographer Meletius and the Chronicle of Dorotheus of Monemvasia. By its side the old classical style, increasingly filled, however, with Turkish words, continued its course, and after 1821 unfortunately eclipsed its rival, and the modern purifying language, the καθαρεύουσα, took shape and became the language of the nation. Its excesses produced the anti-classical movement of Psychari and Pallis, which has certainly had the result of moderating the classical excesses of the purists. It would seem now that Greece has entered upon a fresh period of 'diglossy', by some writers regretted, by others regarded as the only means by which a writer can have at his command the whole resources of the language.

The relations of the Byzantine Greeks with neighbouring peoples naturally made their mark to some extent in the language. But these contacts were never so intimate as to have any influence on the morphology and syntax; the frequent gallicisms in modern phraseology and the quasi-Turkish syntax of the Asia Minor dialects belong entirely to the world of post-Byzantine Greek,[2] and we are left here with nothing to discuss but the loanwords.[3] Space compels us to leave aside the few stray words, many for merchandise, from the Arabian East, and also the mainly rustic words brought in by Slavs and Roumanians and later by Albanian immigrants. Nor can we do more than mention the Frankish words introduced by the Crusaders, notably in Cyprus and the Peloponnese, where Ramon Muntaner, the Catalan writer, was able to say that as good French was spoken as in Paris.[4]

[1] Gregorovius, Geschichte der Stadt Athen im Mittelalter, Bk. I, ch. vii.
[2] For mutual influence of Balkan languages see Kr. Sandfeld, Linguistique balkanique (Paris, 1930).
[3] Collected in the not very critical book of M. A. Triandaphyllidis, Die Lehnwörter der mittelgriechischen Vulgärliteratur (Strassburg, 1909).
[4] Ch. cclxi: e parlauen axi bell Frances com dins el Paris.

These French words have for the most part disappeared, and the immense number of Italian words brought to the Greek East by merchant colonies from Venice and Genoa and by the later Italian conquerors belong only to the end of our period.

But a little more space must be given to the Latin words. Byzantium was a New Rome, and Roman administration, Roman law, and the Roman army system inevitably brought with them a great number of Latin words.[1] How deeply such professional words entered into the language of ordinary life may be doubted; nor can the test of survival be applied, as all such words naturally disappeared when the government fell into the hands of the Turks. But so many Latin words adopted for the common objects of life are still surviving that we may be sure that the Latin element played a real part in the ordinary language of Byzantium, spoken as well as written. We give a few examples of these words as collected by Gustav Meyer:[2] ἀκουμπίζω, *accumbere*; ἄρμα, *fem.*, *arma*; ἀρμάρι, *armarium*; βαρβάτος, *barbatus* (stallion); βίγλα, *vig(i)lare*; βιόλα, *viola*; βοῦλλα, *bulla*; δεφενδεύω, *defendere*; καλίγι, *caliga*. Then come the names of the months: Γενάρις, Φεβρουάρις, and popularly Φλεβάρις under the influence of φλέβα, because of the swelling of the springs, Μάρτις, Ἀπρίλις, and the rest. Further examples are σέλλα, *saddle*; σπίτι; πόρτα; στράτα, *road*; φοῦρνος, *oven*; σκάλα, *steps, landing-place* —Latin words heard every day in Greece, though many of them have always belonged to the spoken rather than to the written language. It is to be remarked, however, that until the nineteenth century the extremest conservatism of Greek was shown rather in matters of morphology and in the preservation of ancient words than in any great dislike of foreign words; Latin words also were so closely entwined with the very centre of Byzantine life that, even if they were recognized as non-Greek, they were regarded as free from the stigma of barbarism which attached itself to later comers.

R. M. DAWKINS

[1] Studied by L. Lafoscade, 'Influence du Latin sur le Grec', in *Bibl. de l'École des Hautes Études*, vol. xcii, followed by Triandaphyllidis's *Lexique des mots latins dans Théophile et les novelles de Justinien*.

[2] In *Neugriechische Studien*, vol. iii (*Sitzungsb. d. k. Akad. d. Wiss. in Wien, Philol.-hist. Kl.*, Band cxxxii (Vienna, 1895).

THE EMPEROR AND THE IMPERIAL ADMINISTRATION

I. THE BYZANTINE AUTOCRACY

FOR more than eleven centuries the absolutism of the Emperors was the mainstay of the State which throughout its history proudly bore the Roman name, although its territory soon became limited to the Greek-speaking East. As the bad years of civil war had at one time opened the way to the Principate of Augustus and so to the monarchy, in the same way the bitter experiences of the third century forced men to set their hopes upon an Emperor whose will alone should be the supreme authority in every department of public life. In internal affairs a closely organized bureaucracy, in foreign affairs an army and a diplomatic corps furthered the execution of the imperial will. Foreign enemies, although they varied in the course of centuries, rarely allowed the Byzantine Empire any considerable period of peace; this pressure explains the fact that the necessity for the imperial autocracy and its instruments was never questioned by the subjects of the Empire, in spite of occasional opposition to individual Emperors.

The Byzantine Emperors considered themselves the true heirs of the Roman Caesars. In this they were right, if we are considering the Roman Emperors of the Diocletiano–Constantinian type. The absolute monarch had developed from the first citizen, the *princeps*, who, by the grant of the name of Augustus, had from the first been raised above common humanity, and who, on his death, had been numbered amongst the gods. Now he was decorated with the diadem of the Hellenistic kings, as if to show by an external sign that the Hellenistic conception of the ruler as a divinity become man had won the day; indeed, in the Eastern provinces the Roman Emperor had been thus regarded from the beginning, and subsequently the view had spread throughout the Empire. For his subjects the Emperor was Lord and God; and, to a greater extent than before, everything connected with his person was regarded as holy. And this remained so, even after Constantine, when the Emperors had become Christian, and when the conception of the God-Emperor had to give way before the belief in a special sanctification of the ruler conferred on him through God's grace. Even then *Adoratio*, the *proskynesis*, remained: every subject when allowed to approach the Emperor—a concession obtained with far greater difficulty than in former times—was obliged to throw himself at his master's feet in an attitude of devotion. This ceremony and indeed the whole punctilious Court ceremonial with its hierarchy of rank were oriental in origin; so, too, were the Emperor's robes, glittering with pearls and jewels. Here Sassanid Persia provided the model; and the general effect of the ceremonial at which both Courts aimed was the same: the superhuman unapproachable character of the Emperor's person was deliberately stressed. In pictures the Emperors are represented with a halo. Resistance to the will of the sovereign was a crime against something inviolably sacred: it was a sacrilege.

The title of the Emperor remained for a time the old one, *Imperator Augustus*, and in the Greek official language *Autokrator Augustos*. Only in 629, after the final defeat of the Persians by Heraclius, was the Emperor called *Basileus*, the Greek word for king, which had always been used for the Emperor in non-official language. The names *Autokrator* and *Augustus* then fell into the background; the Empress was always called *Augusta*. After the coronation of Charlemagne as Emperor, the Byzantine ruler, as the true heir of the Roman Emperors, called himself *Basileus Rhomaion*— 'Emperor of the Romans'. In the tenth century the title of *Autokrator* was again added when the Tsars of the Bulgarians took the title of *Basileus*. Apart from being a title, the word *Autokrator* became the epitome of absolute power: hence our word autocracy.

Another Roman heritage was the method of conferring Empire on the ruler. In principle the Emperor was elective. The Senate, the army, and the people co-operated. When the throne became vacant, the Emperor could be proclaimed either by the Senate, which in course of time had in fact dwindled to a small body consisting of the highest officials of the Empire, or by the army, where again a small part acted for the whole body. The consent of the other electoral body was needed to establish a completely constitutional procedure; hence the acclamation of the people which was represented by the citizens of Constantinople assembled in festal array. This was a right which was maintained until the time of the Palaeologi. Finally, after the reign of Leo I (457), there was added the coronation, an important act which from the seventh century was usually performed in St. Sophia by the Patriarch. However, in contrast with the coronation of Western Emperors, which the Papacy made one of the most important rights of the Church, the Patriarch officiated at the coronation not as representative of the Church but as representative of the electors; and his co-operation was not regarded as essential for the legal institution of the Emperor. But only a relatively small number out of the long line of Emperors came to the throne in this way, for, by ancient usage, the sovereign chosen in that manner had the right to settle the question of succession during his lifetime by the nomination of one or more co-Emperors whom he selected freely according to his own judgement. On such an occasion the reigning Emperor usually performed the ceremony of coronation himself, as he always did when the Empress (Augusta) was crowned. The Emperor, the possessor of the undivided sovereignty, transferred the imperial power by conferring the diadem as symbol of office. On the occasions when the Emperor left the act of coronation to the Patriarch, the latter acted as his master's servant and by his commission. After the seventh century the position of 'co-Emperor' no longer involved active participation in the government. It is true that there were often more Emperors than one at the same time, but there was never more than one ruler. All the co-rulers shared in the imperial honours, but only one possessed the imperial power which passed automatically to his successor at his death. The Emperor frequently crowned his own son. Thus, in spite of the elective principle, it was possible to build up dynasties; for instance there was the dynasty of Heraclius; then the Isaurian dynasty after Leo III; and, most markedly, the Macedonian dynasty of the descendants of Basil I. The subjects of the Empire connected the idea of legitimacy with their feeling for a dynasty. We already find tendencies in this direction in the time of the families of Constantine and of Theodosius the Great. But the idea of legitimacy grew especially strong with the advent of the Macedonian dynasty. The *Porphyrogeniti*, that is to say the children of the reigning sovereign who were born in the Porphyry Chamber of the palace, were regarded more and more as the legitimate successors to the throne. Finally, the succession could be bestowed upon one of the imperial issue simply by the expression of the ruler's desire and without being preceded by a coronation. If the Emperor was under age or lacked the necessary qualities of a commander-in-chief, in the interests of the Empire the way out was found by granting the ruling power to a 'co-Emperor'—the government would then be carried on by him alone or a council of Regency might be appointed; during this time the rights of the legitimate successor to the throne were to be protected. It was certainly a popular step when such a ruler through marriage with an Emperor's widow or with an Emperor's daughter acquired a kind of claim to legitimacy. Loyalty to dynastic succession even brought women to the throne; this happened with the Princesses Zoë and Theodora (1042); their joint rule was the sole instance of a division of the supreme power. When Zoë in the same year took Constantine Monomachus for her third husband, the interlude of female government was ended; but it was revived for a short time after Constantine's death when Theodora was the only sovereign. This brings to mind the Empress Irene, who transformed the guardianship of her son into a personal sovereignty. That personal sovereignty met with no opposition, but the anomaly was expressed in the official titulary where Irene appeared as 'the Emperor' (Basileus). Such cases remained exceptions.

When an Emperor was once on the throne, there was no constitutional way of deposing him. If, however, his rule gave reasonable ground for discontent, recourse was had to the last resort of the subject, i.e. revolution, an expedient which was indeed at times abused. A new Emperor was proclaimed. If the *coup* failed, he met with the shameful death of a usurper; if it succeeded, his victory was the sign that God's favour had abandoned the dethroned Emperor. Not a few Emperors were forced to abdicate, or met a violent death as the result of revolts either in camp or in the palace. Success legitimized the revolution. In a somewhat modified sense Mommsen's description of the Principate—'the imperial power is an autocracy tempered by the legal right of revolution'—is applicable also to the Byzantine Empire.

Another quotation from the same historian is not less applicable here; arguing from the fact that the will of the people both raises the *Princeps* to the throne and overthrows him, he writes: 'the consummation of the sovereignty of the people is at the same time its self-destruction'. For the Emperor, once he was acknowledged, was the only being in whom sovereignty rested. It is true that even as late as the reign of Justinian one can find in the legislation a memory of the fact that all power was conferred upon the Emperor by the people in virtue of an old law, the *lex regia* or *lex de imperio*. Though Leo I in his order of the day to the army might say: 'the almighty Lord *and your choice* have appointed me Emperor', Justinian begins one of his novels with the words: 'since God has placed us at the head of the Roman Empire'. No matter by what means an Emperor had reached the throne, the idea that his sovereignty was derived directly from God was always preserved. He is the ruler whom God has crowned and is greeted as such; and the Emperors themselves make this conception their own. Michael II, writing to Louis the Pious, said that he held his power from God; and Basil I, who had risen from peasant stock, wrote in his advice to his son Leo: 'you receive imperial power from God', and 'you receive the crown from God through my hand'. No wonder that imperial power seemed to the Byzantines to be but an earthly image of the divine power. The thought is as ancient as the Christian Empire itself; it had already been expressed by Eusebius in the fourth century.[1] So Constantine Porphyrogenitus saw in the rhythm and order of the imperial power a reflection of the harmony and order displayed by the Creator of the world. The Emperor was the chosen of God and the Lord's anointed, to whom, like Peter, God

---

[1] Cf. *Annuaire de l'Institut de Philologie et d'Histoire orientales*, vol. ii (1934) (Mélanges Bidez), pp. 13–18.

had given the commission to feed his flock; this belief found its symbolical expression in the anointing of the Emperor, a rite which was probably introduced—though this is not certain—as early as the ninth century. The Patriarch anointed the Emperor with the consecrated oil, and thus gave expression to the divine will.

But God's will could only be that a Christian sovereign should rule over a Christian world. A necessary condition for succession to the throne was membership not only of the Empire but also of the orthodox Church, as well as the full possession of bodily and mental powers. The Christian 'Autokrator' is the heir of the idea of a universal Emperor, and at the same time he is the representative of Christianity, which is also conceived as universal. The whole world, the *oikoumenē*, forms the ideal limit and the goal of his rule. He alone has the right and the claim to be overlord of the universe. In disregard of the facts the theory was still firmly held that other Christian princes could be, as it were, only the representatives of the Christ-loving Emperor, and that territory formerly belonging to the Empire but now in possession of unbelievers must some day return to him, the lawful sovereign, the protector and disseminator of the Christian faith. So the title of *Basileus* was again and again refused to the German Emperors—Isaac Angelus called even Frederick Barbarossa simply *rex Alamanniae*; this clearly expresses the persistent nature of the fiction of the one and only God-guarded Imperium—an Imperium which is represented by the Byzantine Emperor.

His imperial power, founded in this way and fettered by no written constitution, was, theoretically at least, unlimited. Everything was subject to the imperial majesty. As in former times, the Autokrator held the supreme command over the army, and, not being obliged to follow the counsel of his advisers, could himself decide for war or for peace. A long line of capable soldiers exercised this right, down to the last Constantine, who was killed while fighting for his capital. Furthermore, the Emperor was the sole and unrestricted legislator. In this capacity he organized and supervised the administration. He appointed the officials and officers, allocated their powers, and determined their rank. He gave special care to the financial administration, for its successful management was an essential condition for the welfare of the State. He decided what taxes should be levied and how the moneys raised should be applied, and he alone controlled the income of the imperial treasuries. The Emperor was also supreme judge, for he was the final interpreter of the laws.

Another duty of the Christian ruler was the welfare of the Christian Church, whose unity was to be the strong cultural bond which held together the Empire. That conviction had been formulated at the outset by Constantine the Great as one of the axioms of imperial duty. Therefore the regulation of the Church as the support of the State was an essential duty and at the same time a right of the Emperor. The Church had become the State Church; it was within the State and was part of the State organization. Its victory had been gained with the assistance of the Emperors. That fact was never forgotten by the Church of the Eastern half of the Empire; it acknowledged the ruler's authority. But the Emperor drew permanent constitutional conclusions from individual precedents. It is highly significant that Justinian's code, the codification of the imperial legislation in the name of our Lord Jesus Christ, should begin with a section on the sublime Trinity and the Catholic faith, and should combine in the same first book the laws relating to the order of the Church and to defence against its enemies with the laws concerning the position of imperial officials. In this way the Emperor co-operated in the formation of canon law. He did this in another way too: following Constantine's example, he summoned the General Church Councils and presided over their sessions either in person or by deputy. He confirmed their canons, gave them the force of law, and took measures for their execution. Resistance to the decisions of the Councils was heresy, but at the same time it was opposition to the authority of the State. When the Emperor appointed bishops and removed those who opposed him, so long as he did not violate the traditional forms of episcopal elections, he might well count such intervention as part of his duty to maintain good order in the Church.

In this way the State preserved ecclesiastical discipline,

while at the same time it upheld the dogmas of the faith. It is therefore not surprising that Emperors who were interested in theology should also have sought personally to influence the formulation of dogma. Justinian can again be regarded as the model of such an Emperor. The Iconoclast controversy was the main occasion on which the claim of the Emperor to decide ecclesiastical questions by the authority of the State was emphasized.

This autocracy, which expressed itself both in temporal and in ecclesiastical matters, has been described as a Christian caliphate or sacerdotal monarchy; it is more often known by the name of 'Caesaropapism'. But when all is said, it is possible that the resemblance of this autocracy by the grace of God to a theocratic government has been overstressed. It is true that the Emperor Marcian was acclaimed as *Hiereus* (priest) and *Basileus* (king) at the Council of Chalcedon, and before and after him Theodosius II and Justinian were even greeted as *Archiereus*. But the question may at least be raised: How great a part was played by memories of the title *pontifex maximus* borne by earlier Emperors and long since abandoned? Justinian himself clearly distinguishes in a law between *sacerdotium* and *imperium* as two gifts of God's mercy to humanity, a thought which was also on occasion expressed by John Tzimisces. A reminiscence of this idea of the equality of these rival powers seems to live on in the ceremonial of the tenth century when both Emperor and Patriarch pay to each other the tribute of formal *Proskynesis*. Moreover, when in the above-mentioned law Justinian puts forward a claim to the Emperor's right of supervision of the affairs of the *Sacerdotium*, he does so not by virtue of any sacerdotal authority; this is also the case when he makes use of legislation to guard the souls of his subjects from the dangers of heresy. Again, this holds good when his Patriarch Menas expresses the subordination of the Church to the State in the words that nothing should be done in the holy Church contrary to the intention and the will of the Emperor. This does not prove that the Emperor was infallible in the spiritual domain as he was in the temporal. If that had been so, why should Justinian have needed the signatures of the Patriarchs or even of a general council for the recognition of his legislation on points of dogma? Even if an Emperor called himself 'Emperor and priest' in the heat of the Iconoclast controversy, yet at the same time the champions of Church independence were vigorously maintaining the lay character of the imperial power. Not even the fact that the sacred person of the Emperor was admitted to the sanctuary, which was otherwise reserved for the clergy, makes him a priest. And the increasing penetration of ecclesiastical customs into the ceremonies of the Court has a parallel in the daily life of every single Byzantine which is equally regulated by religious usages. Can one really speak of 'Caesaropapism', when one remembers that even in those times when the Church was prepared to recognize the supreme right of imperial supervision over itself, the Patriarch as guardian of the discipline of the Church was able to excommunicate an Emperor? It is true that such an action was directed only against the person of the Emperor, not against the institution. Yet in this right of the Patriarch we may see an indication that arbitrary despotism was kept within limits.

Similar limits restricted the Byzantine imperial dignity in other ways, although the existence of the autocracy was based on the fact that there was no institution of equal authority which could legally oppose its will. For it was expected of the Emperor that he himself should observe the laws, although he was the only lawgiver; yet God had subordinated even the law to him in so far as He sent him to mankind as a 'living' law; in these words of Justinian, we can catch yet another echo of Hellenistic constitutional theory. Justinian's code conformed to this expectation by adopting a passage from an edict issued by Theodosius II, in which the sovereign professed himself bound by the law (*adligatum legibus*): 'for our authority depends on the authority of the law, and in fact the subordination of sovereignty to the law is a greater thing than the imperial power itself'. The law, it is true, included also administrative regulations and in this sphere there were naturally many changes in the course of a long and agitated history. Yet the conservatism which can be traced even in this sphere—and the term 'conservative' does not necessarily mean 'fossilized'—is due to the binding force of legal tradition. Moreover, Byzantine officials may often have felt some sympathy with the opinion of the *quaestor* Proclus who on occasion would oppose his Emperor Justin I with the words: 'I am not accustomed to accept innovations; for I know that in the making of innovations security cannot be preserved.' In this way the Senate could exercise its influence even without constitutional rights, and in particular could impose its will on a weak Emperor, consisting as it did of high dignitaries, and being able to act in its capacity of a Council of State. And it must be remembered that down to the seventh century the people of Constantinople, politically organized in their *demes*, usually known as the parties of the Circus, frequently compelled the Emperor to parley, and even when the *demes* had lost their political significance and played their part only in an inherited ceremonial, the resistance of the people was often expressed in riots and rebellions, in which fanatical monks not seldom took the lead.

A remarkable instance of the limitations imposed by the Emperor on himself was the obligations which the newly chosen ruler undertook towards his electors. Thus Anastasius I took an oath that he would forget former enmities and would govern the Empire conscientiously. Besides this, being suspected of heretical inclinations, he signed, on the demand of the Patriarch Euphemius, a solemn declaration never to introduce innovations into the Church. There was thus a kind of pledge on election which had the effect of binding the Emperor morally, if not legally. Finally—we do not know exactly when—this developed into an arrangement by which a regular coronation oath was sworn. In this oath the Emperor assured the people of his orthodoxy, and promised to preserve inviolate the decrees issued by the recognized Councils, and also the rights and privileges of the Church; furthermore he undertook that towards his subjects he would be a mild and just sovereign, and that so far as possible he would refrain from inflicting the death penalty or mutilation. Justin I had already at his coronation made a similar promise to govern justly and mildly, while his predecessor Anastasius had expressed such sentiments more generally when he implored the Almighty to give him strength to govern in accordance with the hopes of the electors. The later coronation oath shows what the subjects expected from their sovereign. The theme of the Emperor's duties occurs once; but the reference is not to the heavy burden of daily routine work and the toils borne by a painstaking Emperor as the circle of his work widened, but rather to that spirit which was supposed to underlie all his actions. Here again we find an echo of an ancient tradition appearing as one of the principles binding on the autocrat. The conception of the love of mankind, of *Philanthropia*, as conceived by Hellenistic philosophy in its picture of the ideal ruler, is applied to Constantine by Eusebius in his panegyric, and translated into the sphere of the Christian Empire. In the next generation the orator Themistius derived all the duties of the imperial office from this general conception of *Philanthropia*. This subject was taken up again and again. And it did not fail to make an impression on the Emperors. Justinian used similar formulas, including precisely this conception of *Philanthropia*, as the foundation of his legislative activity. In one case where he prescribes the death penalty he gives his reasons in the following words: 'this is not inhumanity (*apanthropia*); on the contrary, it is the highest humanity (*philanthropia*), for the many are protected by the punishment of the few.' From beginning to end the idea persisted that 'philanthropy' was the duty of the Emperor, who saw his task as justice and the protection of his subjects. There were exceptions enough. But the ideal, once accepted, was again and again a restraining force, all the more so since the sovereign's actions were also always kept within certain limits by public opinion. However, neither this latter consideration nor the guidance of a moral standard could really be called a constitutional obligation, any more than the fact that the conception of imperial authority as a gift of God, in accordance with the prevalent religious feeling, could increase the sense of responsibility even of the ablest sovereigns.

The extent to which a Byzantine Emperor was bound by tradition is shown yet more clearly in what might seem at first sight to be mere formalities. The Court ceremonial with its usages set a limit which the arbitrary caprices of the autocrat never broke through. This is all the more re-markable since here in the pomp of these ceremonies the unapproachable majesty of the Emperor found its fullest expression. Constantine Porphyrogenitus indeed, who personally supervised the composition of a 'Book of Cere-monies', gives the motive for this activity, which he classes among the necessary duties; he states that the imperial power shines in greater splendour and rises to greater dignity through a laudable ceremonial; and thus foreigners as well as his own subjects are filled with admiration. This Book of Ceremonies has rightly been called the codification of Court ceremonial and recognized as an essential characteristic of Byzantine statesmanship. The details of the ceremonies which were obligatory on all sorts of occasions pass in a lengthy catalogue before the reader, as for instance the pro-cessions at important Church feast-days, the solemn formali-ties of festivals in the imperial family, the reception of ambassadors, and the part taken by the Court in traditional popular festivities. Whether the matter in hand was the coronation of the Emperor or merely one of His Majesty's excursions, the investiture of a high dignitary or a Court dinner party, all the arrangements were predetermined down to the last detail, with particulars of the time and place, the circle of those taking part, their dress, their behaviour, and their words of salutation. These fixed rules were laid down for the Emperor from the moment of his accession to the throne; they surrounded an imperial prince from the cradle to the grave. The christenings and the celebration of birth-days and weddings follow these rules in the same inevitable way as the funerals and the Court mourning. The attendance of a large imperial household, of numerous dignitaries and servants, of palace guards and of the people, the order of precedence which was always observed, all combined to increase the conservative effect. We discover the importance of such institutions when reading the *kletorologion* of the *Atriklines*, the Court marshal, Philotheus, which is a treatise on the regulations governing precedence at a Court dinner in the year 899. Further proof of the strength of a tradition of many centuries which lasted until the Empire's fall may be seen in the fact that, as late as the fourteenth century, at a time when the splendour of the Empire was already dimmed, a book on the *Offices*, wrongly attributed to Georgius Codinus, discussed the same theme of the ceremonial, of the order of precedence, and of official and Court apparel. But the Emperor always remained the centre. Everything had reference to him; his presence was essential for the ritual and that presence determined the whole ceremonial.

When all this is borne in mind, it becomes difficult, in fact impossible, to place this Byzantine autocracy within any category of the usual modern constitutional theories. It was taken as so much a matter of course by the Byzantines that it did not occur to them to theorize about it. It was so exclusive in its nature that no one ever thought of comparing it with other forms of government. But the fact that this institution as such was never questioned, apart from Utopian experiments in the last period of decline, is a proof that this autocracy in its own particular nature was admirably suited to the circumstances of its time.

II. THE ADMINISTRATIVE SYSTEM

A modification of the administrative system of the Empire was introduced simultaneously with the final autocratic development of the imperial power. This reform was intended to provide means for the defence of the Empire and for the administration of internal affairs, and at the same time to draw together the heterogeneous elements so as to form a united realm; for this purpose it aimed at building up a bureaucracy controlled down to the last detail. The system was centred in the will of the Emperor and the aim of the system was to render the expression of that will effective. Former Emperors had, of course, prepared the way. The permanent principles of the new administrative system were first established under Diocletian and Constantine. In spite of many changes and adaptations in detail these principles continued to be of great service in after years, and even survived the revolutionary reforms of the seventh century. This fact serves to explain a certain rigidity in the system of administration, which was more the result of the pressure of circumstance than of any subtle theorizing. For just as the autocracy was necessary for the existence of the Empire, so external pressure, which hardly ever relaxed, caused a state of continuous strain upon all the resources of the Empire; thus to develop and control all these resources the establishment of the administrative system with its countless bureaucrats was in its turn a necessity. However, the maintenance of this bureaucracy, together with the defence of the Empire and the expense of a magnificent Court, entailed a considerable drain on the finances and was partly responsible for the fact that an inexorable fiscal policy, with all its consequences, gave the State its particular character.

In order to protect the Emperor from a dangerous rivalry, which could have arisen if great military and civil power had been combined in one person, civil and military authority were completely separated. The division of large provinces into small administrative districts served the same purpose, and the governor profited by this arrangement, as he was able to manage his judicial and administrative work with greater efficiency. Several provinces formed a diocese, several dioceses formed a prefecture. There were two prefectures in the Eastern half of the Empire: Oriens with five dioceses (comprising the Asiatic territory, Egypt, and Thrace), and Illyricum with two dioceses (comprising the rest of the Balkan peninsula as far as the Danube). To the Praetorian Prefect, now the highest civil official, fell the supervision of the administration and an extensive jurisdiction, which functioned as the highest court of appeal. He exercised supreme authority over the police, and, above all, controlled the administration of the important land tax, the *annona*, from the revenue of which he had to pay the salaries of the officials and the soldiers, and to feed the army. The dioceses were under the control of the representatives of the Prefect, the *vicarii*, who could also report directly to the Emperor, while an appeal lay from their decisions to the Emperor's court. Similarly the Emperor was in direct communication with the *vicarii* and with the provincial governors, and sent special deputies to inspect the administration when the necessity arose. In this way a system of mutual control was established: such a system, it was true, might produce disputes between rival authorities through overlapping of their spheres of duty or from questions of precedence, but this the

Government was content to accept, in order to increase its own powers of supervision. The same result was produced by the joint responsibility of the subordinates forming the staff (*officium*) of a high official; these subordinates, in the event of any error on the part of their superior officer, were held jointly liable and were therefore exposed to punishments which were often serious. Although decentralization obtained when the system of prefects was introduced in order to lessen the burden of the direct transaction of business by the Emperor, yet there was continuous opposition to all attempts to establish too great an independence of the central Government. In spite of this the influence of the Praetorian Prefects was strong enough to secure in course of time that the officials who were in competition with them became more and more their own executive organs. In particular the officials charged with the collection of the taxes, working under the control of the prefecture, steadily gained in importance at the expense both of the provincial governors and also of the staffs of the central bureaux. The organization of the Taxation Department, which was under the *scriniarii*, increased in size as well as in influence in the civil service, and in the fifth century it had a number of subordinate departments of its own, among which were those for the pay and the commissariat of the army, for public works and arsenals; the prefect's treasury was separated into two sub-departments, a special department for the salaries of the officials directly under the prefecture, and the general pay office for the rest of the salaries. The prefecture of the East had its official seat in Constantinople. The administration of the capital was carried out by the city prefect, who was next in rank below the Praetorian Prefect. He was supreme judge over all senators in civil and criminal causes arising within the boundaries of the capital. He was also responsible for the supervision of food supplies and of the *collegia*, the guilds.

Constantinople, as the seat of the imperial Court, was also the seat of the central administration, with a number of high officials whom we may call ministers, although with some hesitation. Of these the most important was the *Magister officiorum*, who supervised the imperial chanceries (the

Scrinia), the arms factories, and the postal system, and had command over the bodyguard. As master of the ceremonies he also introduced embassies from abroad, thus performing the functions of a foreign minister. Assisted by *Agentes in Rebus*, who were at the same time couriers and secret police, he became the highest instrument of imperial control. From the *Agentes in Rebus* he formed his own staff; and he filled many of the highest posts in the civil and military administration by sending seniors in rank to act as chiefs of staff (*principes*). The *Quaestor Sacri Palatii* was the chairman of the imperial State Council, the *Consistorium*, and minister of justice; in this capacity he drew up drafts of legislation and answers to petitions with the assistance of the staff of the *Scrinia*. Secretaries of State, *Magistri Scriniorum*, were at his disposition for other branches of the imperial correspondence. As finance ministers the *Comes Sacrarum Largitionum* and the *Comes Rerum Privatarum* should be mentioned. The former derived his name from the largesses (*largitiones*) which the Emperor used to distribute to his soldiers on certain occasions. He administered the Treasury proper, which succeeded the *Fiscus*, into which flowed the tribute paid in money, taxes paid by the senatorial order, taxes on trade and industry, and other revenues. Mines and the mint were also under his control. The *Comes Rerum Privatarum* administered the extensive domains belonging to the State, of which one part was set aside for the exclusive use of the Court; he also administered the imperial privy purse. The fact that the lower officials of the central finance departments were known as *Palatini* shows the extent to which these departments were regarded as offices of the Court. It is therefore not surprising that the highest Court official, the Lord Chamberlain, *Praepositus Sacri Cubiculi*, not only enjoyed a rank equal to the highest State officials, but was also at an early date entrusted with the administration of the domains reserved for the upkeep of the Court. Finally a new official arose to manage the Privy Purse, the *Sacellarius*, 'steward of the Privy Purse'. As this Privy Purse had again and again to cover the deficit of the *Comes Sacrarum Largitionum*, inevitably it also became a State Treasury, and the *Sacellarius* finally replaced the *Comes*.

The precedence of the officials was settled comparatively early by dividing them into classes of rank. The high officials belonged to the classes of *illustres*, *spectabiles*, and *clarissimi*. The liberality of the Emperor in distributing titles caused these to become increasingly pompous; 'Magnificence' and 'Excellency' survive to the present day. The original official name of an imperial attendant, *Comes*, also became a title of rank and was graded in three classes. The highest honour which was not connected with an office was that of a Patrician, which had been created by Constantine. It was surpassed only by the Consuls, present and past, known in Greek as the *Hypatoi*, until finally, after the abolition of this magistracy, which for a long time had been an expensive distinction without real administrative authority, the office of honorary consul was turned into a new title of rank, that of *Hypatos*. Furthermore, the names of offices which had not become sinecures could also be granted as honorary titles, and later they, too, could become mere titles of rank.

Admission to office and attainment of the highest honours were open to all, except to those who were bound to another class by hereditary obligation. Further, the lower officials needed the approval of the Emperor before taking their first post. Promotion followed in order of seniority. It must not be forgotten that very important positions could be reached in the staffs of the bureaux, from which promotion to higher posts was possible, and in some cases certain. The number of officials employed in both the Eastern prefectures was reckoned to be about ten thousand. The salaries of the officials formed an important part of the budget. In addition they received all sorts of extra fees (*sportulae*) which can almost be called indirect taxes. The bureaucratic machine was never entirely free from corruption, against which the Emperors struggled with varying success. The administrative organization, when once instituted, showed, both for good and for evil, a capacity for passive resistance to the imperial will which is not to be underestimated. The chief officials were often changed, but their highly trained subordinates were more reliable agents for the effective discharge of business and at the same time jealous guardians of administrative tradition. Johannes Lydus, who had himself worked in the office of the Praetorian Prefect, gives examples of this in his book *On the Magistracies*. And the difficulties with which reforming Emperors had to contend in these offices are reflected in the imperial decrees, even in those of Justinian, although he had received the support of a man as energetic as the Praetorian Prefect John of Cappadocia.

The gradation of the effective offices and of a small number of high ministers and correspondingly high military officers in the central department (see § III) is shown in the State manual, the *Notitia Dignitatum*, which dates from the fifth century, and apart from a few modifications the order remained the same until the sixth century. Philotheus's above-mentioned 'list of court officers', written in the last year of the ninth century, gives us a completely different picture. The number of officials placed directly under the Emperor had considerably increased. The former system of subordination in the administration had been replaced in the course of time by an extensive co-ordination; this did not affect the order of ranks, which by then had been considerably further developed. Heavy fighting with Persia had forced the Emperor Heraclius to introduce a new military organization, the system of themes or military districts (see § III), which had perhaps been borrowed from his Persian opponents. As civil authority had been once more joined with the military command, these military areas had become new administrative districts. The themes took the place of the provinces, and this change was the more conspicuous when smaller districts were formed from the themes which originally had been of very wide extent. The union of civil and military powers had already begun in those Western districts which had been reconquered for the Empire under Justinian; the *exarchs* combined the duties of a Master of Soldiers (*magister militum*; see § III) with those of the Praetorian Prefect. Justinian had also made the same arrangement for some of the Eastern provinces. The new order introduced by Heraclius came fully into operation in the time of the Isaurian Emperors, but neither here nor in the rearrangement of the central offices can any uniform and single plan be traced. The Praetorian Prefecture disappeared. It lost its significance when civil and military jurisdiction were joined. Besides, its financial department had increased to such an extent that it was finally split up into independent offices directly under the Emperor's control. It seems that the intention to do away with the former decentralization and the independence which was its consequence played an important part in these developments. The reduction of the size of the Empire, especially after the Arab conquests, made a strong policy of centralization easier. The gradual dissolution of the all too influential central office of the *Magister Officiorum* is in keeping with this general policy. The duties of the Lord Chamberlain, the *Praepositus Sacri Cubiculi*, were also divided up and carried out by different independent officials. The names of the offices which had thus disappeared remained as titles of rank. While Latin was very much in the background in the naming of the effective offices for which the uniform Greek official language was used, yet a relatively large number of Latin names was retained among the titles of rank. At the beginning of the tenth century there were fourteen such titles, and accordingly there were fourteen classes of rank, apart from those reserved for members of the imperial family and for the eunuchs of the Court. The highest rank was that of a *Magister*; then followed the *Patricii Anthypatoi*, a revival of the Greek name for proconsul; then the *Patricii*, and so on down to the rank of a former prefect (*Apo Eparchon*) or of a general (*Stratelates*). The privileged position of those personally serving at Court is reflected in the precedence granted to eunuchs over others of equal rank. Apart from his official designation, as a rule every higher official bore such a title of rank, which was conferred on him by the Emperor in a ceremonial audience: a diploma or sign of rank (*brabeion*) was given him to be held for life. A *Magister* received a tunic interwoven with golden threads, a cloak laced with gold, and a belt set with precious stones. The *Spatharii* wore a sword with a golden hilt. Others received specially designed necklaces.

The offices were conferred by an order from the imperial Cabinet. The Emperor alone controlled appointments, promotions, and dismissals. The prospect of promotion and with it a rise in rank and salary was the chief way of en-

couraging the ambition of officials. The personal dependence
of high officials on the Emperor was perhaps most clearly
expressed in the scene when in the week preceding Palm
Sunday the Sovereign, in one of the audience-rooms of the
Palace, paid out the salaries with his own hands; this procedure did not fail to make an impression on Bishop Liutprand of Cremona, the ambassador of Otto I. Such a close
connexion with the Court increased the self-respect of the
high officials. There were still offices solely connected with
the Court, mostly belonging to eunuchs, who served the
sovereigns directly and conducted the administration of the
household. At the head of every palace stood a *Papias* (or
Warden of the Gate) and also the *Protovestiarius*, who was
the head of the imperial private wardrobe and of the treasury
connected with it. Largesse was given out of this treasury on
festival occasions. The office of *Praepositus* survived in the
more modest position of a master of ceremonies. The most
influential member of this group was, however, the Grand
Chamberlain, at this time styled the *Parakoimōmenos* (i.e. one
who slept next to the imperial bedchamber). The holders of
this office often enjoyed considerable influence; Basil, for
instance, the all-powerful minister under John Tzimisces
and his successor, made use of his position to acquire a huge
fortune. The possibility of such abuses was not overlooked,
but it was realized that eunuchs were in all circumstances
excluded from the imperial throne, and could therefore
never become usurpers, nor had they descendants on whose
behalf they might exploit their opportunities.

The central imperial administration, with its seat in Constantinople, included only civil offices. The generals stationed in the capital and the admiral of the home fleet had
nothing to do with the administration, not even later when
the *Great Domesticus* had become commander-in-chief of the
army, and the *Great Drungarius* High Admiral. Philotheus
distinguishes in the administration between *Kritai*, judicial
offices, and *Sekretikoi*, chiefly financial offices. This separation never became complete, especially as the tendency to
widen the sphere of the activities of some departments
became in the course of time more and more apparent. The
highest official of the *Kritai* was the City Prefect, the *Eparchos*,

who retained the old title and in the main still continued to discharge his former duties. He was the highest in rank among the civil officials. No eunuch was allowed to hold this office. He was the head of the city after the Emperor, and was addressed as 'father of the city'. He was assisted in his judicial activities by the *Logothete* of the *Praetorium*, and in the administration of the city by the *Symponos*, and also by a numerous staff, as was always the case with the chief offices. The *Eparchikon Biblion*, which deals with the activities of the Prefect in the tenth century, gives detailed information regarding his sphere of duty. He was the chief officer in charge of the guilds, consequently he supervised trade and commerce, controlled the police who guarded roads and buildings, and formed a fire-brigade; he watched over the Sunday rest, and inspected foreigners engaged in trade. The supervision of aliens in the wider sense was under the control of the *Quaestor*, who also kept his former title. But his province was combined with that of an office created by Justinian, the *Quaesitor*. Some of the former imperial secretaries were now transferred to his department and acted as his subordinates. He was the head of a court of appeal, and was a court of first instance for questions of wills and guardianship. The department for petitions was the only one which continued independently in the office called *epi tōn deēseōn*.

The *Sekretikoi*, named after their offices which were called *Sekreta*, were mostly financial officials; their superiors in rank were usually called *Logothetes* (literally accountants); the others were named *Chartularii* (actuaries), and the names of their departments were always specially added. Here the separate offices appear which had developed out of the finance department of the Praetorian Prefecture, though their field of activity could often be widened at the expense of other former offices: thus the *Logothetes tou genïkou* who was responsible for the administration of the land tax, and was therefore a particularly important official, also supervised the contributions for the upkeep of aqueducts and the revenues from mines. There were separate departments in his office for the assessment and for the collection of taxes. The *Logothetes tou Stratiōtikou* controlled the pay and the commissariat of the army; he was thus a kind of Quartermaster-General and chief paymaster. The official named *epi tou eidikou* controlled a special branch charged with the supply of equipment for the troops, for which purpose the State factories were under his control. The *Chartularius tou Vestiariou* may be mentioned next, as he had similar duties, some of which he inherited from the *Comes Largitionum*. He supervised the *vestiarium*, that is, the State wardrobe, from which other kinds of materials for purposes of peace or war were also supplied, and further controlled the imperial mint. A special branch of the office of the *Comes rerum privatarum* was now represented by the *Logothetes tōn agelōn*, who supervised the domains in which stud horses were bred for the needs of the army, and he is accordingly classed by Philotheus as an army official. The *Sacellion*, the origin of which we mentioned above, had gained in importance in that it had also attracted other business besides that of the *Comes sacrarum largitionum*. The independent chief of this State Treasury was the *Chartularius* of the *Sacellion*, originally a subordinate of the *Sacellarius*, who had in the meantime risen to the office of general controller of all *Sekreta*, that is, all offices of finance.

Of those administering the domains we need mention only the *Orphanotrophos*, the director of the large orphanage in Constantinople, who was usually a priest. In general the institutions of social welfare such as hostels, poor-houses, and hospitals were left to the care of the Church; but the Emperors frequently provided property from the domain-lands for their establishment; in spite of the fact that these institutions were run by priests, they remained under the State's financial control and were placed under the administration of an office of the State domains.

The postmaster-general also took the title of *Logothete*, *Logothetes tou dromou*; without properly belonging to the financial administration, he was counted among the *Sekretikoi*. This official contrived to extend his sphere of activity in the same way as had his predecessor, the Magister Officiorum. Like the Magister Officiorum, he, too, became the Minister for Foreign Affairs, and amongst other privileges had a staff of interpreters at his disposal. He was received in audience every day by the Emperor, and finally became a kind of Chancellor, assuming later the title of *Great Logothete*. Some offices were called 'special offices', but they were not of any recognizable significance for the general administration; of these only that of the *Syncellus* need be mentioned. He was a high cleric, frequently succeeding to the Patriarchate, and was appointed by the Emperor in agreement with the Patriarch. He took precedence over all ordinary officials in the hierarchy, and might be regarded as a liaison officer between the Emperor and the Patriarch.

In the administration of the provinces Philotheus knows of twenty-five themes, but at the beginning of the ninth century there were only ten. The number of the themes continued to increase, until in the eleventh century we know of thirty-eight. The extension of frontiers, and even more the desire to check the expansion of these independent districts, had contributed to this development; in troubled times many a military governor had succumbed to the temptation to make use of his power against the Emperor, while the formation of a land-owning military nobility also gave good reason for anxiety. The governors of the themes were mostly called *Strategoi* (generals); thus their purely military origin was indicated in their official title. They were directly subordinate to the Emperor. The themes appear to have been divided into two groups: an Eastern group consisting of those of Asia Minor, with the addition of Thrace and Macedonia, but excluding the maritime themes (see § III) which with the rest of the Balkan themes and those of southern Italy, together with Cherson in the Crimea, formed the Western group. The Eastern *Strategoi* always occupied a superior position. According to Philotheus, they ranked after the *Syncellus* and before the Prefect of the City, who was followed by the Western *Strategoi*. This privileged position accorded to the military officials gave the Byzantine Empire of the middle and late period its special character. The Eastern *Strategoi*, including the maritime ones, received their salaries from the central treasury, whereas those of the West were dependent on the revenues of their provinces. As already explained, the civil administration with its financial and judicial duties was also in the hands of these military governors. The military governor was assisted by a large body of civilian officials in addition to his military staff. But the *Chartularius* of the theme, who supervised the outgoings for the pay of the soldiers, was, while subordinated to him, at the same time responsible to the *Logothetes tou Stratiōtikou*. Moreover, the judge of the theme and the *Protonotary* (who was also counted as an official of the *Chartularius* of the *Sacellion*) were, at least from the beginning of the tenth century, subordinate to the *Strategos*; but this arrangement was subject to a certain reservation, which was expressed in the so-called 'Taktikon of Leo' in the following manner: 'They have to be under the orders of the *Strategos* in some matters, but we consider it safer that they should submit their statements of accounts to our imperial central administration, so as to enable us to know the state of the administration.' It is not known how the duties were divided in detail, but in any case the central office reserved a certain right of supervision, in order to control and restrain the *Strategoi*. The same purpose was served by officials sent out from the central office as overseers and inspectors. In addition to that, the bishops were exhorted to supervise the administrative procedure in their dioceses, and the subjects were encouraged to seek legal redress against oppression.

An appeal lay from the provincial courts. The Emperor remained the supreme court of appeal, and jurisdiction over the highest officials was reserved for him. It is known that some Emperors liked to receive complaints personally. By the side of the Emperor as high judicial authorities stood the Prefect of the City and the Quaestor. In the course of the eleventh century the place of the City Prefect was taken by the *Great Drungarius*. In addition Constantinople had a High Court with twelve judges for important cases. There is, however, plenty of scope for further research in this field. One feature characteristic of the whole period of the Byzantine Empire is the ecclesiastical jurisdiction in civil matters. Since Constantine the Great the bishops had rights of jurisdiction of varying extent. When an ecclesiastic was the accused, the ecclesiastical courts of justice were competent, and this was the case in all civil proceedings, given the consent of both parties. By the end of the eleventh century the competence of these courts had been extended to all matrimonial cases and charitable bequests. After the interlude of the Latin Empire the distinction between lay and ecclesiastical jurisdiction was more and more obscured; and this confusion was the easier since during the last period the Church and the Patriarch played an increasingly important part in the administration. However, administration of justice and legal procedure continued to the end to follow faithfully the ways of juristic thought, although Roman law changed considerably through the penetration of Christian ideas.

The fact that the cruel punishment of mutilation is so frequent in the Byzantine criminal law may at first sight appear inconsistent with such a statement. But mutilation often replaced capital punishment, and may to a sterner age than ours have seemed a mitigation of the former severity; it might be justified by a reference to the words of the Gospel about 'plucking out the eye which offends', or on the ground that it provided the offender with an opportunity for repentance. It must be admitted that, once they had been introduced, punishments such as blinding, cutting out the tongue, and cutting off of hands were also inflicted for offences which had not been previously punishable with death. Other punishments were the confiscation of property and fines. Imprisonment as a punishment was unknown in the old Byzantine law.[1] Only from the twelfth century onwards were many political offenders imprisoned, until a tragic death put an end to their troubles, in the Anemas tower in Blachernae, which was named after the rebel held prisoner there by Alexius I. Banishment to a monastery, a punishment which seems to show more clearly the influence of the penitential system of the Church, had been introduced earlier. The right of granting asylum, which had always been maintained by the Church, implied a certain mitigation of these punishments; when such a right was exercised, ecclesiastical punishment, even though hampered by a number of restrictions, replaced the civil penalty which had been incurred. This right of asylum, however, was denied

---

[1] [On imprisonment as a punishment cf. G. Buckler, *Anna Comnena* (Oxford University Press, London, 1929), pp. 95–6.]

to those charged with high treason and to heretics, who were put on the same level with them; and it was characteristic of the system that defaulting taxpayers and fraudulent tax-collectors were also deprived of it.

The complicated and extensive apparatus of administration continued to function even when repeated disasters abroad fell upon the Empire. The Seljuk invasion of Asia Minor made a reorganization of the themes necessary. The governors now received the official title *Dux*, and their sphere of activity was probably limited. The real position of the administration in the period of the Palaeologi has as yet been inadequately studied. Yet one is inclined to believe that the 'Book of Offices' of the fourteenth century, wrongly attributed to Georgius Codinus, is a picture rather of the outward appearance of the Empire than of the melancholy reality. It seems certain that many of the former offices had only a titular existence. In addition to the Patriarch who exercised wide influence in the civil administration of this period, the *Great Logothete*, together with those occupying the highest military positions, controlled the business of State which had now shrunk to very small proportions.

A particular merit of the Byzantine bureaucracy was the excellent training of its members. The officials benefited by the high standard of general education which their class of society enjoyed at that time. The fact that Constantine Porphyrogenitus granted a salary to the students of his university showed that the State took a great interest in obtaining a well-trained bureaucracy. Legal education as it had been formulated by Justinian had declined in course of time and had been replaced by a narrowly professional instruction, until Constantine IX Monomachus reopened the old school of law in Constantinople. Admission to the influential and lucrative offices was in theory open to everybody; but in actual fact in course of time an aristocracy of office had been formed, which did not make promotion easy for a new-comer. At the same time in Asia Minor there developed another provincial aristocracy of large landowners, and against the growing influence of this landed nobility both Emperors and the highly trained civil service united. This provincial nobility frequently held high military command,

and its popularity with the army only increased the jealousy of the bureaucrats of the capital. It must be admitted that this dislike of the bureaucracy for a military nobility which was always striving for power led finally to a neglect of the army and contributed to the collapse of the Empire's defensive system. Thus the revival under the Comneni resulted in a reaction against the supremacy of the civilians and in consequence the Latin Empire found in the East conditions which were not unlike its own feudal organization. But under the Palaeologi the bureaucracy was still a support to the State which was fighting for its existence.

There is no doubt that this bureaucracy was true to type, and showed a great capacity for resistance; it was partly responsible for the conservative appearance of the Byzantine Empire; but it was flexible enough at all times to perform its allotted task. It provided the means by which the Emperor could realize his policy and it was not its own mistakes that caused the constant complaints of the intolerable burden of taxation, even though in many cases we can trace bribery and selfish exploitation of the subject. For, often enough, these officials were regarded as the link between subjects and Emperor, and as upholders of law and justice. In concert with the Church and perhaps with greater success than the Church, the members of this bureaucracy, whose activities extended over the whole Empire and whose official language was Greek, contributed towards the Hellenization, or, as they themselves would have said, to the Romanization of foreign elements, and in this way helped to promote the unity of the Empire. To sum up: this was a bureaucracy which was costly and not always easy to manage, but it was one that with its inborn capacity for resistance not only gave the Byzantine State through the centuries its special character, but also provided it even in times of crisis with an invaluable support.

III. THE ARMY AND THE FLEET. DIPLOMACY

It is obvious that the army must have been of great importance in an Empire the history of which was for long periods a history of wars, and the organization of which was in large measure designed to meet military requirements.

The army proudly called itself Roman, and this tradition was tenaciously preserved. The link with the military system of the early Empire has once more to be sought in the late period of imperial Rome, and the organization of the army at that time must be shortly outlined. We must return to Diocletian and to Constantine, the latter being this time the chief organizer. Apart from the garrisons stationed on the frontiers, the *limitanei*, which may be compared to a kind of militia of settled peasants in occupation of land which was burdened with the hereditary obligation of military service, there was a mobile field army which accompanied the Emperor and commander-in-chief on campaigns and these troops were therefore called *comitatenses*; while certain 'crack' regiments among them occupied a prominent position as guard regiments, *palatini*. But since Constantine had dissolved the old Praetorian Guard the real bodyguards were the *scholae palatinae*. The officers of highest rank were the commanders-in-chief (*magistri militum*); they came after the prefects, but had the same titles of rank. Originally there had been two: one for the cavalry, who took precedence over the second owing to the superior position of the mounted troops, and one for the infantry. Each was Inspector General for his particular branch of the service, which he commanded under the Emperor when the latter took the field in person; but when holding independent commands each could lead mixed divisions of both cavalry and infantry. From the first this was always the case with the *magistri equitum et peditum* who were appointed for frontier districts of special military importance. Finally, in the Eastern half of the Empire from the time of Theodosius I there were five commanders-in-chief with separate districts under their command; each one was independent of the others and subordinate only to the Emperor; two were *in praesenti* at the Court, and there was one each for the armies of the Orient, Thrace, and Illyricum; to these Justinian added yet another for Armenia. The *dux* held the military command in the provinces. The generals also had an office for the administration of military affairs and for matters of jurisdiction relating to their soldiers. The chief (*princeps*) of their bureaux came from the *agentes in rebus* of the central office.

In spite of the general obligation of military service which still remained in force, conscription was by no means the rule. The sons of soldiers and the rural population were particularly liable to conscription; but the landowners could pay a contribution in money instead of the recruits which they were bound to send from the *coloni* on their domains. Thus recruits were enrolled mainly by voluntary enlistment; in that way many foreigners (*barbari*), especially Germans, were procured for the army, so that the word *barbari* could actually be used for soldiers in the language of the people. *Foederati* were compact divisions under their own leaders raised from tribes which were bound by treaty to supply soldiers. It was only the closing of the frontiers by Attila which compelled the Eastern Government to mobilize once again its own forces. When there was a fresh influx of Germans, Leo I tried to provide a counterbalancing force by using the Isaurians from Asia Minor, who formed later one of the picked regiments of the Empire. But as long as mercenaries were available they were always the main support of the army. The *buccellarii*, named after a kind of baked food, perhaps the soldiers' biscuit, played a special part, which was often not without danger for the State; as household troops of the general they formed the latter's personal following, and were bound by an oath to serve their master as well as the Emperor. On account of their large numbers they formed a prominent *corps d'élite* in Justinian's expeditionary force. But they were a sign of the decline of the Empire, inasmuch as their pay and equipment were left to their master. The distribution of the army still remained the same, except that the divisions of the *comitatenses* (*arithmoi* or *katalogoi*) were called 'Roman soldiers' in the Greek language of the day, in so far as they consisted of subjects of the Empire. The troops which were named after their place of origin, for instance the Isaurians or the Thracians, also belonged to these divisions; and they were held in higher esteem than the other 'Roman' troops because of their magnificent fighting powers. Though they were not excluded from the ranks of the *katalogoi*, yet, owing to their method of recruitment, they had much in common with the *foederati*, whose regiments consisted chiefly of foreign mercenaries. Compact divisions of foreign troops under native leaders were at this time called *symmachoi*, allies. In Justinian's time, however, they were pushed somewhat into the background by the *buccellarii* and the *foederati*. In the meantime the cavalry had become more and more the chief fighting force; it included the mail-clad cavalry regiments formed on the Persian model which were first introduced in the third century. The bow had also been adopted from the Persians as an efficient long-distance weapon for preparing the actual attack.

The weak state of the finances and the appearance of the Avars on the Danube frontier made it increasingly difficult for Justinian's successors to procure mercenaries. The armies of the Emperor Maurice consisted chiefly of subjects of the Empire. Conscription became more and more frequent, especially among the inhabitants of the newly conquered Armenian districts who came of good fighting stock. The *Strategikon*, a military manual ascribed to Maurice, speaks of military service for all subjects until their fortieth year. This book distinguishes between *élite* troups (*epilekta*) and 'weaker' troups (*hypodeestera*). The *buccellarii*, the *foederati*, and the *optimates* belonged to the *élite*. The *foederati* now included also the most warlike contingents raised from within the Empire, such as the Isaurians. The *optimates* were a selection of the best of the other troops. Orders were at this time still given in Latin.

With this army Heraclius fought against the Persians. It provided him with the foundation of the new military organization, which was later to lead to a change in the system of government of the provinces. Being unable to obtain foreign mercenaries, Heraclius decided to settle his troops in the provinces which were most threatened by the Persians, in the hope that their strength would be reproduced in their descendants. He seems to have promised to his soldiers this opportunity of settling on the land before the decisive campaign, so that their desire for victory was considerably increased. We cannot determine the original scope of the Emperor's plans. Their application was restricted to Asia Minor owing to the victorious invasion of the Arabs whose efficient military training was in part due to their former alliance with the Romans and the Persians. In Asia Minor there appear at first three large military districts which were called after the *Themata* (Themes), i.e. the army corps settled there: the *Anatolikon*, the army of the Orient, the *Opsikion* (*Obsequium*, the troops of the former *Magistri militum praesentales*), and the *Armeniakon*, the Armenian army. Their governors, the *Strategoi*, or, in the case of the *Opsikion* division, the *Comes*, may therefore be regarded as the successors of the former *Magistri*, masters of foot and horse. The picked troops from all divisions of the army, however, were established in separate districts which appear later (when the themes were split up) as independent themes; thus the *buccellarii* and the *optimates* were separated from the Opsikion, the *Thrakesioi* (Thracians) from the *Anatolikon*, while the *foederati*, who were also grouped together in one district, always remained with the *Anatolikon*. It is not certain when this organization spread to Europe, but, since the themes of Thrace and Macedonia were assigned to the Eastern group, we may conclude that these two themes were created at an earlier date than that of the other Western themes. For in the final arrangement of the system of themes the Eastern themes always had precedence, originally doubtless owing to their earlier formation, and later on owing to their brilliant defence of Asia Minor against the Arabs. Themes which were established later were given geographical names.

The distribution of the military forces of the Empire was based on this organization into themes and these later developed into military and administrative provinces. Each province supplied one *Thema* (army corps, if we wish to introduce modern terms). The *Thema* was divided according to its size into two or three *turmai*, each under a *turmarch*, who was divisional commander as well as being administrator of one section of the province. The rest of the military scheme is not quite clear and was constantly changing, owing to the different sizes of the themes. The sixth-century division of army corps into *turmai* (divisions), *moirai* (brigades), and *tagmata* (regiments) continued, as is proved by the names *turmai*, *moirai*, and *banda*. The *bandon* was so called after the Germanic word for a banner. In Philotheus's

Kletorologion the *turmarchs*, the *drungarii*, and the *kometes* (*comites*) of the *banda* are under the authority of the *strategoi*. According to a list given by an Arabian source the *strategos* controlled 10,000 men divided into two *turmai*, each of which was composed of five *banda* under a *drungarius*, the *bandon* being divided into five *pentarchies* under a *komes*. Each *komes* had under him five *pentekontarchies* (companies) each consisting of forty men under a *pentekontarchos*, who, as the name indicates, must at times have commanded fifty men; finally, there came the four *dekarchies*, each with ten men.

Further, there were *kleisurai* (commanded by *kleisuriarchs*), which were not included in the theme-system. Literally the word means mountain passes, and therefore refers to particular frontier districts where roads by which invaders might advance had to be protected and barred. As these districts grew in importance they were raised to the rank of themes. The *akritai*, whose name can best be translated by 'frontier defenders' or margraves, were subordinated to them, at any rate from time to time. They carried on perpetual petty warfare on the frontiers. Digenes, the hero of the Byzantine national epic, in which are mirrored the conditions of the tenth century, is such an *akritas*. The continual fighting with the infidel and with robber bands, the *apelatai* (cattle thieves), is the foundation of the *Akritas* sagas.

Besides the army in the provinces, troops were also stationed in Constantinople and in its neighbourhood; these included the four mounted *tagmata*—the *scholarii*, the *excubitores*, the *hikanatai* (each under the command of a *domesticus*), and the *arithmos* or *vigla*, which was the guard of the imperial headquarters, under a *drungarius*. In addition there was an infantry regiment, the *numeri*, under a *domesticus*, and furthermore the troop under the *comes* or *domesticus of the Walls*, a title which probably referred to the Long Walls built by Anastasius I, about forty miles to the west of the capital. With the exception of the Guards of the Walls, these troops went into battle with the Emperor. But his real bodyguard was the *hetairia*, literally the retinue, under the *hetairiarchos*. The *domesticus* of the *scholarii* was the officer of the highest rank after the *strategos* of the *Anatolikon*, and he became the commander-in-chief of the whole army in the tenth century, when the Emperors no longer took the field in person. The estimates of the number of troops in the *tagmata* vary greatly: they range from 4,000 and more down to 1,500. In the ninth century the total number of the troops has been calculated at 120,000, as against 150,000 in Justinian's time; but considering the greatly lessened extent of imperial territory in the ninth century the former figure is a proof of the increased military needs of the Empire.

The pay of the soldiers was relatively small. But it must be remembered that the military landholdings established by the theme system were in themselves a considerable compensation for the owners. In his first year of service the soldier of the themes received one *solidus* in cash; in later years the amount increased until in the twelfth year he received the maximum pay of twelve *solidi*. The soldiers of the *tagmata* and the subordinate officers of the themes probably reached a maximum allowance of eighteen *solidi*. The soldiers' holdings were middle-sized peasant estates and formed the backbone of the whole military system. And for this reason the Emperors did their utmost to protect them from the pressure of the great landowners. It is true that in the end this protection failed, since the aristocracy of Constantinople always sought and found land in which to invest the capital accumulated in their hands. For this reason, and as a result of a certain neglect of the army by the central administration, during the eleventh century the defences of the Empire were weakened; the consequences of the defeat at Manzikert (1071) and the permanent establishment of the Seljuk Turks in Asia Minor led directly to the collapse of the system which had existed up to that time. Therefore when we find 'soldiers' estates' in later years, the words can hardly be used in the original sense, for the owners were, it would seem, the so-called *Pronoiarii*. By the *pronoia* (provision) landed property, to which was attached the obligation of supplying soldiers, was granted to superior officers, and the income from these estates belonged to them during their lifetime, but could not be inherited; this arrangement bears a certain resemblance to the Western feudal system. Moreover, attempts were made to check the depopulation caused in certain parts of the Empire by the raids of the Seljuks, the Serbs, and the Hungarians: to secure this end foreigners were settled in the depopulated districts. The way had been paved for the decline of the old order by the practice, which had already begun to reappear in the tenth century, of purchasing exemption from compulsory military service by money payment (*adaeratio*). Foreign mercenaries, who had always played a prominent part in the *hetairia* (the body-guard), were again engaged in increasingly large numbers. In the course of the centuries Chazars and Patzinaks, Russians and Scandinavians, Georgians and Slavs, Arabs and Turks, and later on 'Latins' of every kind all served together in the imperial army. A crack regiment of the bodyguard was that of the Varangians which, under the Comneni, was for the most part composed of Anglo-Saxons. There was at times a hope of strengthening the defence of the Empire by using these mercenary troops under Byzantine leader-ship, thus counterbalancing the influence of the East Roman military nobles and of the troops of the themes which were dependent upon them; but this hope vanished when the leaders of the mercenaries were admitted to important commands, and, in the manner of condottieri, often enough put their own interests before those of the State. The loyalty of the mercenaries was ultimately a matter of money. One of the principal reasons for the rapid collapse of the Empire in face of the Latin attack in 1204 was the refusal of the foreigners to fight because they had not been paid. In the time of the Palaeologi there was no longer any question of a unified military organization. There was a system of make-shifts, and the army was for the most part a mercenary force.

To return to the Byzantine army proper. The most important weapon remained the cavalry, the *caballaria themata*. The heavy cavalry, the cataphracts, with steel helmet and scale armour or coat of mail over the whole body, carried sword, dagger, lance, and bow. The war-horses were protected by breastplates and frontal plates. These were the squadrons used for attacks in massed formation. The light horse, the *trapezitae*, were used for rapid assault, for recon-naissance, and for harassing the enemy. Their chief weapon was the bow. The light infantry also used the bow, though there were detachments armed with javelins. The mail-clad heavy infantry carried spear, sword, and shield, and often the heavy battle-axe. Each *bandon* had its baggage-train, which frequently included a great number of non-combatants, servants, and slaves. Material for bridging rivers was also brought with the heavy baggage; and military engineering was well developed. The Byzantine army had also its medical service with doctors and ambulance wagons.

A number of military manuals from the fifth century down to the *strategikon* of Cecaumenus in the eleventh century show that the Byzantines regarded the art of war as a practical science; they took into account the particular character of the enemy of the moment when considering the training of the troops, the execution of a campaign, or measures for defence. Stress was laid upon the defensive duty of the army. The conception of attack found full expression only in the orders regulating a siege. The defensive system was still modelled on the late Roman frontier (*limes*) plan, with fortified posts, small forts, and the safeguarding of passes and of roads by which invaders might advance. Towns in the interior were surrounded by ramparts. A system of signals announced the approach of an enemy. If the frontier troops were not successful in warding off the invader, the infantry occupied the roads by which he might retreat, and the light cavalry stuck close to his heels until the *strategos*, who also informed the neighbouring themes, had collected the main troops to repel the attack. Regulations for conduct on the battlefield are given in full detail, but independence and new ideas were expected of the general. The ruling principle was to keep down the number of casualties if any opportunity of success offered itself without the risk of an engagement. The moving of troops and their protection, observation of the enemy, intelligence service and spying, negotiation as a pretext for gaining time, every kind of stratagem, feigned flight, ambuscades: all was considered. Efficient training, strict discipline, and experience in battle made this army an effective weapon in the hands of the Emperors and their generals. The fighting spirit of the troops was sustained by the recognition and the rewarding of special services as well as by drawing attention to the high significance of their task. The 'orators', secular field-preachers, knew how to rouse the enthusiasm of the troops by speaking of the soldiers' duties towards Emperor and Empire, towards God and the Christian religion, and by emphasizing the rewards of valour. The day was begun and finished with prayer; solemn services were held during the campaigns. The Greek war cry 'the Cross has conquered' and the earlier Latin one 'the Lord is with us' show that the ecclesiastical spirit had also penetrated into the camps. At times death on the battlefield was regarded as martyrdom. But Byzantine war songs in the forms of hymns show that in this army's best days the fighting spirit combined trust in God with great self-confidence. In the Epic of Digenes Akritas, where in later times these ideals are wistfully recalled, this spirit of the Byzantine army lives on. Yet here, too, there are still echoes of the indomitable self-assurance of the military nobility which helped to discredit the organiza-tion of the army in the eyes of the Government and the bureaucracy. And yet, despite fluctuations of strength and weakness, to the Byzantine army must be ascribed the honour of having been Europe's chief bulwark against the Arabs. Even when decay had set in, when, too, the Western powers fell upon it from the rear, it could still cripple the onset of the Turks, though it could not any longer stay their advance.

The fleet shares with the army the credit of banishing the danger of the Arab attack. The organization of the fleet was an original creation of the Byzantines. For the Roman Empire the Mediterranean was in actual fact *Mare Nostrum*, and its fleet served more as a police force than as an instru-ment of war. Only when the Vandals took possession of Carthage and became masters of the western waters was the Empire forced for a time to take counter-measures. Yet the fleet played but a subordinate part in Justinian's wars of aggression. When sea battles occurred, as for instance in the Gothic wars, the seamen of the coasts of the eastern Mediter-ranean showed themselves still to be superior in the art of manœuvring. Under Heraclius a small fleet was able to prevent the Persians from crossing the Bosphorus when they planned to attack Constantinople in alliance with the Avars. A little later, when the Arabs threatened the existence of the

Empire, the importance of a fleet first received full recognition, particularly when Muaviah, already in possession of the Syrian coastline, followed the forces of the Empire on the sea, and appeared with his ships before Constantinople. It was not only the Greek Fire which checked the powerful and eager assault of the Arab seamen, but also the fleet, which had been organized as part of the system of the themes in the seventh century, when the militarization of the Empire was carried out.

The commander-in-chief of the fleet was the *Strategos* of the *Carabisiani*, whose name was derived from the *carabos*, a class of ship. Under him were one or two admirals (*Drungarii*). The coast districts of Asia Minor and the Aegean Isles supplied the fleet and the men. Right from the beginning the Cibyrrhaeots, named after the town of Cibyra in Pamphylia, were to the fore. The share taken by the fleet in insurrections as late as the seventh and the beginning of the eighth centuries caused a division of the forces. Alongside of the now independent theme of the Cibyrrhaeots (south and south-west Asia Minor) there was constituted the theme of the Dodecanese or Aegean Sea; each was under a *Drungarius*; the lower rank of the commander is a proof of the inferiority of the naval themes to those of the land army. Under the Isaurian Emperors of the eighth century the importance of the fleet diminished considerably, because pressure from external forces had slackened. The Abbasid caliphs likewise allowed their fleet to deteriorate. Only in the ninth century, when Andalusian Arabs raided the coast as pirates and settled in Crete, and the Aghlabids from Tunis took possession of Sicily, were efforts made to atone for past negligence. The perfected theme system recognized Samos (west Asia Minor) as a third maritime theme; all three themes were now under *Strategoi*. There were also bases for the fleet in the European themes, especially in Cephalonia. In addition there was a fleet under the *Drungarius tou Ploïmou*, who obtained an increasingly influential position under Basil I, and who finally became commander-in-chief of the navy.

Foes of the Empire were once again forced to reckon with the activities of the imperial fleet. When Constantine Porphyrogenitus made a claim to maritime predominance from the Dardanelles to Gibraltar, that may indeed have been on his part but a historical reminiscence, but Nicephorus Phocas, the conqueror of Crete, could tell the ambassador of Otto I with more justification that he alone possessed strong naval forces. The elasticity of the fleet, however, was lost again when demands on it diminished. If the navy had remained even in the days of its glory in the second rank, it now suffered a further setback. The organization of the Asiatic provincial fleet was naturally affected by the invasion of the Seljuks. Later Alexius Comnenus tried once more to restore the navy. The increasing weakness of the fleet is shown by the engagement of mercenaries, and above all by the fact that, whereas the Empire had formerly been able to issue its orders to the Venetians, it now sought their help by granting trade concessions. The consequences of the complete decay of the fleet were quickly apparent. The Doge Dandolo knew only too well that the former master of Venice could not offer resistance to him on the sea. The fleet of the Palaeologi was always too weak to play a decisive part in the fight for predominance in the Mediterranean.

Warships in general were called dromonds. Yet specifically the dromonds were the actual battleships, i.e. boats of different sizes with sails and having two banks of oars, manned by a crew numbering up to 300, of whom 70 were marines, the others rowers and seamen. The average crew may be reckoned as 200 men. Ships of a special construction with two banks of oars were called *pamphyli*; they were of greater speed and could turn more easily; but, in spite of being a type of cruiser, they were also used in set battles. The flagship of the admiral was always a *pamphylus* of a special size and speed. In addition there were lighter ships with only one bank of oars for observation and for carrying dispatches. During the tenth century the fleet at Constantinople was stronger than that of the maritime themes. Yet the figures mentioned in the sources do not give a basis on which to work out a reliable average strength, particularly as trading vessels were also sometimes manned for war, while old ships were brought back into service. The ramming spur of the ships was an excellent weapon, owing to the ease with which the Byzantines manœuvred their vessels.

But the superiority of the East Roman navy rested principally upon the fact that it was armed with the Greek Fire, an invention of the Syrian Greek Callinicus, which was perhaps only a rediscovery, for the employment of a burning material which was inextinguishable was already reported under Anastasius I. The manufacture of this Greek Fire, which had been improved in the course of time, was a strictly guarded State secret. Catapults hurled the fire from the ship's bows; in the end it even seems that a kind of gunpowder in tubes was used for projecting it. The crew carried hand grenades loaded with the fire, which exploded when they hit anything. Yet even so the fleet was used with the same caution as were the land forces, while despite not a few brilliant technical achievements Byzantine naval science never attained to the development which might have been expected when one considers the importance of the fleet for the defence of the Empire.

It remains to say a word on the diplomacy of Byzantium. For East Rome, as for any other State, war was only the continuation of the State's policy with other means. Even to bellicose Emperors it seemed more advantageous to reach their political goal through the art of diplomacy than by the use of the sword. There were as yet no permanent representatives stationed in other countries, and although we have called the *Great Logothete* a kind of Foreign Minister, yet we must not entertain too modern an idea of his position. We can see the machine in action, but we know little of its construction or its working. Ambassadors went to and fro. It was the practice to try to impress foreign envoys or visitors by the splendour of the capital and by the pomp of Court ceremonial; usually these efforts succeeded. The foreigner was led into a magnificent hall in the palace through a crowd of richly clothed dignitaries and through rows of bodyguards with glittering arms. Finally a curtain was drawn back and he gazed on the Emperor clad in his robes of State and seated on his throne. On each side of the throne roared golden lions, mechanical birds sang on a gilded pomegranate tree, and while the visitor prostrated himself, the throne was raised aloft so as to make it unapproachable. Like the image of a saint, the Emperor, motionless, did not himself speak to the astonished stranger; the *Logothete* spoke in his name. Only a few managed to avoid being impressed; Liutprand of Cremona boasted that he was able to do so, but he had to admit that it was only because he had previously made detailed inquiries from those who had seen the spectacle. How much information a Byzantine ambassador was expected to bring back to his sovereign can be deduced from the careful supervision of foreign envoys in order to prevent them from seeing anything that they were not meant to see. Every missionary, every merchant proceeding abroad obtained information which could be of great value in dealing with the rulers of the countries visited, as, for instance, advice concerning the person who should receive presents and the kind of presents which should be chosen. The Byzantines did not necessarily regard it as a humiliation to make regular payments, which were often called tribute by the recipients, to countries with which they wished to live on terms of peace. They tried by subsidies to secure help in times of war. But they also did not hesitate to incite enemies against a peaceful neighbour, though at the same time observing the treaties which they themselves had concluded. They regarded it as a principle of good statesmanship to handicap a real or a potential opponent by placing difficulties in his way. Political marriages also played a part in diplomacy, as indeed did the reception of people whose mere presence at the Byzantine Court could exercise a certain pressure on foreign powers. Christian missions were an effective means of imperial policy, although the neighbouring States which had been converted to Christianity could not always be restrained from their cupidity. On the other hand attempts to achieve a union with the West by means of concessions in dogma were fruitless owing to the resistance of the Emperor's own subjects. One thing is certain: diplomacy called for heavy expenditure in money. But it is precisely in this field that the Byzantines, who have been wrongly accused of clumsiness, showed a capacity for flexibility and for adaptability; although occasionally they did not shrink from objectionable methods, yet this capacity gave the Government a superiority of which full use was often made.   WILHELM ENSSLIN

XI

BYZANTIUM AND ISLAM

BYZANTIUM and Islam have been for many centuries indissolubly connected in both external and internal history. From the seventh century to the middle of the eleventh Islam was represented by the Arabs, from the middle of the eleventh century to the fall of Byzantium in 1453 by the Turks, first the Seljuks and later the Osmanli.

A few years after the formation of Islam in the depths of Arabia about 622 and the death of Muhammad in 632 the Arabs took possession of the Byzantine fortress Bothra (Bosra) beyond the Jordan, a 'trifling occurrence, had it not been the prelude of a mighty revolution'.[1] The Arabian military successes were astounding: in 635 the Syrian city of Damascus fell; in 636 the entire province of Syria was in the hands of the Arabs; in 637 or 638 Jerusalem surrendered and Palestine became an Arab province; at the same time the Persian Empire was conquered; in 641 or 642 the Arabs occupied Alexandria, and a few years later the Byzantine Empire was forced to abandon Egypt for ever. The conquest of Egypt was followed by the further advance of the Arabs along the shores of North Africa. To sum up, by the year 650 Syria with the eastern part of Asia Minor and Upper Mesopotamia, Palestine, Egypt, and part of the Byzantine provinces in North Africa had already come under the Arabian sway. Towards the close of the seventh century the whole of North Africa was conquered, and at the outset of the eighth the Arabs began their victorious penetration into the Pyrenean Peninsula.

The Arabs thus became the masters of a long coastline which had to be protected against Byzantine vessels. The Arabs had no fleet and no experience whatever in maritime affairs. But the Greco-Syrian population of Syria whom they had just conquered was well accustomed to seafaring and

---

[1] Gibbon, *The History of the Decline and Fall of the Roman Empire*, chap. xlv near the end, ed. J. B. Bury, vol. v (London, 1898), p. 95.

had played an extremely important role in Byzantine trade. The first crews of the Arabian vessels, accordingly, were enlisted from the population of the newly won Byzantine provinces. As early as the middle of the seventh century Arabian vessels occupied the island of Cyprus, an important maritime station; then they defeated the Byzantine fleet, reached Crete and Sicily, crossed the Aegean Sea and the Hellespont, and shortly after 670 appeared before Constantinople. All attempts of the Arabian fleet to take the capital failed, however, and in 677 the Arabs departed.

There is no doubt that one of the essential causes of the amazing military success of the Arabs was the discontent of the population of Syria and Egypt. This discontent was religious in character, for the Monophysite doctrine adopted by the great majority of the population of these provinces had been outlawed by the Byzantine Government. Perhaps Nestorianism or Monophysitism affected primitive Islam much more strongly than is usually believed. At first Byzantine theologians viewed Islam as a ramification of Arianism and placed it on a level with other Christian sects. In the eighth century John of Damascus, who lived at the Muhammadan Court, also regarded Islam as but another example of secession from the true Christian faith, similar to other earlier heresies. Recently F. W. Buckler has pointed out that the range of the authority of the Nestorian Patriarchate, which had been established in Babylon (the future Bagdad) in A.D. 499, included the Sassanid Empire, India, China, Arabia, and, from time to time, Egypt. 'After the failure of Nestorius to restore his doctrine within the Christian Church its restoration outside the Church, in Islam, became inevitable.' 'It was by the genius of Muhammad that Nestorius' doctrine was to be restored to the realm of religion.'[1] On the other hand, Professor Grégoire has laid particular stress on the closeness of Islam to Monophysitism; paraphrasing Pirenne's striking but debatable statement that 'Muhammad made Charles the Great', Grégoire declares that Eutyches, one of the founders of the Monophysite doctrine, made Muhammad. Byzantine Christianity,

---

[1] F. W. Buckler, 'Barbarian and Greek—and Church History', *Church History*, vol. xi (1942), p. 17; 'Regnum et Ecclesia', ibid., vol. iii (1934), p. 38.

in all likelihood, in the form of Monophysitism became one of the main foundations of Islam.[1]

In their newly conquered provinces the Arabs found to their hand a well-organized administrative machinery. As of course they had brought nothing of the sort from the desert whence they came, they adopted it, so that the administration of the early Caliphate followed the methods and system inherited from Byzantium and in part from Sassanid Persia.

The Byzantine and Persian provinces which passed into the power of the Arabs were acquainted with Hellenistic culture. Such flourishing cultural centres as Antioch in Syria, Caesarea and Gaza in Palestine, and particularly Alexandria in Egypt with their writers, schools, museums, and general atmosphere of intense intellectual life and old Hellenistic traditions now belonged to the Arabs. Coming into contact with a well-established culture and without possessing a culture of their own, the Arabs naturally fell under the influence of these ancient civilizations. This influence was a powerful stimulus to their own cultural development. Through Hellenism the Byzantine provinces made the Arabs acquainted with the works of ancient learning and art, and introduced them into the circle of nations with an inherited culture.

The final goal of Arab policy in the second half of the seventh century and even more in the first half of the eighth was to gain possession of Constantinople. In 717 the new Isaurian dynasty ascended the throne in Byzantium, and its first representative, the Emperor Leo III, faced one of the most critical moments in the history of his Empire. The Arab land forces marched right through Asia Minor and appeared under the walls of the capital, while a strong Arab fleet surrounded it by sea. In 718 this daring undertaking ended in complete failure for the Arabs. After that defeat the Arabs never attacked the 'God-guarded' city. But the idea of taking Constantinople still persisted. In 838 the Caliph Mutasim, after his military successes in Asia Minor, dreamed of marching on Constantinople.

[1] H. Grégoire, 'Mahomet et le Monophysisme', *Mélanges Charles Diehl*, vol. i (Paris, 1930), pp. 107–19.

Before the Seljuk Turks appeared and established themselves in Asia Minor in the eleventh century, almost continuous fighting took place there between Byzantines and Arabs; Arabic sources mention in almost every year military campaigns, often mere predatory razzias, accompanied by frequent exchanges of captives. Sometimes Byzantium was unsuccessful; e.g. at the close of the eighth century according to the terms of peace the Empire was obliged to pay to the Arabs a considerable amount of money 'which (the Empress Irene) was to pay every year in April and in June'. This agreement gave rise to the erroneous idea that in the year 801 the famous Caliph Harun-al-Rashid was lord of the Roman Empire.[1] The Caliph might call this money tribute, but 'to the Emperor it was merely a wise investment; when he was ready to fight, the payment would cease'.[2] In the Mediterranean, Cyprus (seventh century), Crete, and Sicily (ninth century) passed into the power of the Arabs; some cities were taken in south Italy. Under the pressure of the Arab invasion in North Africa many Greeks fled thence to Sicily, and later, when Sicily was gradually being conquered by the Arabs, many Greeks left Sicily for south Italy and increased the Hellenic element there among the native south Italian population. The Mediterranean Sea, some scholars assert, though not without exaggeration, became the Muslim Lake.

At first sight the interests of these two political and religious enemies seem irreconcilable. But this was not the case. Warlike expeditions put no impenetrable barrier to cultural relations. This period was a long succession of war and peace, ruin and creation, enmity and friendship. There was no race hatred. According to Oriental sources, the Emperor Nicephorus I (802–11) was of Arabian, probably Mesopotamian, origin. Under Leo III (717–41) a mosque was constructed in Constantinople, so that one Greek chronicler refers to this Emperor as the 'Saracen-minded'. In the first half of the tenth century the Patriarch of Constantinople, Nicholas Mysticus, writing to the Emir

[1] The agreement was so interpreted by F. W. Buckler, *Harunu'l-Rashid and Charles the Great* (Cambridge, Massachusetts, 1931), p. 36.
[2] S. Runciman, *Byzantine Civilization* (London, 1933), p. 162.

of Crete, addressed him as 'most illustrious and most honorable and beloved' and said that 'the two powers of the whole universe, the power of the Saracens (Arabs) and that of the Romans, are excelling and shining like the two great luminaries in the firmament. For this reason alone we must live in common as brothers although we differ in customs, manners, and religion.'

As political intercourse with the Arabs, both in the East and in the West, was essential to Byzantium, the ritual of the reception of Arab embassies which were sent to Constantinople during the periods of peace was minutely elaborated, and the ambassadors were welcomed with all sorts of brilliant Court ceremonies, diplomatic courtesies, and the astute display of military strength. In the work on the *Ceremonies of the Byzantine Court* compiled under Constantine Porphyrogenitus in the tenth century are preserved formulas of very cordial welcome to the ambassadors from Bagdad and Cairo. At the imperial table the Agaren 'friends' (Arabs) occupied higher places than the Frank 'friends', and the Eastern Arabs were placed higher than the Western. Moreover, when Byzantine ambassadors made their appearance in Bagdad, e.g. in 917, they were solemnly received by the Caliph with full pomp of Oriental magnificence and military parade. In 947–8 the ambassadors of the Emperor Constantine Porphyrogenitus appeared at the Court of the famous Spanish Caliph Abdar-Rahman III and received a brilliant welcome. Among the gifts presented by the Byzantine ambassadors to the Caliph in the name of their Emperor was a beautiful Greek manuscript containing a medical work, and a Latin manuscript of the *History* of Orosius. Since the Caliph failed to find any Christian in Spain who knew Greek, the medical manuscript remained in his library untranslated.

Treaties of peace between Byzantium and its neighbours, of course including the Arabs, were made for ever, 'as long as the sun shines and the world stands fixed' or 'as long as the sun shines and the world endures henceforth and for evermore'. These flowers of Oriental style have survived up to the nineteenth century. In the agreement between Maskat (Muscat in Arabia) and Great Britain concluded in 1800 we read that 'the friendship of the two States shall remain unshaken until the end of time, till the sun and moon have finished their revolving career'; and in the convention of amity and commerce concluded in 1833 between the United States of America and Siam we find the following clause: 'The Siamese and the citizens of the United States of America shall with sincerity hold commercial intercourse in the ports of their respective nations as long as heaven and earth shall endure.'

The Arab conquests of the seventh, eighth, and ninth centuries resulted in a considerable change in Byzantine trade and commerce. The economic prosperity of the early Roman Empire had been undermined by the internal anarchy of the third century as well as by the barbarian migrations into the Western provinces of the fourth and fifth centuries. In the sixth century the Emperor Justinian gave new life to the foreign trade of his Empire, especially in the East. But a fatal blow to the economic power of Byzantium in the East and South was inflicted by the Arabs, who wrested from the Empire the richest and most vital provinces whose economic life was most highly developed. Arab pirates with headquarters in Crete made the Mediterranean so insecure for sailing that traders were forced to give up their ships and run the risk of long land journeys, which themselves were not always safe or comfortable, in order to escape 'the Mavrousian barbarians', as the *Life of St. Gregory the Decapolite* puts it.[1]

At first sight it might be thought that the whole economic structure of the Near East collapsed, and that trade relations with the East came to a close. But this was not so. In Arabia before the time of Muhammad besides the nomadic Bedouins there had been settled inhabitants of cities and hamlets which had developed along the trade routes, mainly on the caravan road from the south to the north, from Yemen to Palestine, Syria, and the Sinaitic peninsula. The richest among the cities along the route was Mecca (Macoraba in ancient writings), famous long before the time of Muhammad. There were many Jews and Christians among the

[1] *La Vie de Saint Grégoire le Décapolite et les Slaves Macédoniens au IXᵉ siècle*, ed. F. Dvornik (Paris, 1926), p. 53 (par. 9).

merchants in Arabia, and the Meccans were to such an extent absorbed in their commercial affairs that according to one scholar Mecca 'assumed a materialistic, arrogantly plutocratic character'.[1] In other words, before Muhammad Syria and Palestine were economically connected with Arabia. Even in the Koran, if the passage is correctly interpreted, we read that the Quraysh, the tribe to which Muhammad belonged, were busy in sending forth caravans both in winter and in summer.[2] Adequate protection was of special value to the Quraysh in their trading journeys, in summer northward to Syria and in winter southward to Yemen. Moreover, local economic life in the Eastern Byzantine provinces before they were occupied by the Arabs was still well established, which is proved by the fact that under the Arab régime the Byzantine artisans in Syria continued to carry on their business.

Of course Byzantium after losing the Eastern provinces derived no direct advantage from the economic order established there upon the termination of hostilities. But indirectly the advantage was great, for the well-established economic life in Syria and Palestine considerably helped the Empire, as long as it was possible to re-establish commercial relations with the East. In spite of their frequency and intensity the wars in Asia Minor were not continuous, and in the intervals of peace both the Empire and the Caliphate had time enough to realize the importance of establishing trade relations. Byzantine merchants appeared in many Arab cities, and Muslim traders came to Byzantium to transact their business. In the tenth century Trebizond became the most important centre of commercial relations between Byzantine and Muslim merchants; according to an Arab writer of the tenth century Trebizond during its annual fairs was crammed full of Muslim, Greek, Armenian, and other merchants.[3] In 961 after two unsuccessful attempts Crete, the base of the pirate Arabs, was at last restored to the Empire, so that the Emperor Nicephorus Phocas could say

---

[1] Goldziher, *Die Religion des Islams*, p. 103, in *Die Kultur der Gegenwart*, ed. by P. Hinneberg, Teil I, Abt. 3, *Die Religionen des Orients* (1913), part 1, ed. 2.

[2] *Koran*, surah 106, 2. See H. Lammens, 'Mekka', in the *Encyclopédie de l'Islam*, livraison 44 (1931), p. 507.

[3] Maçoudi, *Les Prairies d'or*, ed. Barbier de Meynard, vol. ii (Paris, 1861), p. 3.

to the Italian ambassador Liutprand: 'Nor has your master any force of ships on the sea. I alone have really stout sailors.'[1]

Economic relations with the Arabs were extremely important to Byzantium not only for their own sake but also for the international position of the Empire in relation to western Europe. Before the epoch of the Crusades the commerce of the Muslim East with Europe was carried on mostly through Byzantium, which derived large revenues from her position as intermediary between East and West. But the Crusades established direct commercial relations between Europe and the East, so that soon afterwards the economic prosperity of Byzantium came to a close, and the leading economic role passed to the Italian cities, with Venice and Genoa at their head.

When we approach the problem of the mutual cultural relations between Byzantium and Islam, we must take into account the contribution made by other peoples to the intellectual life of the Arab State. From the middle of the eighth century, when the Abbasids overthrew the Ummayads (Ommiads) and transferred their capital from Damascus to Bagdad, the Persians began to play a preponderant role in the cultural progress of the Caliphate. Then the Arameans acquainted the Arabs with the treasures of Hellenistic culture. In a word the cultural development of the Arabs was mostly due to foreign activities and foreign materials. An eminent German Orientalist remarks: 'Greece, Persia, and India were taxed to help the sterility of the Arab mind.'[2]

During the Middle Ages before the Crusades there were three world cultural centres, one belonging to Christianity, two to Islam: Constantinople on the Bosphorus, and Bagdad and Cordoba on the two opposite borders of the Muhammadan world. Constantinople, 'the city guarded by God', 'the glory of Greece', was the richest and most brilliant city in the medieval world. Bagdad, the city called into existence in the middle of the eighth century 'as by an enchanter's wand', was second only to Constantinople, and the Court of the Abbasids was a real garden of learning, science, and the arts. Cordoba in Spain in the tenth century was the most civilized

[1] Liutprand, *Legatio*, ch. xi.
[2] Ed. Sachau, *Alberuni's India*, vol. i (London, 1888), p. xxviii.

city in western Europe, 'the wonder and admiration of the world'; it contained 70 libraries and 900 public baths.

Hellenistic culture was the common possession which after the conquest by the Arabs of Syria and Egypt could draw together Byzantium and the Caliphate. In the monasteries of Syria humble monks were assiduously translating the works not only of religious but also of secular literature. Among philosophers Aristotle held pride of place; among medical writers Hippocrates and Galen. The Nestorians, persecuted by the Byzantine Government and condemned at the Third Oecumenical Council in 431, found shelter in Sassanid Persia and brought with them the learning of the Greeks. Under the Abbasids many scholars set to work on translations from the Greek and on the search for new manuscripts. Particular attention was devoted to the translation of philosophical, mathematical, and medical works.

When in the eighth century the Iconoclast movement triumphed in Byzantium, one of the most ardent defenders of the icons, John of Damascus, was living under the Caliphate. Although, as good authorities assert, the Ummayad Caliph Yazid II (720–4), the contemporary of the Emperor Leo III (717–41), three years before the date of Leo's edict had issued a decree by which he ordered the destruction of all images in the churches of his Christian subjects, yet John of Damascus was not hampered in his literary work. Among his numerous writings in the fields of dogma, polemics, history, philosophy, oratory, and poetry, his three famous treatises *Against Those Who Depreciate Holy Images* were written under the Caliphate, and became the best weapon of Byzantine defenders of the icons.

Religious tolerance was not a particular trait of the Byzantine system. From the period of Constantine the Great when for the first time Christianity was proclaimed legal, the history of Byzantium affords many striking examples of religious intolerance. Any deviations from the religious credo of the ruling Emperors were outlawed by the Emperors or condemned by the Councils, so that many sects and doctrines which appeared during the Middle Ages within the Christian Church and were important not only religiously but also politically were persecuted and forbidden;

this policy of intolerance sometimes led to serious political complications and important territorial losses. But the attitude of the Byzantine Government towards Islam was different. It is true Byzantine sources sometimes attacked Islam; to brand the Emperor Leo III for his Iconoclast tendencies a Byzantine chronicler, as we have noted above, calls him 'Saracen-minded'; one of the accusations against John of Damascus which was set forth at the Iconoclast council in 754 was that he was 'inclined to Muhammadan-ism'. But on the other hand, as we have seen, a mosque was built in Constantinople under Leo III (717–41).

In 1009 the insane Fatimid Caliph of Egypt, al-Hakim, to whom Palestine belonged, ordered the destruction of the Church of the Holy Sepulchre in Jerusalem. After his death (1020) a period of tolerance towards Christianity set in again. His successor, al-Zahir, in 1027 made an agreement with the Emperor Constantine VIII which is an interesting illustration of the religious relations between Islam and the Empire. It was agreed that the Fatimid Caliph should be prayed for in every mosque in the Byzantine dominions, and permission was granted for the restoration of the mosque in Constantinople which had been destroyed in retaliation for the destruction of the Church of the Holy Sepulchre in Jerusalem, as well as for the institution of a *muezzin*, a Muhammadan priest to call the faithful to prayer. In his turn, al-Zahir agreed to permit the rebuilding of the church in Jerusalem.

The Byzantines were not much addicted to travelling; there are no descriptions of Bagdad, Antioch, Jerusalem, Cordoba, or a number of other places under the Arab sway written by Byzantine visitors. There were few Muhamma-dan travellers either who before the Crusades visited Con-stantinople or other places within the Empire. As far as we know at present, the earliest Muhammadan traveller who described the capital was an Arab, Harun-ibn-Yahya. He visited Constantinople either under the Emperor Basil I (867–86) or under Alexander (912–13);[1] he was neither

[1] A. Vasiliev, 'Harun-ibn-Yahya and his Description of Constantinople'. G. Ostrogorsky, 'Zum Reisebericht des Harun-Ibn-Jahja'. Both studies in *Seminarium Kondakovianum*, vol. v (1932), pp. 149–63, 251–7.

trader nor tourist, but was captured somewhere in Asia Minor and brought by sea to the capital as a prisoner. As an eye-witness he described the gates of the city, the Hippodrome, the imperial palace—where he was particularly impressed by an organ—the solemn procession of the Emperor to the Great Church (St. Sophia), the statue of Justinian, an aqueduct, some monasteries around Constantinople, and some other things. On his way from Constantinople to Rome he visited another important city of the Empire, Salonica (Thessalonica). Harun-ibn-Yahya's description gives us very interesting material for the topography of Constantinople and for some Court and ecclesiastical ceremonies; it would repay further detailed study. In the tenth century another Muhammadan visited Constantinople; this was Masudi, the famous geographer and historian, who spent most of his life in travelling. Anxious to see the capital of 'the Christian kings of Rum',[1] he visited the city during the brilliant period of the Macedonian dynasty and left a succinct description of it. He remarks: 'During the period of the Ancient Greeks and the early period of the Byzantine Empire learning did not cease to develop and increase.'

In spite of the almost continuous warfare in the East between Byzantium and the Arabs, the cultural intercourse between these at first sight irreconcilable enemies always continued, and the Caliphs, recognizing the superiority of Byzantine culture in many respects, as occasion arose, appealed to the Emperors for help in cultural enterprises. The Caliph Walid I (705–15) asked the Emperor to send him some Greek artisans to adorn with mosaics the mosques of Damascus, Medina, and Jerusalem. In the tenth century on the opposite border of the Muhammadan world in Spain, the Ummayad Caliph of Cordoba, al-Hakim II (961–76), wrote to the Emperor of Byzantium begging him to send a mosaicist to adorn the Great Mosque of Cordoba. According-to an Arab historian, al-Hakim 'ordered' the Emperor to send him a capable artisan to imitate what al-Walid had done for the completion of the mosque of Damascus. The Caliph's envoys brought back a mosaicist from Constanti-

---

[1] The word 'Rum' is merely 'Roman'; it was applied by Muhammadan writers to the medieval Byzantine Greeks. 'Rum' was also used as a name for Asia Minor.

nople, as well as a considerable number of cubes of mosaics which the Emperor sent as a present. The Caliph placed many slaves as pupils at the disposal of the mosaicist, so that after his departure al-Hakim had his own group of skilful workers in mosaic. In the tenth century also the Emperor Constantine Porphyrogenitus sent 140 columns to the Spanish Caliph Abd er-Rahman III who at that time was building Medinat ez-Zahra, his favourite residence, in Cordoba. In the ninth century under the Emperor Theophilus, there lived in Constantinople a distinguished mathematician named Leo. Through his pupils he became so famous abroad that the Caliph Mamun, an active promoter of education in his country, asked him to come to his Court. When Theophilus heard of this invitation, he gave Leo a salary and appointed him as public teacher in one of the Constantinopolitan churches. Although Mamun sent a personal letter to Theophilus begging him to let Leo come to Bagdad for a short stay, saying that he would consider this an act of friendship and offering for this favour, as tradition asserts, eternal peace and 2,000 pounds of gold, the Emperor refused to satisfy his request. In the ninth century also the Caliph al-Wathiq (842–7) 'with a special authorization from the Emperor Michael III' sent to Ephesus an Arab scholar to visit the caves in which were preserved the bodies of the seven youths who, according to tradition, had suffered martyrdom under Diocletian. For this occasion the Byzantine Emperor sent a man to serve as guide to the learned Arab. The story of this expedition, told by an Arab writer of the ninth century, that is, by a contemporary, is not to be rejected. It indicates that even at a time when hostilities between Byzantium and the Arabs were very keen and frequent, a sort of joint 'scientific' expedition was possible. The goal of the expedition was in absolute harmony with the medieval mind.

Arabo-Byzantine wars affected the literature of both countries. The military conflicts created a type of national hero, intrepid, valiant, magnanimous; some of these heroes became legendary figures endowed with superhuman vigour and carrying out stupendous deeds. An Arab warrior, Abdallah al-Battal, probably fell in the battle of Acroinon in Asia Minor in 740; later this champion of Islam became the historical prototype of the legendary Turkish national hero Saiyid Battal Ghazi, whose grave is still shown in one of the villages south of Eskishehr (medieval Dorylaeum) in Asia Minor. In the tenth century the Hamdanids at Aleppo in Syria created at their Court a centre of flourishing literary activity; contemporaries called this period of the Hamdanids the 'Golden Age'. The poets of their epoch treated not only the usual themes of Arabian poetry, but also praised the deeds of the Muhammadans in the wars with Byzantium. The famous Byzantine epic on Digenes Akritas, a Byzantine *chanson de geste*, depicting the wonderful exploits of this Greek national hero, goes back to an actual person who apparently was killed fighting against the Arabs in Asia Minor in 788. The tomb of the hero himself is found not far from Samosata. The epic of Digenes Akritas and the so-called Akritic popular songs beautifully and in many cases accurately describe the warfare between the Arabs and Byzantium, especially in the ninth century, when in 838 took place the great military success of the Arab armies over the Byzantine troops at Amorium in Phrygia. Now owing to some recent brilliant studies on Byzantine and Arabo-Turkish epics another extremely interesting problem arises, that of the close connexion between the Greek epic of Digenes Akritas, the Turkish epic of Saiyid Battal which is Turkish only in the language of its last version but is originally Arab, and the *Thousand and One Nights*. The Greek epic *Digenes Akritas* is a priceless mine of information for cultural relations between Byzantium and the Arabs.

On account of the continued intercourse between Byzantium and the Arabs, many Arabic words passed into Greek, and many Greek words into Arabic. These borrowed words, whether Arabic or Greek, have very often taken distorted forms in which it is sometimes not easy to discover the hidden original. Similar borrowings may be observed in the West in Spain, where many Arabic words made their way into Spanish and Portuguese.

The period from the beginning of the Crusades to the fall of Constantinople in 1453 differed considerably from the preceding period so far as mutual relations between Byzantium and Islam are concerned. Three ethnic elements one after another became important in the Near East. In the course of the eleventh century the Seljuk Turks founded in Asia Minor the Sultanate of Iconium (Konia); in the thirteenth century the Mongols defeated the Seljuks; and in the fourteenth and fifteenth centuries the Ottoman Turks established their supremacy, conquering Asia Minor and most of the Balkan peninsula and taking possession of Constantinople in 1453, thus putting an end to the political existence of the pitiful remnants of the Byzantine Empire. During this period political interests were predominant over economic and cultural interests in the relations between Byzantium and Islam.

Before the Seljuks in the eleventh century began their advance through Asia Minor, this country, though it was for long a theatre of stubborn hostilities with Islam, had remained Christian. Only in the eleventh century did the Seljuks bring Islam into this newly conquered country which afterwards became mainly Muhammadan. The political situation in Asia Minor was essentially changed. In 1071 at the battle of Manzikert in Armenia the Seljuks crushed the Byzantine army and captured the Emperor Romanus Diogenes. About the same year the Seljuks took possession of Jerusalem and sacked it. Islam, represented now not by the Arabs but by the Seljuk Turks, became a real danger to Byzantium. It is of course useless to conjecture what would have happened in the Near East towards the end of the eleventh century had the Western Crusaders not made their appearance in Constantinople and thereby turned a new page in the history of the world.

In the eighth century the question arose of the universal conflict of the whole European Christian world with the powerful Muslim State. The latter was the aggressor; the East threatened the West. At the end of the eleventh century a universal conflict of the whole European Christian world with the Islamic world again manifested itself; but in this case the Christian world was the aggressor; the West threatened the East. The epoch of the Crusades began, that epoch so manifold in its political, economic, and cultural consequences, so fatal to the Byzantine Empire, and so fruitful to western Europe. The Muhammadans were perplexed and troubled. According to a contemporary Arab historian, in 1097 'there began to arrive a succession of reports that the armies of the Franks had appeared from the direction of the sea of Constantinople with forces not to be reckoned for multitude. As these reports followed one upon the other, and spread from mouth to mouth far and wide, the people grew anxious and disturbed in mind.'[1]

The position of the Byzantine Empire in the Crusading movement, which was a purely west European enterprise, was very complicated. In the eleventh century no idea of a crusade existed in Byzantium. The problem of recovering Palestine was too abstract and was not vital to the Empire. There was no religious antagonism to Islam; there were no preachers of a crusade in Byzantium. The Eastern Empire was reluctantly involved in the turmoil of the First Crusade. The sole desire of the Empire was to have some aid against the political menace from the Turks, and this had no connexion with the expedition to Palestine.

Extremely interesting from the point of view of the attitude of Byzantium towards the Crusading movement were the years immediately preceding the Third Crusade. In 1187 the Kurd Saladin, ruler of Egypt, a talented leader and clever politician, captured Jerusalem from the Crusaders and succeeded in organizing a sort of counter-crusade against the Christians. This was the turning-point in the history of the Crusades. And at the moment when the Third Crusade started, the Byzantine Emperor Isaac Angelus opened negotiations with Saladin, against whom the crusade was being directed, and formed an alliance with Saladin against the Sultan of Iconium.

Byzantium paid dearly for her forced participation in the west European expeditions against Islam. In 1204 the Crusaders took and sacked Constantinople, and established the Latin Empire. When in 1261 the Palaeologi retook Constantinople, they were too weak to make any serious attempt to recover what they had lost to the Seljuk Turks.

'Had there been in Asia Minor in the latter half of the thirteenth

[1] *The Damascus Chronicle of the Crusades, extracted and translated from the Chronicle of Ibn al-Qalanisi*, by H. A. R. Gibb (London, 1932), p. 41.

century a predominant element, with an historical past and with a strong leader, we might have seen a revival of the Sultanate of Konia. Or we might have seen a revival of Hellenism, a grafting, perhaps, on fresh stock, which would have put new foundations under the Byzantine Empire by a reconquest of the Asiatic themes. But the Mongols and the Crusaders had done their work too well. The Latins at Constantinople, and the Mongols in Persia and Mesopotamia, had removed any possibility of a revival of either Arab Moslem or Greek Christian traditions.'[1]

The last period, from 1261 to 1453, was, as we have noted above, a time of desperate political struggle—a protracted death agony of the remnants of the Empire in its unequal fight against Islam represented this time by the Ottoman Turks.

Accordingly there was almost no cultural intercourse between Byzantium and Islam in the period from the Crusades to the fall of the Empire. Trade was interrupted and ceased to be well organized and regular. Many treasures of Islamic culture perished. Neither the Seljuks nor the Ottomans were at that time ready to carry on or stimulate real cultural work; in particular any co-operation with the Eastern Empire became impossible.

During this period four Arab travellers visited Constantinople and left descriptions of the city. Two of them came to Constantinople during the brilliant rule of the Comnenian dynasty in the twelfth century. In his *Guide to Pilgrimages* Hassan Ali al-Harawy gives a brief account of the most important monuments of the capital and specifies some monuments connected with Islam. He stresses once more the religious tolerance of Byzantium towards Islam. 'Outside of the city there is the tomb of one of the companions of the Prophet (= Muhammad). The big mosque erected by Maslamah, son of Abdel-Melik, is within the city. One can see the tomb of a descendant of Hussein, son of Ali, son of Abu-Thalib.' At the end of his description he says, 'Constantinople is a city larger than its renown proclaims', and then exclaims, 'May God, in His grace and generosity, deign to make of it the capital of Islam!' His wish was fulfilled in 1453. Another Arabian traveller of the twelfth century who

[1] H. A. Gibbons, *The Foundation of the Ottoman Empire* (New York, 1916), pp. 13–14.

visited Constantinople was the famous geographer Edrisi, born in Ceuta, in the west of North Africa. Under the Palaeologi two Arab travellers visited and described Constantinople. At the beginning of the fourteenth century an Arab geographer, Abulfeda, observes some traces of the decline of the capital. He remarks, 'Within the city there are sown fields and gardens, and many ruined houses'.

In the first half of the fourteenth century another famous Arab traveller, Ibn-Batutah (Battuta), who like Edrisi was born in the west of North Africa, at Tangier, visited Constantinople and gave a very interesting and vivid description of it. When his party reached the first gate of the imperial palace they found there about a hundred men, and Ibn-Batutah remarks, 'I heard them saying *Sarakinu, Sarakinu*, which means Muslims'. He was the Emperor's guest, and the people of Constantinople were very friendly to him. One day a great crowd gathered round him, and an old man said, 'You must come to my house that I may entertain you'. But Ibn-Batutah adds, 'After that I went away, and I did not see him again'.

In connexion with the ever-growing danger from the Ottoman Turks we may note some antagonism to Islam in the capital. A Byzantine historian of the fourteenth century says that while a Christian service was being celebrated in the imperial church, the people were angry to see Ottomans who had been admitted into the capital dancing and singing near the palace, 'crying out in incomprehensible sounds the songs and hymns of Muhammad, and thereby attracting the crowd to listen to them rather than to the divine gospels'. The Emperor Manuel II (1391–1425) himself compiled the most thorough refutation of the doctrine of Islam which was written in Byzantine times. He defines Islam as 'a falsely called faith' and 'the frenzy of the mad Muhammad'. In spite of this, on the eve of the final catastrophe the majority of the population was more antagonistic to the Union with the Roman Catholic Church than to the contamination of Islam. The famous words uttered at that time by one of the Byzantine dignitaries, Lucas Notaras, are well known: 'It is better to see in the city the power of the Turkish turban than that of the Latin tiara.'

In 1453 Constantinople, the 'second Rome', fell. Sultan Muhammad II, the 'precursor of Antichrist and second Sennacherib', entered the city. On the site of the Christian Eastern Empire was established the military Empire of the Ottoman Turks. This victory of Islam over Christianity had unexpected repercussions in far-off Russia, where Moscow and the Russian Grand Prince inherited in the imagination of many Russians the cultural legacy of Byzantium and the right and duty of defending the Greek Orthodox faith against Islam.[1]

Finally, perhaps, the cultural influence of both the Byzantine Empire and Islam may be noted in the origin and progress of the so-called Italian Renaissance. Classical knowledge, which was carefully preserved by Byzantium, and various branches of knowledge which were not only preserved but also perfected by the Arabs played an essential role in the creation of the new cultural atmosphere in Italy and became a connecting link between ancient culture and our modern civilization. Here we have an example of the cultural co-operation of the two most powerful and fruitful forces of the Middle Ages—Byzantium and Islam.

A. A. VASILIEV

[1] See Chapter 14 *infra*.

XII

THE BYZANTINE INHERITANCE IN SOUTH-EASTERN EUROPE[1]

It is too much the fashion in western Europe to under-estimate the influence of Byzantium upon the States of south-eastern Europe. In the case of Yugoslavia, Bulgaria, and Albania their Turkish past is emphasized; in that of Roumania Trajan and his 'Roman' legionaries are apt to over-shadow the Byzantine Empire and the Phanariote Princes; in that of Greece the classical past usurps the place of Romans, Byzantines, Franks, and Turks alike. But a survey of the Balkan peninsula from the standpoint of eastern· Europe puts Byzantium in a very different perspective. In Athens, for example, the home of lectures, no lecturer will attract such a large audience as a scholar who has chosen Byzantine history, literature, social life, music, or art for his subject. For the modern Greeks feel with reason that, if they are the grandchildren of ancient Hellas, they are the children and heirs of Byzantium.

To begin, then, with Greece, where the Byzantine tradition is naturally strongest, we find that from the foundation of the Greek kingdom down to the disaster in Asia Minor (1922) of which the Treaty of Lausanne of 1923 was the formal acknowledgement the Greeks were haunted by the spectre of Constantine Palaeologus. Otho and his spirited consort were enthusiastic adherents of 'the great idea', and Athens was long considered as merely the temporary capital of Greece, until such time as Constantinople should be regained. Religion being, as usual in the Near East, identi-fied with national and political interests, Greek participation in the Crimean War on the side of Orthodox Russia, despite the rival Russian candidature for Constantinople, was prevented only by the Anglo-French occupation. The more prosaic George I was compelled by public opinion to follow the same policy in 1866 and 1897, and it was no mere

[1] This chapter was written in 1933, and since Mr. Miller has died I have not attempted to adapt the text of his chapter. N.H.B.

accident that his successor was christened Constantine, who, after his marriage with Sophia, was hailed as the future conqueror of the city which was called after the first, and defended by the last, Emperor of that name. Greece would be more prosperous and better organized to-day had not the lure of the Byzantine heritage monopolized her efforts and strained her resources during all the first and most of the second dynasty. The present friendship with Turkey, which is now the keystone of Greek foreign policy, has apparently ended Byzantine influence upon Greek politics, for the exchange of populations, while it has intensified the internal Hellenism of Macedonia, has ended that 'outside Hellenism', of which the University of Athens and the Greek Church in Turkey were the apostles.

During the Turkish domination over Greece the Orthodox Church of that country depended directly upon the Oecumenical Patriarch at Constantinople. Thus a Byzantine prelate, whose functions Muhammad II had preserved, was the *ethnarches*, or 'National Chief' of the Hellenes, and not only of the Hellenes but of the Orthodox Slavs and Roumanians, for the Turks made religion, not nationality, the distinctive mark of their subjects, so that a 'Greek' meant any member of the Greek Orthodox Church of whatever nationality, just as the writer was once described at a Greek monastery as not a 'Christian' (Greek), but a 'lord' (Englishman). When the Church of the Greek kingdom became autocephalous in 1833, Byzantine influences over it diminished, and the recent inclusion of the Metropolitans of 'New' Greece in the Holy Synod of Athens has further weakened the Byzantine connexion. The Archbishop of Athens and All Greece has now a larger diocese than the Patriarch. Before the expansion of the Greek State in 1912–13 those ecclesiastical dignitaries had been political missionaries, as the history of the Macedonian question showed. The same Byzantine spirit, which has divided the masses on nice questions of dogma and ritual, caused Greek 'Patriarchists' and Bulgarian 'Exarchists' to kill each other in Macedonia in the interests of their rival nationalities, but in the names of their respective ecclesiastical chiefs.

Three societies with three periodicals have diffused

Byzantine learning in Greece, and their members make pilgrimages to the Byzantine sites, which that country possesses in such abundance. Such are the Byzantine Churches of Athens, the adjacent monastery of Daphní, Hosios Loukâs, the aerial monasteries of Metéora, the churches of Arta, Salonica, Hagía Moné in Chios, and, above all, the Greek Ravenna, Mistra, the Medieval Sparta, once the capital of a Byzantine despotat, which was no inconsiderable portion of the waning Byzantine Empire, and like that of Trebizond, its survivor by a few years. The Byzantine castle and city of Mouchli between Argos and Tripolis (explored by Professor Darkó) bears the very name of a monastery at Constantinople. Even in Cyprus, so long under the domination of the Lusignans, and in Crete, still longer under that of Venice, where even then inscriptions were dated by the regnal years of the Byzantine Emperors, Byzantine traditions have been preserved, while the 'Holy Mount' of Athos, a theocratic republic under Greek sovereignty, is the most perfect existing example of Byzantine monasticism, now declining in other parts of Greece. When the monks in 1931 solemnly asked the Greek Foreign Office whether they might be allowed to keep hens, despite the exclusion of the female sex from their sacred peninsula, we were, indeed, transported back to the atmosphere of Byzantine dialectics on dogma. The practice of the Knights of Rhodes of training children to enter the Order was Byzantine, as was originally their hospital in Jerusalem. Byzantine music is still used in the services of the Greek Church, and Byzantine art exercised an influence upon the later Greek painters of the Turkish period, whose works may be seen in the Churches of Kaisariané at the foot of Hymettus and Phaneroméne in Salamis. Byzantine literature served as a stepping-stone between ancient Greek and the 'pure language' of to-day, although the modern school of Greek novelists and poets is far removed from the stilted style and archaisms of some Byzantine historians and theologians, while the contemporary novel can find no models in that—the least successful—form of medieval Greek composition. That the 'language question', now happily less acute than thirty years ago, should have caused two riots and the downfall of the Ministries in

1901–3, is in itself a proof that the Byzantine spirit long survived the establishment of modern Greece. Even in democratic Hellas, where titles are forbidden, and the only titular distinction is to have been 'president' of some council or society, the descendants of Phanariote families still enjoy a certain social prestige, and one Athenian family, that of Ranghabes, traces its descent from a Byzantine Emperor. When, in 1933, a Monarchist organization was founded, it connected its propaganda with the name of the last Emperor of Constantinople, adopted the Byzantine double-eagle as its badge, and sought to justify the return of the Danish Glücksburgs by recalling the achievements of the Palaeologi.

But Byzantium has left traces not only on the Greek State, with which it is linguistically and racially more closely connected, but on the Slav nationalities of the Balkans. There two organizations, the imperial Government and the Orthodox Greek Church, collaborated in their efforts to convert the Slavs into good Byzantine citizens and Orthodox Greek parishioners. Bulgaria, the nearest Slav Balkan State to Byzantium, twice rebelled against this government by aliens, and the first and second Bulgarian Empires were the result, until the all-conquering Turks, availing themselves of the rivalries between these two Christian nationalities, ground the Empire of Trnovo to powder. A recent writer[1] has shown that the 'Byzantinisation and Christianisation of the Balkan Slavs were two aspects of the same process'; Christianity brought Byzantine culture and customs with it, and the language of the primitive Bulgarian Chancery was Greek. For, when Boris was wavering between the Western and the Eastern Churches, the unyielding attitude of the Popes threw him into the arms of the Patriarch, so that the first Bulgarian Empire, and, as a natural consequence, the second, were orientated away from the old towards the new Rome, whence the modern Greeks, even to-day, style themselves in the vernacular, *Romaîoi*. When, largely owing to the educational activities of Clement and Nahum at their Macedonian seminary, Slav priests took the place of Greek, and Slavonic became, instead of Greek, the official language of the Bulgarian State and Church, the traces of Byzantium

[1] Spinka, *A History of Christianity in the Balkans*, p. 185.

in the religious life of Bulgaria became indirect. But Boris's learned son and ultimate successor, Simeon, trained in Greek literature at the palace school of Constantinople, incorporated the Byzantine ideas and literary forms into the language of his own country. The books which he ordered to be translated or adopted were Greek; his Court was copied from Constantinople. Greeks called him 'half a Greek', but, if he was so by culture, he was a Nationalist by policy, in whose reign and at whose instigation Bulgaria for the first time had a Patriarch of her own—an epoch-making event, which centuries later affected her relations with Greece and was one of the causes of the Macedonian question.

Simeon's son and successor, Peter, by his marriage with the masterful Byzantine Princess, Maria, introduced into Bulgaria a new and powerful agent of Byzantine culture; his Court was filled with Greeks and its etiquette modelled on that of the Empress's birthplace. With the fall of the first Bulgarian Empire in 1018 under the blows dealt by Basil 'the Bulgar-slayer', who characteristically celebrated the victory of Byzantium by a service in the christianized Parthenon, the Church of Our Lady of Athens, Byzantine influence, temporal and ecclesiastical, again predominated; the Bulgarian Patriarchate was abolished, and Ochrida, the place to which it had been transferred from Silistria, Great Preslav, and Sofia, became the see of a Greek Archbishop, chosen at Constantinople from the clergy of the capital. Byzantium, however, found a powerful opposition in the adherents of the Bogomil heresy—a thorn in the side of both the Western and Eastern Churches—which, like Welsh Nonconformity and Irish or Polish Catholicism, identified itself with the Nationalist Movement, so that a good Bogomil was also a good Bulgarian. Byzantine persecution, as usual, furthered the cause of the persecuted, and public opinion was ripe for rebellion when, in 1186, the Second Bulgarian Empire arose out of the confusion of the Byzantine State. Even then the peasants were taught to believe that the patron saint of Byzantine Salonica, St. Demetrius, had emigrated from the great Macedonian city to Trnovo, the Bulgarian capital, to protect the brothers Asen. But even under this second Empire with its national rulers the

Byzantine spirit continued to dominate the Court, the army, the administration, and the legal procedure. Although the Bulgarian Patriarchate was restored to Trnovo in 1235, the National Church ceased to lead the nation; in the next century it was, like the Byzantine Church, afflicted with the mystic doctrine of *Hesychasm*, whose founder, Gregory the Sinaite, won many Bulgarian and Serbian followers, chief among them Theodosius of Trnovo. At Trnovo there was established a settlement of *Hesychasts*, modelled on the monastic life of Mt. Athos. This foreign importation led its Bulgarian promoter to take the side of the Oecumenical Patriarch, Callistus I, against his own Patriarch, who had sought to obtain formal, as well as practical, independence by omitting Callistus's name from the prayers and ceasing to obtain the holy oil from him. Thus, theological affinity was a more powerful motive than patriotism. Another important product of *Hesychasm* was the Bulgarian Patriarch Euthymius, an opponent of the Bogomils and a compiler of theological and biographical works, for which Byzantine books were models. Thus, alike in dogma and literature, Bulgaria went back to Byzantium, and originality and nationalism were eclipsed at a time when the Turks were approaching the Balkans. In 1393 Trnovo fell; Bulgaria remained a Turkish province till 1878; the Bulgarian Church was under the Oecumenical Patriarch from 1394 till 1870. The Bulgars were subject to the temporal power of the Turkish Sultan and to the spiritual authority of the Greek Patriarch, who, living at Constantinople, could, as Muhammad II had shrewdly foreseen, be used as an instrument of Ottoman policy in the Balkans. Hence, one of the first acts of the Modern Greek kingdom was to throw off his authority —an act imitated by Bulgaria in 1870, but as the prelude, not as the result, of her liberation.

The history of the southern Slavs has been profoundly marked by the division between the Eastern and the Western Churches, which made the Croats and Slovenes face westward and the Serbs eastward. The Austro-Hungarian Monarchy, which embraced the two first branches of the Yugoslav stock, completed what Virgilius of Salzburg had begun in the case of the Slovenes and Charlemagne in that of the Croats, and the difficulties besetting the later Triune Monarchy of Yugoslavia may be traced in great measure to the struggle between the Papacy and the Oecumenical Patriarchate in the ninth century. Such historical causes have more practical results in the Balkans than with us, for Serbian politicians are apt to speak of Stephen Dushan as if he had lived yesterday, whereas no British statesman would cite Dushan's contemporary, Edward III, as a precedent for the reacquisition of large parts of France. But, when the Balkan States were reborn in the nineteenth century, they naturally and nationalistically looked back to the medieval Serbian and Bulgarian Empires as to their progenitors, and inevitably inherited Byzantine traditions which had been preserved through the dull centuries of Turkish domination. Hence to understand the Balkan questions of to-day it is often necessary to know something of their medieval struggles, whereas to the British politician the reign of Victoria is already 'ancient history'. Stephen Nemanja, by adopting the Eastern creed, instead of the Latin Church, permanently decided the aspect of Serbian culture; his son, Sava, and he himself in his later years, sought inspiration among the Byzantine monks of Mount Athos, and the still-existing Serbian monastery of Khilandar testifies to the connexion between the 'Holy Mountain' and the modern Yugoslav monarchy. Both Alexander of Serbia and Alexander of Yugoslavia visited this foundation, and a recent question, arising between Greece and Yugoslavia out of the expropriation of the lands belonging to Khilandar outside the peninsula of Athos, served as a reminder that the germs of modern Balkan politics are sometimes found in the Middle Ages. The Latin conquest of Mount Athos indirectly assisted the diffusion of Orthodox and Byzantine ideas in Serbia, for Sava, emigrating thence to Studenitza, spread the Eastern ritual among the Serbs, and in 1219 obtained from the Oecumenical Patriarch (then resident at Nicaea) his consecration as 'Archbishop of all the Serbian lands' together with the creation of an autocephalous Serbian Church.

Byzantium's weakness was Serbia's opportunity; as usual in the Balkans politics and religion were yoke-fellows. Sava identified the dynasty with the national religion; Khilandar was the nursery of the Serbian Church, whence came its earliest prelates and priests. Dushan completed the double work of Nemanja and Sava; when he became 'Emperor of the Serbs and Greeks', the imperial crown was placed upon his head at Skoplie by the newly appointed Serbian Patriarch of Petch. The brand-new Serbian Empire, after the fashion of *parvenus*, slavishly copied the ceremonial of the ancient Empire of Constantinople. The Serbian Tsar sought to connect himself with the historical figures of the rulers of Byzantium by assuming the tiara and the double eagle. The officials of the Serbian Court were decorated with grandiloquent Byzantine titles, and contemporary documents reveal to us the existence of a Serbian 'Sebastocrator', 'Great Logothete', 'Caesar', and 'Despot', while Cattaro and Scutari were governed by Serbian 'Counts', and smaller places like Antivari, the seat of the 'Primate of Serbia' in the Catholic hierarchy, by 'Captains'. Thus, as of old, *Graecia capta ferum victorem cepit*. The way had already been prepared by the six marriages of Serbian kings with Greek princesses. Thus, when Stephen Urosh II, 'the Henry VIII of the Balkans', took, through Byzantine theological sophistry, as his fourth wife, Simonis, the only daughter of Andronicus II, his marriage with this Byzantine child was prompted alike by snobbishness and ambition. But the Court of the third Stephen Urosh, also the husband of a noble Byzantine, was ridiculed by the historian Nicephorus Gregoras, who came thither on a diplomatic mission from the Byzantine Empire. 'One cannot expect apes and ants to act like eagles and lions' was his complacent remark when he recrossed the Serbian frontier. But he failed to recognize the sterling natural qualities of the Serbian race which underlay this thin veneer of alien culture. If rough Serbia gained prestige, decadent Byzantium acquired strength from these intermarriages; the only loser was the unfortunate princess, sacrificed to make a diplomatic triumph. In Serbia, as in Greece, the Church became the centre of Nationalism under the Turkish domination; but in 1690 its centre of gravity was transferred from Petch to the more congenial atmosphere of Karlovitz in Austrian territory.

Bosnia and the Herzegovina, now integral parts of Yugo-slavia, had a separate medieval history, in which the Bogo-mils were important figures. Alternately under Byzantine and Hungarian rule in the twelfth century Bosnia found in its concluding decade a strong native ruler in the *Ban* Kulin, who patronized the Bogomils. For a time both his family and over 10,000 of his subjects actually adopted their creed because the sect was opposed alike to Orthodox Byzantium and to Catholic Hungary. Thus the Bogomil heresy became the Bosnian 'national faith', and in the fourteenth century received the official title of 'the Bosnian Church'. Orthodox Byzantium, by provoking opposition, and arousing alarm, combined with its rival, Catholicism, to strengthen Bosnian Nationalism. But the great Bosnian King Tortko I, like Dushan, paid Byzantium the compliment of copying the Court of Constantinople at his rustic residences of Sutjeska and Bobovac, where Bosnian barons held offices with high-sounding Greek names. Thus, in his reign, the Byzantine tradition had spread to the Eastern shores of the Adriatic, from Constantinople to Castelnuovo, his outlet on the sea. But the adoption of Catholicism by King Stephen Thomas Ostojić and the decision to proceed against the Bogomils (1446) caused the wholesale emigration of the persecuted sect to the Duchy of the Herzegovina, and led to the ulti-mate ruin of the Bosnian kingdom. The traitor of Bobovac, who opened its gates to the Turks, was a Bogomil, forcibly converted to Catholicism. Most of the Bogomils preferred Islam to Rome, the Turkish master of Byzantium to the Papacy; many became fanatical converts of Muhamma-danism, preserving thereby their feudal privileges and their lands. Bosnia was for four centuries 'the lion that guards the gates of Stamboul'; even to-day the Bosnian Muslim is a powerful factor among his fellow Yugoslavs of the Christian faith.

The Republic of Ragusa, long under Byzantium, showed fidelity to Byzantine traditions in her coinage and language. It was natural that a trading community like Ragusa, whose 'argosies' were frequent visitors to the Levant, should have been closely affected by the culture and the luxury, the customs and the laws of so wealthy a capital as Constantinople. Yet 'the South Slavonic Athens', as Dubrovnik has been called, has remained Slav rather than Greek or Italian. Albania, with its autochthonous inhabitants and mountainous fastnesses, was too savage a country to be attracted by the civilization of the distant city on the Bosporus. Still Durazzo, the ancient Dyrrhachium, was the capital of a Byzantine theme, and, therefore, governed by officials sent from the new Rome; its wide Byzantine walls were the outward sign of its importance as a bulwark of the East against western invaders; and, even after the break-up of the Byzantine Empire in 1204, a Greek prince, Michael Angelus, included it in the despotat of Epirus which he founded to keep the spirit of Byzantium alive amid the Frankish States of Greece. But the many vicissitudes of Durazzo after his time cut that link with Byzantium, which for centuries had been symbolized by the Via Egnatia. The Albanians, however, after the Turkish conquest, became more closely connected with and more attached to the Sultan than were the other Balkan races. They furnished his best soldiers and were specially selected to form his bodyguard. Ecclesiastically the Orthodox Albanians have only recently freed themselves from the jurisdiction of the Oecumenical Patriarchate at Constantinople, thus cutting their last tie with Byzantium; they now have an Albanian Patriarch.

Roumania was so long connected with Greeks that Byzantine influences were inevitably engrafted upon the native stock in both the Danubian principalities. Their princes dated their official documents by the Byzantine calendar, according to which the year began on 1 September, and those of Wallachia signed, like the Byzantine Emperors, in purple ink, as does the present autocephalous Archbishop of Cyprus—and as did one of its recent governors. In Roumania, as in Bulgaria and Bosnia, Bogomilism played a part and was the national religion till 1350.

Byzantine art, as Professor Iorga has shown, was adapted to Wallachian and Moldavian surroundings, but he considers that 'all art produced within the theoretical boundaries of the Empire, as far west as the Adriatic and east to the Danube is Byzantine'. Long after the fall of Constantinople, the Greek families of the Phanar, Byzantine in ideas and in some cases by descent, furnished the *Hospodars* who ruled over the two principalities during a large part of the eighteenth and nineteenth centuries, and who were regarded as 'the eyes of the Ottoman Empire, turned towards Europe'. Historians have often stigmatized the Phanariote period of Roumanian history, its corruption and its luxury. But these defects must not blind us to the services rendered by the more cultured Phanariote Greeks to the less advanced Roumanian population. The Greek Princes and the Greek priests alike represented this foreign rule, and the Greek Church until the drastic reforms of Cuza in the second half of the nineteenth century held vast properties in Roumania. But even to-day closer ties unite the Greeks to the Roumanians than to any other race of south-eastern Europe, and, although with the spread of modern agricultural methods there are fewer nomadic Koutzo-Wallachs in Greece, there are larger Greek colonies in the Roumanian cities—a relic of the Phanariote days. It was not a mere coincidence that the War of Greek Independence began on the Pruth; to historical and racial causes are due the large donations made to modern Athens by rich Greeks of Roumania.

In Asia Minor Byzantine civilization was continued for a few years after the Turkish capture of Constantinople by the Empire of Trebizond, founded at the time of the Latin conquest of Byzantium. The historian Chalcocondylas emphasizes the fact that the orientation of Trebizond was 'towards the Greek character and mode of life'; it was a Byzantine Government; and, if the popular speech was known as 'Greek of Trebizond', the local scholars wrote in the literary Greek of Byzantium, although the *Chronicle* of Panaretus contains an admixture of foreign expressions. The historical mission of the Trapezuntine Empire was to save the Hellenism of Pontus for over two and a half centuries.

Thus not only in Greece, but in the Slav and Latin States of south-eastern Europe Byzantine forms and traditions have had their share in shaping the national life. The chief instrument in this work was the Church, closely interwoven as it was with the Court and politics of Constantinople. Byzantine art was largely connected with the Church, and worked as one of its handmaidens; Byzantine music was another, while much of Byzantine literature was theological. Even after the Turkish Conquest the Church remained as the heir of the Byzantine tradition in the Near East, as it is on Mount Athos to-day. In little Montenegro till the middle of the last century such was the influence of the ecclesiastical tradition that the Bishop, or *Vladika*, was also the secular ruler. Even now wherever in the Christian East political life is rendered impossible by the form of the Government, the public finds a substitute in ecclesiastical discussion: shall, for instance, the Metropolitan of Rhodes be head of an auto-cephalous Church or dependent upon the Oecumenical Patriarch? The form of Balkan and Aegean Christianity came from Palestine by way of Byzantium; the Oecumenical Patriarch was the propagandist of the Byzantine Empire.

WILLIAM MILLER

XIII

BYZANTIUM AND THE SLAVS

THE great work of the Byzantines in conserving the culture of the ancients is well known and often emphasized. Their achievement, of almost equal importance, in disseminating their own civilization to barbarian nations is less fully recognized, chiefly because the nations which benefited most stand somewhat apart from the main course of European history. These are the nations of the Slavs, in particular the Slavs of the south and the east.

The early history of the Slav peoples is obscure. Their migrations followed in the aftermath of the better-known movements of the Germans, at a time when the Greco-Roman world was distracted by troubles nearer home. Consequently we know little of the process by which they spread from the forests of western Russia that were their original home, till by the close of the sixth century they occupied all the territory eastward from the Elbe, the Bohemian Forest and the Julian Alps into the heart of Muscovy and into the Balkan peninsula. Indeed it is only about their Balkan invasions, which brought them into contact with the authorities of the Empire, that our information is at all precise.

The Slav tribe that first appeared in imperial history was that known by the Romans as the Sclavenes, who gave their name as the generic term for the whole family of tribes. They and a kindred tribe called the Antae were wandering as pastoral nomads north of the Danube in the middle of the sixth century, and more than once during the reign of Justinian I raided the Balkan provinces in the train of other tribes such as the Bulgars. The Antae seem to have become *foederati* of the Empire before Justinian's death; but under Justin II the situation on the Danube frontier was altered by the aggression of the Avars, a Turkish tribe moving up from the east. The Avars conquered the Antae and by 566 were crossing the Danube to attack the Empire.

It was during the Avar wars that the Slavs found the

opportunity of settling south of the Danube. In 558 Justinian came to terms with the Avars and agreed to pay them a yearly subsidy. In 582, after a long siege, the Avars captured the great frontier fortress of Sirmium; and the siege and fall of Sirmium were the signal for a Slav invasion of the peninsula that penetrated as far as the Long Walls outside Constantinople. It is probable that many of these invaders remained permanently within imperial territory. During the next decade the imperial authorities were engrossed with the Persian War; and by the close of the century, when next they could turn their attention to the Danube frontier, they found the Slavs too firmly entrenched in the north-west corner of the peninsula to be dislodged.

In 597 a new wave of Slav invasion swamped the peninsula. On this occasion the invaders' goal was less ambitious than in 582, but more valuable for them. The easiest road from the middle Danube to the sea runs not across the rough mountains that border the Adriatic but from Belgrade or Sirmium up the Morava and down the Vardar to Salonica. To possess Salonica has always been, therefore, the aim of every power on the middle and lower Danube. The invaders of 597 were a motley collection of Slav tribes with a few Avars and Bulgars amongst them. Their ambition was probably only to sack Salonica, but their onslaught was none the less very vehement; and the pious Thessalonians considered that only the personal intervention of their patron saint, St. Demetrius, preserved the city.

Though they failed to take Salonica, it is probably from this campaign that the Slav settlements in the city's hinterland, in Macedonia, begin. The account of the Miracles of St. Demetrius gives a picture of life in Salonica at the time. The Empire was distracted by the anarchy of Phocas's reign and its energies were later fully employed in the wars of Heraclius against the Persians. There was no opportunity for punitive action in the Balkans. So the Slavs poured in across the Danube and the Save, gravitating mainly towards Macedonia, while the Avars protected their flanks by attacking Constantinople. It was seldom safe to wander far from the gates of Salonica. Twice again Slav armies appeared before the walls, though in neither case was a definite siege attempted. Meanwhile the Slavs pressed southward into the Greek peninsula, penetrating even to the Peloponnese and extinguishing the old country life of Greece, while they advanced eastward through Moesia towards the Black Sea. New waves of invaders overran Dalmatia and destroyed its former metropolis Salona. By the fourth decade of the seventh century the whole peninsula, except only the sea coasts, the Albanian mountains, and Thrace, was occupied more or less thickly by Slavs.

The Slav is naturally a democrat, who when he settled down chose to live in small isolated villages where all men were equal save the elected head-man, the *Župan*; and this tendency was enhanced by the fact that during their earlier movements the Slavs were vassals to stronger nations like the Avars who kept them in a state of brute subjection. It was difficult therefore for them to co-operate and set up a central organization, to turn themselves, in fact, from groups of petty tribes into nations. Only the Antae had achieved it, in the sixth century; and they now were gone. The other Slavs waited for an outside stimulus. In the seventh century the Slavs on the German frontiers were moulded together into a kingdom by a renegade Frank called Samo. But Samo's kingdom did not survive his death, and two centuries were to pass before the Slavs of the north-west evolved more stable States of their own, such as the great but short-lived kingdom of Moravia, and the duchies of Bohemia and Poland. Even so the stimulus was the proximity and the influence of the Germans.

The Balkan Slavs were similarly chaotic, and thus provided a unique opportunity for the Empire. Could they be given the blessings of imperial civilization quickly, they might be absorbed into the Empire before they acquired racial and national consciousness. The Emperor Heraclius was aware of the situation. As soon as he was free of the Persian War, he turned his attention to the Balkans. First, probably by some show of force, he induced the Slavs south of the Danube to acknowledge his suzerainty; he then sought to seal their submission by securing their conversion to Christianity.

The invaders had extinguished Christianity as they came.

The lists of Bishops from the Balkans attending the great Councils grow steadily smaller from the middle of the sixth century till by Heraclius's later days scarcely any inland city except Adrianople and Philippopolis seems to have maintained its church. The bulk of the peninsula belonged to the ecclesiastical province of Illyricum, a province as yet under the bishopric of Rome. Heraclius therefore sent to Rome for missionaries to re-establish Balkan Christianity. This was probably a mistake. To the barbarian in the Balkans Constantinople represented the glamour and majesty of imperial civilization. Rome to them was not a reverend city in Italy but an idea personified by Constantinople. Priests from Rome lacked the prestige that priests would have who came from the eastern capital. Moreover the Popes of the seventh century were no great missionaries and had anxieties nearer home to distract them, while the imperial Government, face to face now with the terrible menace of the Saracens, troubled itself no more about its Balkan vassals. The missions faded away; and the only Slavs to become Christian were those whose lives brought them into contact with the Christian cities of the coast. Amongst the Slavs round Salonica St. Demetrius began to be paid a proper reverence; but that was almost all.

The opportunity was missed. It was left to another race to organize the Balkan Slavs, and to lead them against the Empire. The Bulgars were a nation of Hunnic origin who on the decline of the Empire of the Avars established themselves on the northern shores of the Black Sea. After Heraclius's intervention the peninsula seems to have enjoyed a rare interval of tranquillity; but in 679, when attacks from the Chazars had broken up the short-lived kingdom known later as Old Great Bulgaria, a large section of the Bulgars crossed the Danube under their Khan Asperuch and settled in the Delta and the Dobrudja. The Emperor Constantine IV set out to defend the frontier, but an attack of gout brought him home from the war. His leaderless army was forced to retire; the Bulgars followed, and in the course of the year 680 established themselves between the river, the Black Sea, and the Balkan range, roughly from Varna for a hundred miles to the west. The Emperor Constantine made peace granting them this territory; but nine years later his son Justinian II broke the peace and invaded the land that the Greeks were beginning to call Bulgaria, only to be heavily defeated on his return from a successful campaign. As a result Khan Asperuch spread his realm farther to the west, to the river Isker, which flows into the Danube above Nicopolis.

During the next decades the Bulgars steadily increased their power, helped largely by the civil wars of Justinian II. In 716, with the Saracen siege of Constantinople in sight, the Emperor Theodosius III made a peace with them that allowed their frontier to extend south of the Balkan range, from the Gulf of Burgas to the upper waters of the Maritza, gave them a yearly payment of silks and gold, provided for the exchange of prisoners and refugees, and set up free trade between the two countries for all merchants armed with a passport. This peace lasted for nearly forty years. We know little of Bulgarian history during this period. Probably it was spent partly in internal struggles amongst the Bulgars, partly in organizing the Bulgar control of the Slavs.

The Bulgar invasion had been the signal for the Slavs to forget their allegiance to the Empire. From 675 to 677 the Slavs of Macedonia, led by a band of Bulgars coming probably from the middle Danube, besieged Salonica, and, as usual, it needed St. Demetrius himself to save the city. The Serbs and behind them the Croats (who had both reached their present homes in the days of Heraclius) established their independence. But the Slavs of the eastern half of the peninsula found the change of masters a change for the worse. We do not know the numbers of the invading Bulgars but they must have been considerable. They made their headquarters in the rolling plain and among the foot-hills at the north-east end of the Balkan range, between Varna and the Danube. From here round their capital of Pliska the Slavs were entirely driven out, and the population was purely Bulgar; farther afield the Slavs were kept as a broad fence round the Bulgar centre. These Slavs either maintained their old chieftains or soon evolved a native aristocracy encouraged by the Bulgars; but the administration would seem to have been conducted by Bulgar officials.

The Bulgars themselves, like all Finno-Ugrian tribes, were composed of clans, and the Khan was little more than the leader of the most powerful clan, though Asperuch's dynasty, the House of Dulo, enjoyed a special prestige, owing, no doubt, to its probable descent from Attila himself.

How much culture the Bulgars brought with them is uncertain. The buildings erected by the Bulgar Khans in the ninth century are reminiscent of Sassanid architecture and it has been suggested that the Bulgars derived their art from the lands north of the Caucasus where they were settled in the sixth century. But we know that in the ninth century, the date of the earliest Danubian Bulgar buildings, there were many Armenians in the employ of the Bulgar Khan: the Armenians were great builders, and their art long preserved Sassanid features. It is thus probably simplest to explain early Bulgarian architecture as the work of Armenian employees of the Khan. In the other arts nothing has been preserved which might elucidate the problem of the character and sources of early Bulgarian civilization.[1]

The slow encroachment of the Bulgars continued throughout the early years of the eighth century. But in 739 the old royal dynasty, the House of Dulo, died out. Its first successor, a boyar called Kormisosh, managed to maintain himself till his death in 756, but henceforward disputed successions and civil wars became frequent. Moreover the Empire was being reorganized under the great Isaurian sovereigns, and the Saracens had for the moment been checked. In 755 the Emperor Constantine V was ready to turn his attention to Bulgaria. At the time of his death twenty years later after a series of glorious campaigns he had confined the Bulgars to the northern slopes of the Balkan mountains and had refortified a long line of fortresses to hem them in, Mesembria, Develtus, Berrhoea, Philippopolis, and Sardica. Only the *coup de grâce* remained to be given. In 777 the Bulgar Khan himself fled to the imperial Court, and accepted baptism and a Greek bride. Now was the Empire's opportunity. A vigorous missionary policy backed by the imperial army would probably have brought all Bulgaria into a state of political and cultural vassaldom and then absorption could

[1] Except possibly the bas-relief horseman on the cliff side at Madara.

easily have followed. But, as in Heraclius's day, Byzantium
missed its opportunity. The Iconoclast controversy was
dragging on. The Iconoclasts lacked the spirit and the
Iconodules the power to be missionaries. And Bulgaria
seemed no longer a menace of any importance. The matter
could wait.

In the meantime, free from the Bulgar danger, the imperial
Government occupied itself usefully in taming the Slavs.
At the close of the century the Empress Irene, herself an
Athenian by birth, saw to the pacification of the Slavs of the
Greek peninsula. And though a century later there were still
distinctive Slav tribes in the Peloponnese, such as the
Milengi, who might be restive, especially if the Bulgars
approached from the north, henceforward the history of
Greece is mainly one of steady and orderly amalgamation.

But Byzantium was to pay dearly for her inaction towards
Bulgaria. At the turn of the century the Avar kingdom on
the middle Danube was destroyed by Charlemagne. The
Avars had long been declining, but they had served to keep
in check the Slavs and Bulgars of central Europe. Numbers
of Bulgars had been settled in Transylvania for some
centuries under Avar domination. Now they were emancipated, and they found a leader in a certain Krum, probably a
scion of their old ruling house. Krum was ambitious; having
freed his people he succeeded, we do not know how, in
uniting them with the Bulgars of the Balkans in one great
realm under his rule. Nor did his ambitions stop there. He
aimed at further expansion, at breaking through the line of
imperial fortresses that isolated Bulgaria, and he dreamed of
taking Constantinople. In 807 war broke out. In 809 Krum
captured and dismantled the fortress of Sardica; and Bulgars
poured across the frontier to settle amongst the Slavs of
Macedonia. In 811 the Emperor Nicephorus I marched
northward in force and sacked Krum's capital of Pliska, only
to perish with all his men, caught in a narrow defile by the
hordes of Krum.

This battle, which took place on 26 July 811, was comparable in Byzantine eyes only to the rout at Adrianople,
where Valens had fallen, four centuries back. It meant that
Bulgaria was come to the Balkans to stay; and it meant

that the prestige of the Empire was for ever lowered in the eyes of the Balkan nations. Constantinople became an attainable goal. Yet Krum was not to achieve it, nor were any of his successors. The Empire was saved by its admirable organization and by the walls of its city.

War lasted till Krum's death in 814, on the eve of his second expedition against Constantinople. The capital remained unconquered; but he had achieved enough. In the course of the war he had destroyed one by one the great imperial fortresses that hemmed him in, and thus made for Bulgaria an untrammelled passage into Macedonia. Only Adrianople and Mesembria, the guardians of Thrace, were rebuilt by the Emperor. Krum had united Pannonian with Balkan Bulgaria. He apparently performed considerable works of internal reorganization and made a simple codification of the laws. With material stolen from the churches and villas of the Bosphorus and with captive architects he made himself palaces worthy of a great king. When he died Bulgaria was one of the great powers of Europe.

Krum's son Omortag (815–31) made a Thirty Years Peace with the Empire. He wished to consolidate his father's conquests; he feared for his eastern frontier on the Dniester, where the Magyars were pressing; and his territorial ambitions lay in the north-west, in Croatia, where he opposed successfully the Carolingian Franks. His internal policy was, it seems, to enhance his own glory as ruler and to encourage his Slav subjects, playing them off against the aristocratic Bulgars in the interest of his autocracy, a policy probably initiated by Krum. Meantime the peace and the size of his realm gave wonderful opportunities for trade; merchants from the Empire passed to and fro through his dominions as far as Moravia on the north-west frontier, while Bulgarian and Slav merchants paid visits to Constantinople. Byzantine civilization began to spread through Bulgaria, at first in the form of luxuries for the richer classes. But with the merchants came missionaries; and Christianity began to be known in Bulgaria particularly amongst the Slavs. The Bulgar authorities disapproved. To them Christianity seemed merely an insidious branch of imperial propaganda. Omortag indulged freely in persecution; but the virus slowly spread.

It continued spreading under his son Malamir,[1] but as yet to no great extent. Malamir's reign was, rather, remarkable for the development of Bulgaria as a Slav power. It is probably about this time that the Bulgars adopted the Slavonic language; Bulgar names henceforward have a Slavonic form. This slavization was undoubtedly helped by the Bulgarian expansion into Macedonia. Soon after the year 846 (when Omortag's Thirty Years Peace ended) the Bulgarians annexed Philippopolis and steadily moved south-westward till by the end of Malamir's reign the hinterland of Macedonia, hitherto occupied by unruly Slavs, had been given order under the Bulgarian Government. But the Bulgarians could not prevent a small Serbian State from being founded in the Bosnian hills.

The accession of many more Slavs gave the Bulgar Khan fresh support against the Bulgar aristocracy. But the coping-stone was needed to complete the building of autocracy. Christianity in the early Middle Ages was the great ally of monarchy. The monarch was the Lord's Anointed, his authority sanctified by Heaven. Malamir's successor Boris saw its value, and he saw that Christianity need not necessarily mean Byzantine influence. But before he could decide on his plans his hand and the hand of the Emperor at Constantinople were forced by a new situation in European politics.

Charlemagne's destruction of the Avars, that movement which had resulted in the growth of a Greater Bulgaria, had also let loose the Slavs of the Middle Danube. A few decades later the Carolingian conquerors themselves were defeated by the nation of the Moravians, whose King Rostislav, originally a client of the Germans, had by 850 established himself as overlord over roughly the districts that now comprise Austria, Hungary, and Czechoslovakia. Thus the central European situation was very simple. Between the Western Empire of the Carolingians and the Byzantine there were two strong powers, Moravia and Bulgaria.

---

[1] Professor Zlatarski believes that Malamir reigned from 831 to 836 and was succeeded by Presiam who reigned from 836 to 852. Bury maintained that Presiam was Omortag's successor and took the name of Malamir during the slavization of the country. There are disadvantages in both views, particularly the former; and I am inclined to doubt the existence of any Khan called Presiam.

Rostislav, like Boris of Bulgaria, saw the advantage of Christianity for an autocrat. German missionaries had worked in Moravia, but, like the Byzantines in Bulgaria, they were suspected of nationalist propaganda. Rostislav decided to import Christianity from elsewhere. Constantinople had already considerable trade relations with Moravia,[1] and the Moravians probably realized that Byzantine culture was something higher and more splendid than the culture of Carolingian Germany. Moreover Rostislav feared the danger of a Bulgar-Frankish alliance and sought for the help of Bulgaria's natural enemy. Byzantium was not a far-off legendary power in the eyes of the Moravians, as sometimes has been made out, nor was Rostislav's scheme for introducing Christianity from the Byzantine Empire a wildly imaginative experiment. It was merely a natural outcome of the international situation. But it was nevertheless one of the greatest turning-points in the history of the Slavs.

In 863 the embassy reached Constantinople and asked the Emperor Michael III for a teacher who could preach Christianity to the Moravians in their own tongue. The Emperor was fortunate in having such a teacher. There was a Thessalonian called Constantine, better known by his later religious name of Cyril, who had in his varied career been a University professor, a diplomatic agent, and a monk; but his main interests were philology and religion. He had already dabbled in Slavonic studies and had probably evolved an alphabet for the Slavs of the neighbourhood of Salonica. Certainly in a very short time he was ready to set out for Moravia with his brother Methodius bearing a Bible and other liturgical books translated into the language of the Macedonian Slavs, a language that was intelligible to the Moravians and has remained the liturgical language of the Slavonic Churches to this day.

The Moravian alliance forced the Emperor's hand elsewhere. Boris of Bulgaria would be tempted to play a game analogous to Rostislav's and secure his Christianity from the Latin West. The imperial Government acted quickly. The threat of a sharp campaign induced Boris, already aware of

[1] This is borne out emphatically by the excavations at Staré Město undertaken in 1927.

the merits of Christianity, to accept Christianity from Constantinople. There was a wholesale baptism of Bulgars, and
Greek priests flocked into the country. A short heathen
rebellion was firmly suppressed.

By the year 865 Constantinople had established daughter
churches to spread Byzantine influence as far as the frontiers
of Germany, a triumph of ecclesiastical diplomacy all the
more gratifying in that the Patriarch Photius was now in full
schism with Pope Nicholas I. But in the second round Rome
was to win. The Moravian Mission began well. Rostislav
welcomed Cyril and Methodius gladly. But the Moravian
Court was largely Germanophil; German bishops made
trouble from over the frontier. The young Moravian
Church could not stand alone; Cyril decided to counter the
Germans by placing it directly under the supreme bishop of
the West, the Pope of Rome. It was an embarrassing gift
for Rome, for Cyril had taught his converts the usages of the
Church of Constantinople and had introduced its liturgy
translated into Slavonic. Rome desired uniformity and
disliked the use of the vernacular. But the prize was too
valuable to miss. Cyril and Methodius were summoned to
Rome to discuss the organization of the new church; and
there Cyril died.

Meanwhile things went less well in Bulgaria also. Boris,
once the military pressure from the Empire was removed,
began to resent the religious dictation of the Patriarchal
Court. He had meant Christianity to enhance his autocracy;
he had thought that he himself would control the Bulgarian
Church. In 866, in the hope of securing a better bargain, he
sent to ask for priests and a Patriarch from Rome.

The struggle over the Bulgarian Church and the fate of
the Moravian Church belong to the story of the Photian
schism with Rome. In Bulgaria Boris found Rome a stricter
master than Constantinople. Even an Archbishop was
denied him, though twice he found Latin priests to whom, he
pleaded, the post should be given, Formosus and Marinus,
both actually to become Popes themselves. At last, tempted
by the subtle diplomacy of Constantinople, in 869 he cleared
the country of Latin priests and welcomed back the Greeks;
and not all the wiles nor the thunder of Rome would make

him reverse his decision. The Greeks gave him an Archbishop of his choice, and soon would give him greater benefits still.

In Moravia Methodius on his return met with lessening success. In 869 Pope Adrian II consecrated him Bishop of Sirmium, the frontier city of Moravia, intending that he should tempt the Bulgars back to Rome by his Slavonic liturgy. But it was in vain. In 870 Rostislav was deposed by his Germanophil nephew Svatopulk, who disliked Methodius and his ways. Methodius could win no support from Rome, where Adrian's successors were turning against the methods of Cyril, and resented Methodius's firm refusal to add the *Filioque* to the creed; he believed with Photius that it was heresy. Till his death in 885 Methodius struggled on to maintain the Cyrillic Church in Moravia, persecuted by the Court and half-disowned by Rome, but too venerable a figure to be touched himself. After his death the edifice collapsed. German influence won. His more prominent disciples were driven into exile down the Danube to Bulgaria; his humbler followers were sold by the Moravian Government to the slave-dealers of Venice.

Bulgaria accepted what Moravia rejected, and Constantinople gave assistance. The Moravian exiles were received into Bulgaria gladly by Boris; and the imperial Ambassador at Venice bought up their disciples and sent them to Constantinople, where it seems that Photius established them in a School of Slavonic Studies, to be a seminary for providing priests for the Slavs. In the course of the next few years the Bulgarian Church found its solution in becoming a Slavonic Church enjoying autonomy under the suzerainty of the Byzantine Patriarch. Cyril had worked in Moravia, but Bulgaria reaped the benefits, and in so doing Bulgaria bound herself to the Balkans and the civilization of Byzantium.

In particular Macedonia benefited. Boris sent Cyril's disciple Clement to spread Slavonic Christianity there; and Clement organized the Macedonian Church, founding the bishopric of Ochrida. This missionary-work bound Macedonia to Bulgaria with a tie that was to show its strength a century later.

About the same time the conversion of the Serbian tribes was effected. How much it was due to pressure from Constantinople and how much to the enterprise of the Serbian princes we cannot tell. By the early years of the tenth century the various Serbian tribes had their own Cyrillic churches, with the exception of the Narentans, heathen pirates on the shores of the Adriatic, who were only properly subdued and civilized by Venice a century later. To the north and west in Croatia and Dalmatia, Christianity took a different form. There contact with the Franks and with the old Roman cities of Dalmatia had introduced Latin rites. The Slavonic Church spread there, and under the Bishops of Nin (Nona) put up a strong fight for its existence. But after the turn of the century Byzantine influence, the main prop of the Slavonic Church, was barely extant in Croatia, and King Tomislav of Croatia decided at the synods of Spalato (924 and 927) to bring his people unitedly into the Latin fold. And so Byzantium was to play no direct part in building up the civilization of Croatia, which followed rather in the wake of its Catholic neighbours, Italy and Hungary.

Meanwhile Moravia suffered for its desertion of Cyrillism. At the close of the ninth century there was a war between Bulgaria and Byzantium. The Magyars were now living beyond the Bulgarian frontier on the Pruth, and beyond them was another Turco-Ugrian people, the Petchenegs. During the war the Byzantines called in the Magyars against Bulgaria; but during their invasion the Petchenegs were induced by the Bulgars to occupy their vacant home. The Magyars, terrified of the Petchenegs, decided to move elsewhere, and in about the year 900 they crossed the Carpathians. In a very short time not only had they occupied the Bulgarian province of Transylvania, but the whole Moravian kingdom had crumbled away and its surviving inhabitants were restricted to the small district to the north known in later years as Moravia. In its place was the heathen militarist State of the Magyars, Hungary. Constantinople was not displeased. Moravia was punished; the Magyars now would raid western rather than eastern Europe; and, to the relief of the Germans no less than the Byzantines, the great Slav *bloc* stretching from the Baltic to the Adriatic, the Aegean, and the Black Sea was broken in its centre by the Magyars. The Magyars were later to receive their Church and most of their civilization from Germany.

In Bulgaria Byzantine influence, half-disguised as Cyrillism, was now all-triumphant. Under Boris's son Symeon (892–927) Bulgaria reached its zenith. Symeon had been educated at Constantinople and was eager to adapt its culture for his subjects. The arts were patronized. In his capital of Preslav his architects, probably Bulgarians trained in Armeno-Byzantine methods, built him churches and palaces. Books were eagerly translated from Greek into the Slavonic dialect that Cyril had made a literary language; and, in the works of John the Exarch and the Monk Chrabr, signs of native talent were revealed. Commerce was fostered; indeed the war with Byzantium at the close of the ninth century had arisen out of a trade dispute. But it seems that there was never a large commercial middle class in Bulgaria; the traders remained mostly Greek and Armenian. Superficially the administration took on a Byzantine complexion. Government was in the hands of a centralized bureaucracy controlled from the pompous Court of Symeon. But, beneath, the old life endured. In the provinces Bulgar and Slav nobles ruled, in a fashion more resembling the Feudal West, over a primitive peasantry. Even when a centralized system of taxation was introduced, the taxes were paid in kind. There was no money economy in the Bulgarian provinces.

The civilization of Symeon's Bulgaria was thus, like its literature, an attempt to translate Byzantium into Slavonic terms. To what extent the old Bulgar element lingered on we cannot tell. As yet the civilization did not penetrate far below the surface; but the Church was slowly spreading it amongst the people.

Bulgaria was, however, to decline before the penetration was completed. Symeon's ambition rose too high; he was the first great Balkan monarch to fall victim to the dream of Constantinople. He thought to unite in his person the majesty and traditions of Rome with the fresh vigour of the Bulgars and Slavs. The troubled minority of the Emperor

Constantine VII gave him his opportunity. War broke out in 913. In 914 Symeon was before the walls of Constantinople. The attempt of the Empress-Regent Zoë to crush him once and for all failed in the slaughter of her troops at Anchialus. By the end of 919, when Romanus Lecapenus won the imperial throne through marrying his daughter to the young Emperor (thus blocking Symeon's chance of using the same method), Symeon had all the European provinces of the Empire at his mercy. But the walls of Constantinople and Byzantine diplomacy defeated him. Fruitless attempts against the city and continual irritation from Serbs and Petchenegs in his rear wore him out. In 924, after a personal interview with Romanus, he abandoned his ambitious aim. He was still haughty; he assumed an imperial title, Basileus or Tsar; he declared his Church independent, and raised his Archbishop to be Patriarch; but he now turned his attention elsewhere. In 925 he annexed Serbia. In 927 his troops invaded Croatia. But there they met their match. The news of their annihilation brought Symeon to the grave.

Symeon's son and successor, Peter, hastened to make peace with the Empire. The peace was not inglorious. The Tsar and his Patriarch kept their titles; Peter was even given the rare honour of a bride of imperial blood dowered with an annual subsidy from Constantinople. But these terms were given the more willingly since Bulgaria was clearly exhausted; they were only empty honours, and honours tending to increase Byzantine influence at the Bulgarian Court. The Empire of Bulgaria was now an inert mass, worn out before it was adult, a playground for any foreign invader that chose to cross its borders; and many so chose.

The work of civilization continued but at a reduced pressure. The priest Kosma who wrote at the close of the tenth century was more sophisticated than the writers of Symeon's day, but he was an almost isolated phenomenon. Saints, like John of Rila, the patron of Bulgaria, rather than men of letters were the product of the time. Meanwhile the peasantry underwent a reaction against the graecized Court, a reaction that was expressed in Bulgaria's most curious contribution to the religious thought of Europe. In the course of the ninth century rebel Armenian heretics, known as Paulicians, had been settled by Byzantine authorities on the Bulgarian frontier. The Paulicians were styled Manichaeans, a term inaccurately applied in the medieval world to all Dualist sects. They believed in the equality of the Powers of Evil with those of Good, assigning to the former the realms of the Flesh and to the latter the realms of the Spirit. Paulician doctrines apparently spread into Bulgaria; and in Tsar Peter's reign they were preached there in a slightly different, rather simpler, form by a village priest called Bogomil, whose followers were known as Bogomils after him.

By the time of Peter's death (969) the Bogomils were numerous all over Bulgaria amongst the peasant classes. Their crude doctrines, the absence of a priesthood amongst them, their simplicity and purity, all attracted men oppressed by an elaborate hierarchy whose morals they suspected and whose subtleties they could not grasp. But their own practices caused alarm to the State. The Flesh is wicked, therefore abstain as far as possible from the things of the Flesh, meat and drink, marriage and the procreation of children, even manual labour. Amongst them was a special class, the elect, whose abstention was complete. The others did their best. Politically they expressed their views in apathy and passive resistance to authority; and the Bulgarian Government found itself obliged to persecute them. The persecution was ineffective. Bulgaria had to suffer this disease of apathy and hostility within herself at a time when every resource was needed to repel the enemies from outside.

It was not indeed for another three centuries that Bogomilism faded out of Bulgaria, despite the persecutions of Alexius Comnenus, who had also to suppress it in Constantinople whither it had spread. In the meantime it was flourishing farther to the west. In eastern Serbia it met with a qualified success, but in Bosnia and Croatia it found a second home. In Bosnia, indeed, it was the State religion for the greater part of the period from the end of the twelfth century till the Turkish Conquest. From Croatia the heresy reached northern Italy and France, and the Cathari and the Albigensians talked darkly of their Black Pope in Bulgaria.[1]

The canker was especially dangerous in view of the foreign problems that Bulgaria had to face. Peter's reign was peaceable enough, despite two Magyar invasions and one Russian, but at its close the war party came into power and by their insolence provoked an attack from Constantinople. The Emperor Nicephorus Phocas was busy in the East; so he called on the Russians to punish Bulgaria. The Russians did the work all too thoroughly; by 969, when the Emperor was murdered, they had overrun all eastern Bulgaria and were advancing on Constantinople. The next Emperor, John Tzimisces, spent the first year of his reign in driving the Russians back to the Danube. By 972 eastern Bulgaria was liberated from the Russians, only to be annexed to Byzantium. During the war the Bulgars, in helpless apathy, had seen their lands overrun; they made no resistance now.

But John Tzimisces left the work unfinished. The great province of the West, the Rilo country, the valleys of the Vardar and the Morava and Upper Macedonia, remained unconquered. There was probably very little Bulgar blood in these districts, but they had long been part of the Bulgarian realm, and Bulgaria had given them their Slavonic Cyrillic civilization. Their inhabitants considered themselves Bulgarian, and amongst them a new Bulgaria was born.

Its history is the history of its Tsar Samuel (976–1014), a local governor's son, who took advantage of rebellion amongst the Byzantines and the inexperience of the young Emperor Basil II to build up an Empire as extensive as Symeon's. The Eastern provinces were reconquered. The centre of this Empire was in Macedonia by the high mountain lakes of Ochrida and Prespa. Samuel's Court was wilder than Symeon's; it produced little literature and little art. Of his government we know almost nothing, not even on what terms he was with his Bogomil subjects. Given time he might have established his government on a lasting basis; but most of his reign was filled with a struggle for existence.

[1] The connexion between the Bogomils and the Albigensians is sometimes doubted, but to anyone who compares Slavonic Bogomil literature with Albigensian it is obvious.

By 990 Basil II had overcome internal rebellion and was determined to destroy this dangerous Balkan kingdom. After long campaigns, brilliant on either side, the Bulgarians nearly achieving their age-long ambition of capturing Salonica, at last Samuel's army was destroyed by the Emperor in the defile of Cimbalongus (1014) and the old Tsar died broken-hearted.

Samuel's successors were unequal to the task of saving Bulgaria. During their family quarrels Basil advanced and conquered their country. By 1018 the whole Balkan peninsula was his as far as Belgrade and the borders of Dalmatia; and his grateful countrymen surnamed him Bulgaroctonus, the Bulgar-slayer.

Those of the Bulgars whom he spared Basil treated wisely. They were allowed to keep many of their local customs. Their taxation remained taxation in kind at the same rate as before. Their Slavonic Church was left to them. Their Patriarchate was removed, and the Archbishop of Bulgaria, the new head of the Church, was placed under the Patriarch of Constantinople, ranking in the hierarchy after the Patriarchs of the East. A Greek was almost always appointed to the post. But in the less exalted ranks nothing was altered; the Cyrillic liturgy kept alive both the Bulgaro–Slavonic language and national self-consciousness.

The annexation of Bulgaria was followed by the submission of the eastern Serbian princes to the Empire. Their vassalage was never very strict; Serbia developed along her own lines. But politically and culturally the influence of Byzantium was paramount.

Meanwhile Byzantine influence had triumphed elsewhere, with even more far-reaching results. The Russians, like the Bulgars, were a non-Slavonic people who had superimposed themselves on Slavonic territory and had given their subjects the organization that the Slavs so seldom managed to achieve. In the course of the ninth century Swedish adventurers, known to the Eastern world as Varangians or the Russ, overran the districts round Lake Peipus and Lake Ilmen, establishing their rule over the Slavs there and extending it slowly down the River Dnieper towards the Black Sea. In about 860 the semi-legendary Rurik founded a strong State at the old Slavonic town of Novgorod. His successor Oleg added Kiev to the principality and Kiev became the capital of the dynasty of Rurik.

The expansion of the principality was directed by economic considerations. From Novgorod to the Dnieper past Kiev ran the great trade-route from the Baltic to the Black Sea. From the outset commerce was the main interest of the Varangians. Their State had a feudal aspect; each town was the domain of some prince or noble who administered the district and drew military levies from it, and the princes were the vassals of the Great Prince or Grand Duke of Kiev. But the princes were also the chief merchants of their districts, collecting and carrying its merchandise and leading the local contingent on the yearly commercial expeditions to Constantinople. These expeditions soon became a regular feature in Russian life. When exactly they began we do not know. By the middle of the tenth century there was a definite route that the Russians followed, there was a quarter at Constantinople assigned to them for their visits, rules were drawn up determining their rights and obligations there, and these rules were confirmed in the various treaties between the Russians and the Empire.

But the Russians did not always come as peaceful visitors. The wealth of the great capital was a constant temptation; and if their trade was in any way interrupted, they retaliated with an armed attack; indeed to secure new markets or new commercial concessions they would raid as far afield as Persia. Constantinople was several times in the ninth and tenth centuries threatened by a Russian attack; and its statesmen were anxious to find some means of checking the menace. Their solution was to convert the Russians.

Already in the mid-ninth century Photius had sent missions to Kiev, where apparently they met with some initial success but declined on the conquest of Kiev by the Varangian Oleg. In the tenth century missionaries began to work again, helped now by the perfected weapon of the Cyrillic liturgy; and in 954 they made an eminent convert in the person of the Dowager Grand Duchess Olga. Olga's conversion and her subsequent visit to Constantinople did much to popularize Byzantine civilization in Russia. But the bulk of the Russian people remained heathen for another forty years. The Balkan policy of the Emperor Nicephorus II and John Tzimisces brought Byzantium into conflict with Russia, and a little later the conflict was renewed owing to Russian ambitions in the Crimea. In the first conflict the Emperors succeeded in keeping Russia out of the Balkans, but to keep her out of the Crimea was less easy. However, the time was come for a compromise. Olga's grandson, the Grand Duke Vladimir, saw, as so many princes before him, the value of Christianity in building up the autocracy. Already he had done much to assert the authority of Kiev over the other Russian districts. Now, in 989, he agreed to be baptized, and in return he was to receive the hand of the Emperor Basil II's sister Anna.

Vladimir's conversion was of paramount importance in Russian history. It was followed by the rapid conversion of the Russian people—only a few outlying tribes remained heathen; the last of them, the people of Murom, embraced Christianity in the thirteenth century. And the adoption of Christianity, though it could not destroy at once Varangian feudalism, contributed largely to the hegemony of Kiev and the prestige of its ruler, the Emperor's brother-in-law. It led in time, after the Mongol interruption, to the Byzantine autocracy of the Muscovite Empire. It fixed Russia in the politico-cultural system of Byzantium. When a few years later Boleslav of Poland attempted to introduce Latin Christianity into Russia his agents received a rebuff so firm as to discourage any repetition of the attempt.

The influence of Byzantine civilization in Russia reached out in every direction. In art Byzantine pictures, such as the famous twelfth-century icon known as Our Lady of Vladimir, set the model for Russian iconography; Russian architecture is based on Byzantine principles, modified however by direct Caucasian influences, while the characteristic onion-shaped dome of the Russians was probably their own invention to deal with the winter snows. In religious thought, in daily life Byzantine ideas could long be everywhere traced,[1] and the language of St. Cyril became in Russia, as in the Balkans, the basis of the native literature.

[1] Cf. Chapter 14.

But the political influence of Byzantium in Russia was less than might have been expected. Barbarian movements in the twelfth century and the Mongol conquest in the thirteenth cut Russia off from the Black Sea. The centre of Russian life moved northward, to Vladimir, Tver, and Moscow. To the last Constantinople, Tsarigrad, remained in Russian eyes the capital of the world; occasional Russian pilgrims would journey there, and were certain of a welcome from their fellow Orthodox; a Russian princess might even become an Emperor's bride, popular in Constantinople because she was not of hated heretic Latin blood; but contacts grew fewer; Russia was left to develop her Byzantinism in her own less adaptable manner. She remained a potential guardian of the flank of the Orthodox East, but steadily less useful. It was not till the nineteenth century that the Greeks reaped the fruit of their conversion of Russia.

Thus by the eleventh century Byzantium was dominant over the eastern Slavs. But her domination had come too late; nations had already appeared amongst the Slavs, and Byzantium had recognized the fact by using as her method of domination the Cyrillic church-system. The Slavs of Serbia, of Bulgaria, or of Russia would never be absorbed into the Greek Christian world. They would therefore submit to the domination of the Greek Christian world only so long as Constantinople remained the great inviolable city with the power to make her views felt. In the twelfth century this power declined. Attacks from the Seljuk Turks and from the West, the embarrassment of the Crusades, the commercial rivalry of Italy and, to crown it all, the ineptitude of the imperial house of Angelus, brought the Empire to a state of obvious decay.

The southern Slavs had long been restive under the suzerainty of Byzantium; but fear of Hungary and of the strong armies of the Comneni made revolts abortive. The troubles that followed the death of the Emperor Manuel Comnenus in 1180 gave them their opportunity. The leading Serbian figure of the time was the Zupan Stephen Nemanya of the Zeta (Montenegro), who by the time of his abdication in 1196 had made himself Grand Zupan of the Serbs, the independent ruler of all the Serbian lands save the little district of Hum (Herzegóvina) where his brother Miroslav reigned. Farther north, about the same time, the Bosnian Kulin established the independent monarchy of Bosnia. Byzantium was powerless to prevent them. Hungary intervened more effectively for a time in Bosnia and Hum but without any permanent result. In 1186 Bulgaria, for a century and a half an imperial province,[1] was whipped by unjust taxation into revolt, and the brothers John and Peter Asen proclaimed the independence of the country in the little church of St. Demetrius at Trnovo. With the help of the Cumans beyond the Danube and of the Vlachs in the peninsula (the Asen were probably of Vlach origin) they defeated the Byzantine armies and established a kingdom stretching from the Black Sea to Sofia and into Macedonia, and assumed an imperial title.

John Asen was murdered in 1196 and Peter in 1197. Stephen Nemanya retired to a monastery in 1196 and died on Athos in 1200. Kulin died early in 1204. Under their successors an event occurred that made certain the independence of their kingdoms. The capture of Constantinople by the Crusaders in 1204 is a turning-point in the history of the southern Slavs. Hitherto, vassal or free, they had regarded Constantinople as the centre of their universe, the source of their culture and religion. Now suddenly and unexpectedly they were orphaned.

Their first reaction was to believe that the lords of Constantinople must be masters of the world and to make terms with the Latin West. In 1205 the Bulgarian monarch Kalojan, youngest of the Asen brothers, sent to Pope Innocent III and was given by him a royal crown;[2] and similarly, as late as 1217, the second Serbian Stephen, the 'first-crowned', won a royal crown from Pope Honorius III. But by then Bulgaria had evolved a better policy.

The thirteenth century saw the zenith of the Second Bulgarian Empire. The Latin Empire soon showed itself a pathetic farce. The exiled Byzantine Emperors of Nicaea were too busy piecing together the shattered Greek world to

---

[1] There had been Bulgarian revolts in 1040 and 1073 but both had been suppressed without much difficulty.

[2] He had asked for an imperial crown.

be aggressive against the Slavs. The smaller succession-states, Epirus and Salonica, were transient and weak. It was Bulgaria's opportunity to come forward as the leading power, the new centre of the Christian East. Kalojan quickly saw his new role. In 1205 he took Philippopolis from the Latins, defeating and capturing the Latin Emperor Baldwin I before Adrianople. In 1206 he slew the Latin King Boniface of Salonica. But in 1207 he fell himself in a palace intrigue.

The weak reign of the usurper Boril delayed the growth of Bulgaria for eleven years; but in 1218 Kalojan's son John Asen II assumed the throne and his father's aggressive policy. But it was a little late now. The Greeks had recovered much of their lands from the Latins, and the local inhabitant who preferred a Slav to a heretic Westerner was now content under his own fellow countrymen. The goal of every Balkan statesman who has not been deluded by vain hopes for Constantinople is Macedonia and its great port of Salonica. To hold the Balkan hinterland without Salonica is to hold something incomplete. Kalojan had died on the eve of an expedition against Salonica. John Asen II was aware of its importance. Early in his reign he expanded his kingdom towards the south-west. The medley of races in Macedonia (from which the culinary term *macédoine* is derived) could not oppose any strong military invader. But Salonica was a Greek city, and remained beyond his reach. Twice, in 1230 and 1240, it lay almost in his power, but in his fear of the growing Empire of Nicaea he allowed the Angeli of Salonica to retain their rule. Similar complex considerations marred his policy elsewhere. He could not decide whether to win Frankish Thrace by an alliance with Nicaea or to regard Nicaea as a menace to be opposed. He hesitated, and the Nicaeans benefited by his hesitations.

Nevertheless his reign was a great age for Bulgaria. His personality won him the respect even of his enemies, and his international prestige was great. In his Court at Trnovo he ruled with Byzantine pomp and ceremony through a bureaucracy formed on the Byzantine model. The Bulgarian Church was reorganized under the Archbishop of Trnovo, to whom the Patriarch of Nicaea conceded in 1235, as the price of an alliance against the Latins, autonomy and the Patriarchal title. Commerce was encouraged and conducted partly by Greek merchants, as in the old days, but mainly through the Ragusans who had trading rights throughout the Bulgarian Empire and introduced many of the products of the West. But civilization remained fundamentally Byzantine, modified to suit the temperament of the Balkan Slav. Bulgarian buildings such as the churches of Trnovo or Boiana are Byzantine in their conception. Only a greater simplicity in their construction, a cruder touch in the colouring of their decorations, show them to be the work of a different people.

John Asen II died in 1241; and at once Bulgaria began to crumble. Its decline was due partly to the lack of a personality to hold the kingdom together, partly to the growing power of the Nicaeans and their recovery of Salonica in 1246 and of Constantinople in 1261. John Asen's sons Kaliman I (1241–6) and Michael Asen (1246–57) and his nephew Kaliman II (1257–8) were active but unwise; and on Kaliman II's death the Asen dynasty was extinct. For the next twenty years Bulgarian history is the tale of a sequence of usurpers, supported by or reacting against the influence of Constantinople, while Thrace and Macedonia fell from Bulgarian hands.

In 1280 a stronger dynasty was founded by a Cuman, George Terteri, which was to last till 1323, holding its own against Tartar invaders and losing no ground to its Balkan rivals. In 1323 Michael Shishmanitch of Vidin founded the last Bulgarian dynasty. Its career started well; Michael all but captured Constantinople; but in 1330 the Bulgarians were badly defeated by the Serbs on the field of Velbuzd; and Bulgaria became hardly more than a vassal of Serbia. During the reign of John Alexander (1331–61) Bulgaria enjoyed little political power. Defeatism even crept into that great nationalist organization, the Church, where Bulgarian ecclesiastics such as St. Theodosius of Trnovo opposed the attempts of the Bulgarian Patriarch to assert his complete equality with the Patriarch of Constantinople. But it was a period of culture; St. Theodosius and his disciples formed the last literary coterie of medieval Bulgaria. The Tsar caused

works to be translated from the Greek, such as the Historical
Synopsis of Manasses; this translation is now in the Vatican
Library, illustrated in the somewhat crude but no longer
vigorous style of fourteenth-century Bulgaria. Architecture,
too, flourished, but again with neither new inspiration nor
improved technique.

In 1361 John Alexander died, dividing his inheritance.
His elder son, John Sracimir, was left the family fortress of
Vidin; his favourite, John Shishman, inherited the kingdom:
while a usurper, Duvrotik, took the district called the
Dobrudja after him. The division only led to trouble. Five
years earlier the Ottoman Turks had established themselves
in Europe intending to stay.

Meanwhile the hegemony had passed to Serbia. The
Serbian monarchy founded by Stephen Nemanya had been
put on a firmer basis by his sons, Stephen 'the First-Crowned'
and St. Sava. Stephen was crowned first by a papal legate in
1217, then more popularly by St. Sava as Archbishop of
Serbia in 1222. Before his death in 1228 he had reasserted
once more the authority of his line over the other Serbian
princes. St. Sava's work was even more valuable. His
diplomacy and the respect accorded to his high personal
qualities not only made him of great international use to his
brother but also enabled him to reorganize the Serbian
Church and win recognition of its autonomy from Byzantium. St. Sava was a man of wide experience, a traveller and
a scholar. The Serbian Church had hitherto been ruled
from Constantinople or Ochrida with little care or sympathy,
with the result that the Bogomils had vastly increased in
number. Sava understood the essential spirit of Cyrillism
and made Christianity more real to the Serbs by absorbing
many of their national beliefs and customs, and produced a
Church that was popular, linked to the new nationalist
dynasty but still in touch with the higher civilization of
Constantinople. In consequence the Bogomil faith soon
faded out from Serbia. His more political work in favour of
a Balkan *entente* was less permanently successful.

During the reigns of Stephen the First-Crowned's elder
sons, Radoslav and Vladislav, Serbia was overshadowed by
Bulgaria. But in 1243 the youngest, Stephen Uroš I, suc-

ceeded, shortly after the death of John Asen II of Bulgaria. Stephen Uroš I reigned for thirty-three years, a period of peace, during which the natural resources of the country and its commerce were developed, largely by merchants from the neighbouring Dalmatian coast. The King shocked the Byzantines by the crude simplicity of his life; nevertheless they sought his alliance—in vain, as he was disinclined to embark on restless political activities. Moreover, thanks perhaps to his Latin wife, his sympathies were more Latin than Greek.

In 1276 Stephen Uroš was ousted by his son Stephen Dragutin, a fanatical cripple, who eventually gave place to his brother Stephen Milutin, Stephen Uroš II (1281–1321). Dragutin became Duke of Belgrade and Lower Bosnia, a convert to Catholicism and an earnest persecutor of Bogomils. Stephen Uroš II was a man of few scruples. His diplomacy was bewildering in its sudden betrayals; Constantinople, Rome, Naples, and Hungary were all wooed and deserted; Venice was given commercial privileges and then saw the Serb issuing counterfeit Venetian coin. Nevertheless, by the time of his death Stephen had extended his kingdom into Macedonia and Bosnia and down the Adriatic coast. He had even for a while thought of winning Constantinople in the right of his wife, the Byzantine Princess Simonis.

His heir was his bastard Stephen Dečanski, Stephen Uroš III, a worthy disciple of his father's methods. He, too, increased the kingdom, his great feat being the battle of Velbužd, which left Serbia unquestionably supreme amongst the southern Slavs and made the annexation of Bulgaria a matter of practical politics. But Dečanski, probably wisely, preferred to leave Bulgaria a vassal state. A year later, in 1331, Dečanski was deposed and strangled by his son Stephen Dušan (Stephen Uroš IV).

Under Dušan Serbia reached its zenith. His campaigns in Bosnia and on the Adriatic coast were not wholly successful; he neither crushed the former nor conquered all the latter, though his influence was paramount there, as in Bulgaria also. But his main political activities were directed against Byzantium. Like so many great Balkan rulers he dreamed of being Emperor there, and his dream was his people's undoing. The civil war between John V and John Cantacuzenus, which broke out in 1341, furnished the opportunity. By 1345 Dušan had conquered all Macedonia except Salonica; a few years later he was master of western Thrace, and by 1349 of Epirus and Thessaly. In 1355 he marched on Constantinople, with every hope of success; but on the march he died.

Dušan's titles rose with his ambitions. In 1345, in defiance of Constantinople, he raised the Archbishop of Serbia, whose seat was Ipek, to the rank of Patriarch. In 1346 the Serbian and Bulgarian Patriarchs crowned him Emperor or Tsar of the Serbs and the Greeks. As new provinces were added to his Empire so their names were added to his titles. Realizing that Macedonia is the centre of the Balkan peninsula he moved his capital thither, to Skoplie (Uskub); and so Macedonia, once the seat of a Bulgarian Empire, became the seat of the Serbian. But Salonica eluded his grasp. Further to complete the working of his realm he collected the laws of Serbia and issued in 1349[1] his great Zakonnik, or code.

Dušan's code is less important from the purely legal point of view; its significance rests upon the picture that it gives of Serbian civilization. In Dečanski's reign Serbia, though rich, was primitive. The Armenian Archbishop Adam who passed through the country says that there were no walled castles; all houses were of wood except on the Dalmatian coast. The Byzantine writer Gregoras depicts the Serbian Court as highly pretentious, yet sadly wanting in comforts and decencies. But gold- and silver-mines were being worked; the valleys were fertile and the hills well wooded. Dušan's code shows that fortresses and palaces were now being built. The Court has become a Byzantine bureaucracy, each high-titled official with clear-cut functions. The towns were under the Tsar's officials, Counts for the cities and Captains for the smaller towns. But the country-side remained unaffected by Byzantine autocratic methods. There the nobility ruled, limiting the power of the Tsar.

[1] The last sixteen articles of the code were actually issued in 1365, ten years after his death.

There were the *Vlastele*, the great nobles, and under them the *Vlastelićići*. Their fiefs were hereditary and commanded jurisdiction over the peasants and serfs, though the peasants had clearly defined rights so long as they did not meddle in politics; the magnates even controlled the local church, as patrons of every living that they founded. They paid a tithe to the church and a death duty of their best armaments to the Tsar to whom they owed military service. The Tsar, on the other hand, summoned them to a parliament or sobor before he could legislate and maintained a permanent council of twenty-four of the greatest nobles. The Church organization was officially under the Crown; but the Patriarch could count on public support sufficiently to maintain his spiritual freedom. The Code shows Serbia to be a preponderantly agricultural society. The merchant classes were almost all alien and restricted to the Adriatic cities; the mines, mostly state-owned and worked by slave labour, employed only a tiny section of the community. The Code itself displays a diversity of influences. The Church law is purely Byzantine, as are the arrangements for the bureaucracy. The commercial law is Dalmatian in origin. Trial by jury had been introduced by Stephen Uroš II, probably in imitation of the West. The law of the country-side is derived from the ancient customs of the Serbs.

Serbian culture was not very high. Church architecture flourished. At first crudely Byzantine, it had in the mid-thirteenth century undergone an Italo-Gothic influence, due partly to the connexion with Dalmatia and Venice, partly to the work of Stephen Uroš I's Latin queen. By Dušan's time it had developed its own characteristics. The architects were probably usually Ragusans. Their buildings were fundamentally Byzantine but lighter, more fanciful, less classically restrained on the outside, and inside more lavishly if more crudely decorated. Serbian painting copied Byzantine. Serbian literature barely existed, save for the great popular epic-ballads that were now beginning to be sung, poetry that owes nothing to Byzantium.

In 1355 Stephen Dušan died and his Empire crumbled, leaving behind only a memory and an ideal that no Serbian patriot can forget. It crumbled because it was too diverse.

It contained too many races, Bulgarian, Italo-Dalmatian, Vlach, Albanian, and Greek as well as Serb; the Dalmatians and Albanians were largely Catholic, the Bosnians largely Bogomil; the Greeks resented the nationalism of the Serbian Church. Serbian civilization was itself too synthetic to bind this mass together; the ceremonial and hieratic aspects of Byzantium without its traditions, its outward luxuries without its inward culture, superimposed on Serbian agrarian feudalism, ornamented with a touch of Latin chivalry and Italo–Dalmatian commercialism, made up a medley acceptable to no one. Had Dušan won Constantinople with its oecumenical past and prestige, he might have founded a lasting realm, but the Serbian would have been swallowed up in the Byzantine. Had he been content to be a Slav monarch with Macedonia as his centre and Salonica as his port, again his realm might have survived. But his Byzantine ambitions and his failure to acquire Salonica led to the downfall of his Empire.

The rest of the story is the chronicle of the steady Turkish advance and need not be recounted in detail. From 1360 to 1370 the Turks were busy establishing themselves in Thrace. The battle of the Maritza (1371) sealed the fate of Bulgaria; Serbians and Bosnians were crushingly defeated on the field of Kossovo (15 June 1389). The freedom of the Balkans was lost. Four years later Bulgaria was annexed, and Serbia suffered the same fate in 1459. It was not until 1463 that the Turks formally took over Bosnia.

The fourteenth century had seen the rise of another Balkan people, the Roumanians of Wallachia and Moldavia. The Roumanians claimed Roman origin and so were eagerly susceptible to the influence of Byzantium. Moldavia never acquired great political power, though its importance as a mart of Byzantine and Slavonic culture during the next centuries is vast if dimly known. Wallachia had its brief eminence under the house of Bassaraba, but was too tightly wedged between Hungary and the Turks to develop a lasting position. Even its greatest prince, Mircea, was a tributary of Hungary, and its hero John Hunyadi, the White Knight of Wallachia, a soldier in the Hungarian army. But Roumania, despite its Roman and Hungarian–Latin connexions, was firmly attached by religion to the Slavonic world. Its Church had been organized under the Church of Ochrida in the great days of Bulgaria. It was therefore Cyrillic and inappropriately Slavonic-speaking, though it looked to Constantinople as its true metropolis. But the story of Roumanian civilization lies outside the scope of this chapter. It developed after the Turkish Conquest at the close of the fifteenth century, along lines that were very Byzantine, thanks chiefly to the Viceroys that the Sultan provided, scions of the Greek nobility of the Phanar.

Thus all the Balkan nations fell once more into the hands of Constantinople, now the deadening fist of the Turk. It remains to estimate what the old Constantinople, Christian Byzantium, had done for them. It was inevitable that the proximity of Constantinople should make the Slavs regard her as the centre of the world; nor was there in medieval days any other city as rich or as cultured. In art they owed everything to her. Russia and to a lesser extent Serbia evolved their own art from a Byzantine basis; Bulgaria, too close to the source, never succeeded so well. Politically Byzantium failed in her first object, to absorb the Slavs; she missed her opportunities till it was too late. But she succeeded in winning them to her sphere of influence by the most generous and far-reaching of her gifts, the Cyrillic Church. The Slav nations of Russia and the Balkans, with their national churches in communion with one another and deriving from a common source, could co-operate without antipathy, while each preserved its own individuality. It has been argued that the Slavs would have fared better under the ecclesiastical authority of Rome, or that at least Constantinople should not have led them into schism with the West. Then they would have had the full sympathy of the West at the time of crisis in the Ottoman invasions. But the sympathy of the West was of little help to Catholic Croatia; it did not save Hungary at Mohacs. The autocratic tendencies of the Roman Church were incompatible with Cyrillism, and Cyrillism was what the Slavs needed, both to preserve them first against the over-great cultural might of Byzantium and later against the over-great militarist might of the Turks. The nationalism of the Balkans is now to be deplored; but the nationalism supplied by the Cyrillic Churches during the long night of Turkish domination meant hope and a basis on which to build, when the dawn at last should rise.[1] In religion, above all else, Byzantium did well by the Slavs, better perhaps than she intended; and the heroes of the story are the brothers from Salonica, St. Cyril and St. Methodius.

STEVEN RUNCIMAN

[1] The same is true, *mutatis mutandis,* of Russia under the Mongols.

THE BYZANTINE INHERITANCE IN RUSSIA

THE Byzantine inheritance in Russia—to that title objection might with some reason be taken, for the heir comes into his inheritance only after the death of his ancestor, and it is true that East Rome had evangelized Russia centuries before Constantinople fell into the hands of the Muslim. But the phrase may perhaps be justified, since it is also true that it was only after 1453 that Holy Russia became fully conscious that she and she alone could claim as of right the inheritance which the Second Rome had been powerless to defend.

To estimate the range and the intensity of Byzantine influence upon pre-Mongolian Russia one must always bear in mind the historical background. It is now generally recognized that the creation of the Kievan State was the work not of the Slavs but of the predatory Northmen who raided far and wide round the coasts of Europe in the early Middle Ages. The Scandinavian advance was at the first directed towards the south by way of the Volga and it is the Russians of this eastern route who are known to the Arabic geographers. Their statements have been supported by the evidence of archaeology: post-Sassanid ornaments and Arab coins dating from the ninth century have been found in Sweden and Arab coins (A.D. 745–900) in north Russia. But it is with the later western Scandinavian advance that the future lay. Here the Swedes first established themselves in the neighbourhood of Novgorod under the half-legendary figure of Rurik. After a repulse he withdrew to his own country only to be recalled by the disunited tribesmen. Such is the account given in the saga which is preserved in the Russian *Primary Chronicle*. From Novgorod the Northmen made their way southward down the Dnieper under the leadership of Askold and Deir until they reached Kiev which they captured from the Slavs. The invaders found in their path Slav cities: they were not city-founders but organizers, warrior-merchants entering into possession where others had already builded. It was from Kiev that

Askold and Deir following the course of the Dnieper reached the Black Sea and in A.D. 860 delivered the first Russian attack upon Constantinople at a time when the Emperor was campaigning against the Arabs in Asia and the Byzantine fleet was operating in the Western Mediterranean. Photius, the Patriarch of Constantinople, had inspired the successful defence of the capital and when the attack had been repulsed it was ecclesiastical statesmanship which presented to him a vision of a new world to conquer: not only should the Christian message be carried to the Slavs and Bulgars of the Balkans, here was yet another mission-field for the Christian Church. A bishop was consecrated and later Photius could proudly report the progress of the work of conversion. After the fall of Photius his successor Ignatius appointed an arch-bishop for the Russian Church, while the Emperor Basil I sent an embassy which concluded a treaty of peace between the Russians and the Empire.

It was, however, a false dawn. From Novgorod by way of Smolensk there came a new invasion of pagan Northmen, and when Askold and Deir had been treacherously slain Oleg, as guardian of Rurik's young son Igor, ruled in Kiev, and by his successes over the Slav tribes of the south was the real founder of the Russian State. Kiev, said the victorious Oleg, was to be 'the mother of the Russian cities'. The economic and political centre of Russia shifts from the north to the south—from Lake Ilmen to the banks of the Dnieper. The overlordship of the Great Prince of Kiev was recognized, though other Scandinavian princes or Slav tribal chiefs might retain a wide independence. Trade with the Empire was extended and was regulated by a succession of treaties (907, 911, 945, 971) the text of which is preserved only in the Russian *Primary Chronicle*.

'It has never been satisfactorily determined whether the copies preserved in the *Chronicle* represent Old-Russian texts of the treaties made when they were negotiated or whether they are translations afterwards prepared from Greek originals which subsequently came to light in Kiev itself. It is not likely that the Russian princes of the tenth century, who were by no means superior to Scandinavian free-booters elsewhere on the Continent, attached any grave significance to these scraps of paper, and the fact that there is but one Greek allusion to them would indicate that to the Byzantine authorities they were more a gesture than a contract' (S. H. Cross).

Their importance lies in the fact that they permit to Russian merchants during the summer months free access to the capital, while we know that Russians early served as sailors in the Byzantine navy. Thus constant contact was maintained with the Christian civilization of the Empire; Igor's attack upon Constantinople in 941 did but lead after the defeat of the Russian navy to a renewal of the former treaty with Byzantium.

When Igor had been murdered leaving as his successor a young son Svyatoslav, the government was undertaken by Igor's widow Olga, of whose subtlety and diplomatic skill the *Primary Chronicle* gives a lengthy account. While Svyatoslav followed the warrior pagan tradition of the Northmen and engaged in one campaign after another, Olga turned to Christianity: she was received by the Emperor in Constantinople (A.D. 957) and on baptism assumed the Empress's name of Helen. Her son refused to follow her example: his men, he said, 'would laugh him to scorn'.

After Oleg's capture of Kiev we have no further report of any direct missionary activity on the part of the Greek Church, yet Christianity must have gained a foothold in Russia. Southern Slavs would have come in contact with Christians in the imperial outpost of Cherson in the Crimea; we know that there was already a Christian church in Kiev, while in the treaty of 944 the Christian Russians are distinguished from the pagan Northmen. In 969 Olga, the first Christian Russian princess, died and in 972 Svyatoslav fell in battle with the Petchenegs; while his bastard son Vladimir governed Novgorod, the territory of the Great Prince of Kiev was divided between Svyatoslav's two sons. When civil war had broken out between the brothers and one had been killed, Vladimir, fearing an attack from the survivor, Yaropolk, fled to Scandinavia and there gathered a strong force of Northmen. As in the days of Rurik, from Novgorod the Scandinavians advanced against Kiev. Vladimir removed Yaropolk by treachery and re-established the unity of government with Kiev for his capital. And it was Vladimir who accepted Christian baptism and made Christianity the religion of the Russian State. The date and the circumstances of this conversion are disputed. It is strange that there is no mention of Vladimir's baptism in the Greek sources. It would seem, however, that we may accept the account of the Russian *Primary Chronicle* and date the conversion to A.D. 989. According to that account, when the Emperor was hard pressed by the revolt of Bardas Phocas he appealed to Vladimir for military aid. The Russian saw in this appeal an opportunity to rid himself of some of his dissatisfied followers and agreed to send support, but his price was high: he was to be given in marriage a Byzantine princess. The Emperor on his side must have stipulated that Vladimir should accept baptism. But when Vladimir's Northmen had won a victory for the Emperor over his rival, East Rome was unwilling to fulfil the terms of the contract. To force the Emperor to send the princess Anna to Russia Vladimir attacked and captured the imperial city of Cherson. Thereby he carried his point: at Cherson he was baptized and married. At his baptism he assumed the Emperor's name, Basil, as Olga at her baptism had taken the Empress's name of Helen. Vladimir returned to Russia and began the destruction of idols and the imposition upon his subjects of his new faith. Such is the historical framework of delayed conversion within which the introduction into Russia of Byzantine influence must be placed.

Since Christianity was brought to Russia from East Rome the Russian Church followed from the first the Byzantine model. Already within the Empire orthodox dogma had attained to its full expression: the Iconoclast attack upon the tradition of the Eastern Church had been repulsed. That system of dogma was transported in its entirety to Russia and was never questioned. There are no controversies concerning the fundamental issues of the faith within the Russian Church, and to the Russian liturgical forms were part of the same deposit which was hallowed by the authority of the Fathers. The strands of the inherited faith and the liturgical tradition were interwoven and each element in that interweaving was sacrosanct.

The Russia to which Christianity came was a primitive and barbarous land: all culture necessarily emanated from the

Church and in this field there was no rival to contest the ecclesiastical supremacy. Greek architects planned and Greek workmen built the early Russian churches. The decoration of the churches naturally followed the pattern set by Constantinople: through mosaics and icons the Greek view of the ascent by way of the saints and the angelic hierarchy up to the majesty of Christ as Pantokrator—Lord of All—was faithfully reproduced. In time Russia would introduce her own architectural developments such as the characteristic 'onion dome', but however deeply the Greek might later be suspected as a renegade from the faith of the Fathers, the Russian converts did but cling the more tenaciously to the creed which Greek thinkers had formulated in the Seven Oecumenical Councils.

Yet from the outset—from the conversion of Vladimir, 'the new Constantine'—it was clear that the Christian Church on Russian soil was a very different thing from the Church within the Roman Empire. The Christian faith had penetrated East Roman society from below before it had been adopted as his personal belief by the first Christian Emperor. The Church had developed through centuries of conflict and had in the course of that development secured the passionate loyalty of the Byzantine people: it had become an integral part of a long-established social organization. In Russia Christianity was not thus securely founded in history: it had no such deep roots. It was an alien religion set against a pagan world; it had been imposed from above upon Slav and Northman alike. There was no wealth of native tradition to which it could appeal for support. The Christian clergy was therefore, of necessity, bound in close alliance with the Great Princes of Kiev. The Church needed the tithe which the Prince of Kiev granted to it from the revenues of the State: it was the Prince who founded monasteries and built churches; the State placed its powers of compulsion at the service of the bishops who sought to suppress paganism and to turn the 'double faith' of the converts—half-pagan and half-Christian—into a complete allegiance to the ethical demands of the new religion. And since the higher clergy represented culture, the State for its part needed the advice of bishops and monks, needed their intermediation in the ceaseless princely feuds, needed a bishop's consecration when the Prince at his accession 'was set upon his throne' or an episcopal blessing when the ruler started upon a campaign. It was through the Church that provision was made for the poor, the sick, the widow, and the orphan, while it was in monasteries that the Councils of the princes assembled. It was thus imperative that the Russian State and the Russian Church should be closely integrated in mutual defence and co-operation.

What, in the period immediately following on Vladimir's conversion, the relation of the Russian Church to the Patriarchate of Constantinople may have been we do not know; some have suggested that the Russian Church was independent: while it may from the first have had, as it undoubtedly had in the eleventh century, a single Metropolitan appointed by and under the authority of the Patriarch. Thus the Patriarch could summon the Metropolitan to the Byzantine capital for trial and could entertain appeals from the judgement of the Metropolitan; he might write advocating the adoption of the monastery of the common life rather than the system of separate cells for monks, but in general, so far as records show, he did not interfere in the administration of the Russian Church. Of the Metropolitans themselves during the pre-Mongolian period our sources tell us little. We know that the princes, when they had chosen a diocesan bishop, sent him for consecration to the Metropolitan, and while it is regarded as needing no comment in a chronicle that a prince should remove his bishop there is apparently no record of the deposition of a Metropolitan by a Great Prince of Kiev.

Thus through the appointment by the Patriarch of the Metropolitan Byzantine influence in the Church of Russia was continually reinforced; for in the pre-Mongolian period (down to 1237), apart from two exceptional cases, the Metropolitan was always a Greek. Since there only one Metropolitan for the whole of Russia representing the Church in Kiev by the side of the Great Prince, since all claims to appoint a second Metropolitan in the north (as, for example, in Rostov-Suzdal in the twelfth century) were rejected by the Patriarch of Constantinople, the Church acted as a unifying influence in a world of warring princes, while the Metropolitan, being a Greek coming to Russia from the Empire, was committed to neither of contending Russian parties and could thus with impartiality attempt to perform the task of peacemaker, could seek to persuade princes to abide by their oaths which had been solemnized by 'kissing the Cross'.

It would be easy, but it would be false, to idealize the relation between State and Church in early Russia: that relation, it has been said, was rather one of might than of right. If he were strong the Russian prince could and did ignore priestly admonitions; he would imprison outspoken bishops: the formal respect shown to monks and clergy was compatible with actual disobedience which set at nought the threat of excommunication. The Church might, and did, proclaim to the princes that they held their power from God and that this fact imposed upon them the duty of punishing evil-doers, of ruling with mercy and judging with justice, that breach of faith would bring upon them vengeance in this world and perpetual damnation after death, but perjury, it appears, was so general that an archbishop forbade the taking of an oath by the kiss upon the Cross on account of the spiritual danger of broken pledges. In the civil wars monasteries and churches were laid waste or burned down without scruple. One Metropolitan, at least, weary of his failures to control the feuds of the princes, retired disheartened to Constantinople.

The literature of early Russia came of necessity from the Church as the only source of culture. It was naturally a religious and monastic literature. It was fed by Slav translations of Byzantine works and its original compositions were moulded on Byzantine models. Of 240 Russian writers who are known to have lived before the close of the sixteenth century no less than 190 were monks, 20 belonged to the secular clergy, and only 30 were laymen. Such in literature is the debt of Russia to the Church. Byzantine influence can be traced in the Russian *Primary Chronicle*, formerly known as the Chronicle of Nestor, which is our principal source for the history of pre-Mongolian Russia. Scandinavian sagas may have been drawn upon in the early parts of the Chronicle, but its author, a monk from the Kievan monastery of the Caves, probably derived from East Rome the whole conception of writing a continuous history of the Russians, while the annalistic form of his work would have been suggested by Slav translations of Byzantine chronicles—the *Brief Chronography* of Nicephorus, the Patriarch of Constantinople (died A.D. 828), and the Chronicle of Georgius Hamartolus (George the Monk). The author of the *Primary Chronicle* twice quotes by name Georgius Hamartolus, and his debts to this Chronicle have been tabulated by the late Professor S. H. Cross of Harvard University. These borrowings extend from A.D. 858 to A.D. 943, while it is to the same source that the *Chronicle* owes its account of the original apportionment of the earth, of the tower of Babel and the long description of the customs of the alien peoples. Among other debts of the *Chronicle* to Greek sources may be mentioned the lengthy creed taught to Vladimir I; this is translated from a Greek text of the ninth century written by Michael Syncellus, the friend of St. Theodore of the monastery of Studius in Constantinople.

Russia's devotion to Byzantine ascetic and anchoritic ideals is reflected in its hagiography; the monumental collection of Lives of the Saints compiled by Macarius in the sixteenth century fills 27,057 folio pages of script. Anyone who is conversant with the Greek biographies of saints feels that he is on familiar ground when he reads the Life of a Russian Saint such as that of St. Sergius of Radonezh. Indeed one may wonder whether accounts given in such a Life which have customarily been treated as resting upon fact have not been simply incorporated from Greek hagiography. The story of the early difficulties of St. Sergius in learning to read is suspiciously like the similar difficulties experienced by St. Theodore of Edessa. It would be interesting to study such a Life as that of St. Sergius in the light of Greek hagiographic texts: the forms of exorcism, the miracles granted during the celebration of the Eucharist and the injunction to maintain secrecy concerning such miracles during the lifetime of the saint, the protection of the poor and the orphan, the punishment for doubts of the saint's holiness, the warning given to the saint of his coming death, the reception of the saint's soul by angels. Such a comparison would illustrate in detail how faithfully the Russians followed their Greek models.

In the sphere of law the influence of the Byzantine Empire through the Russian Church was paramount. In ecclesiastical law the Kormchaia was based upon a Byzantine Nomokanon,[1] i.e. a digest of canon law and of imperial constitutions affecting the Church, together with the Church ordinances of Vladimir and Yaroslav. The civil law of Russia—the Russkaya Pravda—consists of a brief statement of customary law supplemented by the legislation of the Russian princes and is modelled on the short Byzantine systematic summaries of law of the eleventh and twelfth centuries such as the Procheiros Nomos—the 'handy' lawbook. In Kievan Russia delinquencies which were sins but not crimes were in all cases subject only to the jurisdiction of the Church. Those classes of the population which fell under the description of 'church people' were exempted completely from intervention by the courts of the State. The term 'church people' as defined in detail by Vladimir has a much wider range of application than might have been expected: it embraces not only priests and deacons and the members of their families, abbots, monks, and nuns, but also (amongst others) pilgrims, doctors, freedmen, vagrants, the blind, the lame, and inmates of hospitals and hostels. For all these 'church people' even in criminal cases the Church courts alone are competent, and since the Russkaya Pravda has been preserved together with the Kormchaia it has been contended by Kluchevsky that the texts of the Russkaya Pravda as they have come down to us represent a compilation drawn up by the clergy for application in the courts of the Church. This might serve to explain the absence from our texts of the Russkaya Pravda of any mention of such practices as the judicial duel of which churchmen disapproved. But so far as we know the Church did not attempt any widespread remodelling of Russian customary law. Not

---

[1] It has been suggested that the grant of a tithe by the State to the Church is evidence of Western influence.

otherwise in the fourth century of our era had the Christian
Church of the Roman Empire accepted the law of the pagan
State while developing for its own use through its canons
an independent body of ecclesiastical legislation. Indeed,
ecclesiastical legislation in Russia was forced to modify the
rigour of Byzantine Church law: thus pagan practices and
the resort to astrologers were so deeply rooted in the social
life of Kievan Russia that it was impracticable to enforce the
death penalty demanded by imperial legislations. A Greek
Metropolitan in the eleventh century might lay stress upon
the observance of rules laid down by the Greek Fathers—
'Cleave unto the law of God, not unto the custom of the
land'—but a Russian bishop of Novgorod was more liberal
in his interpretation of canon law, and a rising sentiment of
Russian nationalism as a protest against Byzantine dominance may perhaps be traced in his boast that there was no
need for him to send money 'to another land', i.e. to the
Patriarch of Constantinople. The Church is on the way to
become the Church of the Russian people.

Probably the most potent channel of Byzantine influence
in Russia was Monasticism. One of the earliest of monastic
foundations was the Monastery of the Caves in the neighbourhood of Kiev (1051). Here St. Theodosius (died 1074)
worked, introducing the rule of St. Theodore the Studite and
modelling the ascetic life on the more moderate Palestinian
practice rather than on the extreme forms of Syrian mortifi-
cation. It was only in his youth that St. Theodosius wore
chains. 'He created the model of Russian monastic piety.'
In Russia as in the Empire it is the monk, who need not be a
priest, who awakes popular devotion: the monastery comes
to be regarded as the half-way house between earth and
Heaven—the 'House of the Angels'. It is from the monks
that a father confessor is chosen; it is to the monastery that
the destitute turn for relief. And from the monasteries the
diocesan bishops are drawn: they carry with them the
monastic scale of values and naturally desire to create new
monasteries in or near the capital of their province. In early
Russia most monasteries are placed in the neighbourhood of
the towns: the monastic colonization of the north belongs to a

later period. Up to the middle of the thirteenth century
some seventy monasteries were established in or near towns:
it has been estimated that both Kiev and Novgorod each
possessed some seventeen monasteries. In those monasteries
which had arisen spontaneously through the influence of
some holy man drawing disciples to his retreat the brother-
hood was free to choose its own abbot, but, just as in the
Byzantine Empire, so in Russia there was no little danger
to religious life from the rights possessed by the founder
(Ktitor) of a monastery. It was his generosity which had
called the monastery into being, and it was recognized that
he was entitled to administer the affairs of his foundation:
he could appoint and remove the abbot and his decisions
might be influenced by bribery. The founder's monastery
became the mausoleum of his family. To his monastery the
prince, when death was near, would retire to invest himself
in the sacred robes of the monk: having worn these for a few
days or even a few hours he would pass with better hope
to another world. As in Byzantium, again, the monastery
was the refuge for princesses, for widows, for those who had
made shipwreck of their lives, and once again as in the
Empire of East Rome defeated foes were tonsured and
confined within the monastery walls.

During the twelfth century, it would seem, monasticism
suffered a decline and after the period of subjection to the
Tartars the revival which followed in the fourteenth century
was largely due to St. Sergius of Radonezh: to him eight
monasteries owed their foundation. In the fifteenth century
monasteries acquired from princely donations such large
estates tilled by numerous peasants, their management and
organization required so much time and care that the primary
purpose of the ascetic life was gravely prejudiced. Monasticism had become a part of the world from which it had
professed to withdraw. Pre-Mongolian Russia had early
established contact with Mount Athos; in 1169 a Russian
monastery was founded on the Sacred Mountain, and
St. Panteleimon was another such monastery. The Tartar
invasion severed this connexion, but at the end of the fourteenth and in the fifteenth century a close intercourse was
re-established. It was on Mount Athos that Nil Sorski (born

1433) became acquainted with the mysticism of Hesychasm. On his return to Russia he protested against monastic absorption in worldly interests. Monks should surrender their lands and return to their original profession of poverty. His followers were nicknamed the 'Non-Possessors'. The opposition to Nil Sorski's proposals was led by St. Joseph of the Volokolamsk monastery (1439–1515). The 'Possessors' were able administrators ready to co-operate with the Tsar in the tasks of government: monasteries were to become the nursery of future bishops. If they were to be trained for bishoprics, the monks must be freed from economic anxieties: the possession of lands was a necessity. The Josephites insisted on unquestioning obedience to superiors and a rigorous enforcement of minute details of the external forms of asceticism. Personality was to be reduced by strict discipline to a common level. One's own opinion was 'the mother of all passions: opinions are the second Fall of Man'. The 'Non-Possessors' regarded asceticism as but a means to an end, and their aim was that inner freedom for the activity of the spirit which should lead to the soul's perfection. Through this action of the spirit and through contemplation the monk should ultimately attain by the path of prayer to union with God. Monasticism must be liberated from the control of the State, while the persecution of heretics must cease: heretics should be confined in monasteries until they should come to a realization of the truth. In the thought of Nil Sorski we catch the echo of Byzantine mysticism: introspection and silence, united with a never-sleeping watchfulness over man's vagrant thoughts, will fashion a permanent attitude of the soul so that temptation will lose its power. The fruit of the surrendered life is joy ineffable: prayer unspoken rises spontaneously from the heart. The mind is taken captive by Another's strength. Then doth the soul pray not by asking, but doth rise above asking: it gains a foretaste of eternal felicity and in that bliss forgets itself and everything terrestrial.

But Nil Sorski failed to persuade the monks of Russia: the 'Possessors' held their ground. His disciple Vassian Kossoi stigmatizes in bitter denunciation the avarice and the harshness of the wealthy monastic landlords: his pamphlet may be compared with the picture drawn, in the twelfth century by Eustathius of Salonica, of the monastic landlords of the Empire. At length in 1533 a foreign visitor, Adam Kliment, could estimate that one-third of the agricultural land in Russia was owned by the religious houses. Nil Sorski left the monastery of the ascetic community but did not adopt the life of the solitary; he inaugurated in Russia the monasticism of the 'middle way' (Skitsvo) where two or three monks would live together in a cell—often an old monk and a novice—and all would be under an abbot, receiving food from the monastery and generally meeting for a common service on Saturday evening. The *skete* resembled the Palestinian Laura of St. Sabas. Thus the Josephites triumphed and their influence can be traced in the decisions of the Council of the Hundred Chapters (the Stoglav) of 1551, but the sixteenth century saw a decline in the influence exercised by Russian monasticism: the maintenance of the monastery as the nursery of bishops and the handmaid of the Muscovite State was secured, but the price paid for such support was the stifling of that spiritual passion which Nil Sorski had sought to kindle afresh in Russian asceticism.

Perhaps the outstanding weakness of Byzantine monasticism was its extreme individualism: each monastery was a law unto itself. There were in East Rome no monastic orders which might have given cohesion and control to the separate foundations. The monastery depended too greatly upon the sanctity or the administrative ability of its abbot. Were he a reformer, there was the danger that his reforms would not outlive him. The same would seem to have been true of Russian monasticism, though here the evidence is not perhaps so conclusive as for the Empire.

The strength of the ascetic appeal in Russia is most clearly demonstrated by the reverence and devotion popularly shown to the monk and the solitary. It is the ascete who first penetrated into the Russian forests of the north and with his own hands cleared the ground to secure his support. And then the peasant was drawn as by a magnet to the cell of Christ's athlete and a village was formed and the lands about the upper course of the Volga and the Oka were

peopled. Thus was the Russian frontier extended. Just as
within the Empire Lives of the heroes of asceticism formed
the favourite reading of simple folk, so on Russian soil such
biographies of the holy men were multiplied and the Russian
Church constituted its own national calendar of the sainted
dead.

A Russian psychologist has studied these popular biographies in order to assess which moral values were most
highly esteemed by the common folk. He notes the strength
of will of these ascetes, their humility, their continence and
abstinence, their knowledge of the human heart. It might
be urged that all these virtues are traditional in biographic
literature: they could be paralleled through the whole range
of the Lives of Byzantine saints. As a distinguishing characteristic it has been suggested that the Russian ascete did not
suffer—at least to the same extent—from those sins of the
flesh which tortured the monks living in a Mediterranean
climate. It is indeed instructive to consider who were the
heroes of the faith whom the Russian people chose for
canonization. Under Ivan IV the Metropolitan Macarius
summoned two Councils to determine what names should
be added to the list of the 22 holy dead already recognized
as 'national' saints in the Russian calendar. Thirty-nine
were canonized by the Councils of 1547 and 1549. Amongst
these 61 saints there were 16 princes and princesses, 1 boyar,
3 Lithuanian martyrs, 14 higher dignitaries of the Church,
and 23 founders or superiors of monasteries. Amongst the
saints canonized between the Macarian Councils and the
constitution of the Holy Synod (1721) the founders or
superiors of monasteries numbered 74 out of 146. Thus is
reflected the veneration of the Russian people for the ascetic
life.[1]

In art the debt of Russia to East Rome is obvious. Byzantium had not only moulded dogma and ritual but it had
created types to which the mosaicist and the painter were

[1] Of the 39 canonizations of the Macarian Councils, 30, it would seem, were
'national' saints while 9 were 'local' saints (revered within one diocese or a single
monastery or group of monasteries), formally canonized as such. I desire to
acknowledge the help of the Warden of All Souls College, Oxford, on the disputed
question of the number of Russian saints. N.H.B.

bound. Russian art, like Byzantine art, is not illusionist or naturalistic: it permits of no free play for individual fancy save in its glorious colouring. It does not attempt to represent the realism of this world, but seeks to transport the worshipper into the world of a supernatural tranquillity—into that peace of soul which our troubled existence here can neither give nor take away. In its bold simplicity the icon can make its appeal to all alike; it calls for no secret gnosis for its understanding. It speaks a universal language and in this it does but reflect the universality of the Christian faith.

The first great Russian victory over the Tartars was the battle of Kulikovo Pole, 8 September 1380. St. Sergius of Radonezh had bidden the Russians 'go forward and fear not. God will help you', and the saint's words had been put to a triumphant test. In 1472 Ivan III married Sophia Palaeologus, the niece of the last East Roman Emperor. In 1480 Ivan renounced his subjection to the Tartar and adopted the title of Tsar or autocrat: he was no longer the vassal of any alien power.

In the early history of Russia there is no developed theory of sovereignty, nor could there be in a land where the feuds of the princes made unity impossible, where the authority of the Great Prince of Kiev depended upon his power to enforce it by arms. The developed theory of sovereignty came with the establishment of the autocracy of the princes of Moscow after the liberation from the Tartar domination. But though that theory was derived from the Byzantine Empire, it did not, it would seem, come to Russia directly from Constantinople, but indirectly by way of Bulgaria. The second Bulgarian Empire with its centre at Trnovo had for a time controlled the Balkans (see Ch. 13); its rulers had styled themselves Tsar and Autokrator and at their Court there had been a literary revival when Greek works were translated into Bulgarian. Among these translated works was the verse chronicle of Manasses. In this chronicle the decline of the Roman power in western Europe was described: the old Rome of the West had failed, but Constantinople had taken its place and still stood young and vigorous. In the Bulgarian version Constantinople disappears, and in its stead the chronicler's praise is transferred to 'our new Tsarigrad' and the Bulgarian Tsar. Trnovo claimed for itself the imperial glory of the city of Constantine. In 1393 the Bulgarian Empire fell before the attack of the Turks and many exiles fled from Bulgaria to Moscow. A Bulgarian, Kiprian, at this time became Metropolitan of Moscow. It looks as if these *émigrés* had carried with them the imperial theory which on Bulgarian soil had been shattered by the Turkish victory. It was Kiprian who, when a dispute had arisen between Moscow and the Empire, wrote to the Patriarch of Constantinople: 'We have a Church but no Emperor, and we do not recognize him.' Byzantium replied by a reassertion of its sole claim to imperial sovreignty. In 1438-9 came the Council of Florence and the Union of the Eastern and Western Churches. Orthodoxy had been betrayed by the Greeks: the Metropolitan Isidor who had played the traitor's part at the Council was cursed as a renegade. In 1453 Constantinople itself fell into the hands of the Turks. The lesson thus taught by history was obvious: here was the hand of God. Already in 1458-9 the contrast is drawn between heretical Greece and orthodox Russia: there only remains one truly orthodox Church on earth—the Russian Church. In 1492 Ivan, Tsar in Moscow, has become the new Constantine in the new city of Constantine. In 1504 a Council formulated in its Sixteen Chapters the duty of the Tsar: the office of the sun is to give light to the whole creation, the office of the Tsar is to care for all his subjects. 'Thou hast received the sceptre from God: be mindful to satisfy Him Who gave it thee. . . . By nature the Tsar is like any other man, but in power and office he is like the Highest God.' Thus did the Russian Church echo the words of Chrysostom (*Homilia in Epist. ad Rom.* xxiii. 689E. Migne, *Patrologia Graeca*, vol. lx, col. 618). The chronographer of 1512 writes: 'Constantine's city is fallen, but our Russian land through the help of the Mother of God and the saints grows and is young and exalted. So may it be, O Christ, until the end of time!' The words which the Bulgarian translator of Manasses had applied to Trnovo are here claimed for Moscow. The new doctrine finds its final expression in the writings of Philotheus of the monastery of Pskov. In a letter dating from the first quarter of the sixteenth century we read:

'I wish to add a few words on the present orthodox Empire of our ruler: he is on earth the sole Emperor (Tsar) of the Christians, the leader of the Apostolic Church which stands no longer in Rome or in Constantinople, but in the blessed city of Moscow. She alone shines in the whole world brighter than the sun. . . . All Christian Empires are fallen and in their stead stands alone the Empire of our ruler in accordance with the prophetical books. Two Romes have fallen, but the third stands and a fourth there will not be.'

When Constantinople united with the Latins the 'Woman' of the twelfth chapter of the Apocalypse fled to the Third Rome, that is, the 'new Great Russia'. When Heberstein in the middle of the sixteenth century composed his famous description of Russia he could write: 'Fatentur publice voluntatem Principis Dei esse voluntatem et quicquid Princeps egerit ex voluntate Dei agere.' Men said: 'Deus scit et magnus Princeps.' At the Council of the Hundred Chapters (Stoglav) held in 1551 it was declared that the orthodoxy of Moscow was the pattern for the whole of the Eastern Church. In 1589 the Metropolitan of Moscow received the title of Patriarch and after long negotiation this was recognized by the Eastern Patriarchates. In the charter of installation, when in Moscow the Patriarch of Constantinople, Jeremiah, elevated the Metropolitan to the Patriarchate of all Russia, the words of Philotheus were reaffirmed:

'Because the old Rome has collapsed on account of the heresy of Apollinaris, and because the second Rome which is Constantinople is now in possession of the godless Turks, thy great kingdom, o pious Tsar, is the Third Rome. It surpasses in devotion every other, and all Christian kingdoms are now merged in thy realm. Thou art the only Christian Sovereign in the world, the Master of all faithful Christians.'[1]

From February 1498 dates the first Russian order of coronation founded on Byzantine models. At the coronation of Ivan IV in 1547 we hear for the first time that the regalia had been sent to Russia by the Emperor Constantine Mono-

[1] This translation is taken from N. Zernov, *The Russians and their Church* (S.P.C.K., 1945), p. 71.

machus (1042–54). But this is not enough: the dynasty of Rurik traces its descent from the brother of Augustus. Thus did Russia become the heir of Rome and of Byzantium, the sole defender of the orthodox faith. 'Holy Russia' was born: Christian Tsar and Christian Church were united in a common mission. The faith of the Byzantine Caesars, the confidence that their rule was stayed on God, was planted securely, as men thought, on Russian soil.

Likewise Russia made its own the Byzantine theory of imperial authority. The Muscovite Tsar as defender of the faith summons the Councils of the Church, determines their composition, propounds the subjects for their discussion, and gives to their decisions the force of law. 'As God in Heaven, so is on earth the Tsar', says the Russian proverb. And then wider horizons opened up: in reunion with the Greek Church the Tsar could take the lead as defender of the Eastern Patriarchates, as liberator of the Balkans from the rule of the Turk. But union with the Greeks carried with it the revision, on the basis of Greek texts, of the service books of the Russian Church. The guardian of orthodoxy—'Holy Russia'—was to go to school with those who had betrayed the faith at the Council of Florence. And western currents began to flow eastwards: a new spirit of inquiry and research led to the opening of schools in Moscow; the teaching of Greek and Latin grammar, the study of rhetoric invaded the world of tradition. New naturalistic icons were painted 'with red lips, curly hair and thick muscles'. Literature for the Russian had meant in a word edification (Jagoditsch), and as for the new spirit of inquiry blowing from the West the traditionalists had their answer: 'Do not seek learning, seek humility.' 'The fishermen of the Gospels were not learned in books: they had found wisdom through the Holy Ghost and thus were given the power to draw to themselves the whole world.' Profane learning was the breeding-ground of arrogance: 'learning is the coming of Anti-christ.'

The new age found its embodiment in Nikon appointed Patriarch of Russia in 1652. Nikon, the Russian Cerularius, who sought to set the Church above the State, began ruth-

lessly to enforce Greek forms—Greek chants, Greek vestments, Greek texts—upon the Church. After the appalling
devastation of the 'Time of Troubles' the movement which
had begun as a reform, initiated through the preaching of
the parochial clergy, became with Nikon a crusade of violence
against the treasured inheritance of the centuries. 'I am a
Russian', was his confession, 'but my faith is Greek.' In the
sixteenth century the traditional shape of Russian life in
State and Church had been formulated in the *Stoglav* (at
the Council of the Hundred Chapters) and of life in the
family in the *Domostroi*, itself framed on a Byzantine model,
and now that statement was challenged, and the issue of that
challenge was the Great Schism. The Schism meant the
destruction of the unity of the Russian civilization of the
Middle Age based upon a Byzantine tradition; in the heroic
grandeur of the resistance of the Old Believers there is
demonstrated how deeply that tradition had taken root.
And it is a singular good fortune that the modern student
can re-live that tragedy in the autobiography of Avvakum
(*c.* 1620–82) the one great literary masterpiece which has
been bequeathed to us by early Russia.

Without any previous politic explanation of his action
Nikon issued an order which spread dismay through the
Church: instead of making the sign of the Cross with two
fingers it was to be made with three; instead of a double
Alleluia a triple Alleluia was to be sung. Both practices had
been pronounced heretical by the Council of the Hundred
Chapters (1551). The faithful met together and took counsel: 'It was as if winter was of a mind to come; our hearts
froze, our limbs shook.' The order aroused widespread
resistance: the body of the 'Old Believers' was formed, and
against them Nikon waged a bitter persecution. 'Wife', asks
Avvakum, 'what must I do? The winter of heresy is at the
door. Am I to speak or to hold my peace?' Her answer was:
'Christ is strong and He will not abandon us. Get thee gone,
get thee gone to Church, Petrovich. Unmask the whore of
Heresy.' Superficially it may seem an insufficient change
to justify the splitting of a Church in two. But it is easy to
overlook the significance of the *physical* act in worship: it is
the habitual physical act which awakes the response of the

spirit. Religion is bound up with profound emotions which are impervious to logic. Russians have often pointed to the aesthetic character of Russian religion and in such a sphere a very slight change may effectually break the link of association.

'Religious apprehension', Kluchevsky has written, 'is distinguished from apprehension based upon logic or upon mathematics by the fact that, in it, an idea or a motive is indissolubly bound up with the form through which it is expressed. . . . The law of psychological association causes an idea or a motive to become organically one with the text, the rite, the form, the rhythm or the sound through which that idea or that motive is expressed. Forget the picture or the musical combination of sounds which has evoked in you a given frame of mind— and instantly you find yourself powerless to reproduce that mental attitude.'[1]

A translation of the New Testament in modern speech may be closer to the original text, but for the Christian in this country it can never have the same value as the familiar words of the Authorized Version. In his loyalty to the past the Old Believer was preserving a Byzantine tradition: 'Even the smallest neglect of the traditions leads to the complete contempt of dogma.' These words of Photius found their echo in Russia. The passion which had inspired Byzantine monks in their defence of the icons animated the Old Believers during the persecution of Nikon.

'Blessed are those who die for the Lord,' wrote Avvakum, 'and even if they do begin to scourge you or to burn you, all the more glory to God for that! For this we came out of our mother's womb You will not be very long burning in the fire—just the twinkling of an eye— and the soul is free. Are you afraid of the furnace? Play the man, spit at it, do not be afraid! Fear comes before the fire; but once you are in it, you forget it all. You catch fire, and here they are—Christ and the hosts of angels with Him; they take your soul out of the body and carry it to Christ, and He, the good Lord, blesses it and fortifies it with divine force. It is no longer heavy, but becomes as though winged; it flies off in company with the angels, it hovers like a bird, glad to be free from its prison.

'The Nikonites have massacred myriads of people, believing it to be agreeable to God. And I rejoice that they should have done so; they

[1] A History of Russia (London, Dent, 1913), vol. iii, p. 298.

have hallowed the Russian land with Martyrs' blood. . . . Run and jump into the flames. Here is my body, Devil. Take and eat it. My soul you cannot take.'

The resistance of the faithful no brutality could overcome: banished to Siberia, their tongues cut out, executed, mutilated, burnt alive, they welcomed death in the cause of their Lord, and even an amputated hand miraculously brought together its two fingers to make the Sign of the Cross in the fashion hallowed by the Fathers of the Church. The East Roman had preferred the triumph of the Turk to the victory of the papal tiara: similarly Avvakum hopes for a second Titus to destroy the New Jerusalem (Nikon's monastery) and the heretical city Moscow. 'I trust in God that he will raise the Turk to avenge the blood of our Martyrs.' To the Tsar Theodore he writes: 'If you let me have my way, I would lay them all low in a single day as did Elijah. . . . This would not have sullied my hands, but sanctified them. . . . We would begin by quartering the dog Nikon and afterwards all the Nikonites.' With God's prophet Avvakum could claim: 'I have been very jealous for the Lord God of Hosts.' Devotion to the Lord of life and for the Nikonite blasting scorn: 'All we need to do is to spit on their doings and their ritual and on their new-fangled books, then all will be well.' And thus in the Cathedral Church, in the presence of the Tsar, Login, Archpriest of Murom, 'was consumed with the zeal of God's Fire and he defied Nikon and spat across the threshold to the altar straight into his eyes, and loosening his girdle he tore off his shirt and flung it at the altar into Nikon's face'.

But despite the passionate loyalty of the Old Believers to the traditional faith Anti-Christ triumphed. Though Nikon was forced to withdraw from Moscow to a monastery, the Nikonites carried the day. At the Council of 1666 Nikon was condemned and imprisoned, but Avvakum and the Old Believers were excommunicated, and at the same Council the Russian bishops under the influence of the Patriarchs of Alexandria and Antioch were constrained to disavow the Council of 1551 which had proclaimed Russian orthodoxy as the pattern for the Church of the East: 'the Metropolitan Macarius and those with him had acted and made their decisions in ignorance and without reason.' The claim of Russia to be the Third Rome was surrendered, and before many years had passed Peter the Great would inaugurate the new age of Westernization.

In course of time the Scandinavian conquerors learned to speak the tongue of their Slav subjects, and perhaps the greatest and the most permanent gift of East Rome to Russia was the Byzantine liturgy in the Slav language. In the west of Europe during the early centuries of our era there had been only one universal language, Latin, and that language the Church naturally adopted in its services; gradually usage hardened into a theory of the illegitimacy of native languages for the celebration of the liturgy. The Eastern Church was more liberal: it had already recognized Armenian and Syriac; its missionaries were thus prepared to employ a Slav language in their work of evangelization. The Slav liturgy was one of the most important factors in promoting unity within the national Church of Russia; it was on the ground of liturgical errors that the Church waged its conflict with the Latins; it is the liturgy which to-day is the common possession of the national Slav Churches. It is true that since there was no need for the Russian clergy to know either Latin or Greek, they were cut off from the thought of western Europe: the theological discussions of Scholasticism have no parallel in Russia; the Latin language in which those discussions were conducted acted as an iron curtain. But there is much to be set on the other side. The Russian Christian seeks the satisfaction of his religious need not through reason—that is transcended—but in the spiritual awareness of the Divine Presence: 'We do not consider God, we experience Him.' Religion is Christocentric and at its heart are the Passion and the Resurrection of the Lord of Life as they are re-lived in the drama of the liturgy. It is through Byzantine forms of worship that 'the splendour of eternity breaks into the reality of to-day and the worshipper is borne aloft into the sphere of the invisible and the eternal'. It was through attending East Roman rites that the envoys sent to Constantinople by Vladimir were persuaded that the true glory rested there and not with Bulgars or Germans: 'The Greeks led us', they said, 'to the edifices where they worship their God and we knew not whether we were in heaven or on earth. For on earth there is no such splendour or such beauty, and we are at a loss how to describe it. We only know that God dwells there among men and their service is fairer than the ceremonies of other nations. For we cannot forget that beauty.' And through the centuries the Russian Church has remembered that beauty.

BARON MEYENDORFF AND NORMAN H. BAYNES

BIBLIOGRAPHICAL APPENDIX

A SELECT bibliography like the present can satisfy no one, not even the compiler, but nevertheless it is hoped that this Appendix may prove to be of some service. Only works in West European languages are included, and those subjects which are likely to be of special interest to students have been treated most fully.

N. H. B.

INTRODUCTION

ARNOLD J. TOYNBEE, *A Study of History*, especially vol. iv, pp. 320–408. London, Oxford University Press, 1939.

A. HEISENBERG, 'Die Grundlagen der byzantinischen Kultur', *Neue Jahrbücher für das klassische Altertum*, xxiii (1909), pp. 196–208.

N. H. BAYNES, *The Byzantine Empire* (in the *Home University Library*), revised 1943. London, Oxford University Press.

Id., *The Hellenistic Civilization and East Rome* (a lecture). Ibid., 1946.

Id., *The Thought World of East Rome* (a lecture). Ibid., 1947.

I

THE HISTORY OF THE BYZANTINE EMPIRE

EDWARD GIBBON, *The Decline and Fall of the Roman Empire*, ed. J. B. Bury (new edition). London, Methuen, 1900, 7 vols. (Gibbon's masterpiece is still essential for the history of the Roman Empire until the seventh century.)

GEORGE FINLAY, *A History of Greece*, 7 vols. Oxford, Clarendon Press, 1877. (Vols. i–iii cover the Byzantine Empire.) There is a reprint in Everyman's Library: vol. i, *Greece under the Romans*; vol. ii, *History of the Byzantine Empire* (down to 1057).

L. BRÉHIER, *Le Monde byzantin. Vie et Mort de Byzance* (in the series *L'Évolution de l'Humanité*, ed. Henri Berr). Paris, Michel, 1947.

J. B. BURY, 'Roman Empire, Later', in the *Encyclopaedia Britannica*, 11th ed., vol. xxiii, pp. 510–25. Cambridge University Press, 1911.

The Cambridge Medieval History, vols. i–ii and specially vol. iv, *The Eastern Roman Empire (717–1453)*. Cambridge University Press, 1923.

GEORG OSTROGORSKY, *Geschichte des byzantinischen Staates*. Munich, Beck, 1940.

A. A. VASILIEV, *Histoire de l'Empire byzantin*, 2 vols. Paris, Picard, 1932. It is understood that the English translation published at Madison (= *University of Wisconsin Studies in the Social Sciences and History*, nos. 13 & 14, 1928–9) is now being revised and will be reissued.

C. W. C. OMAN, *The Byzantine Empire* (in the series *The Story of the Nations*). London, Fisher Unwin, 1892.

CH. DIEHL, *Histoire de l'Empire byzantin*. Paris, Picard, 1919.

H. GELZER, 'Abriss der byzantinischen Kaisergeschichte' in Karl Krumbacher, *Geschichte der byzantinischen Litteratur*, 2nd ed. Munich, Beck, 1897.

CHARLES DIEHL and GEORGES MARÇAIS, *Le Monde oriental de 395 à 1081* (=
Histoire générale, ed. G. Glotz, *Histoire du Moyen Âge*, vol. iii). Paris,
Les Presses universitaires de France, 1936; and in the same series vol. ix,
1st part, *L'Europe orientale de 1081 à 1453*, by Charles Diehl, R.
Guilland, L. Oeconomos, and R. Grousset, ibid., 1945.

ERNST STEIN, *Geschichte des spätrömischen Reiches*, vol. i. Vienna, Seidel,
1928. (A valuable work of reference.)

ANDRÉ PIGANIOL, *L'Empire chrétien 325–395* (in G. Glotz, *Histoire générale*,
Histoire romaine, tome iv, 2ème partie). Paris, Presses universitaires de
France, 1947.

H. ST. L. B. MOSS, *The Birth of the Middle Ages, 395–814*. Oxford, Clarendon Press, 1935.

O. SEECK, *Geschichte des Untergangs der antiken Welt*. 6 vols. with separate
Anhang of notes to each (vol. i, 4th ed., 1921–2; vols. ii–v, 2nd ed.,
1921–3; vol. vi, 1920–1). Stuttgart, Metzler.

CHRISTOPHER DAWSON, *The Making of Europe*. London, Sheed and Ward,
1932.

FREDERIC HARRISON's Rede Lecture (1900) should be read and his paper on
the Eastern Roman Empire: both are to be found in his *Among My Books*.
London, Macmillan, 1912.

J. B. BURY, *Selected Essays*, ed. Harold Temperley. Cambridge University
Press, 1930.

Id., *History of the Later Roman Empire*, 2 vols. London, Macmillan, 1923.

J. W. HOLMES, *The Age of Justinian and Theodora*. London, Bell, 2 vols.,
1905, 1907.

CHARLES DIEHL, *Justinien et la Civilisation byzantine au VIe siècle*. Paris,
Leroux, 1901.

J. B. BURY, *A History of the Eastern Roman Empire* (A.D. 802–867). London,
Macmillan, 1912.

STEVEN RUNCIMAN, *The Emperor Romanus Lecapenus and his Reign. A Study
of Tenth-Century Byzantium*. Cambridge University Press, 1929.

GUSTAVE SCHLUMBERGER, *Un Empereur byzantin au dixième siècle*. Paris,
Firmin-Didot, 1890. (The later reprint lacks the valuable illustrations.)

Id., *L'Épopée byzantine à la fin du dixième siècle*, 3 vols. Paris, Hachette,
1896, 1900, 1905. (A magnificent work.)

CH. DIEHL, *Dans l'Orient byzantin*. Paris, Boccard, 1917.

Id., *Choses et Gens de Byzance*. Paris, Boccard, 1926.

Id., *Byzance. Grandeur et Décadence*. Paris, Flammarion, 1919.

Id., *Études byzantines*. Paris, Picard, 1905.

Id., *Théodora Impératrice de Byzance*, reprint, no date. Paris, Boccard.

Id., *Figures byzantines*, 2 vols. Paris, Colin, 1906, 1908.

Id., *L'Égypte chrétienne et byzantine* (= Gabriel Hanotaux, *Histoire de la
Nation égyptienne*, vol. iii, pp. 401–557). Paris, Plon, no date. With this
cf. H. I. Bell, *Journal of Egyptian Archaeology*, iv (1917), pp. 86–106.

Id., *L'Afrique byzantine. Histoire de la Domination byzantine en Afrique
(533–709)*. Paris, Leroux, 1896.

Id., *Les Grands Problèmes de l'histoire byzantine*. Paris, Colin, 1943.

STEVEN RUNCIMAN, *Byzantine Civilisation*. London, Arnold, 1933.

N. Turchi, *La Civiltà bizantina*. Torino, Bocca, 1915.

Heinrich Gelzer, *Byzantinische Kulturgeschichte*. Tübingen, Mohr, 1909.

N. Iorga, *Histoire de la vie byzantine*, 3 vols. Bucharest, 1934.

G. Manojlović, 'Le Peuple de Constantinople' (written in 1904), *Byzantion*, xi (1936), pp. 617–716.

A. H. M. Jones, *The Greek City from Alexander to Justinian*. Oxford, Clarendon Press, 1937.

D. C. Hesseling, *Essai sur la Civilisation byzantine*. Paris, Picard, 1907.

A. Rambaud, *Études sur l'histoire byzantine*. Paris, Colin, 1912.

K. Dieterich, *Byzantinische Charakterköpfe*. Leipzig, Teubner, 1909.

J. Laurent, *Byzance et les Turcs Seldjoucides dans l'Asie occidentale jusqu'en 1081* (= *Annales de l'Est*, 28ᵉ année, fasc. 2). Paris, Berger-Levrault, 1919.

Charles Diehl, *La Société byzantine à l'époque des Comnènes*. Paris, Gamber, 1929.

Carl Neumann, *Die Weltstellung des byzantinischen Reiches vor den Kreuzzügen*. Leipzig, Duncker & Humblot, 1894. Also in a French translation: *La Situation mondiale de l'Empire byzantin avant les Croisades*. Paris, Leroux, 1905. (Extrait de la *Revue de l'Orient latin*, tome x.)

Ernest Barker, *The Crusades*. London, Oxford University Press, 1923.

R. A. Newhall, *The Crusades*. London, Bell, 1930.

R. Grousset, *Histoire des Croisades et du Royaume franc de Jérusalem*, 3 vols. Paris, Plon, 1934, 1935, 1936.

Id., *L'Epopée des Croisades*. Paris, Plon, 1939.

D. C. Munro, *The Kingdom of the Crusaders*. New York, Appleton–Century Company, 1935.

William Miller, *The Latins in the Levant. A History of Frankish Greece*. London, Murray, 1908.

Id., *Essays on the Latin Orient*. Cambridge University Press, 1921.

W. B. Stevenson, *The Crusaders in the East*. Cambridge University Press, 1907.

K. Neumann, 'Die byzantinische Marine', *Historische Zeitschrift*, N.F., xlv (1898), pp. 1–23.

The literature on the history of Venice is very extensive; here it may suffice to cite F. C. Hodgson, *The Early History of Venice* (to A.D. 1204). London, Allen, 1901; and Ch. Diehl, *Une république patricienne. Venise*. Paris, Flammarion, 1913.

Edwin Pears, *The Fall of Constantinople; being the story of the Fourth Crusade*. London, Longmans, 1885.

Walter Norden, *Der Vierte Kreuzzug im Rahmen der Beziehungen des Abendlandes zu Byzanz*. Berlin, Behr, 1898.

Ernst Gerland, *Geschichte des lateinischen Kaiserreichs von Konstantinopel*, Part I (1204–16). (No more published.) Homburg v. d. Höhe, 1905.

Conrad Chapman, *Michel Paléologue Restaurateur de l'Empire byzantin (1261–1282)*. Paris, Figuière, 1926.

Alice Gardner, *The Lascarids of Nicaea. The Story of an Empire in Exile*. London, Methuen, 1912.

BIBLIOGRAPHICAL APPENDIX 395

William Miller, *Trebizond: the last Greek Empire*. London, Society for Promoting Christian Knowledge, 1926.

Sir Rennell Rodd, *The Princes of Achaia and the Chronicles of Morea*, 2 vols. London, Arnold, 1907.

D. A. Zakythinos, *Le Despotat grec de Morée*. Vol. i: *Histoire politique*. Paris, Les Belles Lettres, 1932. (No more published.)

E. Pears, *The Destruction of the Greek Empire and the Story of the Capture of Constantinople by the Turks*. London, Longmans, 1903.

G. Schlumberger, *Le Siège, la Prise et le Sac de Constantinople par les Turcs en 1453*. 4th ed., Paris, Plon-Nourrit, 1915.

II and III

THE ECONOMIC LIFE OF THE BYZANTINE EMPIRE. PUBLIC FINANCES

For studies in the Slav languages see the bibliography of G. Ostrogorsky, *The Cambridge Economic History of Europe*, vol. i. Cambridge University Press, 1941, ch. 5 ('Agrarian Conditions in the Byzantine Empire in the Middle Ages', pp. 194–223, 579–83); and cf. his *Geschichte des byzantinischen Staates*. Munich, Beck, 1940.

For the trade of the Mediterranean in the Middle Ages see:

W. Heyd, *Histoire du Commerce du Levant au Moyen Âge*. French translation: Réimpression, 2 vols. Leipzig, Harrassowitz, 1923.

Adolf Schaube, *Handelsgeschichte der Romanischen Völker des Mittelmeergebiets bis zum Ende der Kreuzzüge*. Munich and Berlin, Oldenbourg, 1906.

Rudolf Kötzschke, *Allgemeine Wirtschaftsgeschichte des Mittelalters*. Jena, Fischer, 1924.

For the economic history of the Empire see:

L. Brentano, 'Die byzantinische Volkswirtschaft', *Schmollers Jahrbuch*, Jahrgang 41, Heft 2 (1917), pp. 7–52.

G. I. Brătianu, *Études byzantines d'histoire économique et sociale*. Paris, Geuthner, 1938.

G. Ostrogorsky, 'Die wirtschaftlichen und sozialen Entwicklungsgrundlagen des byzantinischen Reiches', *Vierteljahrschrift für Sozial- und Wirtschaftsgeschichte*, xxii (1929), pp. 129–43. (With bibliography.)

For the silk industry cf. R. Hennig, *Byzantinische Zeitschrift*, xxxiii (1933), pp. 295–312; R. S. Lopez, *Speculum*, xx (1945), pp. 1–42. (With valuable bibliographical material.)

L. M. Hartmann, *Ein Kapitel vom spätantiken und frühmittelalterlichen Staate*. Stuttgart, Kohlhammer, 1913.

Erik Gren, *Kleinasien und der Ostbalkan in der wirtschaftlichen Entwicklung der römischen Kaiserzeit* (= *Uppsala Universitets Årsskrift*, 1941, No. 9). Uppsala, Lindequist, 1941. (Especially for Constantinople as a centre both of production and consumption, pp. 156–64.)

K. DIETERICH, 'Zur Kulturgeographie und Kulturgeschichte des byzantinischen Balkanhandels', *Byzantinische Zeitschrift*, xxxi (1931), pp. 37–
57, 334–50.

E. STEIN, 'Untersuchungen zur spätbyzantinischen Verfassungs- und
Wirtschaftsgeschichte', *Mitteilungen zur osmanischen Geschichte*, ii
(1923–5), pp. 1–62.

A. ANDRÉADÈS, 'L'Empire byzantin et le Commerce international',
*Annali della R. Scuola Normale Superiore di Pisa. Lettere, Storia e
Filosofia*, serie 2, vol. iv (1935), pp. 139–48.

G. MICKWITZ, 'Un problème d'influence: Byzance et l'économie de
l'Occident mediéval', *Annales d'histoire économique et sociale*, viii (1936),
pp. 21–8. (On *emprunts maritimes* of the West from the Byzantine
Empire.)

For the Byzantine taxation system:

G. OSTROGORSKY, 'Das Steuersystem im byzantinischen Altertum und
Mittelalter', *Byzantion*, vi (1931), pp. 229–40.

JOHN DANSTRUP, 'Indirect Taxation at Byzantium', *Classica et Mediaevalia*, viii (1946), pp. 139–67.

L. M. HARTMANN, *Untersuchungen zur Geschichte der byzantinischen
Verwaltung in Italien (540–750)*. Leipzig, Hirzel, 1889. (Finanzverwaltung, pp. 74–105, 165–75.)

F. DÖLGER, 'Das Aerikon', *Byzantinische Zeitschrift*, xxx (1929–30), pp.
450–7 (for bibliography of studies upon this tax).

For administration and taxation in Egypt see:

S. LE ROY WALLACE, *Taxation in Egypt from Augustus to Diocletian* (=
Princeton University Studies in Papyrology, no. 2, ed. A. C. Johnson).
Princeton University Press, 1938.

GERMAINE ROUILLARD, *L'administration civile de l'Égypte byzantine*, 2nd
ed. Paris, Geuthner, 1928. Cf. *Gnomon*, vi (1930), pp. 401–20 (a
review by Ernst Stein).

H. I. BELL, 'The Byzantine Servile State in Egypt', *Journal of Egyptian
Archaeology*, iv (1917), pp. 86–106.

L. WENGER, *Volk und Staat in Ägypten am Ausgang der Römerherrschaft*.
Munich, Bayerische Akademie der Wissenschaften, 1922.

E. R. HARDY, Jun., *The Large Estates of Byzantine Egypt* (= *Studies in
History, Economics, and Public Law*. Edited by the Faculty of Political
Science of Columbia University, no. 354). Columbia University Press,
1931.

On Byzantine Finances and a money economy see:

HANS GEISS, *Geld- und naturalwirtschaftliche Erscheinungsformen im staat-
lichen Aufbau Italiens während der Gotenzeit* (= *Vierteljahrschrift für
Sozial- und Wirtschaftsgeschichte*, Beiheft 27). Stuttgart, Kohlhammer,
1931.

A. ANDRÉADÈS, 'Les Finances byzantines', *Revue des sciences politiques*, 3me
série, 26e année, 1911, pp. 268–86, 620–30.

Id., 'De la monnaie et de la puissance d'achat des métaux précieux dans l'Empire byzantin', *Byzantion*, i (1924), pp. 75–115.

On the Byzantine budget: E. STEIN, *Studien zur Geschichte des byzantinischen Reiches*, Stuttgart, Metzler, 1919, pp. 141–60, and *Byzantinische Zeitschrift*, xxiv (1924), pp. 377–87.

G. OSTROGORSKY, 'Löhne und Preise in Byzanz', *Byzantinische Zeitschrift*, xxxii (1932), pp. 293–333.

F. DÖLGER, *Beiträge zur Geschichte der byzantinischen Finanzverwaltung besonders des 10. und 11. Jahrhunderts* (= *Byzantinisches Archiv*, ed. August Heisenberg, Heft 9). Leipzig, Teubner, 1927; and see the reviews of recent work which Dölger published in *Byzantinische Zeitschrift*, xxxvi (1936), pp. 123–61.

Id., 'Zum Gebührenwesen der Byzantiner', *Études dédiées à la Mémoire d'André Andréadès*, Athens, 1939, pp. 35–59.

E. STEIN, 'Vom Altertum im Mittelalter. Zur Geschichte der byzantinischen Finanzverwaltung', *Vierteljahrschrift für Sozial- und Wirtschaftsgeschichte*, xxi (1928), pp. 158–70.

On the *Book of the Prefect* see:

JULES NICOLE, *Le Livre du Préfet ou l'Édit de l'Empereur Léon le Sage sur les Corporations de Constantinople*. Geneva, H. Georg, 1893 (with a Latin translation); with the same title Nicole published a French translation in 1894.

There is an English translation by A. E. R. BOAK in the *Journal of Economic and Business History*, i (1929), pp. 597–619, and another by E. H. FRESHFIELD in his book *Roman Law in the Later Roman Empire. Byzantine Guilds, professional and commercial*. Cambridge, 1938.

A. STÖCKLE, *Spätrömische und byzantinische Zünfte* (= *Klio*, Beiheft 9). Leipzig, 1911.

P. S. LEICHT, *Corporazioni romane e arti medievali*, ch. 3. Torino, Einaudi, 1937.

G. MICKWITZ, *Die Kartellfunktionen der Zünfte* (= Societas Scientiarum Fennica, *Commentationes Humanarum Litterarum* 8, Fasc. 3), chs. 7 and 8. Helsingfors, 1936.

For a useful bibliography cf. G. OSTROGORSKY, *Geschichte des byzantinischen Staates*, Munich, 1940, pp. 177–8 and cf. *Byzantinische Zeitschrift*, xxxiii (1933), pp. 376–80.

For the problem of landownership, the peasantry, and the *potentiores* see:

F. MARTROYE, 'Les patronages d'agriculteurs et de vici au IVe et au Ve siècles', *Revue historique de droit français et étranger*, 4e série, vii (1928), pp. 202–48.

W. ASHBURNER, 'The Farmer's Law', *Journal of Hellenic Studies*, xxx (1910), pp. 85–95 (with an English translation of the law). Cf. G. Vernadsky, *Byzantion*, ii (1926), pp. 169–80.

N. H. BAYNES, *The Byzantine Empire*, ch. vi, pp. 99–113. London, Oxford University Press, 1925, revised 1943.

G. STADTMÜLLER, 'Oströmische Bauern- und Wehrpolitik', *Neue Jahrbücher für deutsche Wissenschaft*, xiii (1937), pp. 421–38.

G. STADTMÜLLER, 'Landesverteidigung und Siedlungspolitik im oströmi-schen Reich', *Bull. de l'Inst. archéol. bulgare*, ix (1935), pp. 392–9.

F. DÖLGER, 'Die Frage des Grundeigentums in Byzanz', *Bulletin of the International Committee of Historical Sciences*, v (1933), pp. 5–15.

For the growth of a 'féodalité administrative' in Italy within the exarchate of the sixth century see C. DIEHL, *Études sur l'administration byzantine dans l'Exarchat de Ravenne 568–751* (= *Bibliothèque des Écoles fran-çaises d'Athènes et de Rome*, Fasc. 53), pp. 292 ff. Paris, Thorin, 1888.

A. VASILIEV, 'On the Question of Byzantine Feudalism', *Byzantion*, viii (1933), pp. 584–604.

G. TESTAUD, *Des Rapports des Puissants et des petits Propriétaires ruraux dans l'Empire byzantin au Xe siècle* (Thèse, Faculté de Droit de l'Uni-versité de Bordeaux). Bordeaux, 1898.

For the political aim of the Emperors in their legislation against the 'powerful' see ERIK BACH, 'Les Lois agraires byzantines du Xe siècle', *Classica et Mediaevalia* (Copenhagen), v (1942), pp. 70–91.

A. ANDRÉADÈS, 'Floraison et décadence de la petite propriété dans l'em-pire byzantin', *Mélanges Ernest Mahaim*, Paris, Recueil Sirey, 1935, pp. 261–6.

H. MONNIER, 'Études de Droit byzantin. I. De l'Ἐπιβολή', *Nouvelle revue historique de droit français et étranger*, xvi (1892), pp. 125–64, 330–52, 497–542, 637–72; xviii (1894), pp. 433–86; xix (1895), pp. 59–103. II. *Méditation sur la constitution* 'ΕΚΑΤΕΡΩΙ *et le Jus Poenitendi*. Paris, Larose, 1900. (On the 'Puissants'.)

On the continuance of the epibolē at least until the twelfth century see FRANZ DÖLGER in *Studi in memoria di Aldo Albertoni*, vol. ii, pp. 1–11. Padova, Cedam, 1937.

M. G. PLATON, *Observations sur le droit de ΠΡΟΤΙΜΗΣΙΣ en Droit byzantin*. Paris, Fontemoing, 1906.

G. OSTROGORSKY, 'Die ländliche Steuergemeinde des byzantinischen Reiches im X. Jahrhundert', *Vierteljahrschrift für Sozial- und Wirt-schaftsgeschichte*, xx (1927), pp. 1–108.

E. STEIN, 'Paysannerie et grands domaines dans l'Empire byzantin', *Recueil de la Société Jean Bodin*, Brussels, 1937, pp. 123–33.

R. GAIGNEROT, *Des Bénéfices militaires dans l'Empire romain et spécialement en Orient et au Xme siècle*. Bordeaux, Cadoret, 1898.

A. FERRADOU, *Les Biens des Monastères à Byzance*. Bordeaux, Cadoret, 1896.

N. A. CONSTANTINESCU, 'Réforme sociale ou Réforme fiscale? Une hypothèse pour expliquer la disparition du servage de la glèbe dans l'empire byzantin', Académie Roumaine, Bucharest, *Bulletin de la Section historique*, xi (1924), pp. 94–109.

Id., 'La Communauté de village byzantine et ses Rapports avec le petit "Traité fiscal byzantin"', ibid. xiii (1927), pp. 160–74.

For the position of the Jews in the Empire see:

JOSHUA STARR, *The Jews in the Byzantine Empire 641–1204* (= *Texte und Forschungen zur byzantinisch-neugriechischen Philologie*, ed. N. A. Bees, No. 30). Athens, 1939.

A. Andréadès, 'The Jews in the Byzantine Empire', *Economic History*, iii (1934), pp. 1–23. (Supplement to the *Economic Journal*.)

P. Browe, 'Die Judengesetzgebung Justinians', *Analecta Gregoriana* (Rome), viii (1935), pp. 109–46.

F. Dölger, 'Die Frage der Judensteuer in Byzanz', *Vierteljahrschrift für Sozial- und Wirtschaftsgeschichte*, xxvi (1933), pp. 1–24.

IV

THE BYZANTINE CHURCH

L. Duchesne, *Histoire ancienne de l'Église*. Paris, Fontemoing, 1906–8, 3 vols. Several editions. The English translation is from the 4th ed.: *Early History of the Christian Church*, vol. i (1909), vol. ii (1912), vol. iii (1924). London, Murray.

Id., *L'Église au VIème siècle*. Paris, Fontemoing, 1925.

Id., *Églises séparées*. 2me éd., Paris, Fontemoing, 1905.

H. von Schubert, *Geschichte der christlichen Kirche im Frühmittelalter* (published in two parts). Tübingen, Mohr, 1917, 1921.

F. Heiler, *Urkirche und Ostkirche*. Munich, Reinhardt, 1937. (With full bibliographies.)

J. Pargoire, *L'Église byzantine de 527 à 847*. Paris, Lecoffre, 1905.

L. Bréhier, *L'Église et l'Orient au Moyen Âge. Les Croisades*. 2me éd., Paris, Lecoffre, 1907.

J. M. Hussey, *Church and Learning in the Byzantine Empire 867–1185*. London, Oxford University Press, 1937.

Heinrich Gelzer, 'Das Verhältnis von Staat und Kirche in Byzanz', *Ausgewählte kleine Schriften*. Leipzig, Teubner, 1907, pp. 57–141.

In the *Histoire de l'Église* edited by A. Fliche and V. Martin, Paris, Bloud & Gay: vol. iii (1936) by J. R. Palanque, G. Bardy, and P. de Labriolle covers the period *De la Paix constantinienne à la Mort de Théodose*; vol. iv (1937) by P. de Labriolle, G. Bardy, G. de Plinval, and L. Bréhier the period *De la Mort de Théodose à l'élection de Grégoire le Grand*; vol. v by L. Bréhier and R. Aigrain (1938) is entitled *Grégoire le Grand, les états barbares et la conquête arabe 590–737*; vol. vi by E. Amann (1937) covers *L'époque carolingienne*; vol. vii by E. Amann and A. Dumas (1942) entitled *L'Église au pouvoir des laïques (888–1057)* treats of the eleventh-century schism between the East and the West.

A. Fortescue, *The Orthodox Eastern Church*, 3rd ed. London, Catholic Truth Society, 1911.

W. F. Adeney, *The Greek and Eastern Churches*. Edinburgh, Clark, 1908.

H. F. Tozer, *The Church and the Eastern Empire*. London, Longmans, 1888.

Sir W. M. Ramsay, *Luke the Physician*, ch. iv. London, Hodder & Stoughton, 1908.

Mary Hamilton, *Incubation or the Cure of Disease in Pagan Temples and Christian Churches*. St. Andrews, Henderson, 1906.

Stefan Zankov, *The Eastern Orthodox Church*. London, Student Christian Movement Press, 2nd ed., 1930.

SERGIUS BULGAKOV, *The Orthodox Church*. London, The Centenary Press, 1935.

A. E. BURN, *The Council of Nicaea*. London, Society for Promoting Christian Knowledge, 1925.

A. D'ALÈS, *Le Dogme de Nicée*. Paris, Beauchesne, 1926.

Id., *Le Dogme d'Éphèse*. Ibid., 1931.

R. V. SELLERS, *Two Ancient Christologies*. London, Society for Promoting Christian Knowledge, 1940. (On the schools of Alexandria and Antioch.)

W. A. WIGRAM, *The Separation of the Monophysites*. London, Faith Press, 1923.

G. OSTROGORSKY, 'Les Débuts de la Querelle des Images' in *Mélanges Charles Diehl*, i, pp. 235–55. Paris, Leroux, 1930.

E. J. MARTIN, *A History of the Iconoclastic Controversy*. London, Society for Promoting Christian Knowledge (no date).

L. BRÉHIER, *La Querelle des Images*. Paris, Bloud, 1904.

KARL SCHWARZLOSE, *Der Bilderstreit*. Gotha, Perthes, 1890.

ERICH CASPAR, *Geschichte des Papsttums*, vol. ii, *Das Papsttum unter byzantinischer Herrschaft*. Tübingen, Mohr, 1933. (Fifth to eighth century.)

M. JUGIE, *Le Schisme byzantin*. Paris, Lethillieux, 1941.

F. DVORNIK, 'Le second Schisme de Photios. Une mystification historique', *Byzantion*, viii (1933), pp. 425–74.

W. NORDEN, *Das Papsttum und Byzanz* (down to 1453). Berlin, Behr, 1903.

F. X. SEPPELT, *Das Papsttum und Byzanz* (= *Kirchengeschichtliche Abhandlungen*, ed. M. Sdralek, vol. ii). Breslau, Aderholz, 1904.

L. BRÉHIER, *Le Schisme oriental du XIᵉ siècle*. Paris, Leroux, 1899.

JEAN DANIÉLOU, *Platonisme et Théologie mystique. Essai sur la doctrine spirituelle de Saint Grégoire de Nysse*. Paris, Aubier, 1944.

IRÉNÉE HAUSHERR, *Vie de Syméon le nouveau Théologien* (= *Orientalia Christiana* xii, no. 45, 1928). Rome, Pont. Institutum Orientalium Studiorum.

Symeon der neue Theologe, Licht vom Licht, Hellerau, Hegner, 1930. (Translation of Symeon's Hymns by Kilian Kirchhoff.)

N. ARSENIEV, *Mysticism and the Eastern Church*. London, Student Christian Movement, 1926.

V. LOSSKY, *Essai sur la Théologie mystique de l'Église d'Orient*. Paris, Aubier, 1944.

Orthodox Spirituality by A Monk of the Eastern Church. London, Society for Promoting Christian Knowledge, 1945.

M. JUGIE, 'Les origines de la méthode d'oraison des Hésychastes', *Échos d'Orient*, xxx (1931), pp. 179–85.

I. HAUSHERR, *La méthode d'oraison hésychaste*. (*Orientalia Christiana* ix, Part 2, 1927 [cf. ibid. xx (1930), pp. 179–182].)

M. JUGIE, 'Palamas', *Dictionnaire de Théologie catholique*, ed. A. Vacant, &c., xi (1931), cols. 1735–76.

Id., 'Palamite (Controverse)', ibid., cols. 1777–1818.

Id., *Theologia dogmatica Christianorum Orientalium*, vol. ii, Paris, 1932, pp. 47–183; and cf. *Échos d'Orient*, xxx (1931), pp. 396–421.

FATHER BASIL (BASIL KRIVOSHEIN), 'The Ascetic and Theological Teachings of Gregory Palamas', *Eastern Churches Quarterly*, iii (1938), pp. 26–33, 71–84, 138–56, 193–214. Cf. J. Gouillard, *Échos d'Orient*, xxxvii (1938), pp. 424–60.

CLEMENT LIALINE, 'The Theological Teaching of Gregory Palamas on Divine Simplicity', *Eastern Churches Quarterly*, vi (1946), pp. 266–87.

A. M. AMMANN, *Die Gottesschau im palamitischen Hesychasmus. Ein Handbuch der spätbyzantinischen Mystik* (= *Das östliche Christentum*, ed. Georg Wunderle, Heft 6–7). Würzburg, Rita Verlag, 1938.

There is a series of translations of the writings of Byzantine mystics recently published in Paris (*Sources Chrétiennes*, Éditions du Cerf): the series includes French versions from the work of Maximus the Confessor, Nicetas Stethatos, and Nicolas Cabasilas.

The Orthodox Liturgy. London, Society for Promoting Christian Knowledge, 1939.

J. M. NEALE, *Hymns of the Eastern Church.* London, Society for Promoting Christian Knowledge, 1918.

E. HERMAN, 'Le Professioni vietate al clero bizantino', *Orientalia Christiana Periodica* (Rome, Pont. Institutum Orientalium Studiorum), x (1944), pp. 23–44.

V

BYZANTINE MONASTICISM

KARL HEUSSI, *Der Ursprung des Mönchtums.* Tübingen, Mohr, 1936.

H. LECLERCQ, 'Cénobitisme', in *Dictionnaire d'Archéologie et de Liturgie*, t. ii, cols. 3047–248.

On the part played by monasticism in the life of the Empire cf. KARL HOLL, *Preussische Jahrbücher*, xciv (1898), pp. 407–24; J. M. HUSSEY, *History*, N.S. xxiv (1939), pp. 56–62.

De Monachico Statu iuxta Disciplinam byzantinam. Vatican Press, 1942 (= *Sacra Congregazione per la Chiesa Orientale, Fonti*, Serie II, Fasc. 10), ed. P. Placidus de Meester. (An encyclopaedic work.)

ATHANASIUS, *Life of Antony*: Translated in *A Select Library of Nicene and Post-Nicene Fathers of the Christian Church*, 2nd series, edd. Henry Wace and P. Schaff, vol. iv, pp. 188–221. Oxford, Parker, 1892.

Pachomius: L. TH. LEFORT, *Les Vies coptes de S. Pachôme.* Université de Louvain, Bibliothèque du Muséon, Louvain, 1943.

J. PARGOIRE, 'Les Débuts du Monachisme à Constantinople', *Revue des Questions historiques*, N.S. xxi (1899), pp. 67–143.

ABBÉ MARIN, *Les Moines de Constantinople (330–898).* Paris, Lecoffre, 1897.

C. BUTLER, *The Lausiac History of Palladius* (= *Texts & Studies*, ed. J. Armitage Robinson, vol. vi, nos. 1 and 2), 2 vols. Cambridge University Press, 1898, 1904.

W. K. L. CLARKE, *The Ascetic Works of Saint Basil.* London, Society for Promoting Christian Knowledge, 1925. (An English translation of the works.)

W. K. L. CLARKE, *St. Basil the Great. A Study in Monasticism.* Cambridge University Press, 1913.

E. F. MORISON, *St. Basil and his Rule.* London, Oxford University Press, 1912.

P. HUMBERTCLAUDE, *La Doctrine ascétique de Saint Basile de Césarée.* Paris, Beauchesne, 1932.

W. H. MACKEAN, *Christian Monasticism in Egypt to the Close of the Fourth Century.* London, Society for Promoting Christian Knowledge, 1920.

P. VAN CAUWENBURGH, *Étude sur les Moines d'Égypte depuis le Concile de Chalcédoine (451) jusqu'à l'Invasion arabe.* Paris, Geuthner, 1914.

DOM J.-M. BESSE, *Les Moines d'Orient antérieurs au Concile de Chalcédoine (451).* Paris, Oudin, 1900.

R. GÉNIER, *Vie de Saint Euthyme le Grand (377–473). Les Moines et l'Église en Palestine au Ve siècle.* Paris, Gabalda, 1909.

H. DELEHAYE, *Les Saints stylites* (= Société des Bollandistes, *Subsidia Hagiographica,* xiv), Brussels, 1923.

H. S. ALIVISATOS, *Die kirchliche Gesetzgebung des Kaisers Justinian I* (= *Neue Studien zur Geschichte der Theologie und der Kirche,* edd. N. Bonwetsch and R. Seeberg, Heft 17), Berlin, Trowitzsch, 1913, pp. 98–112; and for the legislation of Leo the Wise Granić in *Byzantinische Zeitschrift,* xxxi (1931), pp. 61–9.

W. NISSEN, *Die Regelung des Klosterwesens im Rhomäerreiche bis zum Ende des 9. Jahrhunderts.* Hamburg, Gelehrtenschule des Johanneums, 1897.

K. HOLL, *Enthusiasmus und Bussgewalt beim griechischen Mönchtum.* Leipzig, Hinrichs, 1898. (A masterly study.)

J. M. HUSSEY, *Church and Learning in the Byzantine Empire 867–1185,* chs. ix–xi. London, Oxford University Press, 1937.

L. OECONOMOS, *La Vie religieuse dans l'Empire byzantin au Temps des Comnènes et des Anges,* chs. vii–xi. Paris, Leroux, 1918.

ROBERT CURZON, *Visits to Monasteries in the Levant* (many editions). London, Murray. (A classic.)

KIRSOPP LAKE, *The Early Days of Monasticism on Mount Athos.* Oxford, Clarendon Press, 1909.

There are many recent descriptions of monastic life on Mount Athos as, e.g., H. GELZER, *Vom heiligen Berge und aus Makedonien.* Leipzig, Teubner, 1904; F. W. HASLUCK, *Athos and its Monasteries.* London, Kegan Paul, 1924; R. BYRON, *The Station. Athos: Treasures and Men.* London, Duckworth, 1928; F. SPUNDA, *Der heilige Berg Athos, Landschaft und Legende.* Leipzig, Insel-Verlag, 1928 (good photographs); R. M. DAWKINS, *The Monks of Athos.* London, Allen & Unwin, 1936; R. BREWSTER, *The 6000 Beards of Athos.* London, Duckworth, 1939.

For Greek monasticism in Italy: J. GAY, *L'Italie méridionale et l'Empire byzantin (867–1071)* (= *Bibliothèque des Écoles françaises d'Athènes et de Rome,* Fasc. 90). Paris, Fontemoing, 1904; D. L. RASCHELLÀ, *Saggio storico sul Monachismo italo-greco in Calabria.* Messina, 1925.

J. VON ZHISHMAN, *Das Stifterrecht (τὸ κτητορικὸν δίκαιον) in der morgenländischen Kirche.* Vienna, Holder, 1888.

F. HERMAN, 'Ricerche sulle istituzioni monastiche bizantine. Typika ktetorika, caristicari e monasteri "liberi" ', *Orientalia Christiana periodica*, vi (1940), pp. 293–375.

H. Delehaye, *Deux Typica byzantins de l'Époque des Paléologues*. Brussels, Hayez, 1921.

W. Nissen, *Die Diataxis des Michael Attaliates von 1077*. Jena, 1894. A dissertation (philosophische Fakultät) of the University of Jena.

P. S. Hilpisch, *Die Doppelklöster. Entstehung und Organisation* (= *Beiträge zur Geschichte des alten Mönchtums und des Benediktinerordens*, ed. I. Herwegen, Heft 15). Münster, Aschendorff, 1928.

A. Ferradou, *Les Biens des Monastères à Byzance*. Bordeaux, Cadoret, 1896.

For original texts on monastic life see *Bibliotheca Hagiographica Graeca*, 2nd ed. Brussels, Société des Bollandistes, 1909.

For Byzantine Mysticism and Hesychasm see the bibliography of Chapter IV.

VI

BYZANTINE ART

In the series *Monuments de l'Art byzantin*, Paris, Leroux, there have been published:

1. G. Millet, *Le Monastère de Daphni. Histoire, Architecture, Mosaïques*. 1899.
2. G. Millet and others, *Monuments byzantins de Mistra. Matériaux pour l'étude de l'architecture et de la peinture en Grèce aux 14e et 15e siècles*. 1910.
3. J. Ebersolt and A. Thiers, *Les Églises de Constantinople*. 1913.
4. Ch. Diehl and others, *Les Monuments chrétiens de Salonique*. 1918.
5. G. Millet, *Monuments de l'Athos*. I. Les Peintures. 1927.

(These magnificent publications can be seen in the Library of the British Museum.)

General works

For the background:

O. Beyer, *Die Katakombenwelt*. Tübingen, Mohr, 1927.

M. Rostovtzeff, *Dura-Europos and its Art*. Oxford, Clarendon Press, 1938.

J. H. Breasted, *Oriental Forerunners of Byzantine Painting*. University of Chicago Press, 1924. (On Dura.)

Ch. Diehl, *Manuel d'Art byzantin*, 2 vols., 2nd ed. Paris, Picard, 1925, 1926. (The best general treatment of the subject.)

C. R. Morey, *Early Christian Art. An outline of the evolution of style and iconography in sculpture and painting from antiquity to the eighth century*. Princeton University Press, 1942.

M. Laurent, *L'Art chrétien primitif*, vol. ii, chaps. xii–xvi. Paris, Vromant, 1911.

Ch. Diehl, *L'Art chrétien primitif et l'Art byzantin*. Paris and Brussels, Van Oest, 1928.

O. M. DALTON, *Byzantine Art and Archaeology*. Oxford, Clarendon Press, 1911.

Id., *East Christian Art*. Oxford, Clarendon Press, 1925.

Id., *Catalogue of Early Christian Antiquities and Objects from the Christian East*. British Museum, 1901.

A Guide to the Early Christian and Byzantine Antiquities in the Department of British and Mediaeval Antiquities, 2nd ed. British Museum, 1921 (15 plates, 105 illustrations).

ERNST KITZINGER, *Early Medieval Art in the British Museum*. British Museum, 1940.

100 Masterpieces. Early Christian and Mediaeval. Victoria and Albert Museum, 1930.

The Victoria and Albert Museum has published *A Picture Book of Byzantine Art*. (6d.)

D. TALBOT RICE, *Byzantine Art*. Oxford, Clarendon Press, 1935.

H. PEIRCE and R. TYLER, *Byzantine Art*. London, Benn, 1926. The French edition is fully illustrated: *L'Art byzantin*. Paris, Librairie de France, 1934 (2 vols., 208 pls.).

L. BRÉHIER, *L'Art chrétien: son développement iconographique*. Paris, Laurens, 1918, chaps. iii–vi.

Id., *L'Art byzantin*. Paris, Laurens, 1924.

L'Art byzantin (in the series *La Grammaire des Styles*). Paris, Ducher, 1930.

A. GRABAR, *L'Art byzantin*. Paris, Les Éditions d'Art et d'Histoire, 1938.

P. VOLBACH, GEORGES SALLES, and GEORGES DUTHUIT, *Art Byzantin, Cent planches*. Paris, Éditions Albert Lévy, no date. (Exposés techniques by G. Duthuit, pp. 9–29.)

GEORGES DUTHUIT, *Byzance et l'Art du XIIe siècle*. Paris, Librairie Stock, 1926.

O. WULFF, *Die altchristliche Kunst* (to the middle of the first millennium). Berlin-Neubabelsberg, Athenaion, 1913. (A *bibliographisch-kritischer Nachtrag* was published in 1939.)

O. WULFF and W. F. VOLBACH, *Die altchristlichen und mittelalterlichen byzantinischen und italienischen Bildwerke*. 3rd vol., *Ergänzungsband* of *Staatliche Museen: Beschreibung der Bildwerke der christlichen Epochen*, 3rd ed. Berlin, De Gruyter, 1923.

H. GLÜCK, *Die christliche Kunst des Ostens*. Berlin, Bruno Cassirer, 1923.

M. HAUTTMANN, *Die Kunst des frühen Mittelalters*. Berlin, Propyläen-Verlag, 1929.

CH. BAYET, *Recherches pour servir à l'histoire de la Peinture et de la Sculpture chrétiennes en Orient avant la Querelle des Iconoclastes* (= *Bibliothèque des Écoles françaises d'Athènes et de Rome*, Fasc. 10). Paris, Thorin. 1879.

Constantinople

A. VAN MILLINGEN, *Byzantine Constantinople. The Walls of the City and adjoining Historical Sites*. London, Murray, 1899.

A. VAN MILLINGEN and others, *Byzantine Churches in Constantinople, their History and Architecture*. London, Macmillan, 1912.

W. Goble and A. van Millingen, *Constantinople*. London, Black, 1906.

E. Diez and H. Glück, *Alt-Konstantinopel*. Munich, Roland-Verlag, 1920.

W. R. Lethaby and H. Swainson, *The Church of Sancta Sophia. A Study of Byzantine Building*. London, Macmillan, 1894.

E. H. Swift, *Hagia Sophia*. New York, Columbia University Press, 1940.

M. C. Charles, 'Hagia Sophia and the Great Imperial Mosques', *The Art Bulletin*, xii (1930), pp. 321–46.

Thomas Whittemore, *The Mosaics of St. Sophia at Istanbul*. Three Preliminary Reports on (i) the Mosaics of the Narthex, (ii) the Mosaics of the Southern Vestibule, (iii) the Imperial Portraits of the South Gallery. Oxford University Press for the Byzantine Institute, 1933, 1936, 1942 (Supplementary sheet of corrections to iii); and id., 'On the Dating of some Mosaics in Hagia Sophia', *Bulletin of the Metropolitan Museum of Art*, New York, n.s., v (1946), pp. 34–45 (illustrated).

G. Brett, 'The Mosaic of the Great Palace in Constantinople', *Journal of the Warburg and Courtauld Institutes*, v (1942), pp. 34–43.

W. S. George and others, *The Church of Saint Eirene at Constantinople*. London, Oxford University Press (for The Byzantine Research and Publication Fund), no date (preface dated Nov. 1912).

M. Aga-Oglu, 'The Fatih Mosque at Constantinople', *The Art Bulletin*, xii (1930), pp. 179–95.

Alexander Rüdell, *Die Kahrie-Dschamisi in Konstantinopel. Ein Kleinod byzantinischer Kunst, mit 10 Farben- und 21 Lichtdruck-Tafeln*. Königliche Technische Hochschule zu Berlin. Berlin, Wasmuth, 1908. (The reproductions are specially of value for Byzantine ornament. There is a copy in the Victoria and Albert Museum Library.) And see Th. Schmit (Russian form), Schmitt (French form): the album published at Munich in 1906, a magnificent series of plates: copy in the Victoria and Albert Museum Library.

Michael Alpatov, 'Die Fresken der Kachrije Djami in Konstantinopel', *Münchner Jahrbuch der bildenden Kunst*, n.f. vi (1929), pp. 345–64. (With photographs.)

For photographs and reconstructions of the Land Walls of Constantinople: Fritz Krischen, *Die Landmauer von Konstantinopel*. Berlin, De Gruyter, 1938 (45 plates, 5 figures).

Mosaics (see under *Constantinople*)

A. Blanchet, *La Mosaïque*. Paris, Payot, 1928.

M. van Berchem and E. Clouzot, *Mosaïques chrétiennes du IVme au Xme siècle*. Geneva, 1924.

Otto Demus, *Die Mosaiken von San Marco in Venedig 1100–1300*. Baden bei Wien, Rohrer, 1935 (50 reproductions).

E. Diez and O. Demus, *Byzantine Mosaics in Greece. Hosios Lucas & Daphni*. Harvard University Press, 1931 (reproductions in colour).

Reale Istituto di Archeologia e Storia dell' Arte: Monumenti: Tavole storiche dei Mosaici di Ravenna. Testo di C. Ricci. Atlas of plates. 1930–7 (in Victoria and Albert Museum Library). Plates I–LXXV.

C. R. Morey, *The Mosaics of Antioch*, New York, Longmans, 1938.

Architecture

J. A. HAMILTON, *Byzantine Architecture and Decoration*. London, Batsford, 1933.

J. W. CROWFOOT, *Early Churches in Palestine* (= Schweich Lectures, 1937). London, Oxford University Press, 1941 (fourth to seventh centuries).

H. W. BEYER, *Der syrische Kirchenbau* (= *Studien zur spätantiken Kunst-geschichte*, no. 1, edd. R. Delbrück and H. Lietzmann). Berlin, De Gruyter, 1925.

SIR W. M. RAMSAY and GERTRUDE L. BELL, *The Thousand and One Churches*. London, Hodder & Stoughton, 1909.

E. HÉBRARD and J. ZEILLER, *Spalato. Le Palais de Dioclétien*. Paris, Massin, 1912. (A fine album of restorations of the palace.)

F. BULIĆ, *Kaiser Diokletians Palast in Split*. Zagreb, 1929.

ADOLF STRUCK, *Mistra. Eine mittelalterliche Ruinenstadt*. Vienna and Leip-zig, Hartleben, 1910 (with reproductions of photographs).

R. WEIR SCHULTZ and S. H. BARNSLEY, *The Monastery of Saint Luke of Stiris, in Phocis*. London, Macmillan, 1901. (Cf. Ch. Diehl, *Études byzan-tines*, Paris, Picard, 1905, pp. 370–91 on the mosaics.)

OSKAR WULFF, *Die Koimesiskirche in Nicäa und ihre Mosaiken nebst den ver-wandten kirchlichen Baudenkmälern. Eine Untersuchung zur Geschichte der byzantinischen Kunst im 1. Jahrtausend*. Strassburg, Heitz, 1903.

THEODOR SCHMIT, *Die Koimesis-Kirche von Nikaia. Das Bauwerk und die Mosaiken*. Berlin, De Gruyter, 1927 (35 pls.).

Ed. R. WEIR SCHULTZ, *The Church of the Nativity at Bethlehem*. London, Batsford (for the Byzantine Research Fund), 1910.

H. T. F. DUCKWORTH, *The Church of the Holy Sepulchre*. London, Hodder & Stoughton, [1922]. (The history of the church.)

BRUNO MOLAJOLI, *La Basilica Eufrasiana di Parenzo*, 2da edizione. Padova, Le Tre Venezie, 1943 (finely illustrated).

Painting

J. EBERSOLT, *La Miniature byzantine*. Paris and Brussels, Vanoest, 1926.

H. GERSTINGER, *Die griechische Buchmalerei*. Vienna, Oesterreichische Staatsdruckerei, 1926. Vol. i, Text; vol. ii, Plates.

KURT WEITZMANN, *Die byzantinische Buchmalerei des IX. und X. Jahr-hunderts*. Berlin, Mann, 1935 (Archäologisches Institut des deutschen Reiches: Abteilung Istanbul).

H. OMONT, *Miniatures des plus anciens Manuscrits grecs de la Bibliothèque Nationale du VIe au XIVe siècles*. Paris, Champion, 1929. 2nd ed., vol. i, Text; vol. ii, Plates.

C. R. MOREY, 'Notes on East Christian Miniatures', *The Art Bulletin*, xi (1929), pp. 5–103 (119 figs.).

H. GERSTINGER, *Die Wiener Genesis*. Vienna, Filser, [1931]. Vol. i, Text; vol. ii, Plates.

Hugo Buchthal, *The Miniatures of the Paris Psalter. A Study in Middle Byzantine Painting* (= *Studies of the Warburg Institute*, ed. F. Saxl, no. 3). London, The Warburg Institute, 1938.

G. de Jerphanion, *Une nouvelle province de l'art byzantin. Les Églises rupestres de Cappadoce*. Paris, Geuthner, 2 vols., each in two parts; 3 Albums, 1925–42.

D. Talbot Rice and others, *The Icons of Cyprus*. London, Allen & Unwin, 1937.

G. Millet and D. Talbot Rice, *Byzantine Painting at Trebizond*. London, Allen & Unwin, 1936.

Portrait Sculpture and Minor Arts

For sculpture see H. P. L'Orange and A. von Gerkan, *Der spätantike Bildschmuck des Konstantinsbogens* (= *Studien zur spätantiken Kunstgeschichte*, No. 10, edd. H. Lietzmann and G. Rodenwaldt), text volume and a magnificent album of plates. Berlin, De Gruyter, 1939; and in the same series of Studies R. Delbrück, *Antike Porphyrwerke*, No. 6, Berlin, 1932; id., *Spätantike Kaiserporträts von Constantinus Magnus bis zum Ende des Westreichs*, No. 8. Berlin, 1933; id., *Die Consulardiptychen und verwandte Denkmäler*, No. 2. Berlin, 1929. (With an album of reproductions.)

J. Ebersolt, *Sanctuaires de Byzance. Recherches sur les anciens Trésors des églises de Constantinople*. Paris, Leroux, 1921.

Id., *Les Arts somptuaires de Byzance. Étude sur l'Art impérial de Constantinople*. Paris, Leroux, 1923.

L. Bréhier, *La Sculpture et les Arts Mineurs byzantins* (in the *Histoire de l'Art byzantin*, ed. Ch. Diehl). Paris, Les Éditions d'Art et d'Histoire, 1936.

Ivories

W. F. Volbach, *Mittelalterliche Elfenbeinarbeiten* (in the series *Orbis Pictus*). Berlin, Wasmuth, no date.

R. Goldschmidt and Kurt Weitzmann, *Die byzantinischen Elfenbeinskulpturen des X.–XIII. Jahrhunderts*. 2 vols. Berlin, B. Cassirer, vol. i, Kästen, 1930; vol. ii, Reliefs, 1934. On the revolutionary dating in this magnificent book cf. A. S. Keck and C. R. Morey, *Art Bulletin*, xvii (1935), pp. 397–406.

O. M. Dalton, *Catalogue of the Ivory Carvings of the Christian Era*. British Museum, 1909.

Decoration

A. Grabar, *La Décoration byzantine*. Paris and Brussels, Van Oest, 1928.

Otto von Falke, *Decorative Silks*, 3rd ed. London, Zwemmer, 1936 (5 coloured plates, 537 reproductions).

G. Millet, *Broderies religieuses de style byzantin* (= *Bibliothèque de l'École des Hautes Études, Sciences religieuses*, vol. lv), Fasc. 1, Album (40 plates). Paris, Leroux, 1939.

For the motifs of Byzantine illuminated ornament: M. A. Frantz, *The Art Bulletin*, xvi (1934), pp. 43–76 (25 plates).

Silverwork

L. Matzulewitsch, *Byzantinische Antike. Studien auf Grund der Silber-gefässe der Ermitage* (= *Archäologische Mitteilungen aus russischen Sammlungen*, vol. ii). Berlin, De Gruyter, 1929 (50 plates, 51 figures).

Pottery

D. Talbot Rice, *Byzantine Glazed Pottery*. Oxford, Clarendon Press, 1930.

C. H. Morgan, *Corinth*, vol. xi, *The Byzantine Pottery*, American School of Classical Studies in Athens, Harvard University Press, 1942 (53 plates).

Jewellery, &c.

W. Dennison and C. R. Morey, *Studies in East Christian and Roman Art*, part 2. New York, Macmillan, 1918.

For the radiation of Byzantine Art (and see bibliography to Chapter XIV):

J. Ebersolt, *Orient et Occident. Recherches sur les influences byzantines et orientales en France avant les croisades*. Paris and Brussels, Van Oest, 1928; vol. ii for the period 'pendant les croisades', ibid., 1929 (full bibliographies).

Ch. Diehl, *L'Art byzantin dans l'Italie méridionale*. Paris, Librairie de l'Art, 1894.

É. Bertaux, *L'Art dans l'Italie Méridionale*, tome i: *De la Fin de l'Empire Romain à la Conquête de Charles d'Anjou*. Paris, Fontemoing, 1904.

W. R. Zaloziecky, *Die Sophienkirche in Konstantinopel und ihre Stellung in der Geschichte der abendländischen Architektur* (= *Studi di antichità cristiana*, No. 12). Città del Vaticano, Pontificio Istituto di archeologia cristiana, 1936.

Id., *Byzanz und Abendland im Spiegel ihrer Kunsterscheinungen*. Salzburg-Leipzig, Pustet, 1936.

P. Schweinfurth, *Die byzantinische Form: ihr Wesen und ihre Wirkung*. Berlin, Florian Kupferberg Verlag, 1943 (126 plates, 180 figures).

S. Der Nersessian, *Armenia and the Byzantine Empire. A Brief Study of Armenian Art and Civilization*. Harvard University Press (London, Oxford University Press), 1945.

In the series *Orient et Byzance*, ed. G. Millet, there have been published (Geuthner, Paris):

(i) A. Grabar, *La Peinture religieuse en Bulgarie*. Text vol. and Album, 1928.

(iv) *L'Art byzantin chez les Slaves. Les Balkans*, 2 vols., 1930.

(v) *L'Art byzantin chez les Slaves. L'ancienne Russie, Les Slaves catholiques*. 2 vols., 1932.

M. J. Pupin, *South Slav Monuments*: (i) *Serbian Orthodox Church*. London, Murray, 1918.

G. Millet, *L'Ancien Art serbe. Les Églises*. Paris, Boccard, 1919.

B. Filow, *Early Bulgarian Art*. Berne, Haupt, 1919.

B. Filow, *Geschichte der altbulgarischen Kunst* (down to the Turkish conquest). Berlin and Leipzig, De Gruyter, 1932. (More fully illustrated.)

Id., *L'Ancien Art Bulgare*. Paris, Alcan, 1922.

Addenda.

C. Stewart, *Byzantine Legacy*. Allen & Unwin, 1947.

The Great Palace of the Byzantine Emperors. London, Oxford University Press, 1947 (58 plates, 6 plans).

VII

BYZANTINE EDUCATION

John W. H. Walden, *The Universities of Ancient Greece*. London, Routledge, 1913.

Louis Bréhier, 'Notes sur l'histoire de l'enseignement supérieur à Constantinople', *Byzantion*, iii (1927), pp. 73–94; 'L'enseignement supérieur à Constantinople dans la dernière moitié du XIe siècle', *Revue internationale de l'Enseignement*, xxxviii (1899), pp. 97–112; 'L'enseignement classique et l'enseignement religieux à Byzance', *Revue d'Histoire et de philosophie religieuse de la Faculté protestante de l'Université de Strasbourg*, 1941, pp. 34–69.

Friedrich Fuchs, *Die höheren Schulen von Konstantinopel im Mittelalter* (= *Byzantinisches Archiv*, ed. August Heisenberg, Heft 8). Leipzig, Teubner, 1926.

Georgina Buckler, *Anna Comnena*, pp. 165–221. London, Oxford University Press, 1929.

J. M. Hussey, *Church and Learning in the Byzantine Empire 867–1185*, pp. 22–116. London, Oxford University Press, 1937.

For special studies of the East Roman schools of learning:

Antioch: Albert Harrent, *Les Écoles d'Antioche. Essai sur le Savoir et l'Enseignement en Orient au IVe siècle*. Paris, Fontemoing, 1898.

Athens: on the University of Athens in the fourth and fifth centuries, Fritz Schemmel, *Neue Jahrbücher für das klassische Altertum*, xxii (1908), pp. 494–513.

Berytus: id., *Philologische Wochenschrift* for 10 March 1923, cols. 236–40; Paul Collinet, *Histoire de l'École de Droit de Beyrouth*. Paris, Recueil Sirey, 1925.

Constantinople: in the fourth century, Fritz Schemmel, *Neue Jahrbücher für das klassische Altertum*, xxii (1908), pp. 147–68; id., *Die Hochschule von Konstantinopel vom V. bis IX. Jahrhundert* (= Wissenschaftliche Beilage zu dem Jahresbericht des Königl. Wilhelms-Gymnasiums in Berlin). Berlin, 1912; from the ninth to the eleventh century: id., *Philologische Wochenschrift* for 29 Dec. 1923, cols. 1178–81; from the twelfth to the fifteenth century: id., ibid., 21 Feb. 1925, cols. 236–9; and for the eleventh century cf. Chr. Zervos, *Un philosophe néoplatonicien du XIe siècle, Michel Psellos: sa vie, son œuvre, ses luttes philosophiques, son influence*. Paris, Leroux, 1920.

For Salonica, O. Tafrali, *Thessalonique au quatorzième Siècle.* Paris, Geuthner, 1913.

For the University of Constantinople as a training ground for service in the administration of the State see A. Andréadès, 'Le Recrutement des fonctionnaires et les Universités dans l'empire byzantin', *Mélanges de droit romain dédiés à Georges Cornil,* Paris, 1926, pp. 17–40.

For the use of the Latin and Greek languages cf. L. Hahn, *Rom und Romanismus im griechisch-römischen Osten.* Leipzig, Dieterich, 1906 (for the early Empire); id., 'Zum Sprachenkampf im römischen Reich. Bis auf die Zeit Justinians. Eine Skizze', *Philologus Supplementband* X, Heft 4, 1907, pp. 675–718; H. Zilliacus, *Zum Kampf der Weltsprachen im oströmischen Reich,* Helsingfors, 1935 [on this cf. F. Dölger, *Byzantinische Zeitschrift,* xxxvi (1936), pp. 108–17]; for Latin words in the popular speech of the Byzantine Empire as evidenced by the biographies of the Saints see Zilliacus, *Byzantinische Zeitschrift,* xxxvii (1937), pp. 302–44, xxxviii (1938), pp. 333–50.

For the strength of Hellenism in Asia Minor see Karl Dieterich, *Hellenism in Asia Minor.* New York, Oxford University Press, 1918.

For references to the original texts of biographies of Saints see *Bibliotheca Hagiographica graeca,* ed. 2, Brussels, 1909. For the Law School of Berytus in the fifth century our best source is the Syriac Life of Severus written by Zacharias the Scholastic; of this there is a French translation by M.-A. Kugener in *Patrologia Orientalis,* vol. ii, fasc. 1, Paris, 1903; an earlier French translation was published by Nau in the *Revue de l'Orient chrétien,* iv (1899), pp. 343–53, 544–71, v (1900), pp. 74–98, 293–302. The only account of the teaching of arithmetic in an elementary school would seem to be given by Mesarites: of this there is a German translation in August Heisenberg, *Grabeskirche und Apostelkirche,* Teil 2, p. 21. Leipzig, Hinrichs, 1908.

VIII

BYZANTINE LITERATURE

There does not appear to be any history of Byzantine literature in English. The essential work is Karl Krumbacher, *Geschichte der byzantinischen Litteratur (527–1453),* 2nd ed., Munich, Beck, 1897 (in the *Handbuch der klassischen Altertumswissenschaft,* ed. Iwan von Müller, vol. ix, first part).

There is a short Italian work: G. Montelatici, *Storia della Letteratura bizantina (324–1453).* Milan, Hoepli, 1916.

For the patristic period of Byzantine literature see Aimé Puech, *Histoire de la Littérature grecque chrétienne,* vol. iii. Paris, Les Belles Lettres, 1930, and Otto Bardenhewer, *Geschichte der altkirchlichen Literatur,* vols. iii–v. Freiburg im Breisgau, Herder, 1912–32.

And for reference to recent work: Berthold Altaner, *Patrologie.* Freiburg im Breisgau, Herder, 1938.

F. A. Wright, *A History of Later Greek Literature* (down to A.D. 565). London, Routledge, 1932.

M. GUIGNET, *Saint Grégoire de Nazianze et la Rhétorique*. Paris, Picard, 1911.

M. PELLEGRINO, *La Poesia di S. Gregorio Nazianzeno*. Milano, Vita e Pensiero, 1932.

F. M. PADELFORD, *Essays on the Study and Use of Poetry by Plutarch and Basil the Great* (= *Yale Studies in English*, no. 15). New York, Holt, 1902. (Contains an English translation of Basil's Address to Young Men on the Right Use of Greek Literature.)

A. VENIERO, *Paolo Silenziario. Studi sulla Letteratura bizantina del VI. secolo*. Catania, Battiato, 1916.

For a translation of Paul the Silentiary's poem cf. W. R. LETHABY and HAROLD SWAINSON, *The Church of Sancta Sophia Constantinople*, London, Macmillan, 1894, pp. 35–65.

J. B. BURY, *A History of the later Roman Empire*, London, Macmillan, 1889, vol. i, pp. 310–30; vol. ii, pp. 175–94; pp. 254–7; pp. 518–34. (These sections are not reproduced in the edition of 1923.)

HEINRICH GELZER, 'Ein griechischer Volkschriftsteller des 7. Jahrhunderts', *Ausgewählte kleine Schriften* (Leipzig, Teubner, 1907), pp. 1–56. (On Leontios who wrote the Life of St. John the Almsgiver, Patriarch of Alexandria.)

MARY H. ALLIES, *St. John Damascene on Holy Images*. London, Baker, 1898 (an English translation), and cf. H. MENGES, *Die Bilderlehre des hl. Johannes von Damaskus*. Münster, Aschendorff, 1938.

On Theodore the Studite monk see:

ALICE GARDNER, *Theodore of Studium*. London, Arnold, 1905.

L'ABBÉ MARIN, *Saint Théodore (759–826)*, in the series 'Les Saints'. 2me éd., Paris, Lecoffre, 1906.

For Anna Comnena see:

ELIZABETH A. S. DAWES, *The Alexiad of the Princess Anna Comnena*. London, Kegan Paul, 1928. (An English translation of the Alexiad.)

BERNARD LEIB, *Anne Comnène, Alexiade* (Greek text and French translation). 3 vols. Paris, Les Belles Lettres, 1937, 1943, 1945.

GEORGINA BUCKLER, *Anna Comnena: A Study*. London, Oxford University Press, 1929.

NAOMI MITCHISON, *Anna Comnena*. London, Howe, 1928.

WILLIAM MILLER, 'A Byzantine Blue Stocking: Anna Comnena' in *Essays on the Latin Orient*, pp. 533–50. Cambridge University Press, 1921.

History

The works of Procopius have appeared in a complete English translation by H. B. Dewing (together with the Greek text) in the Loeb Classical Library, 7 vols. London, Heinemann.

For Psellus's history of his own time: J. B. BURY, *Selected Essays*, ed. H. Temperley, pp. 126–214. Cambridge University Press, 1930. Émile Renaud has given a French translation of the history (with the Greek text) in *Psellos, Chronographie*. 2 vols. Paris, Les Belles Lettres, 1926, 1928.

CARL NEUMANN, *Griechische Geschichtschreiber und Geschichtsquellen im zwölften Jahrhundert*. Leipzig, Duncker & Humblot, 1888.

WILLIAM MILLER, 'The Historians Doukas and Phrantzes', *Journal of Hellenic Studies*, xlvi (1926), pp. 63–71.

Id., 'The Last Athenian Historian: Laonikos Chalkokondyles', *Journal of Hellenic Studies*, xlii (1922), pp. 36–49.

R. GUILLAND, *Essai sur Nicéphore Grégoras*. Paris, Geuthner, 1926.

H. F. TOZER, 'Byzantine Satire', *Journal of Hellenic Studies*, ii (1881), pp. 233–70.

J. W. McCRINDLE, *The Christian Topography of Cosmas* (= The Hakluyt Society, vol. 98). London, 1897.

Poetry and Drama

For Syriac influences on Byzantine hymnography see E. WELLESZ, *Journal of Theological Studies*, xliv (1943), pp. 41–51, and see his book *Eastern Elements in Western Chant* (= *Monumenta Musicae Byzantinae*, American Series, vol. i). Byzantine Institute, Boston, 1947. It is expected that his book *A History of Byzantine Music and Hymnography* will be published by the Clarendon Press, Oxford.

There is an Italian translation of some of the hymns of Romanus in CAMMELLI, *Romano il Melode. Inni*. Florence, 1930; and for works on Romanus see the bibliography in E. MIONI, *Romano il Melode*. Torino, Paravia, 1937.

GUSTAV SOYTER, *Byzantinische Dichtung* (fourth to fifteenth century, Greek texts with German verse translations) (= Texte und Forschungen zur byzantinisch-neugriechischen Philologie, ed. N. A. Bees, no. 28). Athens, 1938.

W. R. PATON, *The Greek Anthology*: in the Loeb Classical Library. 5 vols., London, Heinemann, 1916–18. (A complete English translation of the Anthology together with the Greek text.)

J. W. MACKAIL, *Select Epigrams from the Greek Anthology* (new and revised edition). London, Longmans, 1906.

F. A. WRIGHT, *The Poets of the Greek Anthology* (in the series *Broadway Translations*). London, Routledge, no date.

Id., *The Girdle of Aphrodite. The Complete Love-Poems of the Palatine Anthology* (in the series *Broadway Translations*). London, Routledge, no date.

ARTHUR S. WAY, *Greek Anthology, Books V–VII*. London, Macmillan, 1939.

A. VOGT, 'Études sur le Théâtre byzantin. Un Mystère de la Passion', *Byzantion*, vi (1931), pp. 37–74.

S. BAUD-BOVY, 'Sur un "Sacrifice d'Abraham" de Romanos et sur l'existence d'un Théâtre religieux à Byzance', ibid., xiii (1938), pp. 321–34. (Cf. Hubert Pernot, *Études de Littérature grecque moderne*, Paris, Maisonneuve, 1916, pp. 231–70.)

G. LA PIANA, *Le Rappresentazioni sacre nella letteratura bizantina dalle origini al sec. IX con rapporti al teatro sacro d'Occidente*. Grottaferrata, 1912.

Id., 'The Byzantine Theater', *Speculum*, xi (1936), pp. 171–211 in which there is a discussion of Vénétia Cottas, *Le Théâtre à Byzance*. Paris, Geuthner, 1931.

MARJORIE CARPENTER, 'Romanos and the Mystery Play of the East', *University of Missouri Studies (Philological Studies in honour of W. Miller)*, xi (1936), pp. 21–51; and for the origins of the Western liturgical drama MARIA SOFIA DE VITO, *L'origine del Dramma liturgico*. Milan, Albrighi Segati & C., 1938.

For the Byzantine theatre see:

A. MÜLLER, 'Das Bühnenwesen in der Zeit von Constantin d. Gr. bis Justinian', *Neue Jahrbücher für das klassische Altertum*, xxiii (1909), pp. 36–55.

A. VOGT, 'Le Théâtre à Byzance et dans l'Empire du IVe au XIIIe siècle: Le théâtre profane', *Revue des Questions historiques*, cxv (1931), pp. 257–96.

Id., *Byzantion*, vi (1931), pp. 623–40.

On Belthandros and Chrysantza, and Libistros and Rhodamne: CHARLES DIEHL, *Figures byzantines*, 2me sér., pp. 320–53, Paris, Colin, 1908. and on Libistros and Rhodamne: D. C. HESSELING, *Uit Byzantium en Hellas*, pp. 51–81. Haarlem, Willink & Zoon, 1911.

For Digenes Akritas:

SALVATORE IMPELLIZERI, *Il Digenis Akritas. L'Epopea di Bisanzio*. Florence, Sansoni, 1940. This contains an Italian translation of the text of the MS. of Grottaferrata.

C. SATHAS and E. LEGRAND, *Les Exploits de Digénis Acritas*. Paris, 1875. This contains a French translation of the Trebizond version of the epic.

A. RAMBAUD, 'Une épopée byzantine au Xe siècle', in the *Revue des deux mondes*. Paris, 1875; reprinted in his *Études sur l'histoire byzantine*, pp. 63–108. Paris, Colin, 1912.

CHARLES DIEHL, 'Le Roman de Digénis Akritis', *Figures byzantines*, 2me sér., pp. 291–319. Paris, Colin, 1908.

J. B. BURY, *Romances of Chivalry on Greek Soil*. Oxford, Clarendon Press, 1911.

H. PERNOT, *Études de Littérature grecque moderne*, pp. 1–70. Paris, Maisonneuve, 1916.

The epic and the ballads associated with it have been studied in many articles published since 1929 by Professor Grégoire and scholars who have followed his initiative. A summary of the earlier results which, it was claimed, had been established by these studies is given by Grégoire and R. Goossens in 'Les Rec' rches récentes sur l'Épopée byzantine', *L'Antiquité classique* (Louvain), i (1932), pp. 419–39; ii (1933), pp. 449–72; and cf. the following papers by Grégoire: 'L'épopée byzantine et ses rapports avec l'épopée turque et l'épopée romane', *Bulletin de la Classe des Lettres et des Sciences morales et politiques de l'Académie royale de Belgique*, 5e sér., tome 17 (1931), pp. 463–93; 'L'Âge héroique de Byzance', *Mélanges offerts à M. Nicolas Iorga*, pp. 382–97. Paris, Gamber, 1933; 'Études sur l'épopée byzantine',

Revue des Études grecques, xlvi (1933), pp. 29–69; and the reviews of these and other articles by R. Goossens in *Byzantion*, vol. ix (1934). In addition it may suffice to cite the following articles which have appeared in *Byzantion* (where further references can be found): xi (1936), pp. 571–5; on the Slav version of the epic, x (1935), pp. 301–39; xi (1936), pp. 320–4; xiii (1938), pp. 249–51; *Nouvelles chansons épiques des IXe et Xe siècles*, xiv (1939), pp. 235–63; illustrations of the epic, xv (1940–1), pp. 87–103; historical elements in the epics of East and West, xvi (1942–3), pp. 527–44.

X

THE EMPEROR AND THE IMPERIAL ADMINISTRATION

(See also the bibliography on Chapters I, II, III.)

J. B. Bury, *The Constitution of the Later Roman Empire*. Cambridge University Press, 1910; reprinted in *Selected Essays of J. B. Bury*, pp. 99–125. Cambridge University Press, 1930.

E. Stein, *Studien zur Geschichte des byzantinischen Reiches*. Stuttgart, Metzler, 1919.

O. Karlowa, *Römische Rechtsgeschichte*, vol. i. Leipzig, von Veit, 1885.

F. Dölger, 'Rom in der Gedankenwelt der Byzantiner', *Zeitschrift für Kirchengeschichte*, lvi (1937), pp. 1–42.

N. H. Baynes, 'Eusebius and the Christian Empire', *Annuaire de l'Institut de Philologie et d'Histoire Orientales*, ii (1933–4), pp. 13–18. Brussels, 1933.

W. Ensslin, 'Das Gottesgnadentum des autokratischen Kaisertums der frühbyzantinischen Zeit', *Studi Bizantini e Neoellenici*, v (1939), pp. 154–66.

Id., 'Gottkaiser und Kaiser von Gottes Gnaden', *Sitzungsberichte der Bayerischen Akademie der Wissenschaften, Philosophisch-historische Abteilung*, Jahrgang 1943, Heft 6.

O. Treitinger, *Die oströmische Kaiser- und Reichsidee im höfischen Zeremoniell*. Jena, Biedermann, 1938.

J. Straub, *Vom Herrscherideal in der Spätantike* (= *Forschungen zur Kirchen- und Geistesgeschichte*, edd. E. Seeberg, W. Weber, and R. Holtzmann, vol. xviii). Stuttgart, Kohlhammer, 1939.

A. Grabar, *L'Empereur dans L'Art byzantin. Recherches sur l'art officiel de l'Empire d'Orient*. Paris, Les Belles Lettres, 1936.

L. Bréhier and P. Batiffol, *Les Survivances du culte impérial romain*. Paris, Picard, 1920.

W. Sickel, 'Das byzantinische Krönungsrecht bis zum 10. Jahrhundert', *Byzantinische Zeitschrift*, vii (1898), pp. 511–57.

F. E. Brightman, 'Byzantine Imperial Coronations', *Journal of Theological Studies*, ii (1901), pp. 359–92.

Cf. A. E. R. Boak, *Harvard Studies in Classical Philology*, xxx (1919), pp. 37–47; P. Charanis, *Byzantion*, xv (1940–1), pp. 49–66.

K. Voigt, *Staat und Kirche von Konstantin dem Grossen bis zum Ende der Karolingerzeit*, i Teil, chs. i–iv. Stuttgart, Kohlhammer, 1936.

H. Gelzer, 'Das Verhältnis von Staat und Kirche in Byzanz', *Ausgewählte kleine Schriften*, pp. 57–141. Leipzig, Teubner, 1907.

A. Gasquet, *L'Autorité impériale en matière religieuse à Byzance*. Paris, Thorin, 1879.

J. Ebersolt, *Mélanges d'Histoire et d'Archéologie Byzantines* (extract from the *Revue de l'Histoire des Religions*, vol. lxxvi). Paris, Leroux, 1917.

J. B. Bury, *The Imperial Administrative System in the Ninth Century* (= The British Academy, *Supplementary Papers*, i). London, Oxford University Press, 1911.

A text, and a translation by A. Vogt (together with a commentary) of the *De Ceremoniis* of Constantine VII is in course of publication in the Budé *Collection byzantine*, vol. i (in two parts), 1935, vol. ii (in two parts), 1939, 1940. Paris, Les Belles Lettres.

A. E. R. Boak, 'The Roman *Magistri* in the Civil and Military Service of the Empire', *Harvard Studies in Classical Philology*, xxvi (1915), pp. 73–164.

Id., *The Master of the Offices in the Later Roman and Byzantine Empires* (= *University of Michigan Studies. Humanistic Series*, vol. xiv). New York, Macmillan, 1919.

J. E. Dunlap, *The Office of the Grand Chamberlain in the Later Roman and Byzantine Empires* (= *University of Michigan Studies. Humanistic Series*, vol. xiv). New York, Macmillan, 1924.

Ch. Diehl, 'Un haut fonctionnaire byzantin: le Logothète', in *Mélanges offerts à M. Nicolas Iorga*, Paris, Gamber, 1933, pp. 217–27 [and see *Byzantinische Zeitschrift*, xxxiv (1934), pp. 373–9].

R. Guilland, 'Les Eunuques dans l'Empire Byzantin', *Études Byzantines*, i (1943)—published by the Institut français d'Études byzantines de Bucarest—pp. 197–238; ii (1944), pp. 185–225; iii (1945), pp. 179–214.

G. Rouillard, *L'Administration civile de l'Égypte byzantine*, 2e éd. Paris, Geuthner, 1928.

For the Byzantine army see:

R. Grosse, *Römische Militärgeschichte von Gallienus bis zum Beginn der byzantinischen Themenverfassung*. Berlin, Weidmann, 1920.

W. Ensslin, 'Zum Heermeisteramt des spätrömischen Reiches', *Klio*, xxiii (1929), pp. 306–25; xxiv (1930), pp. 102–47, 467–502.

J. Maspero, *Organisation militaire de l'Égypte byzantine*. Paris, Champion, 1912.

F. Aussaresses, *L'Armée byzantine à la fin du VIe siècle*. Paris, Fontemoing, 1909.

On the Themes see:

H. Gelzer, 'Die Genesis der byzantinischen Themenverfassung', *Abhandlungen der Kgl. Sächsischen Gesellschaft der Wissenschaften, Philol.-hist. Klasse*, xviii, no. 5. Leipzig, 1899.

Charles Diehl, 'L'origine du régime des thèmes dans l'empire byzantin', *Études byzantines*, pp. 276–92. Paris, Picard, 1905.

Ernst Stein, *Studien* (see above), pp. 117–40.

There is a map of the Byzantine themes in the ninth century in E. W. Brooks's paper: *Journal of Hellenic Studies*, xxi (1901), pp. 67–77.

C. W. C. OMAN, *The History of the Art of War. The Middle Ages*. London, Methuen, 1898.

For diplomatic usage see:

G. OSTROGORSKY, 'Die byzantinische Staatenhierarchie', *Seminarium Kondakovianum*, viii (1936), pp. 41–61.

XI

BYZANTIUM AND ISLAM

M. CANARD, 'Les Expéditions des Arabes contre Constantinople dans l'Histoire et dans la Légende', *Journal asiatique*, ccviii (1926), pp. 61–121.

GAUDEFROY-DEMOMBYNES and PLATONOV, *Le Monde musulman et byzantin jusqu'aux Croisades* (= *Histoire du Monde*, ed. M. E. Cavaignac, vii¹). Paris, Boccard, 1931.

A. A. VASILIEV, *Byzance et les Arabes*, Tome i. *La Dynastie d'Amorium (820–867)* (= *Corpus Bruxellense Hist. Byzant.*, vol. i). Brussels, 1935.

XII AND XIII

BYZANTIUM AND THE SLAVS

THE BYZANTINE INHERITANCE IN SOUTH-EASTERN EUROPE

W. MILLER, *The Balkans* (in the series *The Story of the Nations*). London, Fisher Unwin, 1896.

L. NIEDERLE, *Manuel de l'Antiquité slave*, tome i, *L'Histoire*; tome ii, *La Civilisation*. Paris, Champion, 1923, 1926.

M. SPINKA, *A History of Christianity in the Balkans*. Illinois, American Society of Church History, 1933.

From the vast literature on Cyril and Methodius may be cited:

L. K. GOETZ, *Geschichte der Slavenapostel Konstantinus (Kyrillus) und Methodius*. Gotha, Perthes, 1897.

F. DVORNIK, *Les Slaves, Byzance et Rome au IXᵉ siècle*. Paris, Champion, 1926 (with bibliography).

Id., *Les Légendes de Constantin et de Méthode vues de Byzance*. Prag, 'Orbis', 1933.

For the origin of the Cyrillic and Glagolitic scripts: E. H. MINNS, 'Saint Cyril really knew Hebrew' in *Mélanges Paul Boyer*, pp. 94–7. Paris, Champion, 1925.

I do not know of any modern English history of Croatia or Bosnia: I can refer only to F. VON ŠIŠIĆ, *Geschichte der Kroaten*, Part I (to A.D. 1102). Zagreb, Matica Hrvatska, 1917.

IVAN VON BOJNIČIĆ, *Geschichte Bosniens* (down to 1463). Leipzig, Friedrich, 1885.

AUGUST NAEGLE, *Kirchengeschichte Böhmens*, vol. i, part i, *Einführung des Christentums in Böhmen*. Vienna & Leipzig, Braumüller, 1915.

H. W. V. TEMPERLEY, *History of Serbia*. London, Bell, 1919.

WILLIAM MILLER, 'The Mediaeval Serbian Empire' in *Essays on the Latin Orient*, pp. 441–58. Cambridge University Press, 1921.

MILOCHE MLADENOVITCH, *L'État serbe au Moyen Âge: son caractère*. Paris, Bossuet, 1931.

C. JIREČEK, *La Civilisation serbe au Moyen Âge*. Paris, Bossard, 1920.

Id., *Geschichte der Serben*, vol. i (1911), vol. ii, part i, down to 1537 (1918). Gotha, Perthes.

Id., *Staat und Gesellschaft im mittelalterlichen Serbien. Studien zur Kulturgeschichte des 13.–15. Jahrhunderts*. 4 parts (= *Denkschriften der kaiserlichen Akademie der Wissenschaften in Wien, philosophisch-historische Klasse*, vol. lvi, Abh. 2, 1912; Abh. 3, 1912; vol. lviii, Abh. 2, 1914; vol. lxiv, Abh. 2, 1919).

JOSEF MATL, 'Der heilige Sava als Begründer der serbischen Nationalkirche. Seine Leistung und Bedeutung für den Kulturaufbau Europas', *Kyrios*, ii (1937), pp. 23–37.

Reference may be made to the Kossovo popular ballad: translation in D. SUBOTIĆ, *Jugoslav Popular Ballads: their Origin and Development*. Cambridge University Press, 1932; OWEN MEREDITH, *Serbski Pesme*. London, Chatto & Windus, 1917; HELEN ROOTHAM, *Kossovo*. Oxford, Blackwell, 1920.

STEVEN RUNCIMAN, *A History of the First Bulgarian Empire*. London, Bell, 1930.

G. SONGEON, *Histoire de la Bulgarie*. Paris, Nouvelle Librairie Nationale, 1913.

W. N. SLATARSKI, *Geschichte der Bulgaren*, Teil I (679–1396). Leipzig, Parlapanoff, 1918.

C. J. JIREČEK, *Geschichte der Bulgaren*. Prag, Tempsky, 1876.

XIV

THE BYZANTINE INHERITANCE IN RUSSIA

For the historical background of Kievan Russia: M. ROSTOVTZEFF, *Iranians and Greeks in South Russia*. Oxford, Clarendon Press, 1922, and see in particular ch. 9, 'The Origin of the Russian State on the Dnieper'.

S. R. TOMPKINS, *Russia through the Ages. From the Scythians to the Soviets*. New York, Prentice-Hall, 1940 (Bibliography, pp. 725–74).

V. O. KLUCHEVSKY, *A History of Russia*, translated by C. J. Hogarth. London, Dent, vol. i (1911), vol. ii (1912), vol. iii (1913). On Kluchevsky cf. Alexander Kiesewetter in *The Slavonic Review*, i (1923), pp. 504–22.

B. H. SUMNER, *Survey of Russian History*. London, Duckworth, 1944.

LEOPOLD KARL GOETZ, *Staat und Kirche in Altrussland. Kiever Periode 988–1240*. Berlin, Duncker, 1908.

HILDEGARD SCHAEDER, *Moskau das Dritte Rom* (= *Osteuropäische Studien* herausgegeben vom Osteuropäischen Seminar der Hamburgischen Universität, I). Hamburg, De Gruyter, 1929.

NICOLAS ZERNOV, *Moscow The Third Rome*. London, Society for Promoting Christian Knowledge, 1937.

A. A. VASILIEV, *The Russian Attack on Constantinople in 860*. The Mediaeval Academy of America, 1946.

LUBOR NIEDERLE, *Manuel de l'Antiquité slave*, tome ii, *La Civilisation*. Paris, Champion, 1926.

KAREL KADLEC, *Introduction à l'Étude comparative de l'Histoire du Droit public des Peuples slaves*. Paris, Champion, 1933.

For translated sources and criticism see:

S. H. CROSS, *The Russian Primary Chronicle* (= *Harvard Studies and Notes in Philology and Literature*, vol. xii). Harvard University Press, 1930. (With an admirable introduction.)

For a translation of the 'Testament of Vladimir Monomach' (12th century) see ARTHUR PENRHYN STANLEY, *Lectures on the History of the Eastern Church*, 2nd ed., pp. 313-14. London, Murray, 1862.

ROBERT MICHELL and NEVILL FORBES, *The Chronicle of Novgorod* (= Royal Historical Society, Camden Series 3, vol. xxv), 1914.

NICOLAS ZERNOV and ADELINE DELAFIELD, *St. Sergius—Builder of Russia*. London, Society for Promoting Christian Knowledge, no date. (Contains a translation from the Russian of the Life of St. Sergius.)

JANE HARRISON and HOPE MIRRLEES, *The Life of the Archpriest Avvakum*, translated by. London, The Hogarth Press, 1924.

RUDOLF JAGODITSCH, *Das Leben des Protopopen Awwakum von ihm selbst niedergeschrieben* (Translation, Introduction, Commentary). Berlin, Ost-Europa Verlag, 1930.

P. PASCAL, *La Vie de l'archiprêtre Avvakum écrite par lui-même* (Translation, Introduction, and Notes), 2nd ed. Paris, Gallimard, no date (printed Nov. 1938).

Id., *Avvakum et les Débuts du Raskol. La Crise religieuse au XVIIe siècle en Russie* (= *Bibliothèque de l'Institut français de Léningrad*, tome xviii). Paris, Champion, 1938.

LEOPOLD KARL GOETZ, *Kirchenrechtliche und kulturgeschichtliche Denkmäler Altrusslands nebst Geschichte des russischen Kirchenrechts* (= *Kirchenrechtliche Abhandlungen*, ed. Ulrich Stutz, Heft 18-19). Stuttgart, Enke, 1905.

E. DUCHESNE, *Le Stoglav ou Les Cent Chapitres. Traduction avec Introduction et Commentaire* (= *Bibliothèque de l'Institut français de Petrograd*, tome v). Paris, Champion, 1920.

Id., *Le Domostroï (Ménagier Russe du XVIe siècle). Traduction et Commentaire*. Paris, Picard, 1910.

NEVILL FORBES, 'The Composition of the Earlier Russian Chronicles', *The Slavonic Review*, i (1922), pp. 73-85.

For the conversion of Vladimir see:

GERHARD LAEHR, *Die Anfänge des russischen Reiches. Politische Geschichte im 9. und 10. Jahrhundert* (= *Historische Studien*, ed. E. Ebering, Heft 189). Berlin, Ebering, 1930.

N. DE BAUMGARTEN, *Aux Origines de la Russie* (= *Orientalia Christiana Analecta*, no. 119). Rome, Pont. Institutum Orientalium Studiorum, 1939.

G. Fedotov, 'Le Baptême de saint Vladimir et la Conversion de la Russie', *Irénikon* (Prieuré d'Amay-sur-Meuse, Belgium), xv (1938), pp. 417–35.

N. de Baumgarten, *Saint Vladimir et la Conversion de la Russie* (= *Orientalia Christiana*, vol. xxvii, no. 1). Rome, Pont. Institutum Orientalium Studiorum, 1932.

V. Laurent, 'Aux Origines de l'Église Russe. L'établissement de la Hiérarchie byzantine', *Échos d'Orient*, xxxviii (1939), pp. 279–95.

M. Jugie, 'Les Origines romaines de l'Église russe', *Échos d'Orient*, 40ᵉ année (1937), no. 187, pp. 257–70.

George Vernadsky, 'The Status of the Russian Church during the first half-century following Vladimir's Conversion', *Slavonic and East European Review*, xx (1941), pp. 294–314.

I. Stratonov, 'Die Krim und ihre Bedeutung für die Christianisierung der Ostslaven', *Kyrios* (Königsberg), 1936, Heft 4, pp. 381–95.

É. Amann and A. Dumas, *L'Église au pouvoir des laïques* (= *Histoire de l'Église*, edd. A. Fliche and V. Martin, vol. vii), pp. 440–51. Paris, Bloud & Gay, 1942.

For the Scandinavian Background and the influence of Western Europe:

S. H. Cross, 'The Scandinavian Infiltration into Early Russia', *Speculum*, xxi (1946), pp. 505–14.

Id., 'Yaroslav the Wise in North Tradition', ibid. iv (1929), pp. 177–97, 363.

Id., 'Mediaeval Russian Contacts with the West', ibid. x (1935), pp. 137–44.

Id., with K. J. Conant and H. V. Morgilevski, 'The Earliest Mediaeval Churches of Kiev', ibid. xi (1936), pp. 477–99 (9 plates, 3 figures).

T. J. Arne, *La Suède et l'Orient. Études archéologiques sur les relations de la Suède et de l'Orient pendant l'âge des Vikings*. Thèse. Uppsala, Appelberg, 1914.

Ad. Stender-Petersen, *Die Varägersage als Quelle der altrussischen Chronik* (= *Acta Jutlandica* vi¹). *Aarsskrift* for Aarhus Universitet, 1934.

Stuart R. Tompkins, 'The Varangians in Russian History' in *Medieval and Historiographical Essays in Honor of James Westfall Thompson*, pp. 465–90. University of Chicago Press, 1937.

N. de Baumgarten, *Olaf Tryggwison Roi de Norvège et ses Relations avec Saint Vladimir de Russie* (= *Orientalia Christiana*, vol. xxiv, no. 1). Rome, Pont. Institutum Orientalium Studiorum, 1931.

A. M. Ammann, *Kirchenpolitische Wandlungen im Ostbaltikum bis zum Tode Alexander Newski's. Studien zum Werden der russischen Orthodoxie* (= *Orientalia Christiana Analecta*, no. 105). Rome, Pont. Institutum Orientalium Studiorum, 1936.

A. A. Vasiljev, 'La Russie primitive et Byzance', in Gabriel Millet, *Orient et Byzance*, tome iv, pp. 9–19. Paris, Geuthner, 1930.

B. Leib, *Rome, Kiev et Byzance à la fin du XIᵉ siècle (1088–1099)*. Paris, Picard, 1924 (foreign marriages, pp. 143–78).

Georg Florovskij, 'Westliche Einflüsse in der russischen Theologie',

Kyrios (Königsbérg), ii (1937), pp. 1–22. (Western influences in Russian theology must be overcome: there must be a return to the Hellenic theology of the Fathers of the Church.)

For Asceticism in early Russia see:

LEOPOLD KARL GOETZ, *Das Kiever Höhlenkloster als Kulturzentrum des vormongolischen Russlands*. Passau, Waldbauer, 1904.

IGOR SMOLITSCH, *Das altrussische Mönchtum (11.–16. Jahrhundert). Gestalter und Gestalten* (= *Das östliche Christentum*, ed. Georg Wunderle, Heft 11). Würzburg, Rita-Verlag, 1940.

Id., *Leben und Lehre der Starzen*. Vienna, Hegner, 1936.

N. F. ROBINSON, *Monasticism in the Orthodox Churches, being an Introduction to the Study of Modern Hellenic and Slavonic Monachism*, &c. London, Cope & Fenwick, 1916.

For the Church in Russia see:

ARTHUR PENRHYN STANLEY, *Lectures on the History of the Eastern Church* (1861). 2nd ed., London, Murray, 1862. Reprinted in *Everyman's Library*. London, Dent [1907].

W. H. FRERE, *Some Links in the Chain of Russian Church History*. London, Faith Press, 1918.

NICOLAS ZERNOV, *The Church of the Eastern Christians*. London, Society for Promoting Christian Knowledge, 1942.

Id., *The Russians and their Church*. London, Society for Promoting Christian Knowledge, 1945.

For Nicon see the account in A. P. STANLEY, op. cit., pp. 345–79.

The immense work compiled by WILLIAM PALMER on Nicon, *The Patriarch and the Tsar. Services of the Patriarch Nicon to the Church and State of his Country and their Requital* (London, Trübner, 1871–6, 6 vols.), I have not read. The pages of the copy in the British Museum are still for the most part uncut.

The Orthodox Liturgy. London, Society for Promoting Christian Knowledge, 1939.

For the psychology and the thought-world of the Russian people see:

KARL HOLL, 'Die religiösen Grundlagen der russischen Kultur' in *Russlands Kultur und Volkswirtschaft*, ed. Max Sering, pp. 1–20. Berlin & Leipzig, Göschen, 1913. Reprinted in his *Gesammelte Aufsätze zur Kirchengeschichte*, vol. ii (Tübingen, Mohr, 1928), pp. 418–32.

FELIX HAASE, *Die religiöse Psyche des russischen Volkes* (= Osteuropa-Institut in Breslau: *Quellen und Studien, Fünfte Abteilung, Religionswissenschaft*, Heft 2). Leipzig, Teubner, 1921.

Id., *Volksglaube und Brauchtum der Ostslaven* (= *Wort und Brauch*, edd. Theodor Siebs & Max Hippe, Heft 26). Breslau, Märtin, 1939.

ROBERT STUPPERICH, 'Zur Geschichte der russischen hagiographischen Forschung (von Ključevskij bis Fedotov)', *Kyrios* (Königsberg), 1936, Heft 1, pp. 47–56.

P. A. PALMIERI, 'La Psicologia dei Santi Russi', *Bessarione*, ser. 3, vol. ii (1907), pp. 234–51.

G. P. Fedotov, *The Russian Religious Mind. Kievan Christianity*. Harvard University Press, 1946.

P. Bratsiotis, 'Die Grundprinzipien und Hauptmerkmale der orthodoxen Kirche', *Procès-Verbaux du Premier Congrès de Théologie Orthodoxe*, ed. H. S. Alivisatoss, Athens, 'Pyrsos', 1939, pp. 115–26 (with a short bibliography) or printed in *Kyrios* (Königsberg), 1936, pp. 331–42 (for the significance in the Church of tradition, θέωσις and the Incarnation, &c.).

For Law see Goetz and Kluchevsky in books cited *supra*, pp. 417–18.

For Art see:

Louis Réau, *L'Art russe des Origines à Pierre le Grand* (104 plates). Paris, Laurens, 1921.

N. P. Kondakov, *Die russische Ikone*, vol. i (1928) 65 coloured plates, vol. ii (1929) 136 plates (not in colour) [vol. 3: Text is in Russian]. Prag, Seminarium Kondakovianum.

Id., *The Russian Icon*. Translated by Ellis H. Minns. Oxford, Clarendon Press, 1927, and cf. *Quarterly Review* for July 1928.

Oskar Wulff and Michael Alpatoff, *Denkmäler der Ikonenmalerei in kunstgeschichtlicher Folge*. Hellerau bei Dresden, Avalun-Verlag, 1925. (There is a copy of this sumptuous work in the library of the Victoria and Albert Museum.)

M. Alpatov and N. Brunow, *Geschichte der altrussischen Kunst*. Textband and Tafelband (with 341 reproductions). Augsburg, Filser, 1932. (There is a copy in the Library of the Victoria and Albert Museum.)

Ed. Michael Farbman, *Masterpieces of Russian Painting*. London, Europa Publications, no date (? 1930). (20 colour plates and 43 monochrome reproductions of Russian icons and frescoes from the eleventh to the eighteenth centuries.)

P. Mouratow, *L'Ancienne Peinture russe* (translated by A. Caffi). Rome, Stock, 1925.

A. A. Hackel, *Das altrussische Heiligenbild. Die Ikone* (= *Disquisitiones Carolinae*, ed. Th. Baader, tomus x). Noviomagi, 1936.

I. Dirks, *Les Saintes Icones*, 2ᵐᵉ éd. Prieuré d'Amay-sur-Meuse (Belgium), 1939. (With bibliography and list of icons reproduced by the Priory.)

F. W. Halle, *Alt-russische Kunst* (in the series *Orbis Pictus*). Berlin, Wasmuth (no date).

Y. A. Olsufiev, 'The Development of Russian Icon Painting from the 12th to the 19th Century', *The Art Bulletin*, xii (1930), pp. 347–73.

K. J. Conant, 'Novgorod, Constantinople and Kiev in Old Russian Church Architecture', *Slavonic and East European Review*, xxii (1944), issue 2, pp. 75–92.

A LIST OF EAST ROMAN EMPERORS[1]

Constantine the Great, dies 337.
Constantius II, 337–61.
Julian the Apostate, 361–3.
Jovian, 363–4.
Valens, 364–78.

Theodosian Dynasty

Theodosius the Great, 379–95.
Arcadius, 395–408.
Theodosius II, 408–50.
Marcian, 450–7.

Leonine Dynasty

Leo I, 457–74.
Leo II, 474.
Zeno, 474–91.
Anastasius, 491–518.

Justinianean Dynasty

Justin I, 518–27.
Justinian I, 527–65.
Justin II, 565–78.
Tiberius II, 578–82.
Maurice, 582–602.
Phocas, 602–10.

Heraclian Dynasty

Heraclius, 610–41.
{ Constantine III, 641 (dies).
{ Heracleonas, 641 (overthrown).
Constans II, 641–68.
Constantine IV, 668–85.
Justinian II, 685–95 (is banished).
Leontius, 695–8.
Tiberius III, 698–705; restoration of.
Justinian II, 705–11.

Decline of Imperial Power

Bardanes, 711–13.
Anastasius II, 713–16.
Theodosius III, 716–17.

Isaurian Dynasty (Iconoclasts)

Leo III, 717–41.
Constantine V, 741–75.
Leo IV, 775–80.
Constantine VI, 780–97 (blinded and overthrown by his mother).
Irene, 797–802 (end of the Dynasty).
Nicephorus, 802–11.
Stauracius, 811.
Michael I, 811–13.
Leo V, 813–20.

Phrygian Dynasty

Michael II, 820–9.
Theophilus, 829–42.
Michael III, 842–67.

Macedonian Dynasty

Basil I, 867–86.
Leo VI,   } 886–912.
Alexander, } 886–913.
Constantine Porphyrogenitus, 912–59.
Romanus I, 919–44.
Romanus II, 959–63.
Basil II,   } 963–1025.
Constantine VIII, } 963–1025; sole ruler 1025–8.
Nicephorus II, 963–9.
John I Tzimisces, 969–76.
Romanus III, 1028–34.
Michael IV, 1034–41.
Michael V, 1041–2.
Zoe and   } 1042.
Theodora, }
Constantine IX Monomachus, 1042–55.
Theodora, 1055–6.
Michael Stratioticus, 1056–7.

[1] See N. H. Baynes, *The Byzantine Empire*, London, Oxford University Press, 1944, ch. iii.

End of the Macedonian Dynasty

Isaac I Comnenus, 1057–9 (abdicates).
Constantine X Ducas, 1059–67.
Romanus IV Diogenes, 1067–71.
Michael VII Ducas, 1071–8.
Nicephorus III Botaniates, 1078–81.

Comnenian Dynasty

Alexius I Comnenus, 1081–1118.
John II, 1118–43.
Manuel, 1143–80.
Alexius II, 1180–3.
Andronicus, 1183–5.

Dynasty of the Angeli

Isaac II, 1185–95 (dethroned).
Alexius III, 1195–1203.
Isaac II, restored with } 1203–4.
Alexius IV,
1203–4.
Alexius V Ducas Murtzuphius, 1204.
The Fourth Crusade: Capture of Constantinople.

East Roman Emperors in Nicaea

Theodore I Lascaris, 1204–22.
John III Ducas Vatatzes, 1222–54.
Theodore II Lascaris, 1254–8.
John IV Lascaris, 1258–61.
Michael VIII Palaeologus, 1259–82.

1261. Recapture of Constantinople.

Dynasty of the Palaeologi

Michael VIII, 1261–82.
Andronicus II, 1282–1328.
Michael IX, 1293–1320.
Andronicus III, 1328–41.
John V, 1341–76.
John VI, 1341–54.
Andronicus IV, 1376–9.
John V (restored), 1379–91.
John VII, 1390.
Manuel II, 1391–1425.
John VIII, 1425–48.
Constantine XI Dragases, 1449–53.

1453. Capture of Constantinople by the Turks.

INDEX

It is not easy to guess to what heading a reader seeking a reference will naturally turn, but it is hoped that this index will furnish an adequate guide to the contents of the book.

MAPS

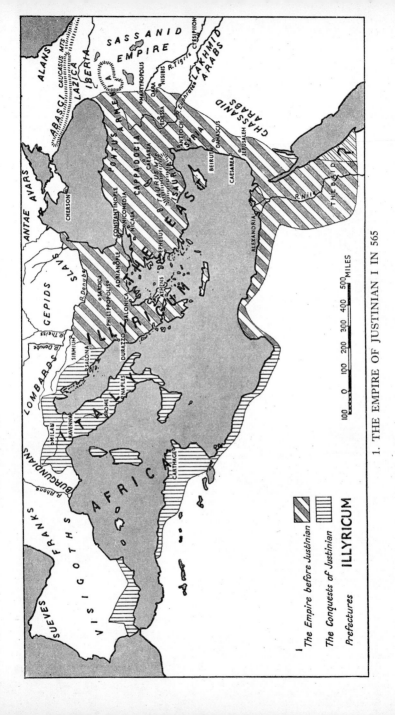

1. THE EMPIRE OF JUSTINIAN I IN 565

ILLYRICUM

The Empire before Justinian
The Conquests of Justinian
Prefectures

100   0   100   200   300   400   500 MILES

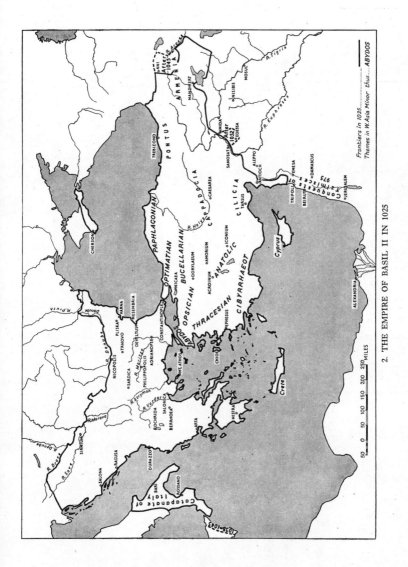

2. THE EMPIRE OF BASIL II IN 1025

Frontiers in 1025 ....
Themes in W. Asia Minor thus .... ABYDOS

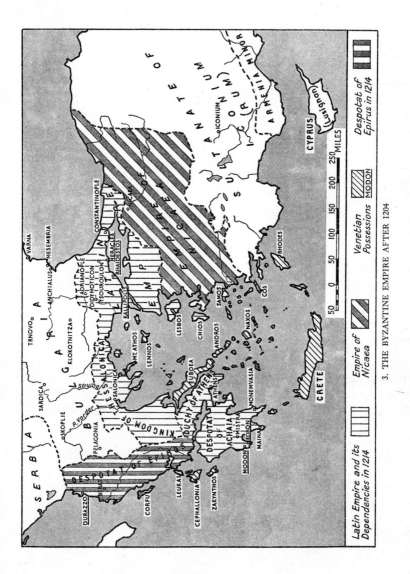

3. THE BYZANTINE EMPIRE AFTER 1204

Latin Empire and its Dependencies in 1214

Empire of Nicaea

Venetian Possessions

Despotat of Epirus in 1214

SERBIA

TRNOVO

VARNA
ANCHIALUS
MESEMBRIA

SARDICA

KLOKOTNITZA

SKOPLIE

R. Vardar

PELAGONIA

BULGARIA

ADRIANOPLE
Didymoticon
Tsourouloi
CONSTANTINOPLE
HERACLEA
RHAIDESTOS
KALLIPOLIS

LATIN EMPIRE

DURAZZO

BERAT

CORFU

LEUKAS

DESPOTAT OF EPIRUS

MT. ATHOS
Struma
THESSALONICA

LEMNOS

LESBOS

CHIOS

SAMOS

EMPIRE OF NICAEA

SULTANATE OF

ICONIUM (RUM)

ARMENIA MINOR

CEPHALLONIA

ZAKYNTHOS

KINGDOM OF THESSALONICA

DUCHY OF ATHENS

ATHENS

DESPOTAT OF ACHAIA

MISTRA

MAINAI
KORON
MODON

MONEMVASIA

ANDROS

NAXOS

COS

RHODES

CYPRUS
(Lusignan)

CRETE

MILES
50   0   50   100   150   200   250

PLATE 2

WALLS OF CONSTANTINOPLE

PLATE 3

TEKFUR SERAI. CONSTANTINOPLE
13th–14th century

PLATE 4

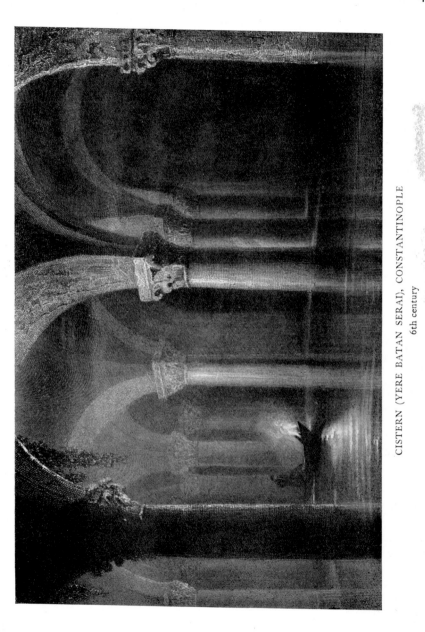

CISTERN (YERE BATAN SERAI), CONSTANTINOPLE

6th century

PLATE 5

ST. SOPHIA, CONSTANTINOPLE. EXTERIOR

(p. 167.) 532–7

PLATE 6

ST. SOPHIA, CONSTANTINOPLE. INTERIOR
(*p.* 168.) 532–7

PLATE 7

KALAT SEMAN, SYRIA
(p. 172.) End of 5th century

PLATE 8

CHURCH AT AGHTHAMAR, ARMENIA
915–21

PLATE 9

CHURCH AT KAISARIANI, NEAR ATHENS

End of 10th century

PLATE 10

CHURCH OF THE HOLY APOSTLES, SALONICA
(*p.* 180.) 1312–15

PLATE II

CHURCH AT NAGORIČINO, SERBIA
(*p.* 194.) Early 14th century

PLATE 12

CHURCH OF THE HOLY ARCHANGELS, LESNOVO, SERBIA
(*p.* 194.) 1341

PLATE 13

FETIYEH DJAMI, CONSTANTINOPLE

(*p.* 192.) Early 14th century

PLATE 14

MOSAIC. JUSTINIAN AND SUITE (*detail*)
San Vitale, Ravenna (*p.* 176). 526–47

PLATE 15

MOSAIC. THEODORA *(detail)*
San Vitale, Ravenna *(p. 176).* 526–47

PLATE 16

MOSAIC. EMPEROR KNEELING BEFORE CHRIST (*detail*)
Narthex of St. Sophia, Constantinople (*p.* 168, *note*). *Circa* 886–912

PLATE 17

MOSAIC. THE VIRGIN BETWEEN THE EMPERORS CONSTANTINE AND JUSTINIAN

Southern Vestibule of St. Sophia, Constantinople (p. 168, *note*). *Circa* 986–94

PLATE 18

MOSAIC. ANASTASIS

St. Luke of Stiris, Phocis (*p.* 184). Early 11th century

PLATE 19

MOSAIC. COMMUNION OF THE APOSTLES (*detail*)
St. Sophia, Kiev (*p.* 184). 1037

PLATE 20

MOSAIC. THE MOUNT OF OLIVES

St. Mark's, Venice. *Circa* 1220

PLATE 21

MOSAIC. SCENE FROM STORY OF THE VIRGIN

Kahrieh Djami, Constantinople (p. 193). Early 14th century

PLATE 22

FRESCO. DORMITION OF THE VIRGIN (*detail*)
Catholicon of the Lavra, Mt. Athos (*p.* 196). 1535

PLATE 23

FRESCO. THE SPIRITUAL LADDER

Refectory of Dionysiou, Mt. Athos (*p.* 196). 1546

PLATE 24

REFECTORY. LAVRA, MT. ATHOS
(p. 196.) 1512

PLATE 25

FRESCO. PARABLE OF THE TALENTS
Monastery of Theraponte, Russia. *Circa* 1500

PLATE 26

a

b

MINIATURES. STORY OF JOSEPH
Vienna Genesis (*p.* 176). 5th century

PLATE 27

MINIATURE. PARABLE OF THE TEN VIRGINS
Rossano Gospel (*p.* 177). Late 6th century

PLATE 28

MINIATURE. ABRAHAM'S SACRIFICE
Cosmas Indicopleustes. Vatican Library (*p.* 176). 7th century

PLATE 29

MINIATURE. ISAIAH'S PRAYER

Psalter. Bibliothèque Nationale, Paris (*p.* 186). 10th century

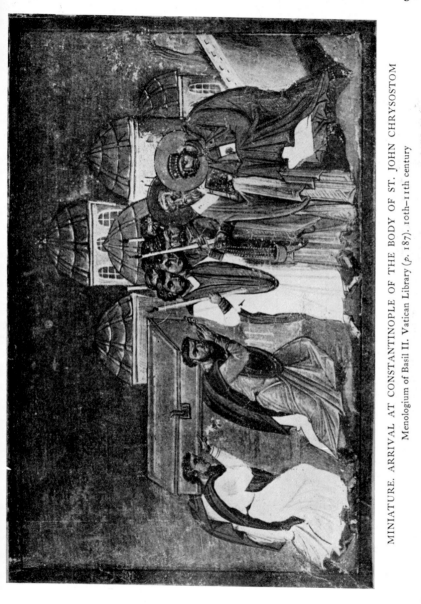

PLATE 30

MINIATURE. ARRIVAL AT CONSTANTINOPLE OF THE BODY OF ST. JOHN CHRYSOSTOM
Menologium of Basil II. Vatican Library (p. 187). 10th–11th century

PLATE 31

MINIATURE. ST. JOHN THE EVANGELIST. GOSPEL
British Museum. 11th century

PLATE 32

MINIATURE. THE EMPEROR BOTANIATES

Homilies of St. Chrysostom. Bibliothèque Nationale, Paris (*p.* 186). Late 11th century

PLATE 33

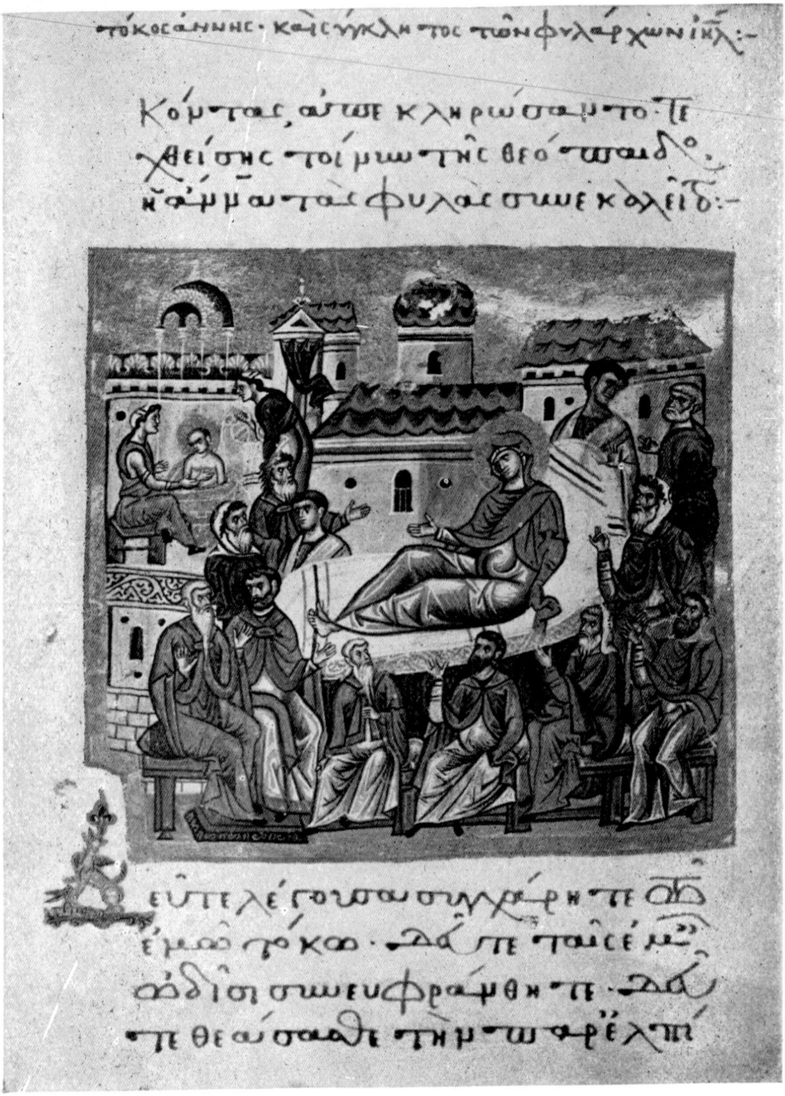

ΤΟΚΟΣ ΑΝΝΗC · ΚΑΙ ΣΥΓΚΛΗ ΤΟC ΤΩΝ ΦΥΛΑΡΧΩΝ ΙΗΛ :-

Κομ ταc, αὔτως κληρωσαμ το τε
ζειʼσηc · τοι μυω τηʼc βεοʹ τταιδο.
ν αʹ μμα ταc φυλαc σωεκαλειʹδ:-

εὐτελεʹτοτσασσωχρέη ττε ος
εʼμασ ρʹκασ · λαʹ ττε ταισέ μʼ
ωʹδιʹσι σωευφραʹμθη ττ · λαʹ
ττε θεαʹ σαλι τηʹμ ω αʹρέχτιʹ·

MINIATURE. STORY OF THE VIRGIN

Homilies of the Monk James. Bibliothèque Nationale, Paris (*p.* 187). 12th century

PLATE 34

MINIATURE. SCENE OF FEASTING

Commentary on Job. Bibliothèque Nationale, Paris. 1368

PLATE 35

MARBLE SARCOPHAGUS
Istanbul Museum. 4th–5th century

PLATE 36

IVORY. ARCHANGEL
British Museum (*p.* 177). *Circa* 500

PLATE 37

BARBERINI IVORY. TRIUMPH OF AN EMPEROR
Louvre (*p.* 177). Early 6th century

PLATE 38

IVORY. 'THRONE OF MAXIMIAN'
Ravenna (*p.* 177). 6th century

PLATE 39

IVORY. STORY OF JOSEPH
'Throne of Maximian.' Ravenna (p. 177). 6th century

PLATE 40

IVORY. ROMANUS AND EUDOCIA CROWNED BY CHRIST
Cabinet des Médailles, Paris (*p.* 187). 10th century

PLATE 41

IVORY. SCENES FROM THE LIFE OF CHRIST
South Kensington. 11th–12th century

PLATE 42

SILVER DISH FROM KERYNIA, CYPRUS
David and Goliath. Metropolitan Museum, New York (*p.* 177). 6th century

PLATE 43

RELIQUARY
Esztergon, Hungary (*p.* 188). 12th century

PLATE 44

a

b

WOOL TAPESTRIES FROM EGYPT
a. Hunting Scene. South Kensington
b. Nereids riding on sea-monsters. Louvre
(*p.* 177). 4th–6th century

PLATE 45

SILK TEXTILE. RIDERS ON WINGED HORSES
Schlossmuseum, Berlin. 10th century

PLATE 46

'DALMATIC OF CHARLEMAGNE'
Vatican Treasury (*p.* 197). 14th century

PLATE 47

EPITAPHIOS OF SALONICA (detail)
Byzantine Museum, Athens (p. 105) 14th century

PLATE 48

ST. NICHOLAS, METEORA, THESSALY

316